Dorothy Gillespie

Radford University Foundation Press

Preface

As an artist, Dorothy Gillespie shapes sculptures. As a caring and committed person, she shapes lives.

Radford University, which now honors Gillespie with this publication, has been the privileged recipient of her generous spirit, both as an artist and as an arts advocate. Her paintings and sculptures enliven our campus, and her dedicated teaching has touched many.

Gillespie began Radford University's now well-established permanent collection by taking an "art van" to her friends' studios to collect pieces from the many prominent artists. As she puts it, "I think permanent collections are important, and I like to start things."

That simple statement reveals much about this dedicated artist. Gillespie shares her considerable energy and expertise without reservation, enriching the world through art and education. Her vision extends beyond the present to the future, enabling her to transcend momentary distractions and reach deeper, to art's basic elements. Rather than following fads, she blazes trails.

Whether or not they realize it, artists through the ages will owe much to Gillespie. She was among those who transformed the art world, opening doors for women artists. She forged her own style, expressing a vision to which people responded, visually and viscerally. She pioneered many collaborative efforts. And through it all, she has consistently been a beacon of the best of humanity, both as an individual and as a person who will leave a valuable artistic legacy.

Douglas Covington, Ph. D.
President, Radford University

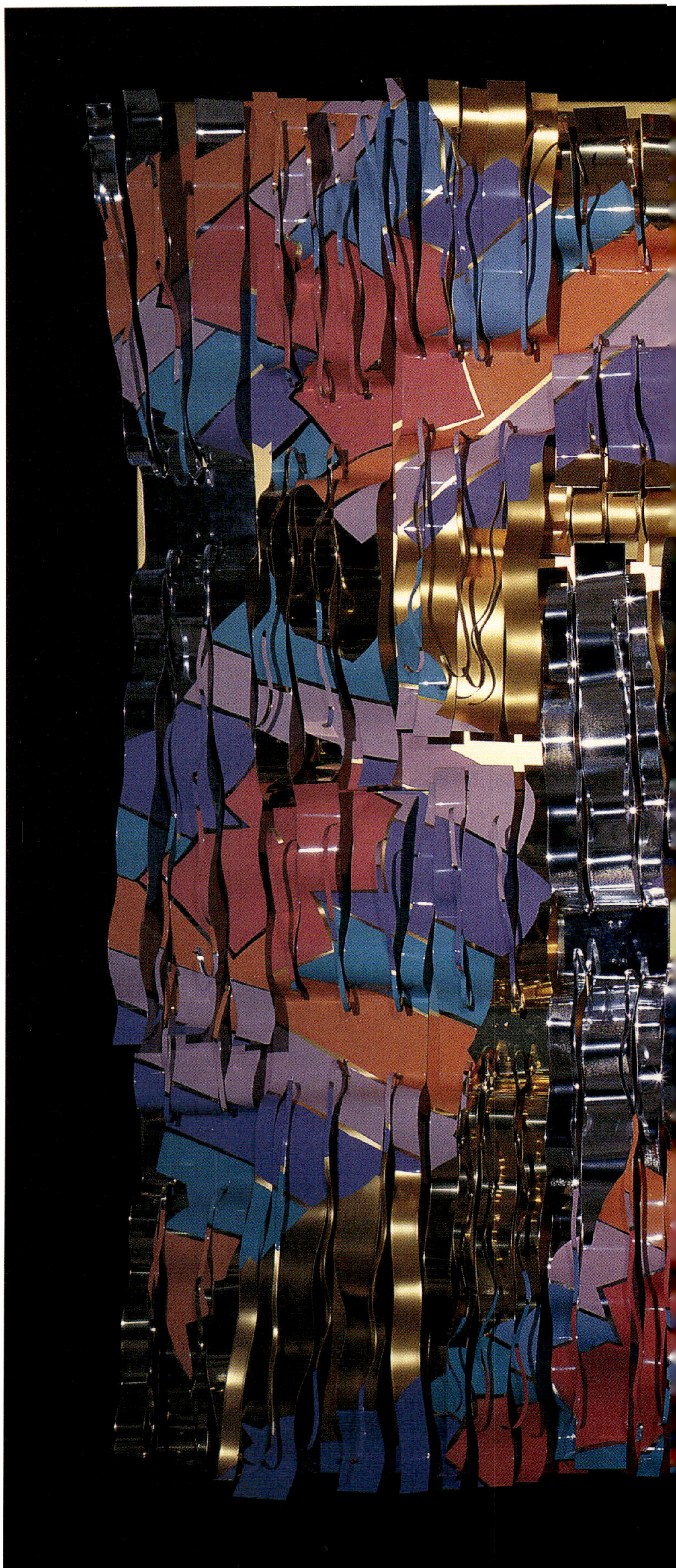

Royal Concerto II, 1992, enamel on aluminum, 64" x 80" x 10"

Detail of *Colorfall: Garden* (pages 100–101) →

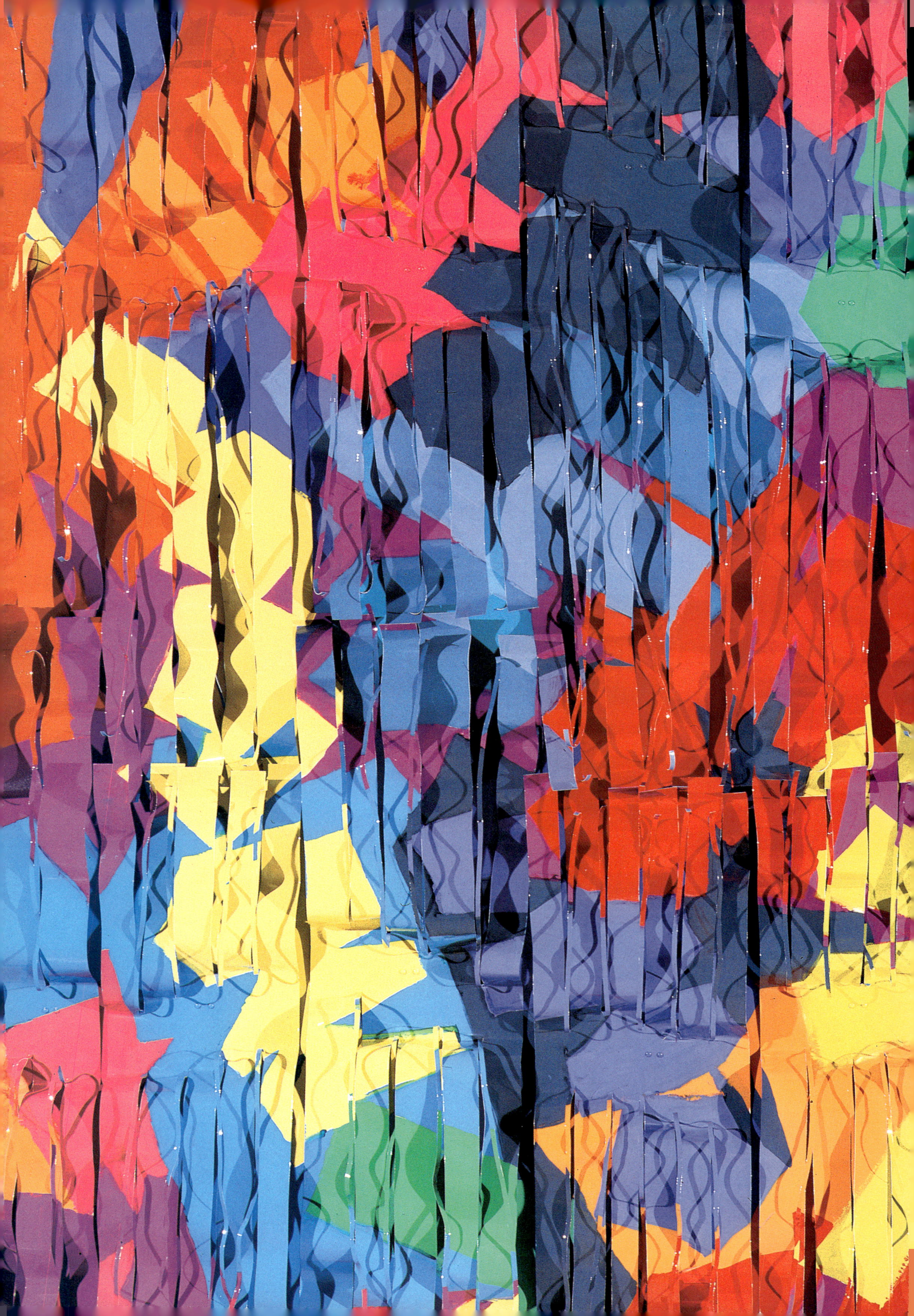

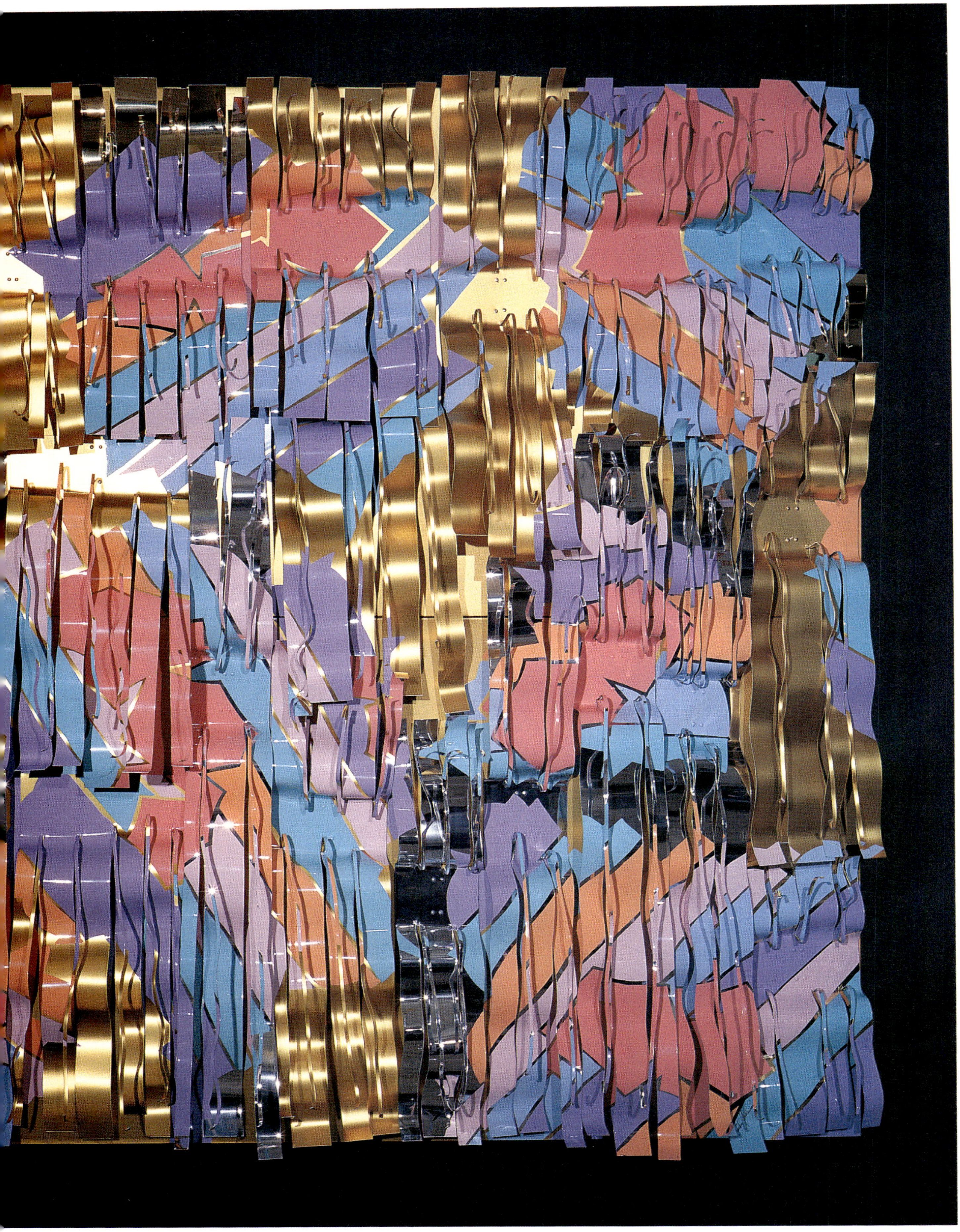

Richard Martin

It may seem a simple truism that an artist's work resides in the achievement of material objects as works of art and in an identity, a personality, or a self as represented in the body of the work when viewed over a period of time. Too often, however, we see myopically only that which is immediately in front of us. Dorothy Gillespie's art tests the truism, so clearly defined is the character of her works of art and so committed, too, the character and integrity of the artist through the course of the work. As we are particularly drawn to artists just now who consider the conditions of moral art in this time, not in massive matters of honor, but in the smaller discourses about truth in our history and truth in our time, the example of Gillespie becomes particularly pointed and especially important.

Gillespie once said, "I never teach religion or politics." In this avowal, she is specifically right, but demonstrably wrong as well. For Gillespie's art is a comprehensive vision of the rightness of making art and the justice of ideas surrounding art. Her art and her art world are a moral universe, a place wherein the promptings of feminism in the 1970s have been sustained in both an individual growth and a collective conviction, a civic spirit that is rare in contemporary art.

In the 1970s, Gillespie was asked by the New School for Social Research to create a pioneering course she called "Functioning in the Art World," initially taught in collaboration with the late Alice Baber. Its objective was comprehension of how the art world works, an intellectual and emotional attainment in seeing how the system one is engaged in actually operates. Many art schools and related institutions came to offer corresponding courses, though more often oriented by title and content to the "business of art" or "making it in the art world." Once asked if her course addressed "making it," Gillespie candidly admitted that it did not and suggested that her approach was personal understanding, not some external standard of success. Two decades ago, few saw Gillespie's motives and enterprise as clearly as she. The College Art Association offered a panel in the late 1970s on "making it" in the art world, and Gillespie was rightly indignant. Her ideas had been subverted in a way so deeply pernicious that we are only now coming to grips with the damage we have all done to a world we cherish in allowing ourselves to be part of the business and commercializing mechanisms of a new, more cynical, crasser art scene.

She expanded on her original concept with an annual workshop at the New School and once at the Maryland Institute, College of Art (her alma mater), called "Art and the Community." The workshop was a sublime expression of faith in the world of art as a single community, surpassing boundaries among curators, collectors, artists, art handlers, dealers, advisers, and many more. There were always a few who attended for the purpose of "getting ahead," but Gillespie's vision was steadfastly on getting knowledge, getting to know some people, and getting to know how other people viewed art.

In retrospect, "Art and the Community" was one of the last idealistic convergences in the New York art world. In the demise of her workshop and its almost Bauhaus-theoretical conviction, what has followed is another kind of art world and another prevailing view. As Dan Cameron has rightly argued in the *New Art Examiner* (October 1987), "hype" is an inevitable presence in contemporary art and art culture. That it may or may not vitiate the art and the system that fosters art remains to be seen, but the change in values that places the names of the collectors on all art world lips even before the names of the artists is a significant shift. Contemporary art must – and will, I am certain – finally be seen beyond the current hype and the obsessive interest in the conditions of the marketplace and collecting. Gillespie's "Art and the Community" can be seen only as one of the last great art-world bulwarks against the world of over-assessed values and hyperbole in our current art.

Today, "community" is an awkward word for the world of art, perhaps too redolent of ideas of civic virtue or those senses of community invoked at the end of the Second World War, when Franklin D. Roosevelt exhorted Americans to become "members of the human community" and Robert Maynard Hutchins responded to the threat of the atomic bomb by invoking a "world community" as the only means to survival. In the ebb and flow of the values tangent to art, Gillespie's "Art and the Community" workshops continued into the early 1980s, but a sea-change was already contributing to their cessation. What Gillespie had sought in deep knowledge rather than easy success, in community rather than commercialism, had lost its moment. It has not lost its value.

When Gillespie says that she does not teach religion or politics, she fails to mention that she teaches a kind of moral politics about art and its conditions. She insists on the possibility of women artists and women's issues; the education of artists as evident in her participation in the Governor's summer program in art at Radford University in Virginia; the dissemination of art and its information to and from New York even as her travels demand unrelenting hard work away from the studio and the hard work of returning immediately to her own art; the possibilities of art for enlightenment, therapy, and joy; and the achievement of dialogue among the parties involved with contemporary art and art history.

Indefatigable as a juror, unceasing as an artist, friend to countless curators, critics, historians, and artists, Gillespie is the embodiment of a civic and moral spirit in contemporary art. She used to respond, when asked about the common ground of the lawyers, curators, artists, dealers, and collectors she would convene for a morning or afternoon, that all of them "love art." She resisted a cynical view of the dealer, a commerce in art-as-investment on the part of the collectors, or superficial fashionability on the part of curators. In defining the art world as a part of art values and of a covenant with art as much as with one another, Gillespie offered a passionate idealism in "Art and the Community." Few who participated can forget their involvement, even more so for the changes in art-world principles and interests since the "Art and Community" series ended. Nonetheless, the conditions of her own art have remained unchanged for several decades, suggesting a like set of values. The integrity of the work, meaning its continuity as a whole and its moral wholeness, has stayed and flourished.

Gillespie likes to describe her process of making her paper pieces, which are formed while wet with water and pigment: "They bloom just a little." So, too, Gillespie's art. At first glance, it might seem that Gillespie's art is of several incompatible styles – abstract painting into sculpture to representational painting – but the styles are reconciled by their idealism and their convincing compatibility in Gillespie's development. Moreover, while Gillespie's art and accomplishments seem to be so much about art-world values, one of their strengths is that she transcends the art world to address others. Working in performance art in the 1960s and early 1970s, Gillespie created circumstances and objects, many of which demonstrated responsiveness to the viewer. For example, an exhibition in 1966 at the Gertrude Stein Gallery was summarized by Gillespie as "the audience was the show." Gillespie played the role of interlocutor and psychologist in basing the exhibition on devices of the flag and Americana. But her conclusion is overly deferential. Indeed, if Gillespie's show, *U.S.*, is really only the audience, then Jasper Johns's *Flag* is also only the spectator, as any major work of art offering multiple readings might be. Gillespie invited the audience to participate and valued their participation and their responses, but the art was undeniably Gillespie's.

A John Philip Sousa room with Mylar stars invoked all the senses as well as patriotic fervor; a room filled with flag variations required a viewer's participation and a room with two videos and the incessant playing of all-news radio promising up-to-the-minute news played in this third room. Playing with both art as a permanent image and the immediacy of current events (as does Johns's *Flags*), Gillespie opened up post-Vietnam ideas of American community and values. In her claim not to address politics, Gillespie considers that this exhibition was not politically prompted. Her distinction is, however, not correct. There are healing politics, there is a moral statement, and there is a new beginning in what Gillespie offers. That new beginning could serve the spectator to reexamine the meaning of patriotic images as well as the meaning of America, but it was also a watershed work for Gillespie, bringing her performance art to the moral plane where she was likewise confronting issues of the women's movement.

Gillespie's piece for the 1973 group show Erotic Garden was likewise a work of moral dimension and of the participation of the spectator. Once again, Gillespie engaged the spectator by soliciting him or her to use knowledge or information of a basic kind to become engaged in the work. While Gillespie claims she "did it instinctively," the Erotic Garden work is exemplary of Gillespie's art and convictions. That is, it is based on knowledge and it promotes a new collective knowing. Gillespie offered flowers and vegetables for association with gender with the rather predictable results of women associated with tomatoes and men linked with cucumbers. Sounds were also gender-selected with options of boat whistles, trains, and lions' roars among others, and Gillespie tabulated results from the spectators' participation to see that men preferred thunder and rain whereas women most wanted to hear the surf. Most erotic flowers were selected, a process that anticipates Gillespie's 1980s works that implicitly speak of flowers as organic forms. The spectator could feel that he or she was participating in a game (later on, Gillespie would participate in the Games show of 1974-75 and create a witty and challenging women's art crossword puzzle) but also realize that he or she was sharing with others in that game and in the assignment of values to bodies, flowers, sounds, and the like.

In the probing of information that Joseph Kosuth, Robert Morris, and others made in the 1960s and 1970s, we have a natural kinship to what Gillespie was proposing in the same period. Surely in part because they are the work of a male artist devoted to male-oriented themes, we all know Morris' *I-Box* or *Litanies*, but few have acknowledged Gillespie's Erotic Garden as a work in which ideas are generated by the seeming disavowal of aesthetic experience only to return us to the essential role of the aesthetic experience as an idea. Furthermore, Gillespie made her work provisionally and spiritually, not dogmatically and not permanently. Her questioning of the spectator led to a result other than that with which she began. Her scientism did not suppose that she had all the answers; she posed and questioned and allowed the answers to happen.

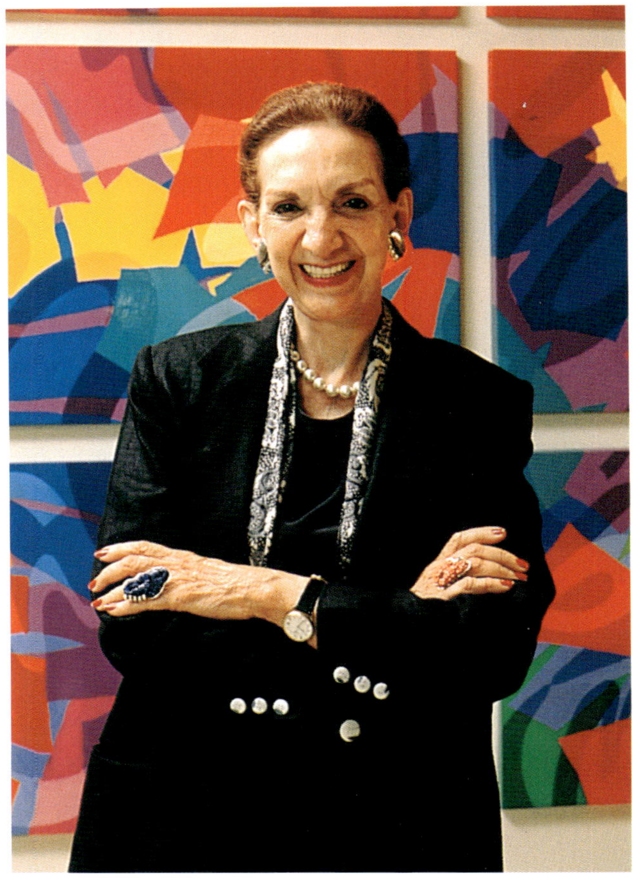

In this, we have the discrepancies between Gillespie and the male artists. Gillespie did not seek her answers from a high semantics and assumptions of philosophical speculation; she sought her answers in common knowledge, in the joys and sense of the spectators. Her results arise from the everyday and become symbolic as opposed to the results of others that have their origins in assumptions of the symbolic and aesthetic. Picking sensations is an idea we would more frequently associate with a children's museum than with the rarefied aesthetic experience of adults, but in that assumption, Gillespie drives home her strong sense of art and its community.

At the same time, having allowed such participation to define art, her "content" is gender. Once again, Gillespie's work can only begin to be assessed with full clarity decades later. Her concern in the women's movement was with women's rights and women's art, but not, despite her founding and sustained participation in the Women's Interart Center in New York City, with women alone. Gender or difference, the issue that now animates much of the academic discourse in women's studies according to Catherine Stimpson and others, was the essential question of Gillespie's work. Men perceiving women and vice versa as well as women seeing themselves and men seeing themselves in reference to objects and sensations is a statement beyond the women's movement in any parochial form.

The women's movement in art is an important factor in Gillespie's work even as she has conscientiously never sought to exploit her work in the movement for personal benefit. Gillespie sees her works on paper as especially indebted to the women's movement not only for the simplistic sense of paper being an available medium to women and resembling or extending the decorum of women allowed to be illustrators or genteel watercolorists (in fact, extending dainty watercolors to 12-foot rolls of paper), but also for the adventures of putting together shows of women's work as they might travel around the country by quick and efficient cargo services. Her own idea for a 1976 exhibition at New York University, more informal than her other works previously shown there, was rolls and rolls of paper unfurled and creating a colorful and exuberant space at a minimum of cost. As her metal sculptures manifest a defiance of gravity, seeming to curl on unseen trampolines of legerdemain, her paper pieces extend the ideas of a floating sculpture. Gillespie coyly points out that the NYU students welcomed a show on paper that could be taken down on the Friday preceding a planned Saturday night rock concert (and, for Gillespie, easily transported to the Jersey City Art Museum for another show). But Gillespie again invests the circumstances with great value and depreciates the innovation and imagination of the art. To be sure, she insists on guiding her own artistic career and takes pride in exhibition direction of many of her own shows, but that role in the art community does then have a direct feedback into the character of the art. An artist who passes up a show because he or she would be obligated to move it out in a day in order to accommodate a rock concert misses the opportunity that Gillespie seizes, both for the exhibition and for the creativity of her work.

Gillespie cites the formative influence of the Atelier 17 printmaking studio, with its ethos of never quite completing, always experimenting in the matter of making art. Gillespie has therefore spoken of the artist making her or his world anew in the manner of stepping off the edge of the world into a vast uncertainty with every gesture and with every mandate of being an artist. Art as an experiment is also a concept perhaps out of favor over the past few years, when certainty prevailed among an elite group of artists of apparent success. Like the results of her Erotic Garden, the factor of the uncertain, the yet-to-be-proved is ever strong in Gillespie's art. It is evident in the unceasing experimentation she brings to the color, materials, and form of the paintings and sculptures of the past two decades that make up the centerpiece of this monograph. Her sculptural color, once hard-edged, has become blurred and softly diffused. Her materials vary at one time from aluminum to paper and her contexts from the decors she has done for the Cleveland Ballet to indoor works, portable pieces, and large-scale outdoor sculptures. Her forms are necessarily uncertain in their flowing penetration into space, tentacles curling outward from a center. One more crimp creates another sculpture; another twist resolves a matter of form so deftly that one realizes her gift for composition.

Has Gillespie, then, moved in this body of work away from involvement of the spectator that is her surrogate for the community, her expression of the engaged art? No. On the contrary, she has created a body of highly suggestive works that moves across all patterns of resemblance and expectation as if to provide us with the reading of our minds and senses as clearly as her experimental involvement of the viewer in the pieces of the early 1970s. The sculptures are sea creatures, dancers, polychromed and playful spiders, meteorites, chrysanthemums, sculptures, cartoon octopuses plus extra legs, and all that one can think of. They recognize so much that is familiar and suggestive and they transform it into art. Their reading in architectural installations creates a perfect interstice between architecture and animation, creating a free flow and joyous balance between the wall as structure and a climbing, alternatively cascading disassembly of the architecture. As much as ever, Gillespie's art encourages the viewer to see options. Those options may seem to be the wonders of the spectator's imagination, but they exist in the art of Gillespie.

When Gillespie saw the great Picasso retrospective at the Museum of Modern Art, she returned to her work empathetic to the pain and anguish of an artist who was constantly experimenting, never satisfied, always questioning. Her own work has those characteristics. To this day she maintains a steadfast and enlightened view of the community of art, and she is an exemplary citizen in that community. At the same time, she is an artist who engages the community of art and the spectator not only in her worldly ventures, but also in an invitation to enter into a world of beautiful objects. Her good citizenship has never contradicted her artistic originality. Her art has never been banal polemics. Indeed, when Gillespie says, "I never teach religion or politics," she is right only in a literal sense. Dorothy Gillespie's work and her life teach all of us a spirit about art and a moral principle about the community of art that are the most important and most precious lessons one can learn.

Return from the Journey, 1978, acrylic on canvas, 60" x 60"

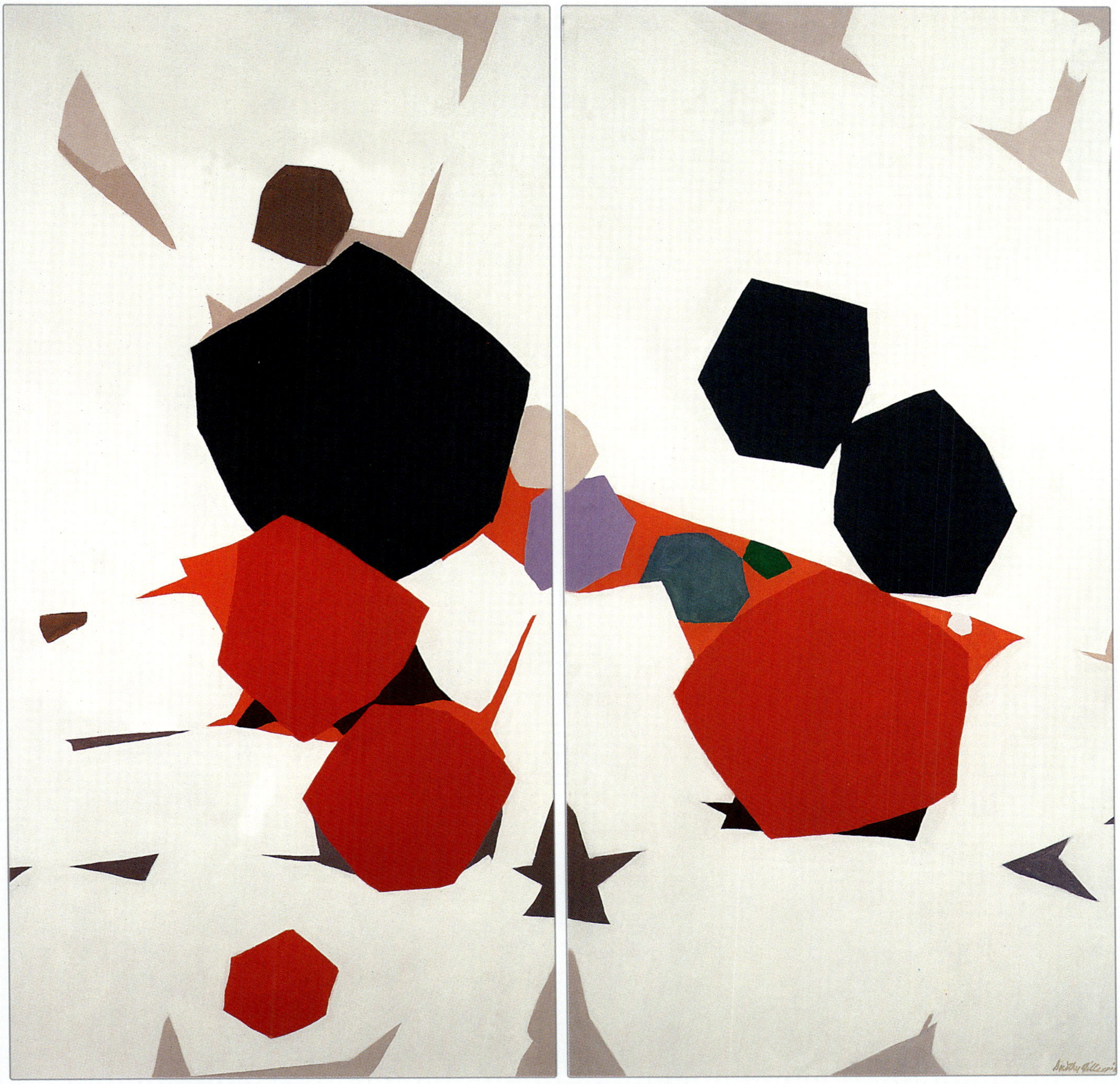

Shadows of the Evening Clouds, 1979, acrylic on canvas, 56" x 59"

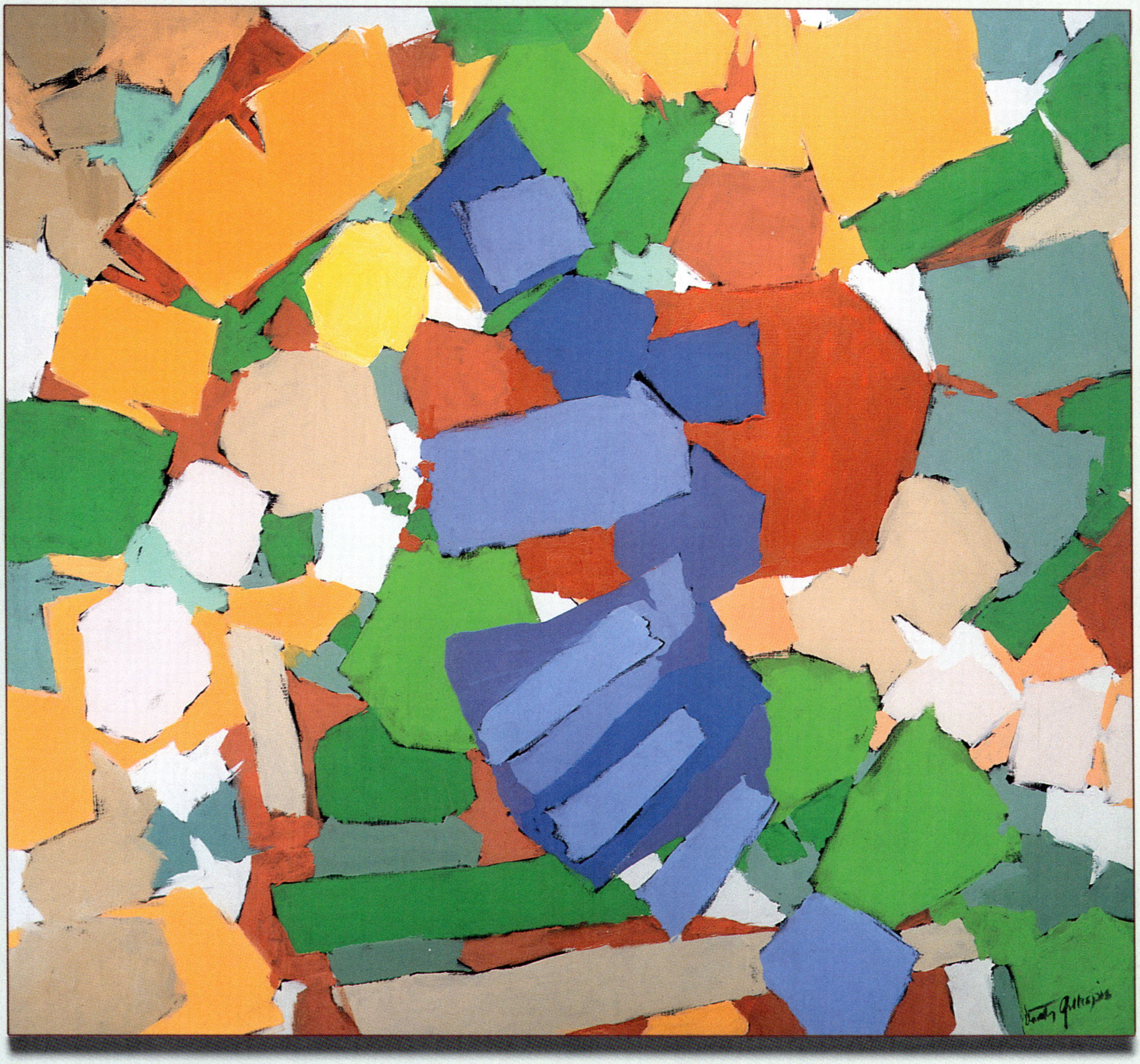

Rearrangement, 1981, enamel on aluminum, 87" x 64"

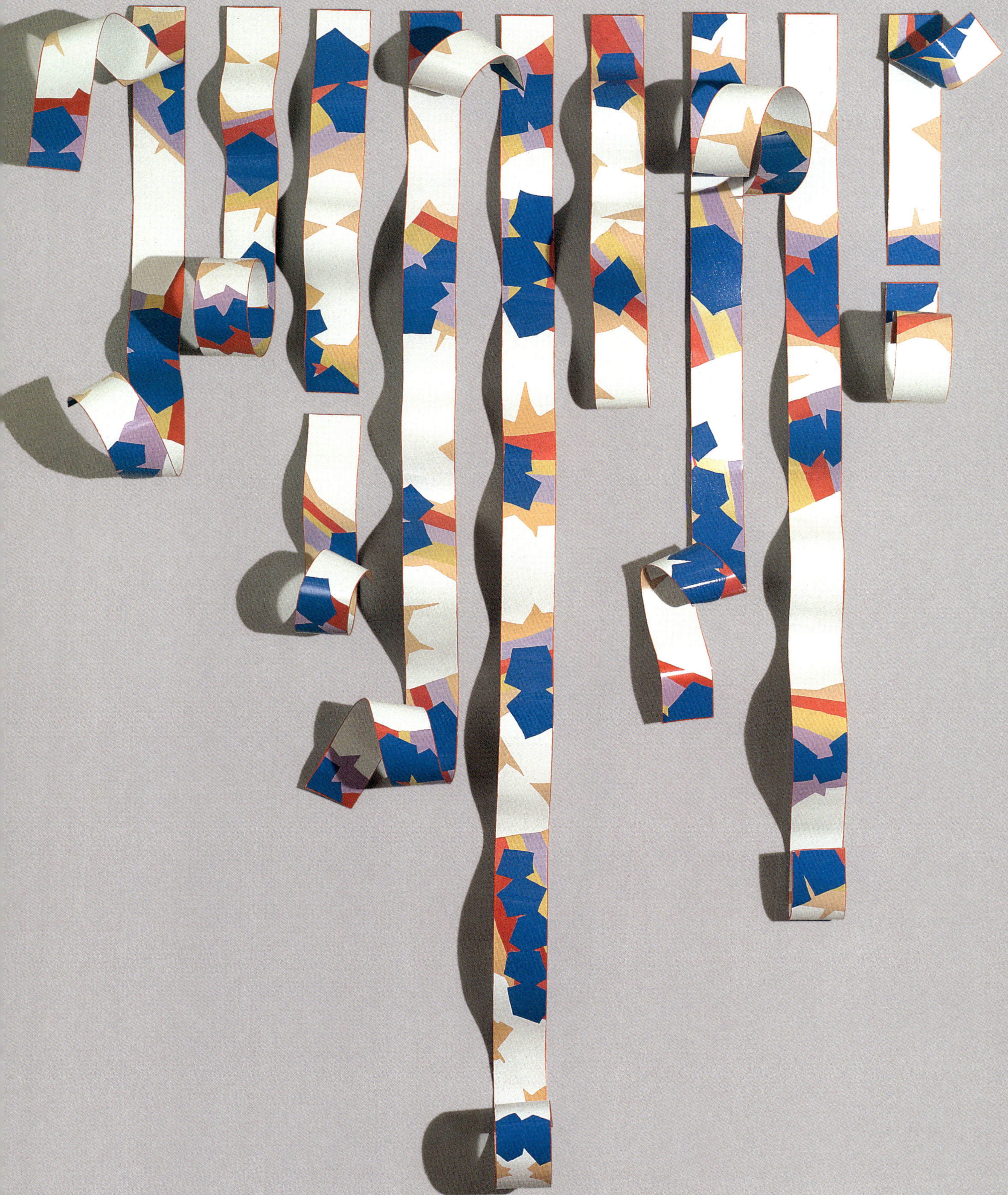

Conjured Image #2, 1982, enamel on aluminum, 74" x 25" x 30"

Conjured Image #1, 1982, enamel on aluminum, 82" x 33" x 30"

Conjured Image #3, 1982, enamel on aluminum, 79" x 30" x 30"

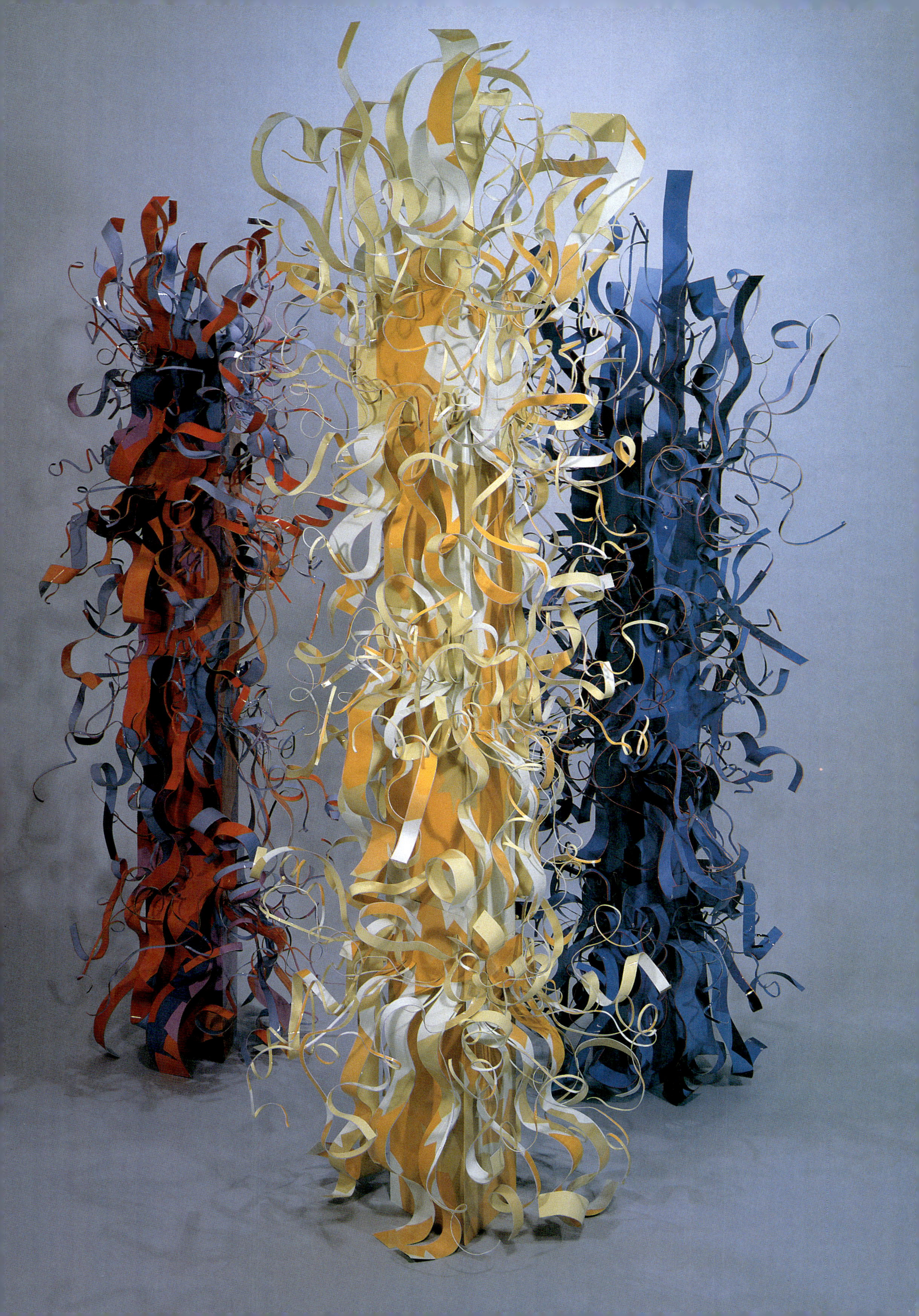

Festival Concerto, 1982, enamel on aluminum, 43" x 46" x 8"

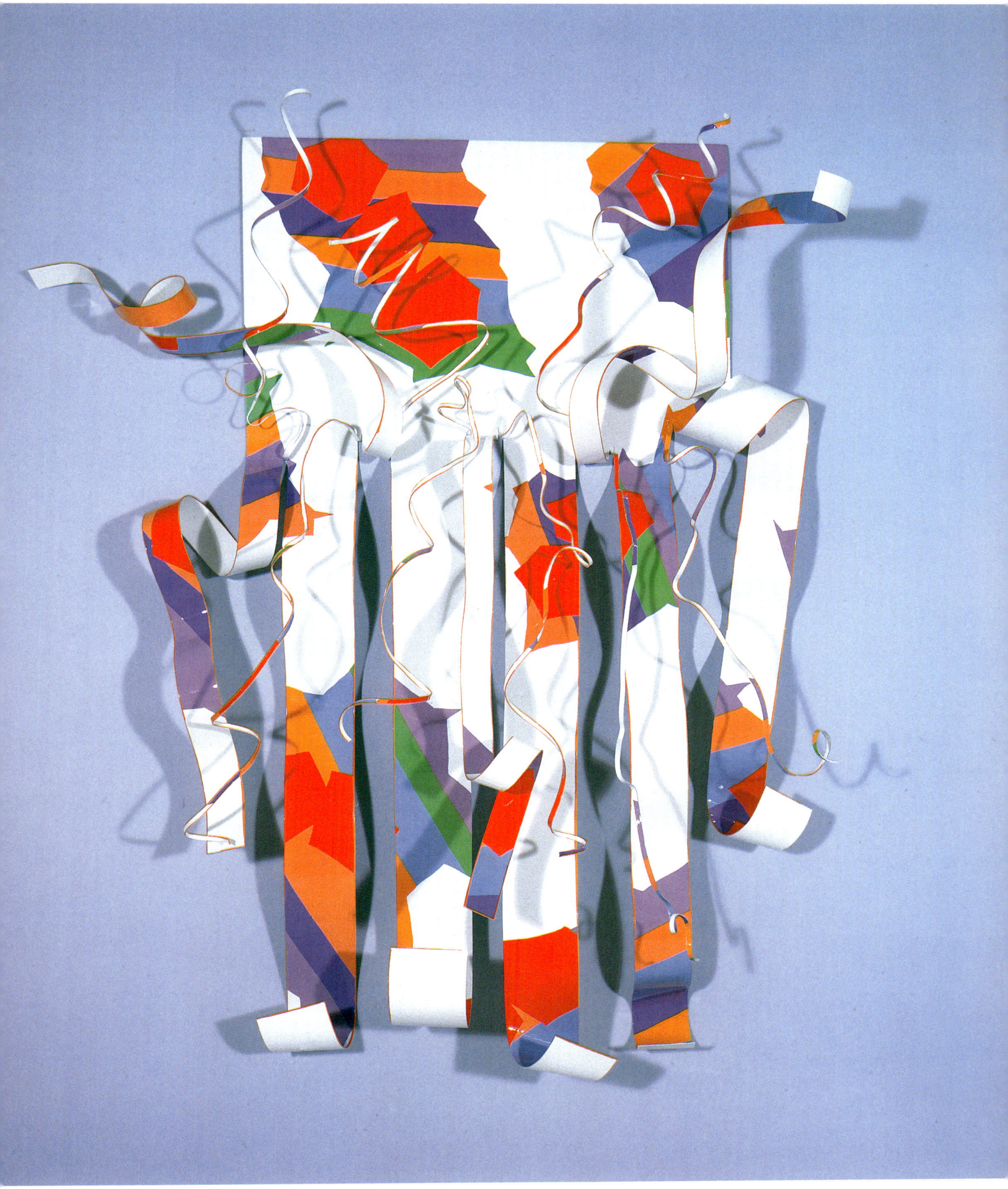

Conjured Image, 1984, enamel on aluminum, 42" x 33" x 30"

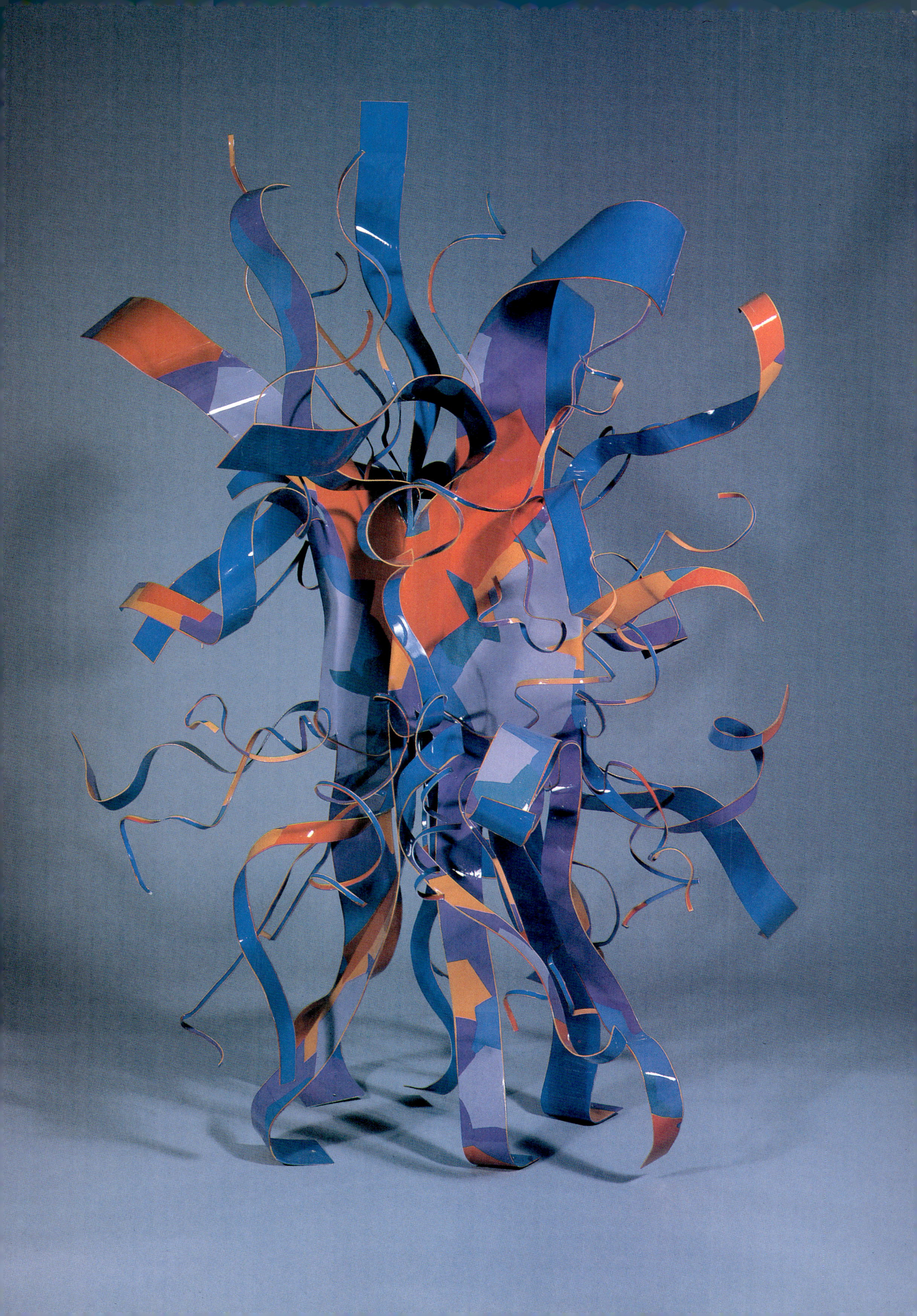

Ballet Royale I, 1985, enamel on aluminum, 58" x 16" x 3"

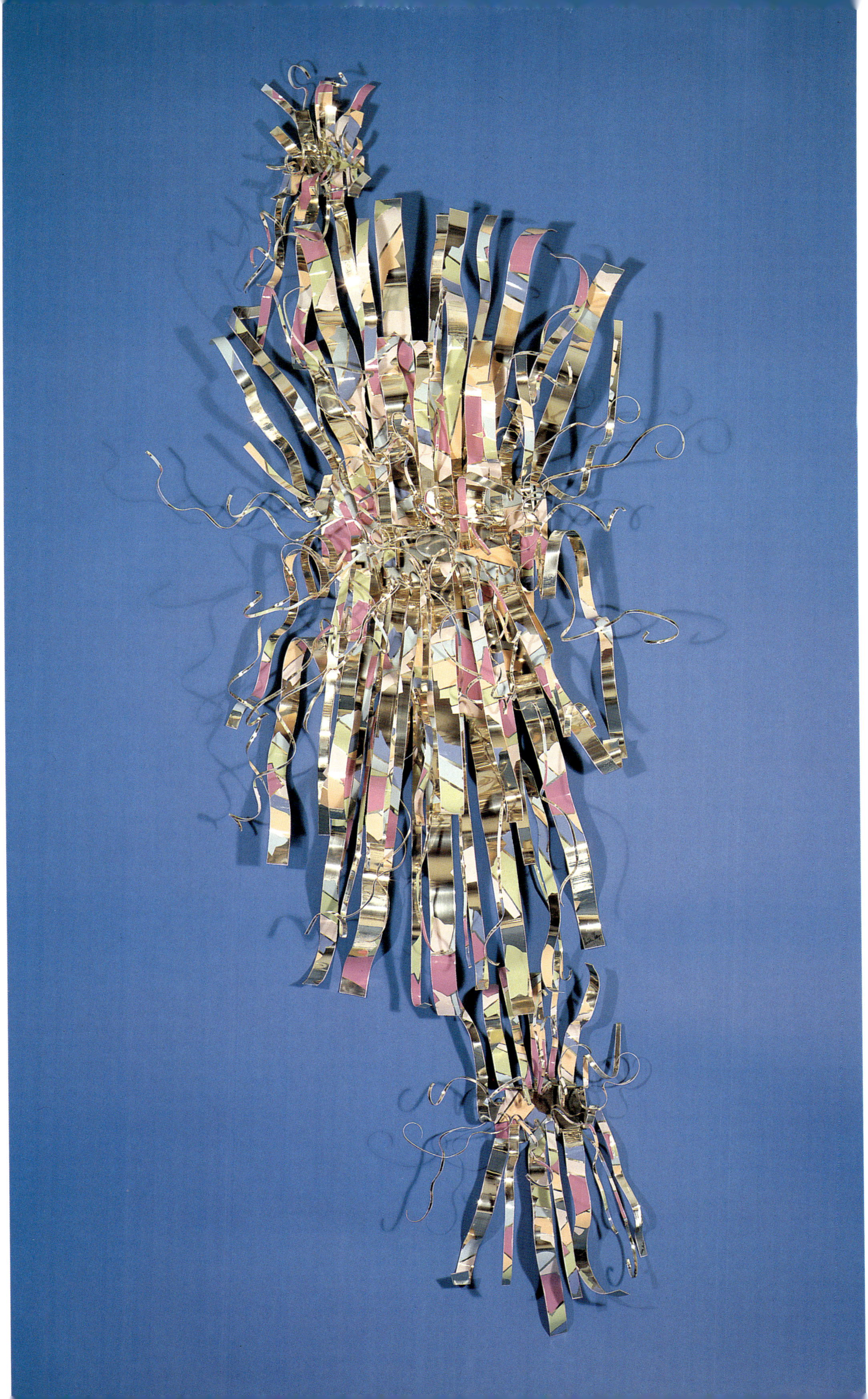

Encounter with a Distant Past, 1985, enamel on aluminum, 59" x 46" x 6"

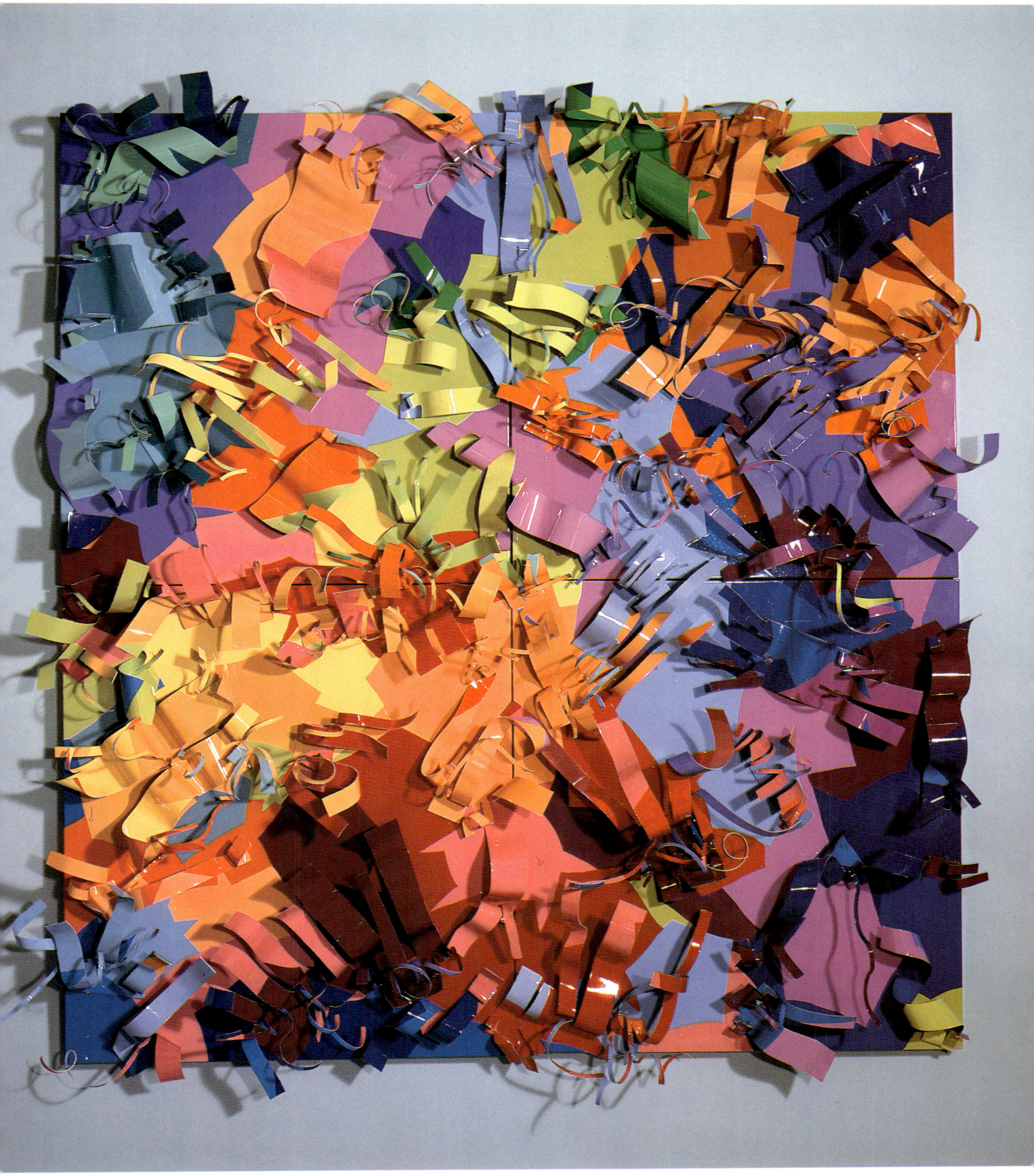

Night at the Fair, 1986, silk screen on aluminum, 36" x 20" x 8"

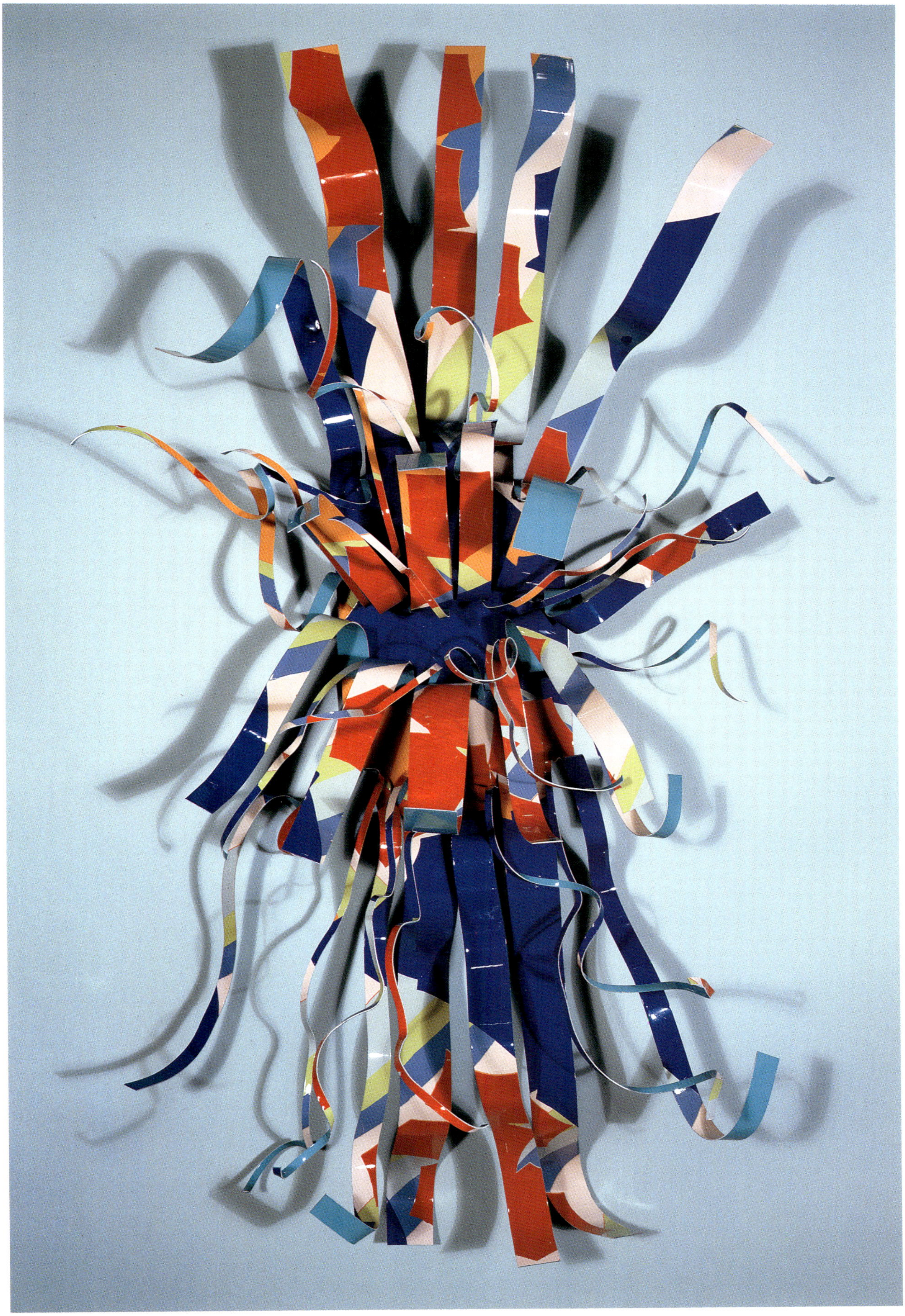

Magic Carpet Slides, 1987, enamel on aluminum, 96" x 48" x 20"

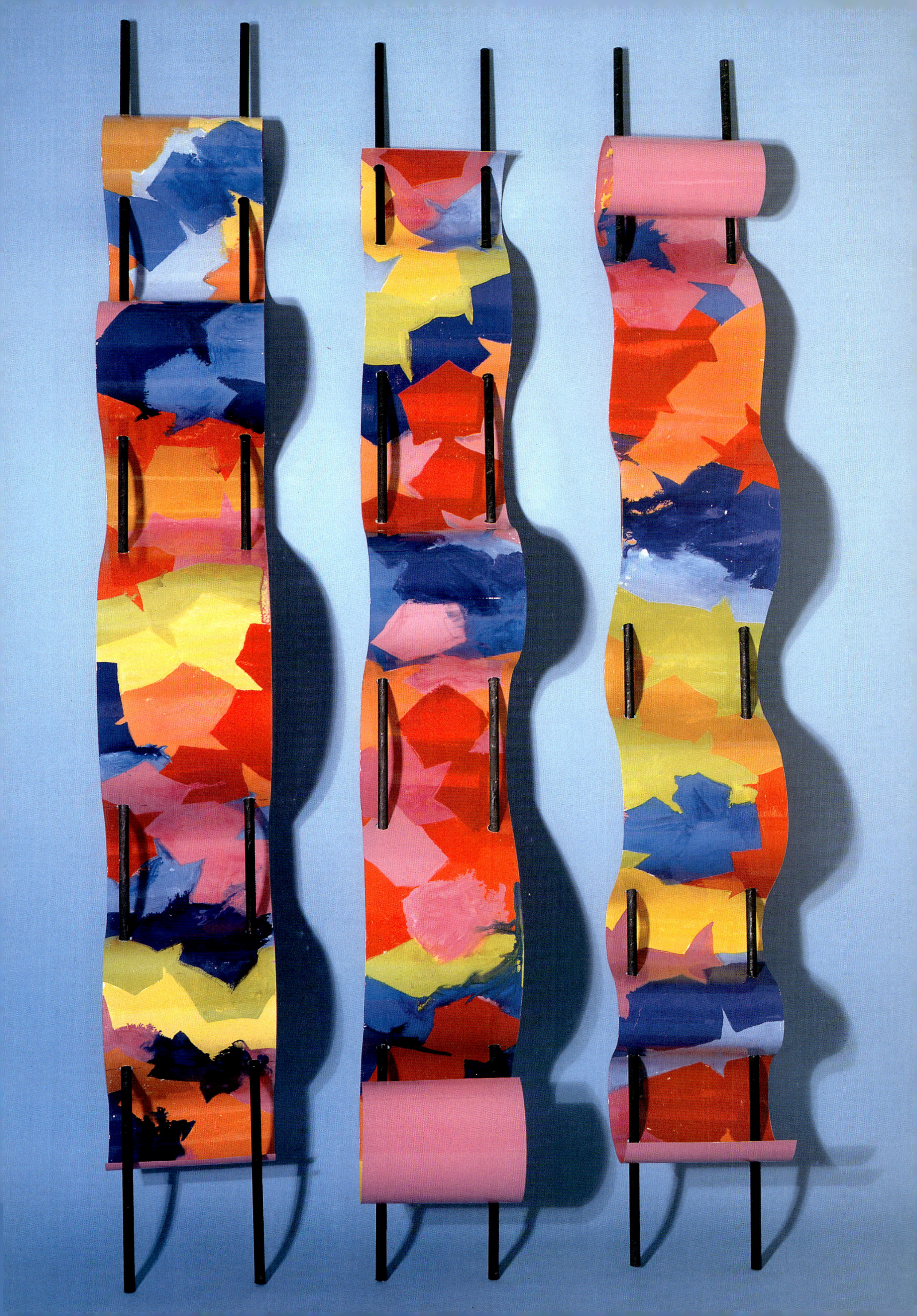

Rain Dance II, 1987, enamel on aluminum, $77\frac{1}{2}$" x 29" x 12"

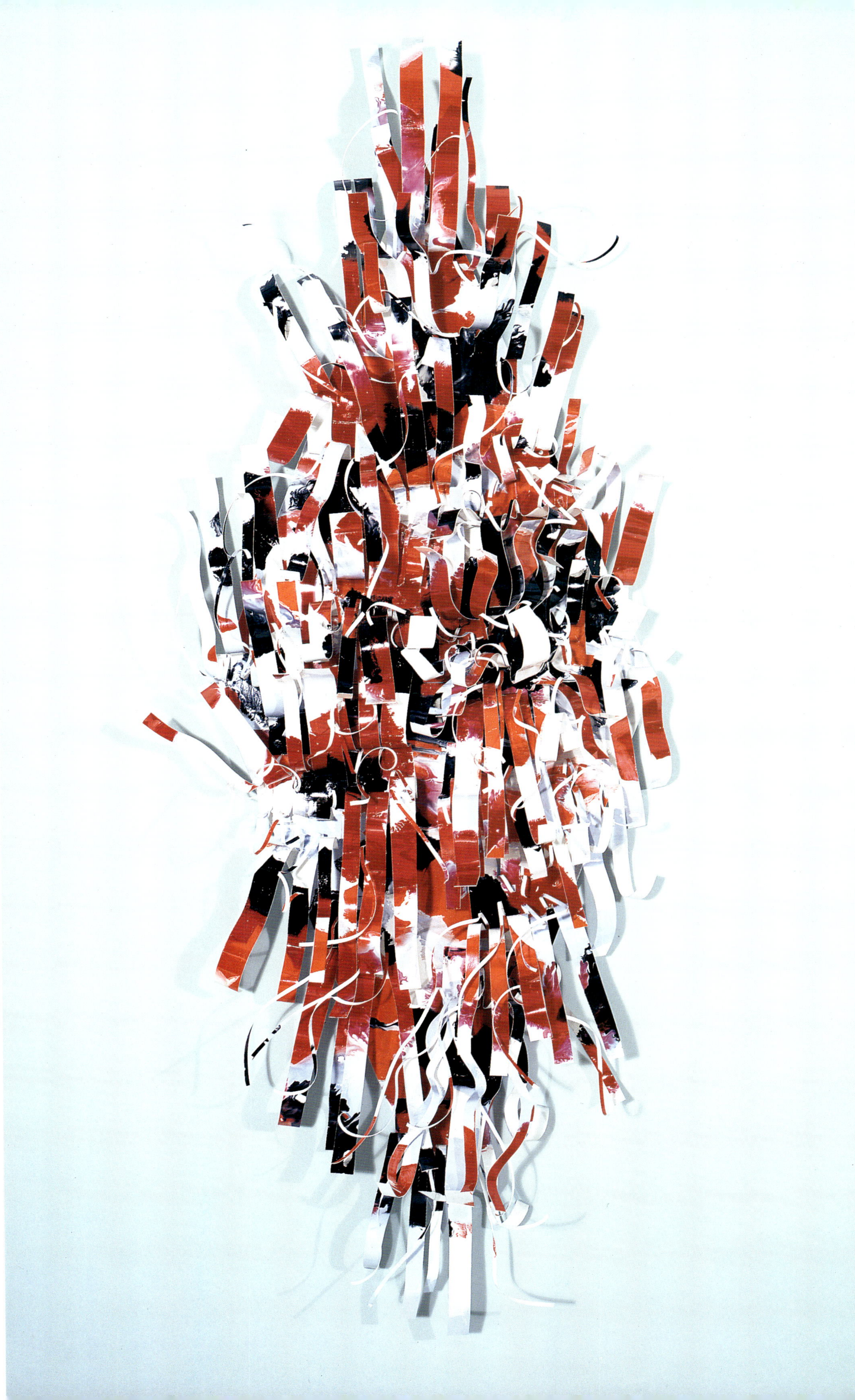

Rain Dance III, 1987, enamel on aluminum, 44" x 40" x 15"

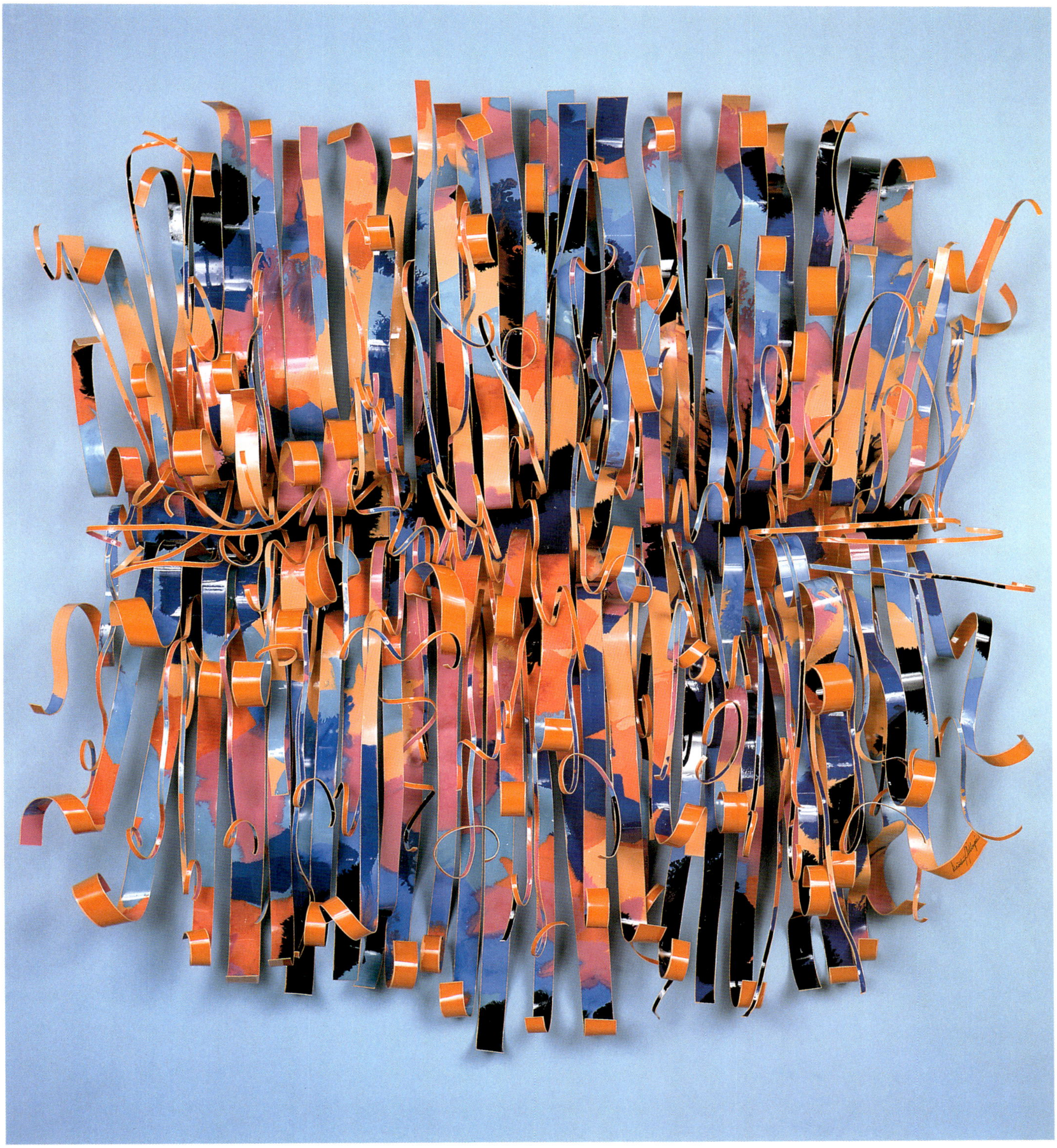

Sounds of the Rain Dance, 1988, enamel on aluminum, 68" x 58" x 14"

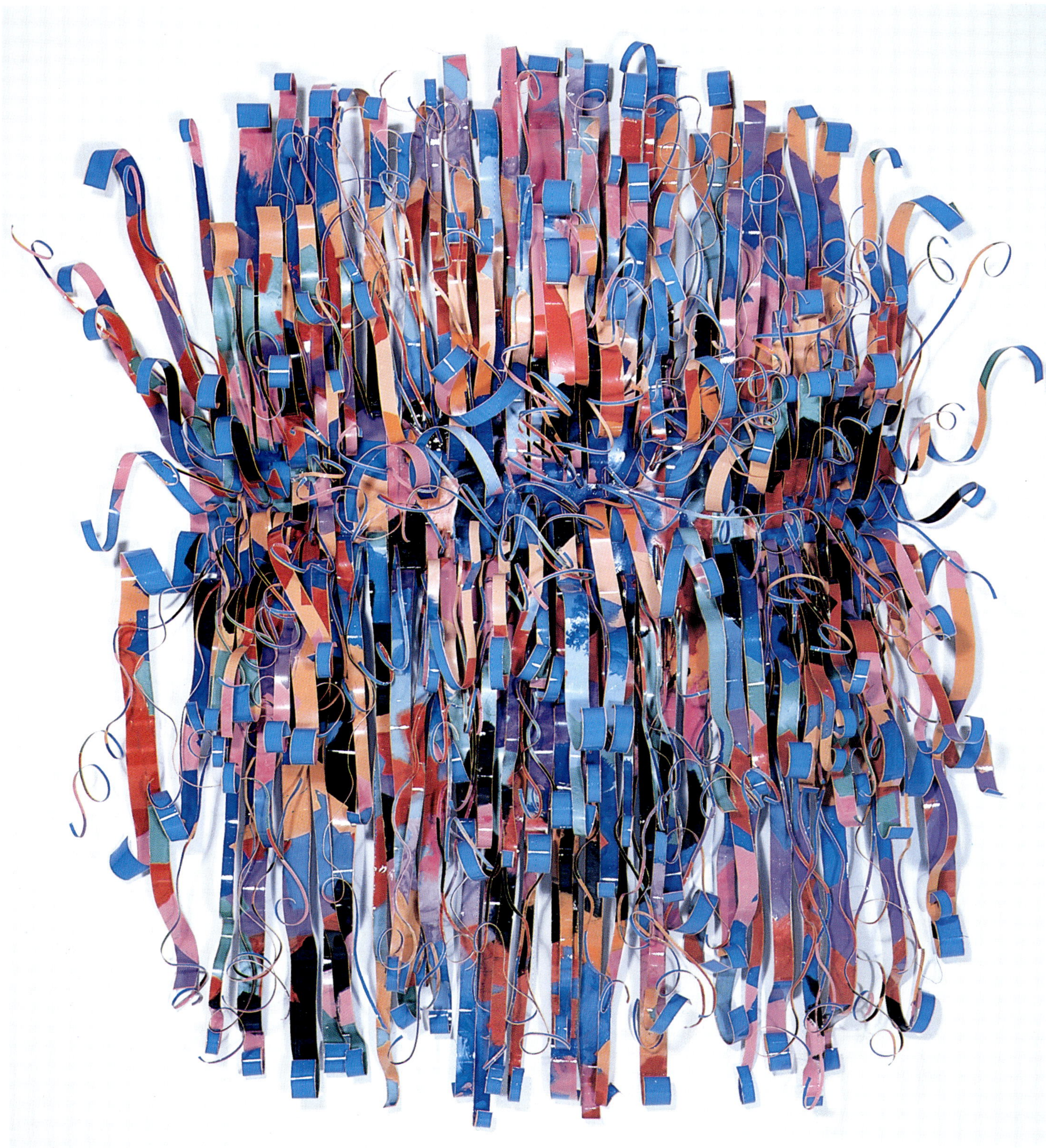

Penelope's Tree, 1987, enamel on aluminum, 9' x 6' x 6'

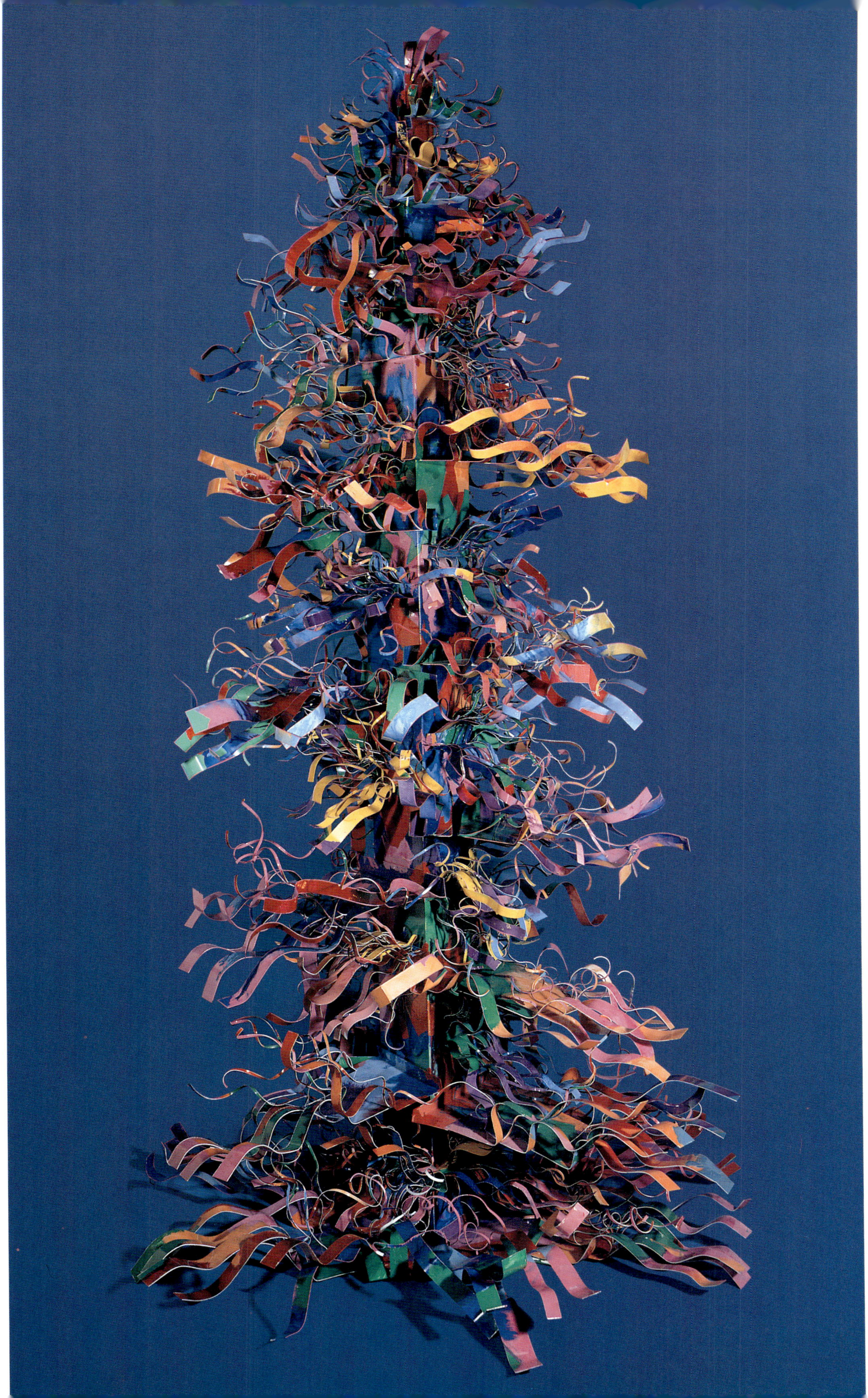

Celestial Journey, 1987, enamel on aluminum, 58" x 40" x 15"

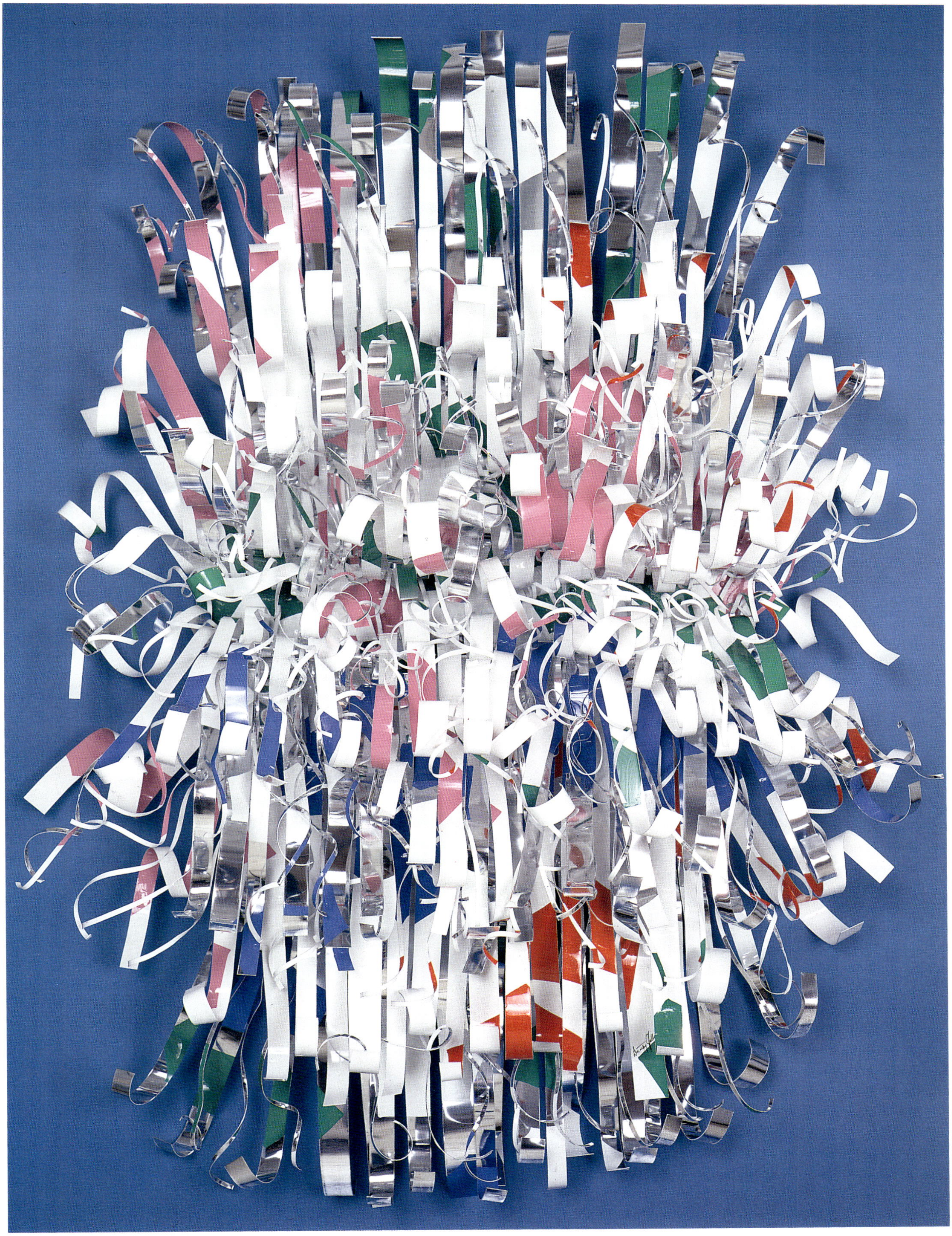

Once upon a Royal Moonbeam, 1988, enamel on aluminum, 48" x 28" x 10"

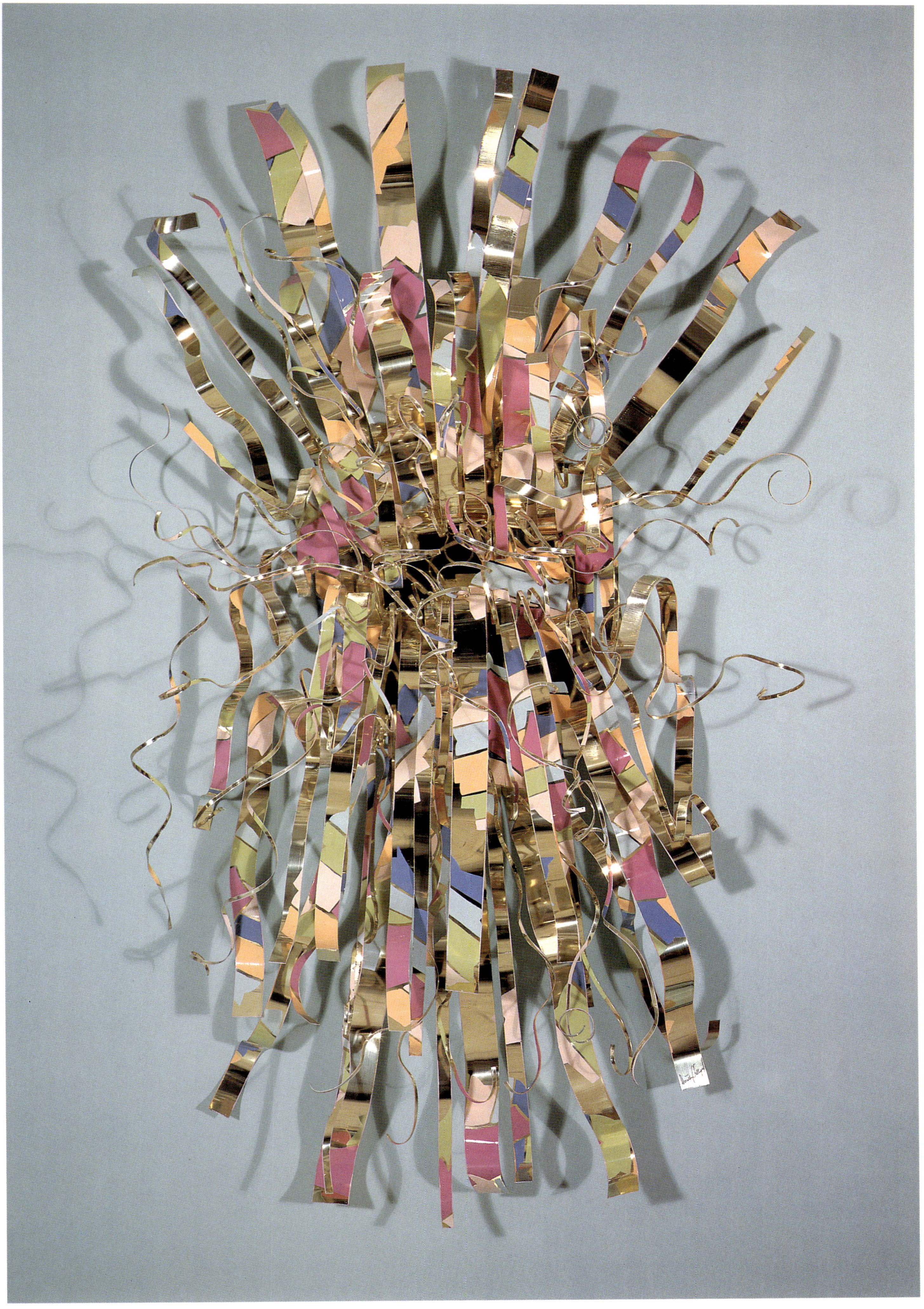

Royal Sentinel, 1984–1988, enamel on aluminum, 72" x 28" x 20"

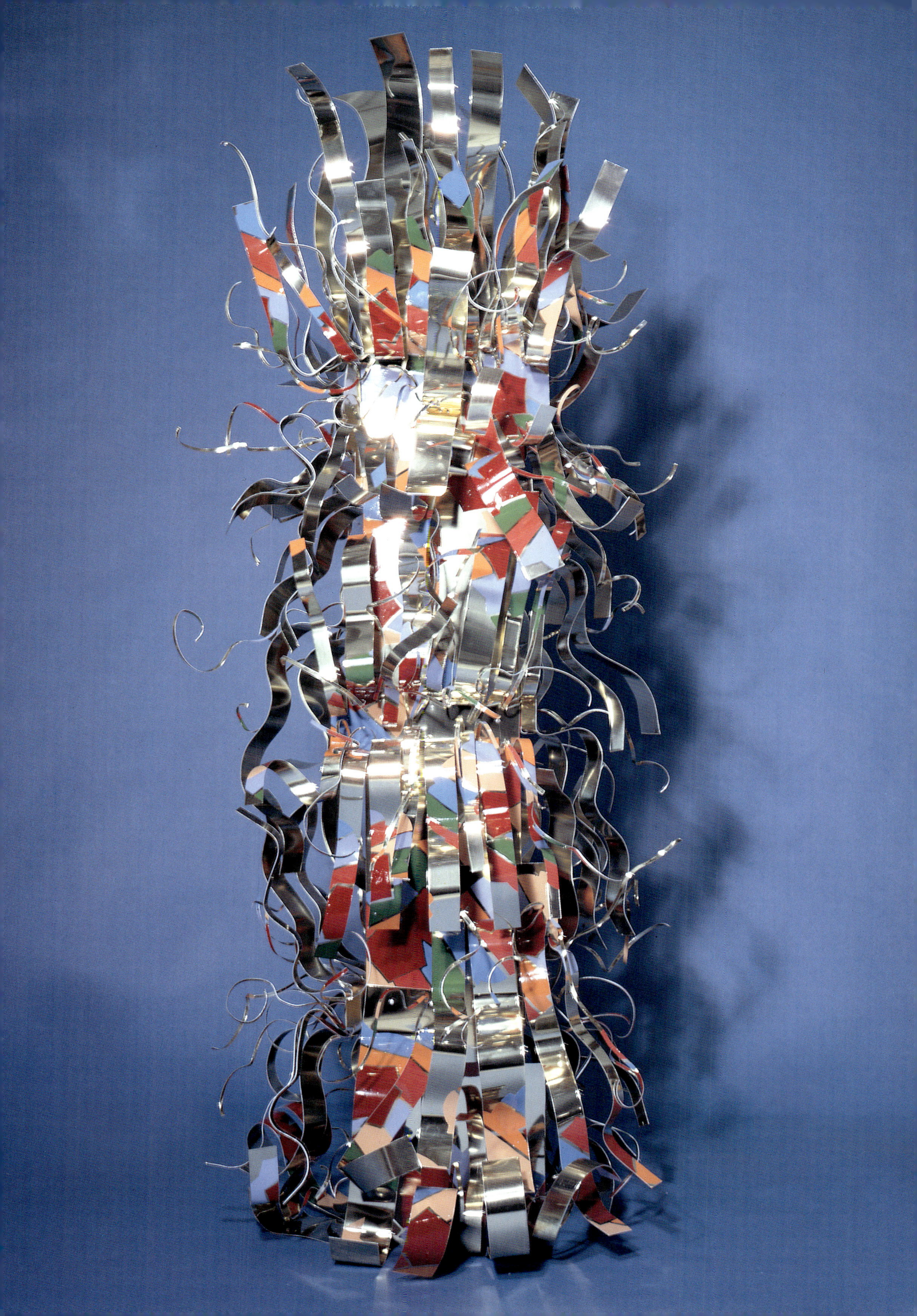

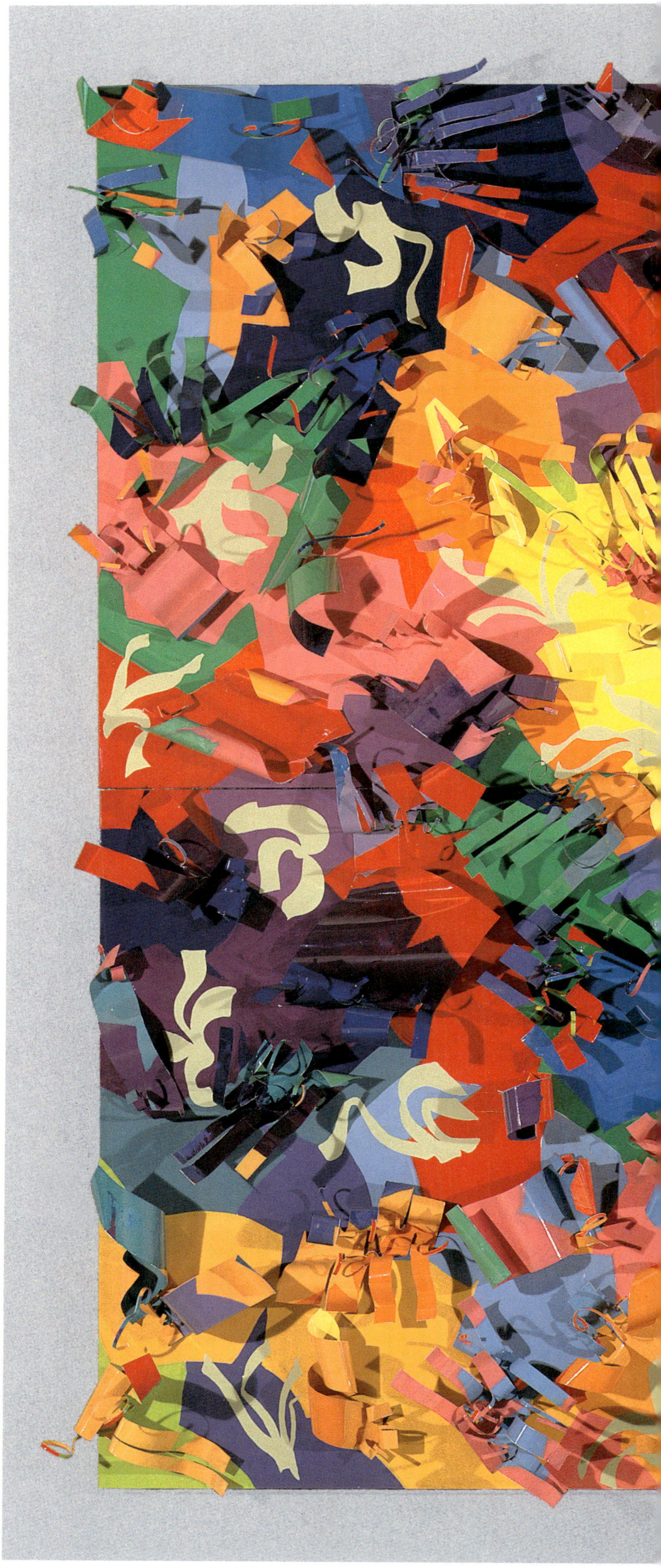

Encounter with a Past Presence, 1988, enamel on aluminum, 76" x 96" x 12"

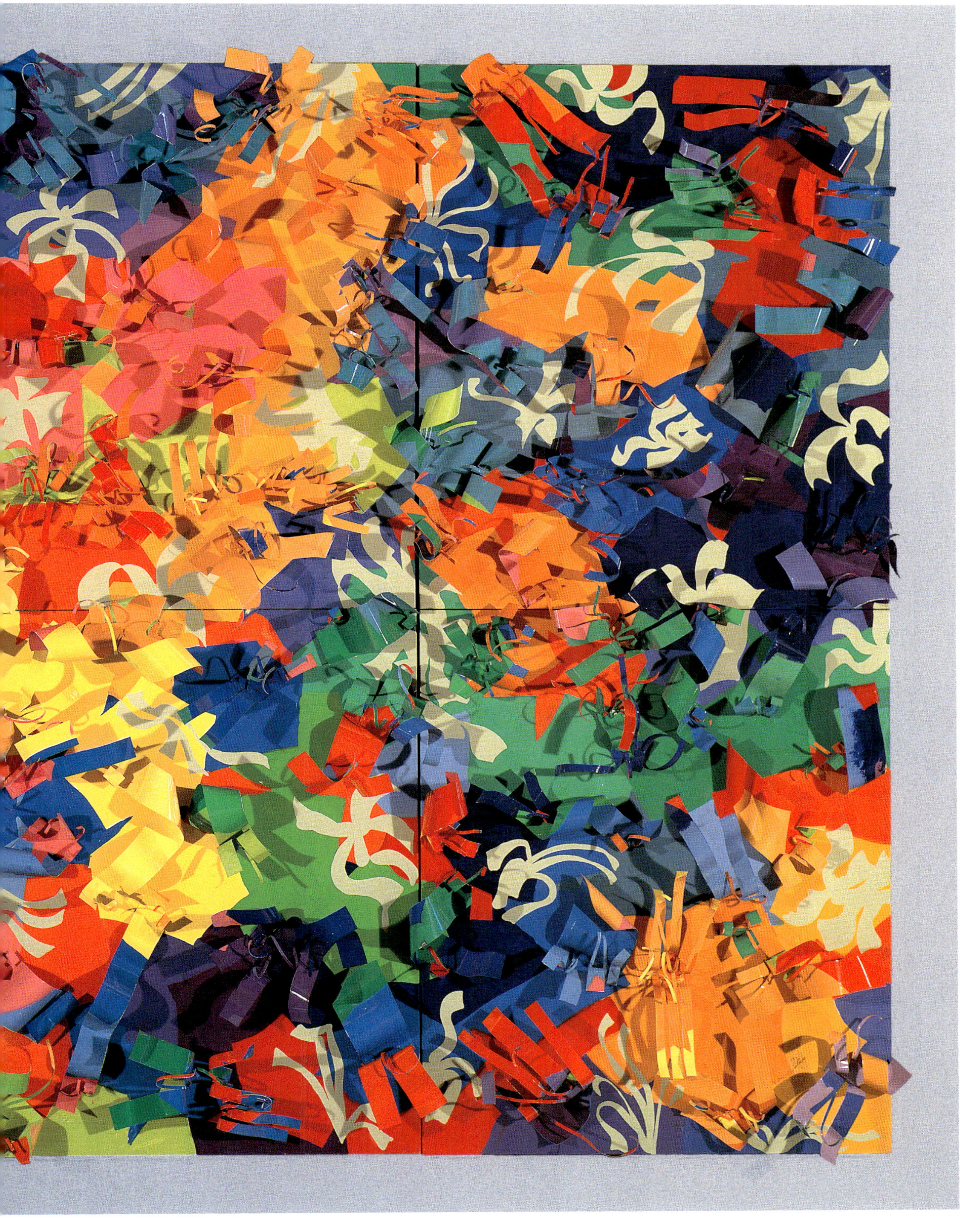

Festival: Sierra Sunset, 1988, enamel on aluminum, 53" x 36" x 8"

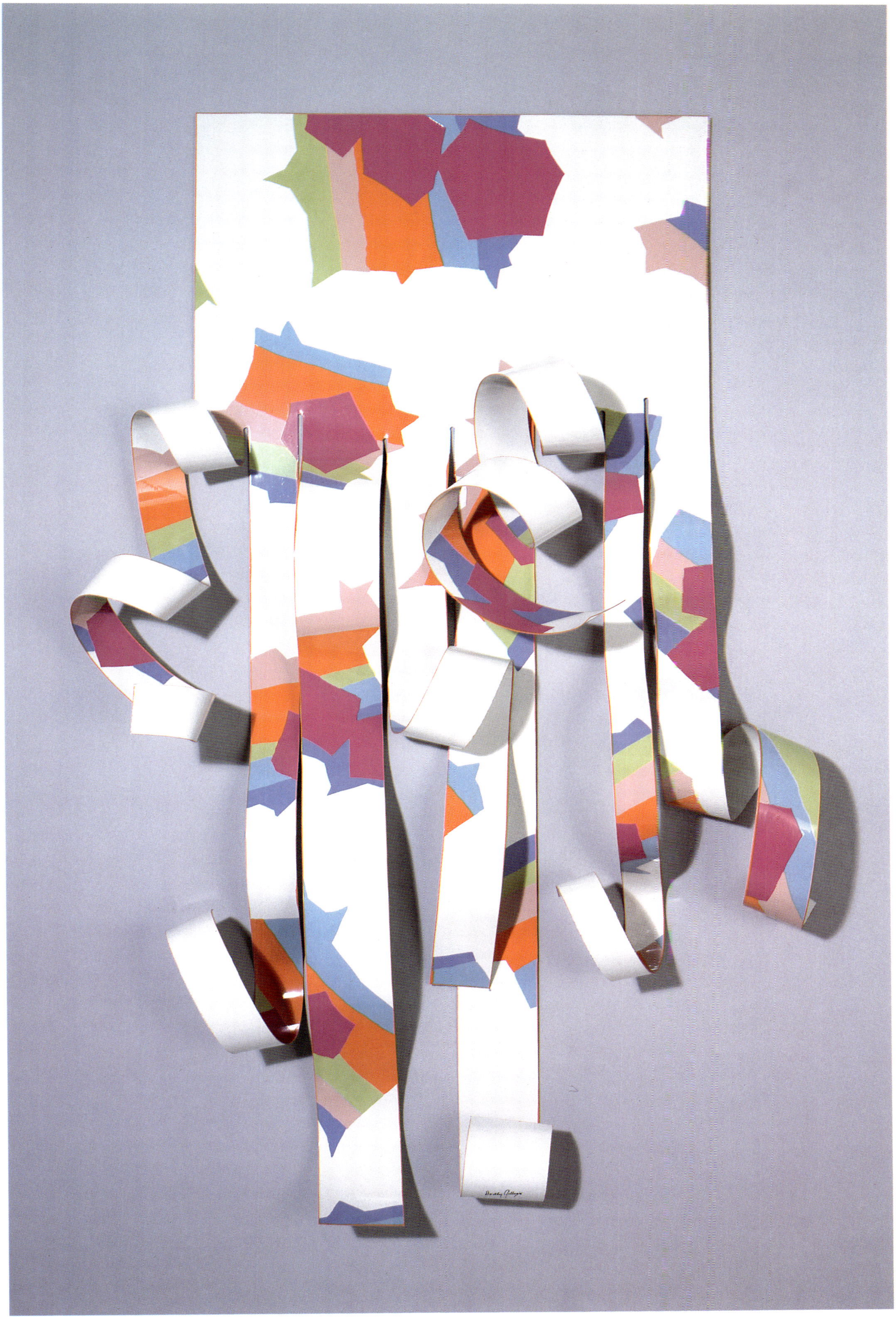

Festival Concerto, 1988, enamel on aluminum, 48" x 27" x 7"

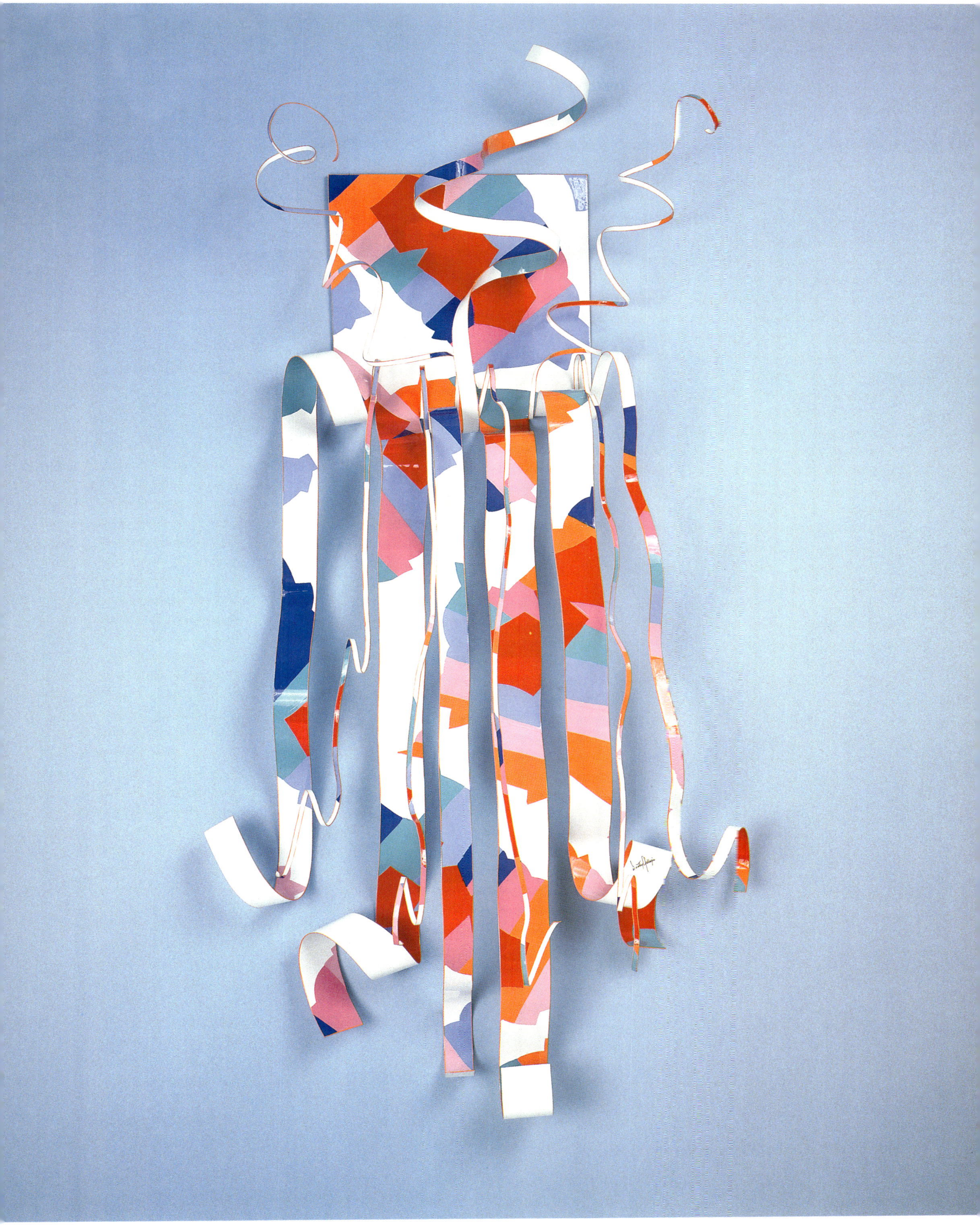

Harlequin Song, 1989, silkscreen on aluminum, 16" x 16" x 16"

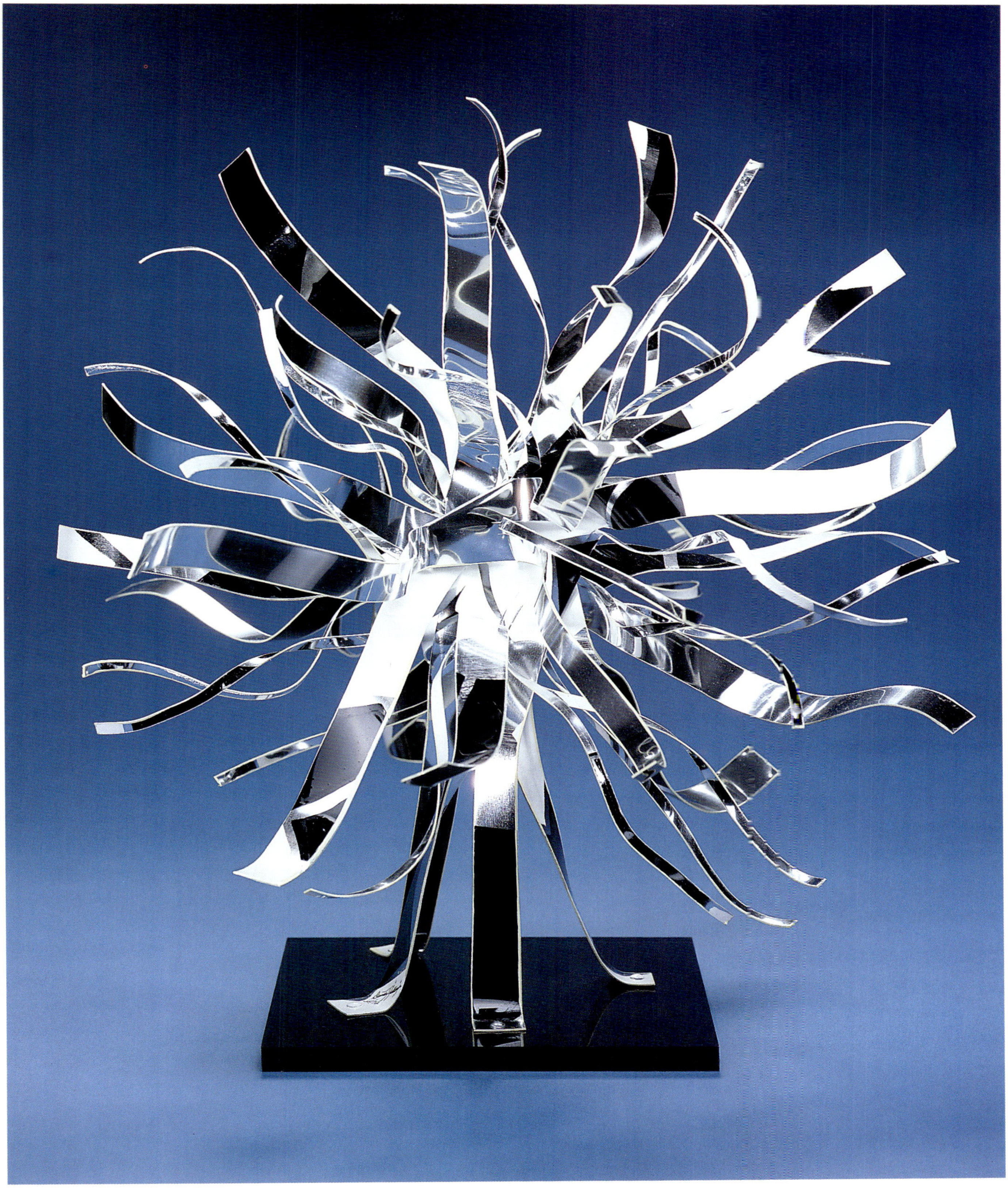

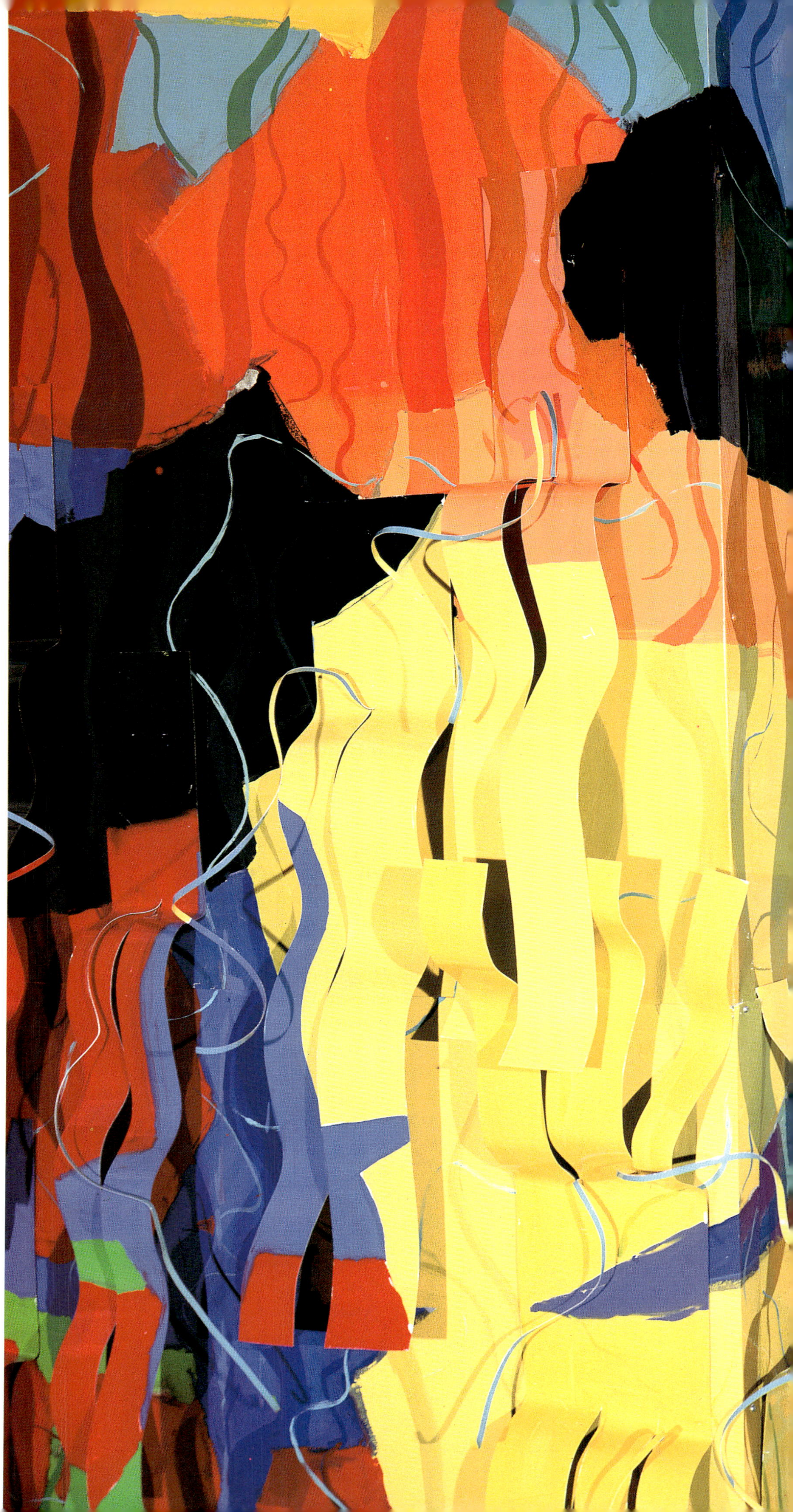

Detail of *Colorfalls* (page 145), 1989, enamel on aluminum, 42' x 11' x 3'

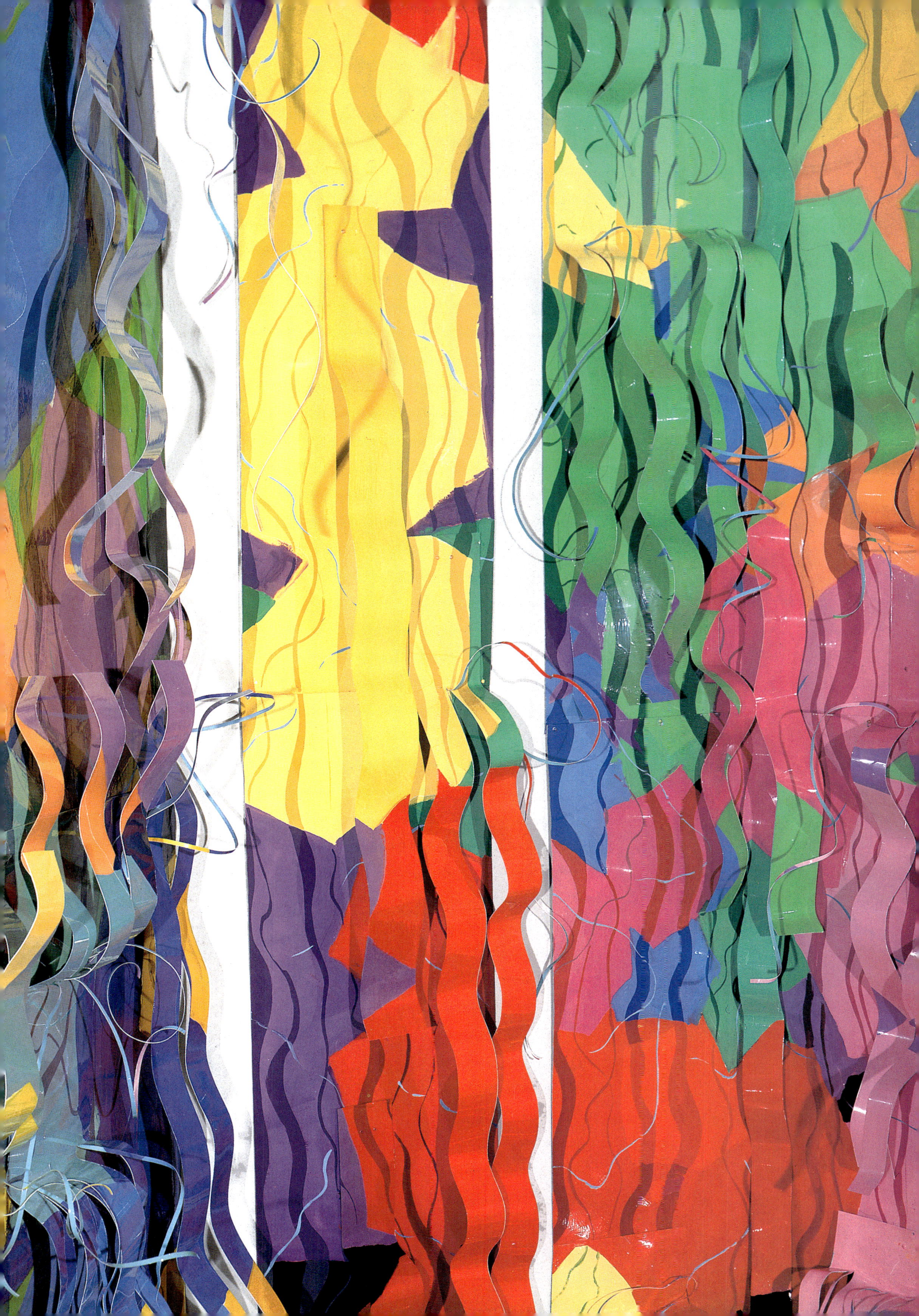

Winter Jazz, 1989, enamel on aluminum, 35" x 29" x 29"

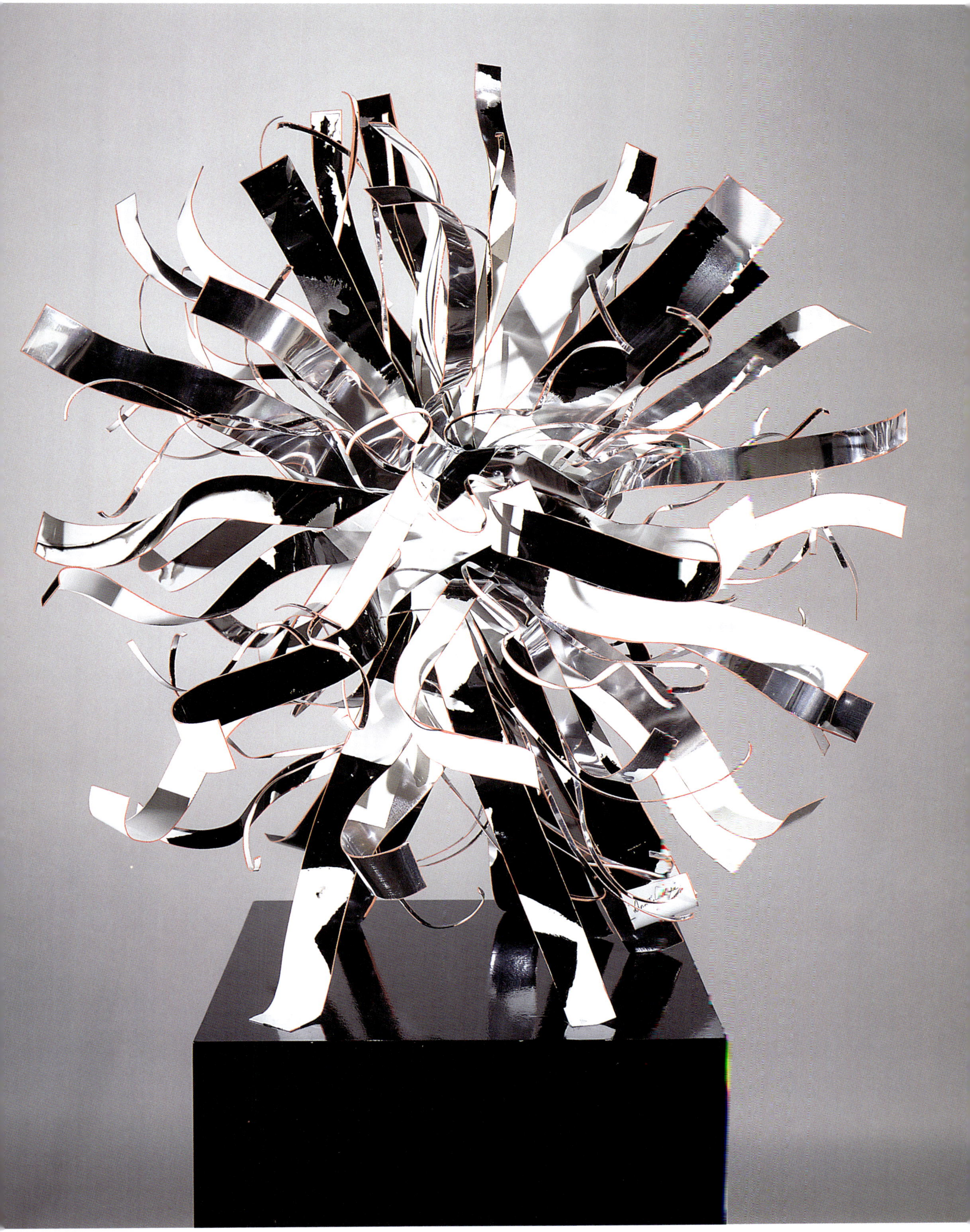

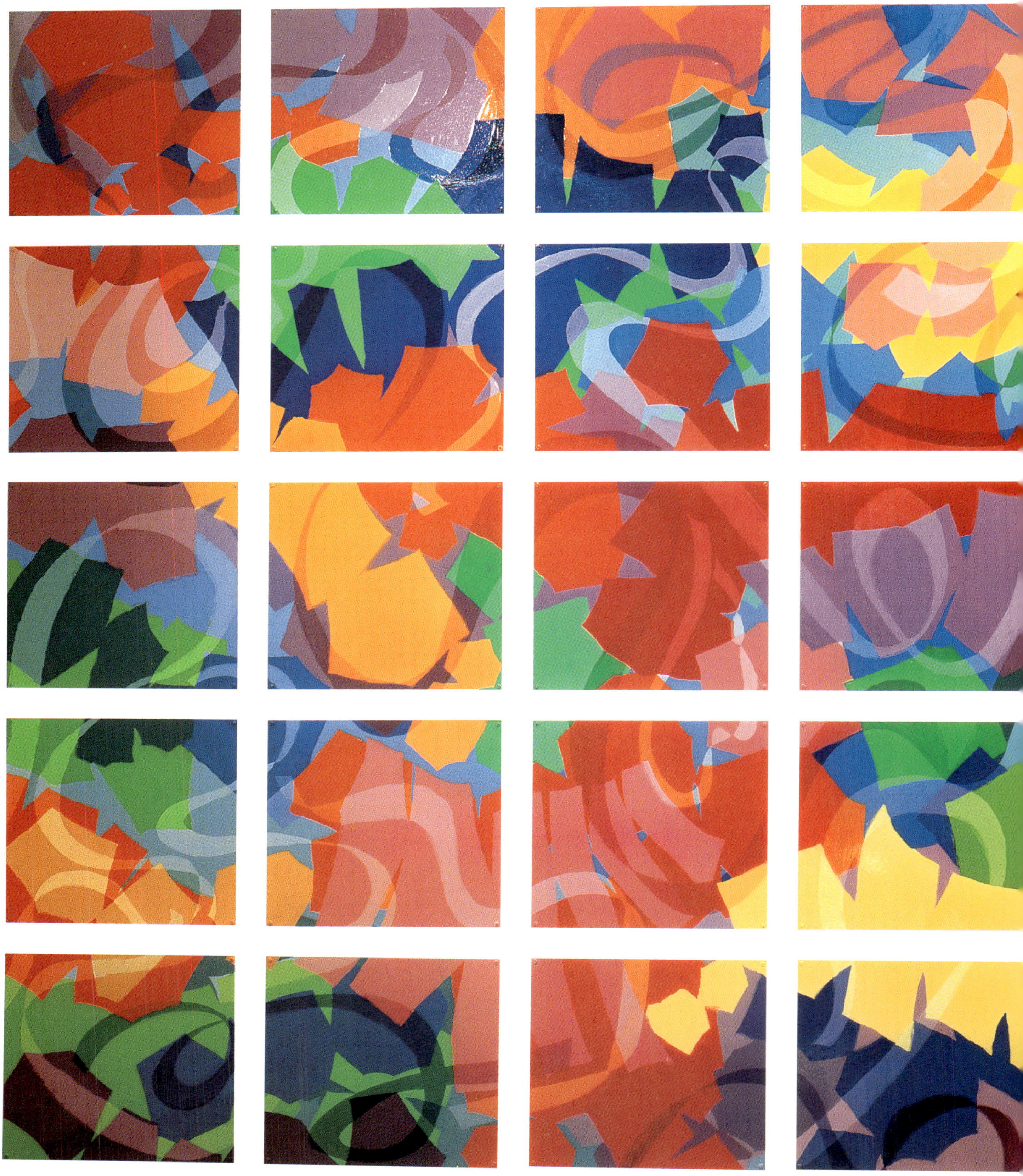

Color and Forms in Flight, 1989, enamel on aluminum, 12'2" x 22'2"

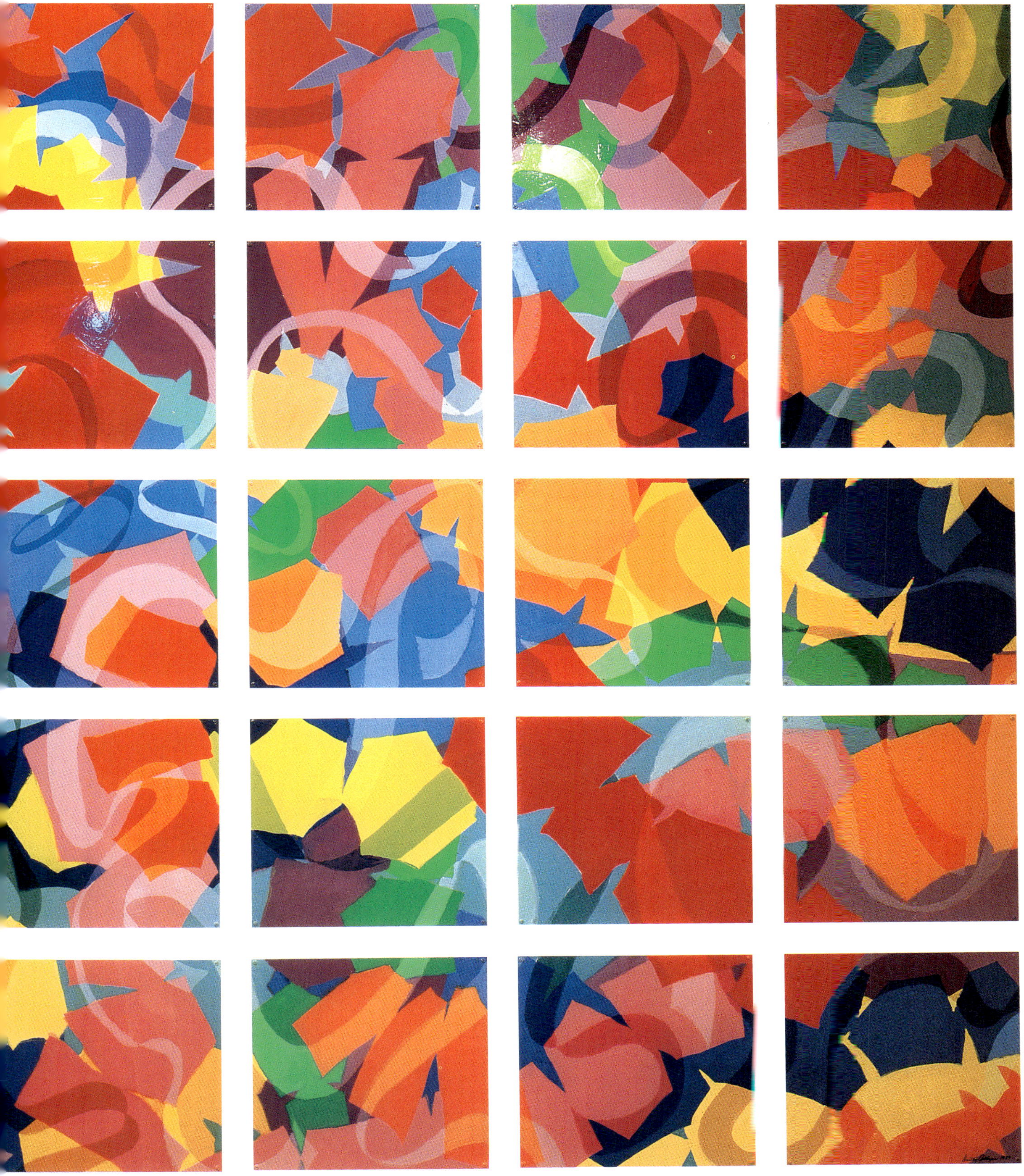

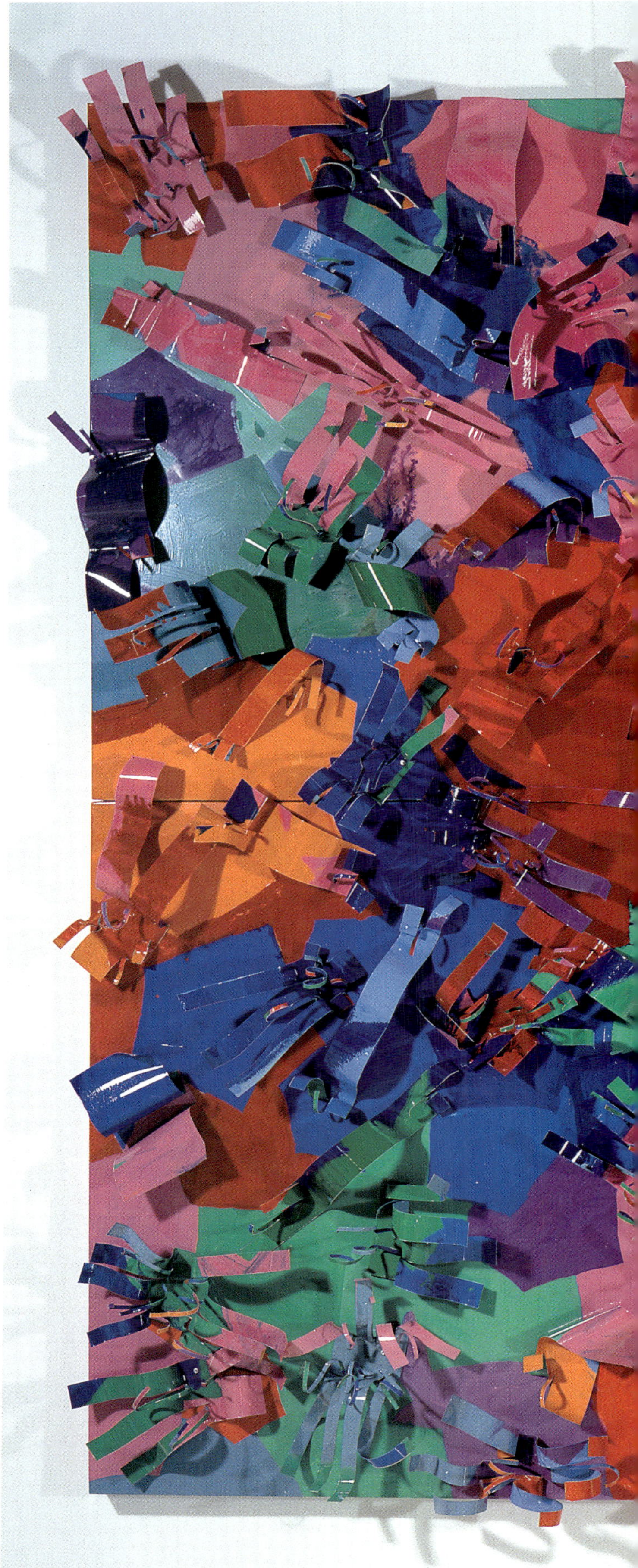

Encounter with a Future Promise II, 1989, enamel on aluminum, 64" x 80" x 8"

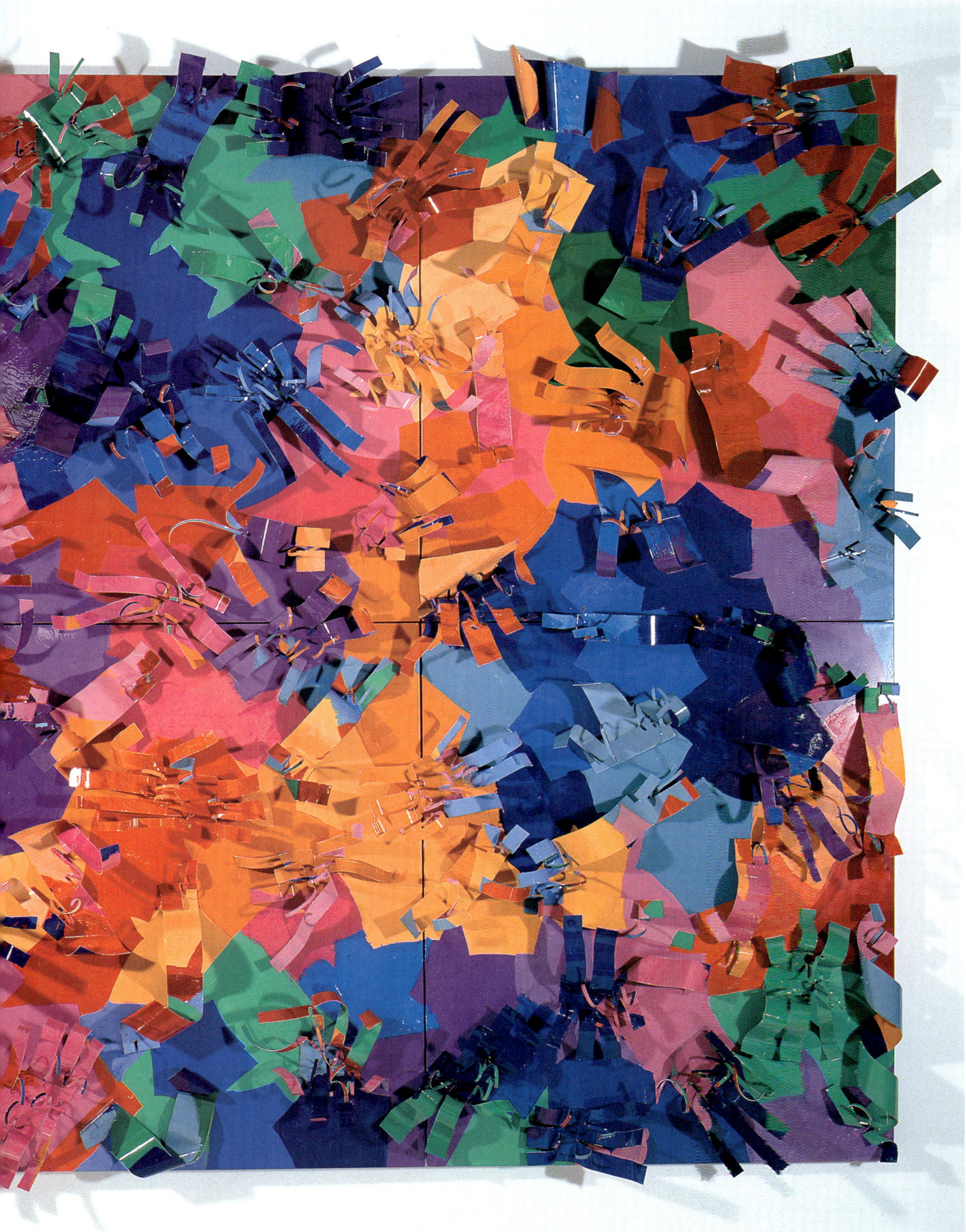

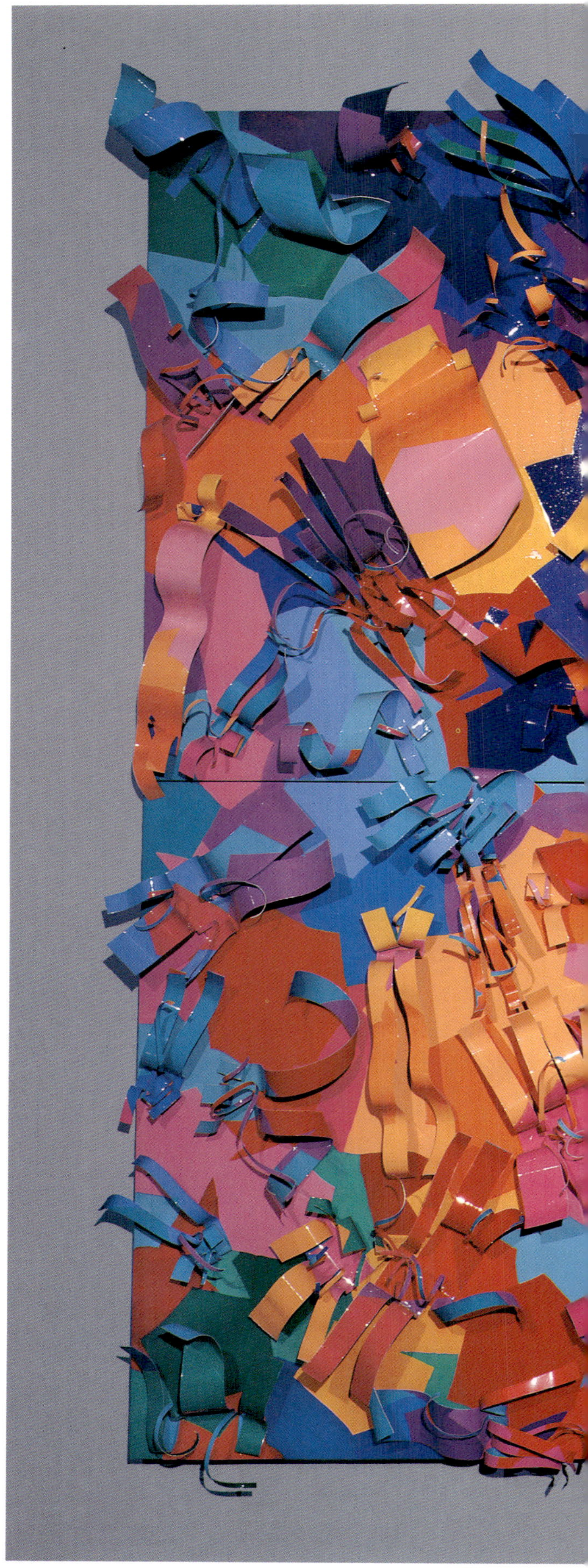

Encounter with a Future Promise III, 1989,
enamel on aluminum, 64" x 80" x 10"

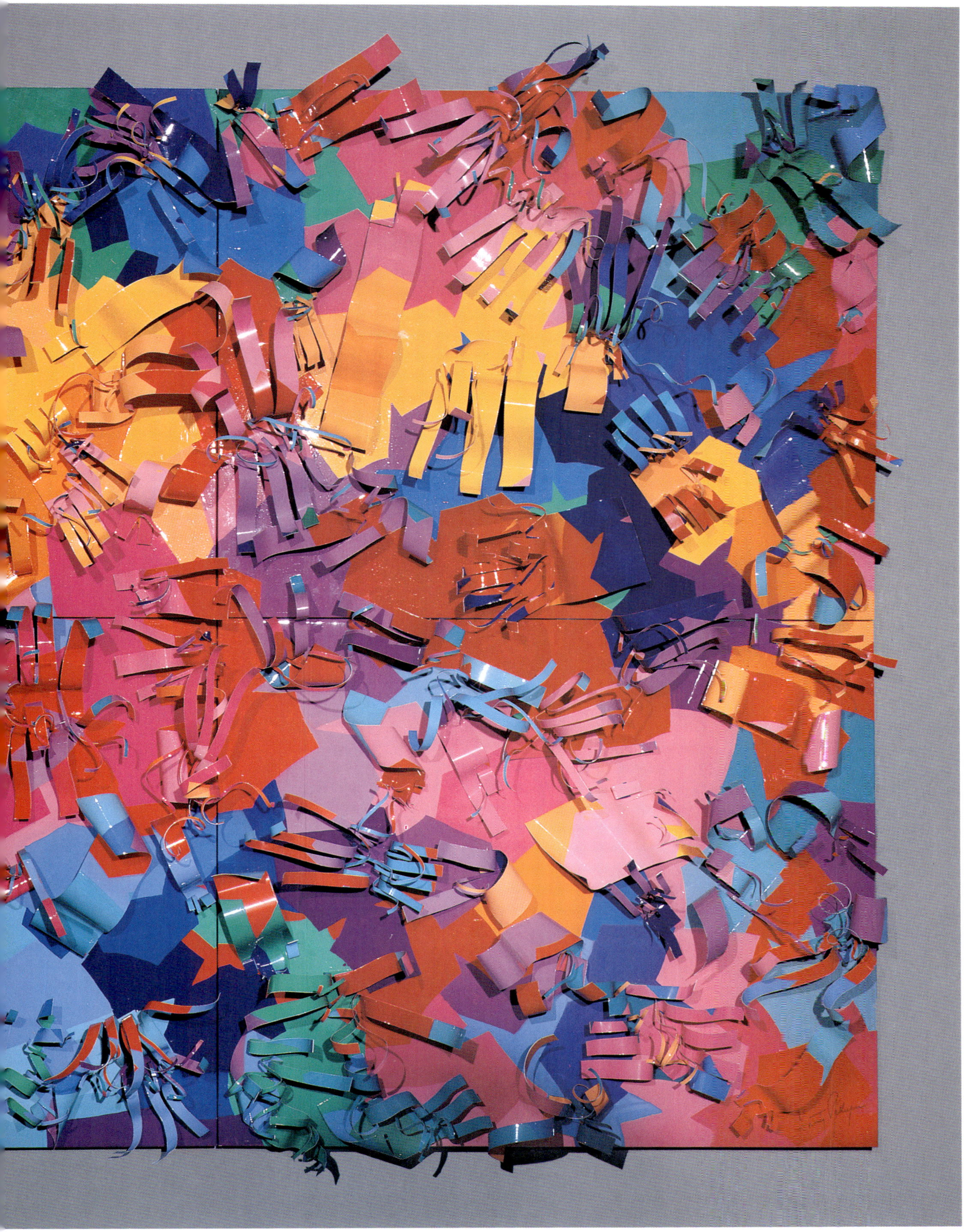

Colorfall: Landscape, 1990, enamel on aluminum, 48" x 40" x 7"

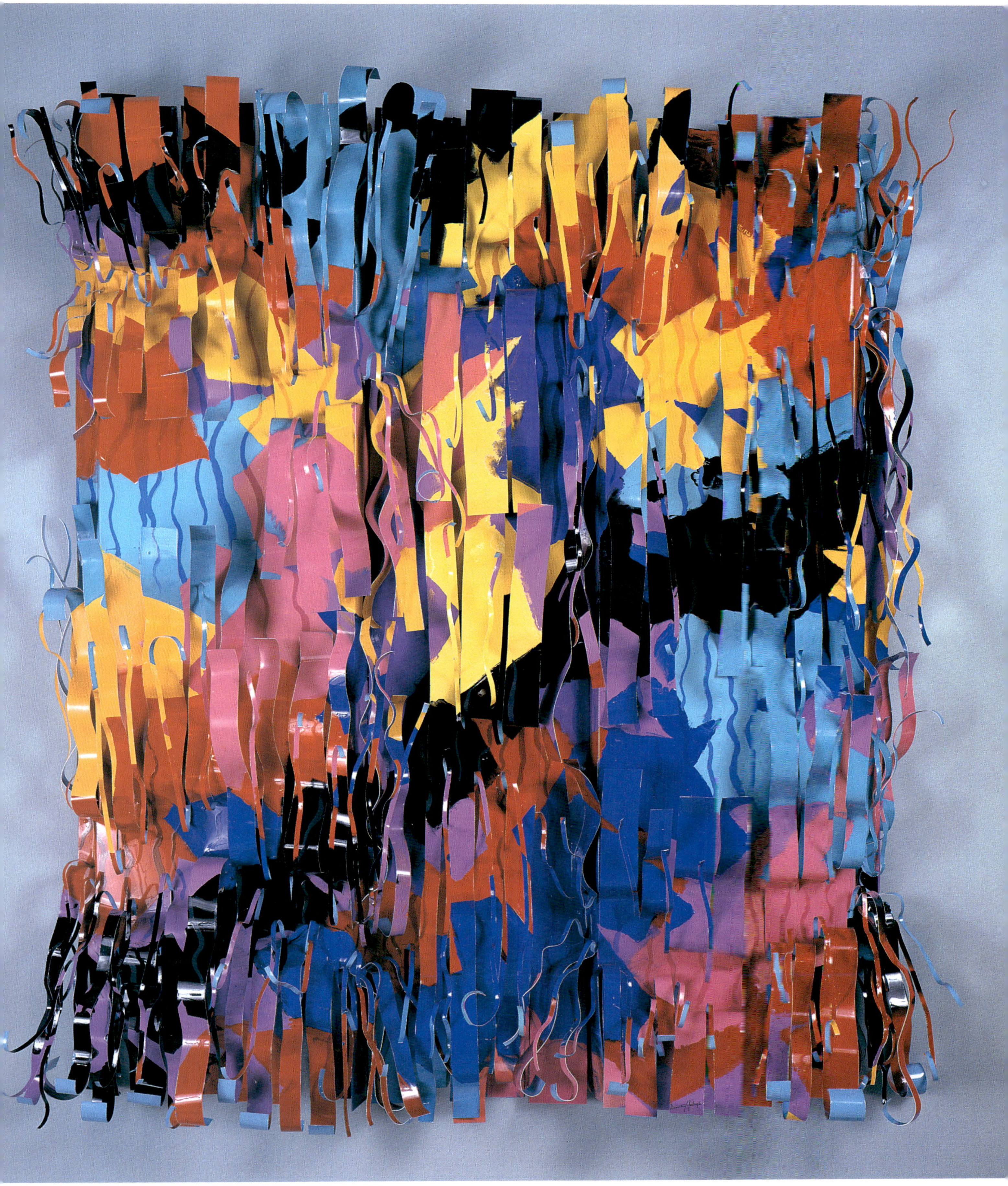

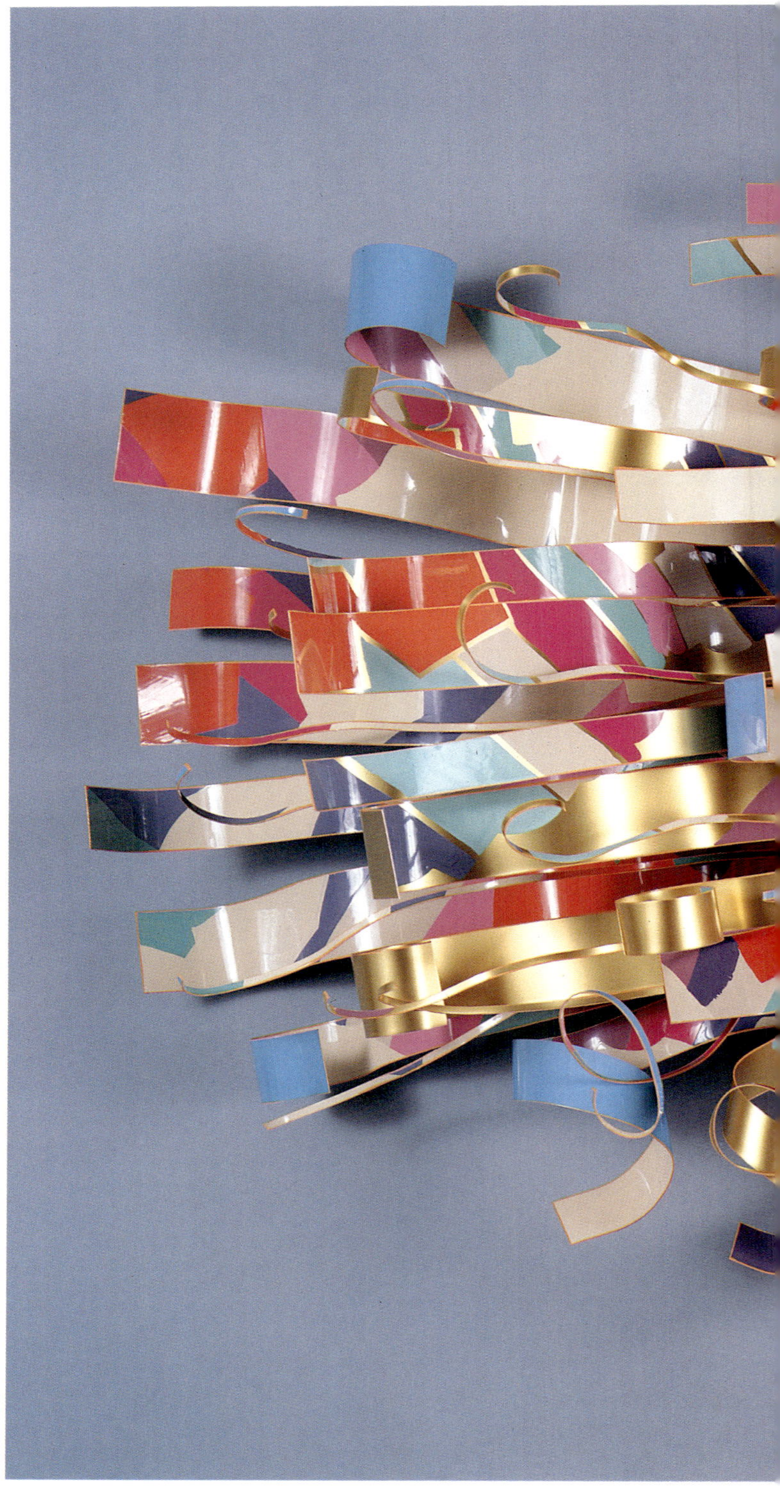

Royal Garden Crest, 1990, enamel on aluminum, 35" x 54½" x 16"

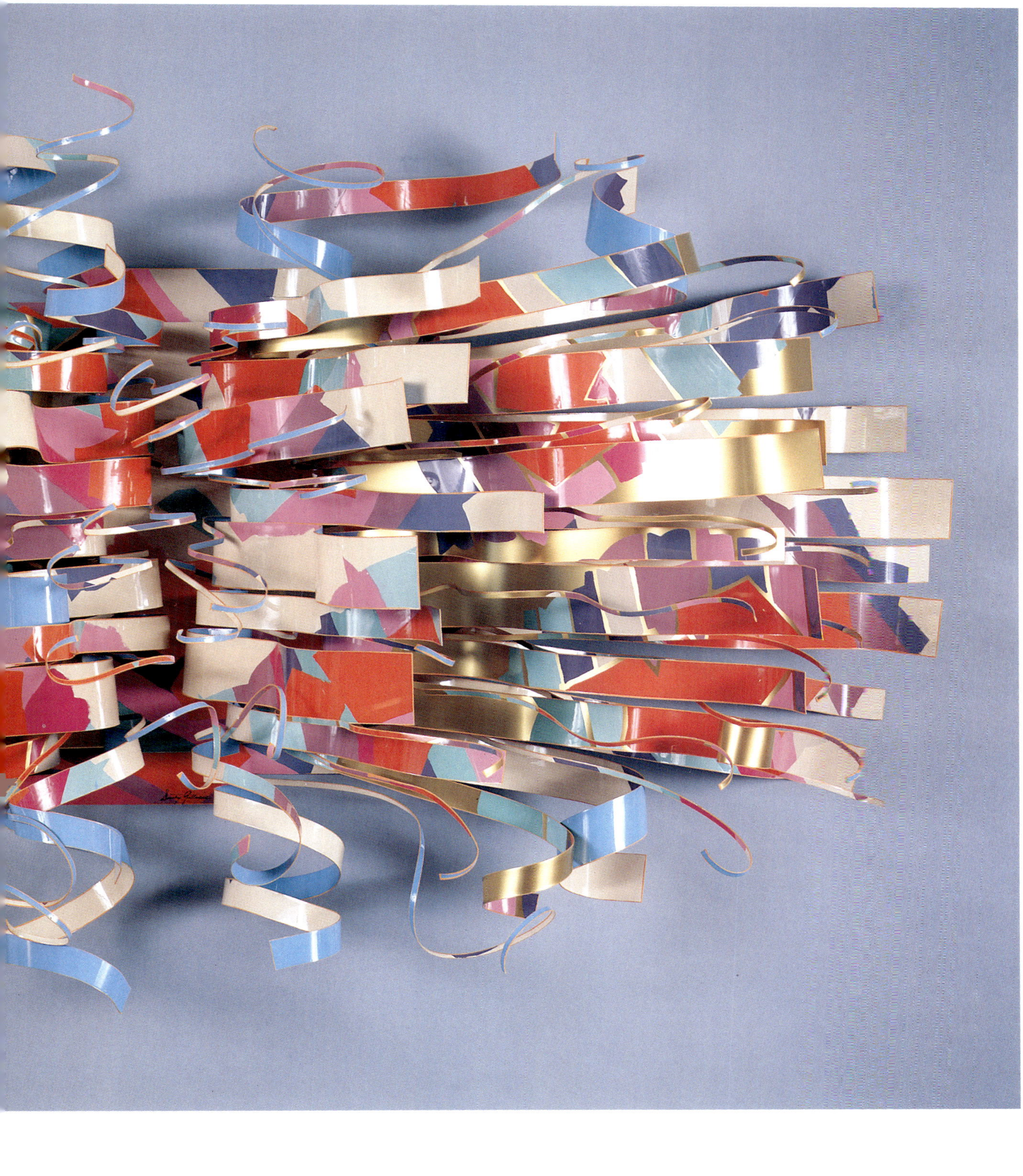

Autumn Beanstalk, 1990, enamel on aluminum, 96" x 23" x 10"

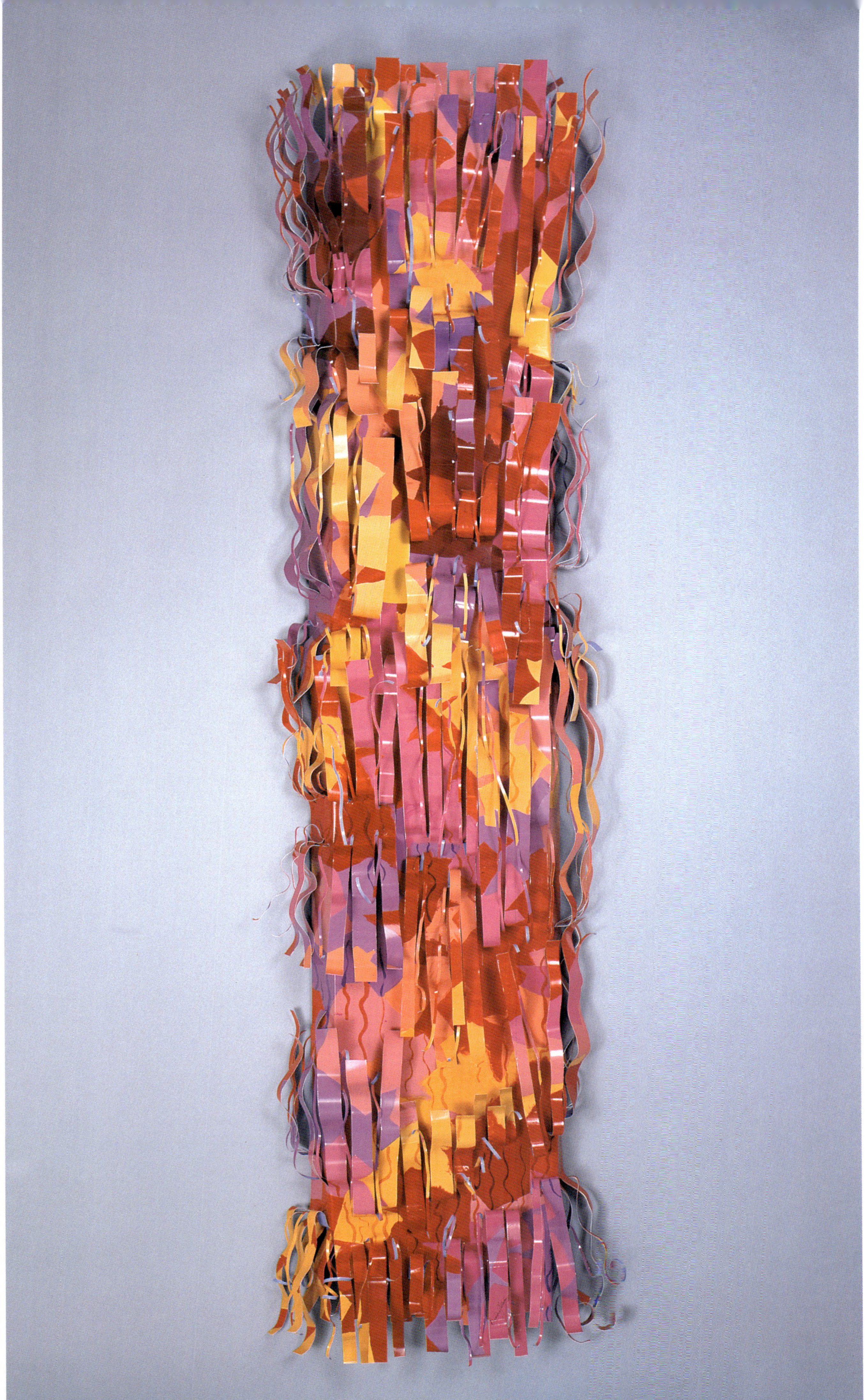

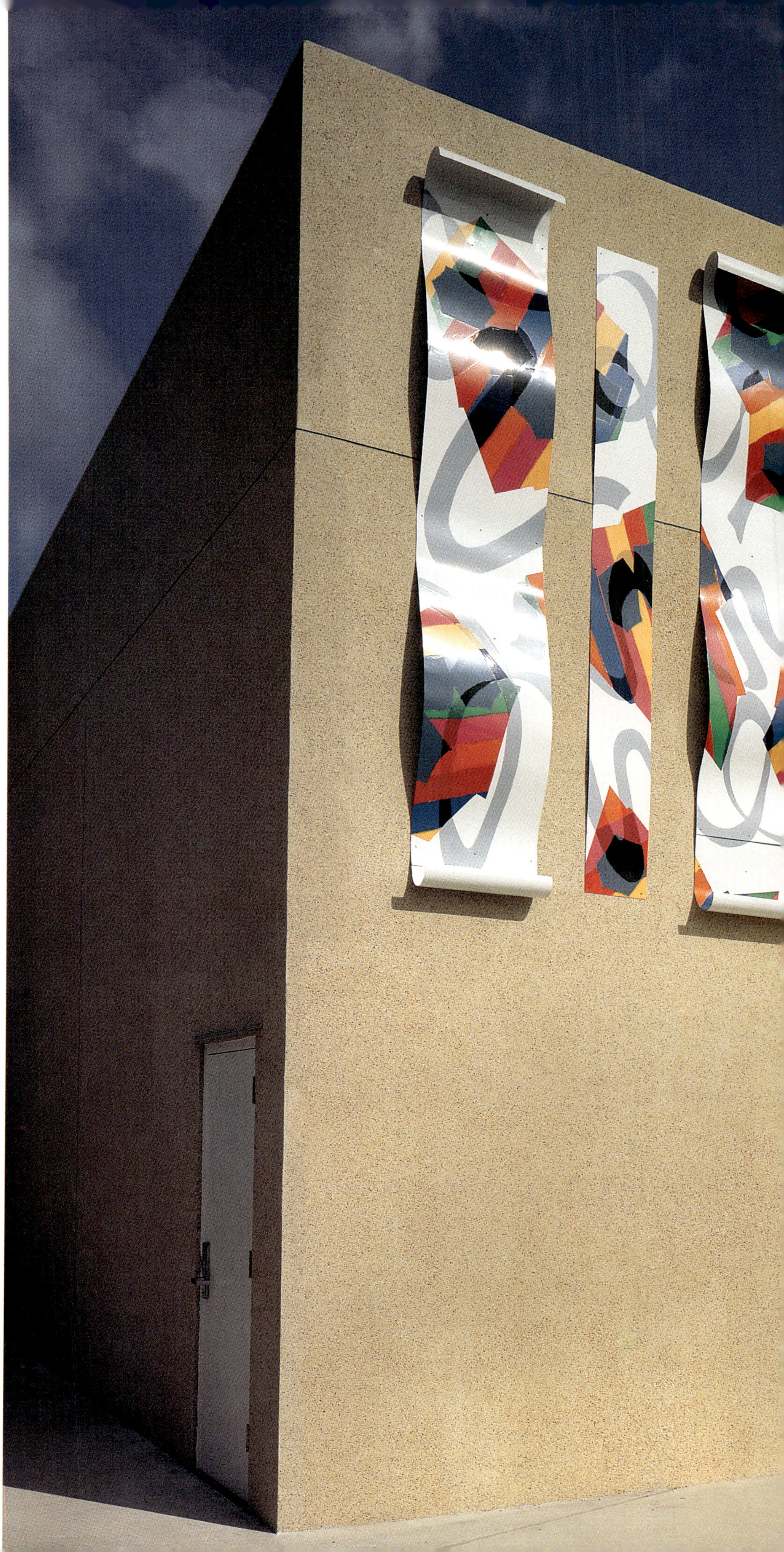

Color Clouds and Ribboned Currents, 1990, enamel on aluminum, 10' x 20' x 10"

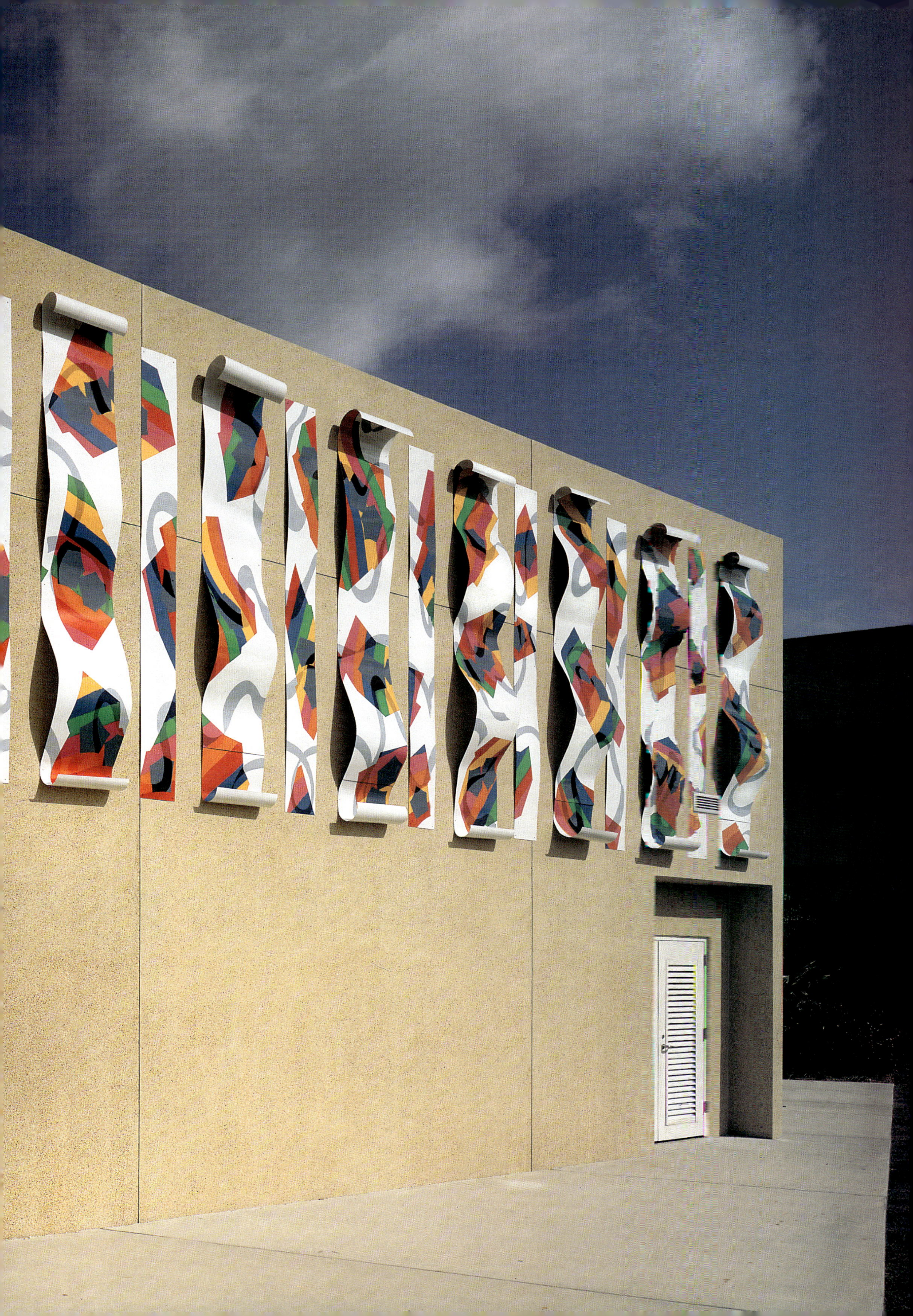

Rite of Spring, 1990, enamel on aluminum, 102" x 53" x 53"

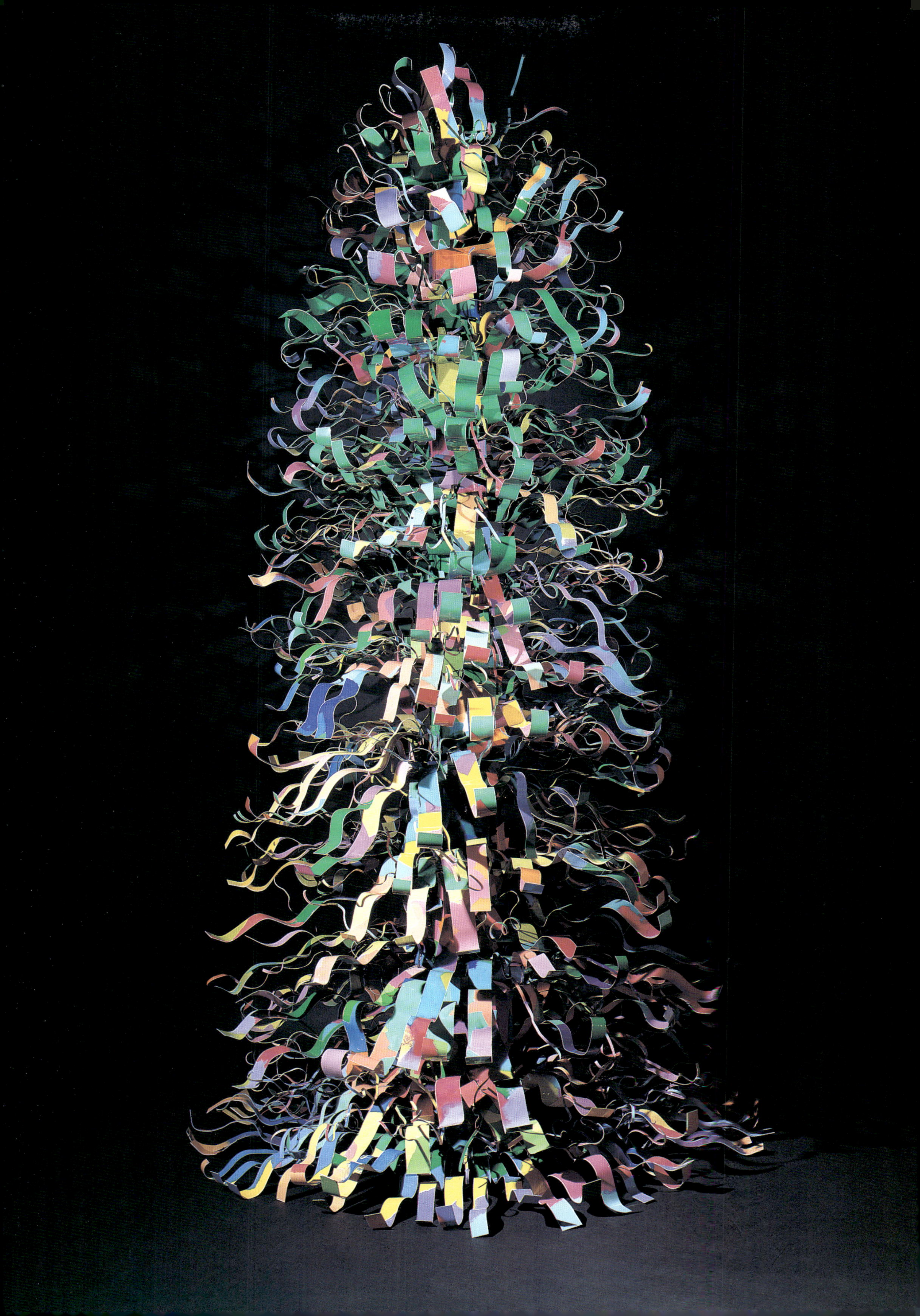

Shaman II, 1990, enamel on aluminum, 89" x 24" x 16"

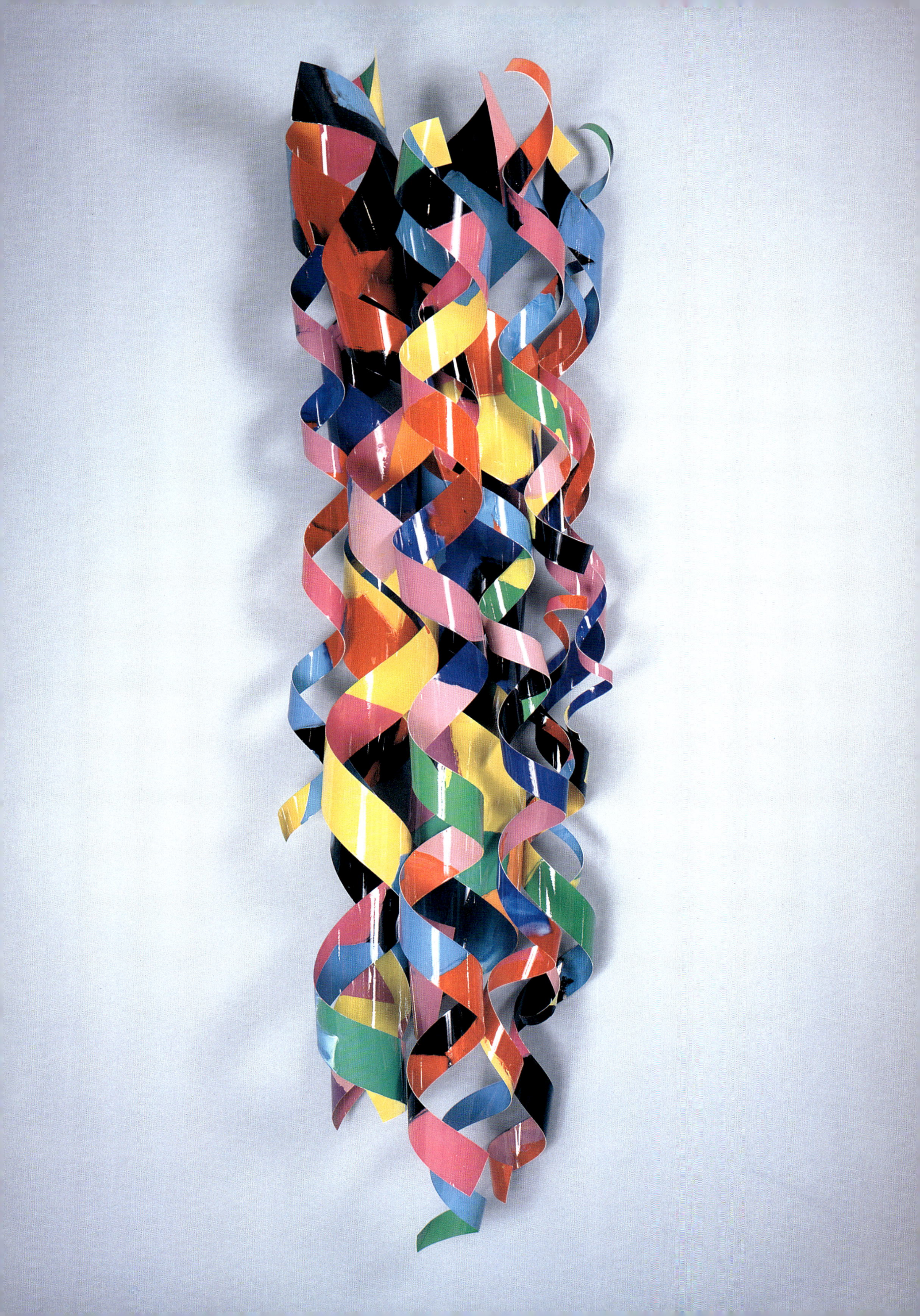

Crayolas, 1990, enamel on aluminum, 44" x 29" x 12"

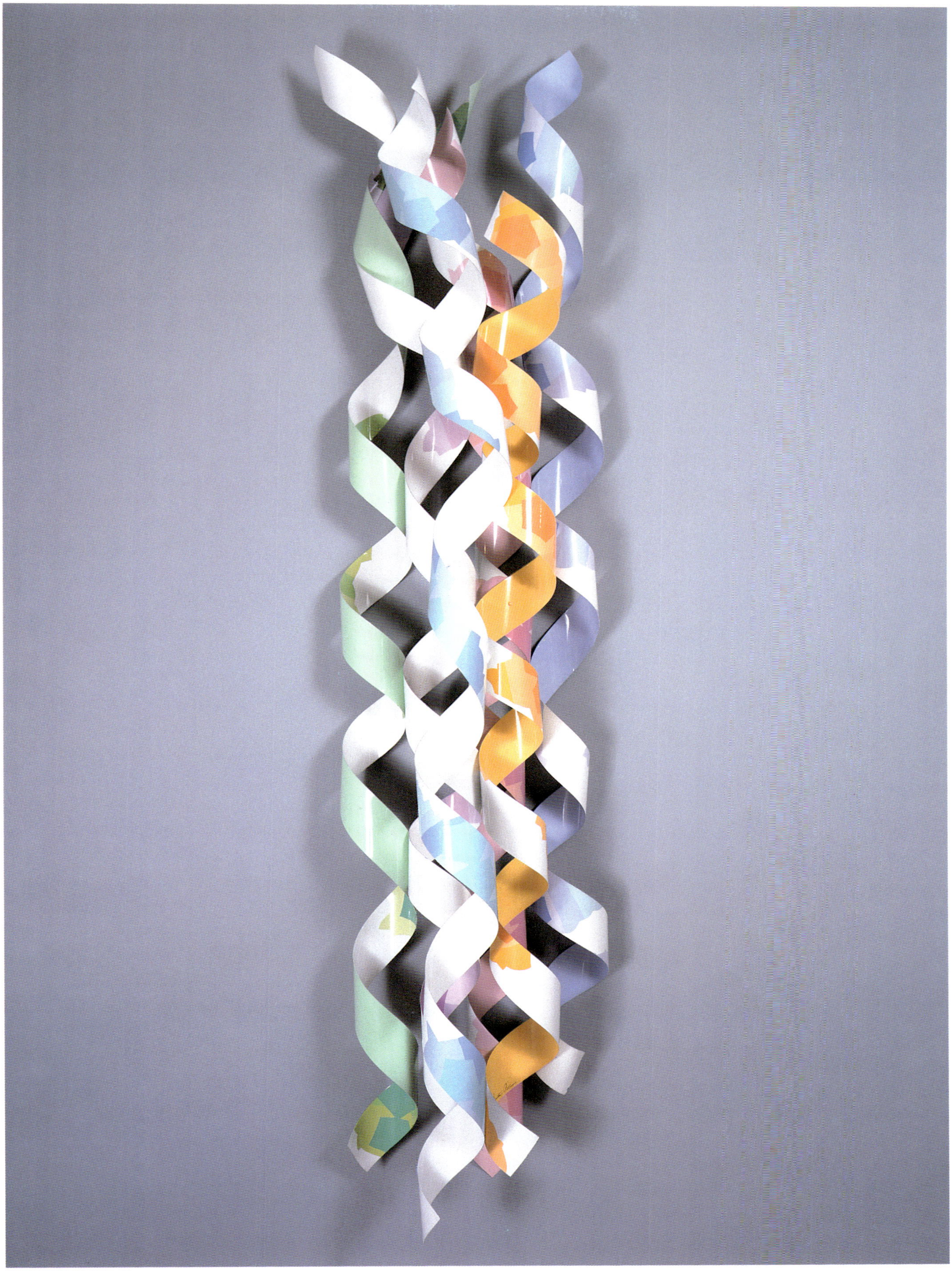

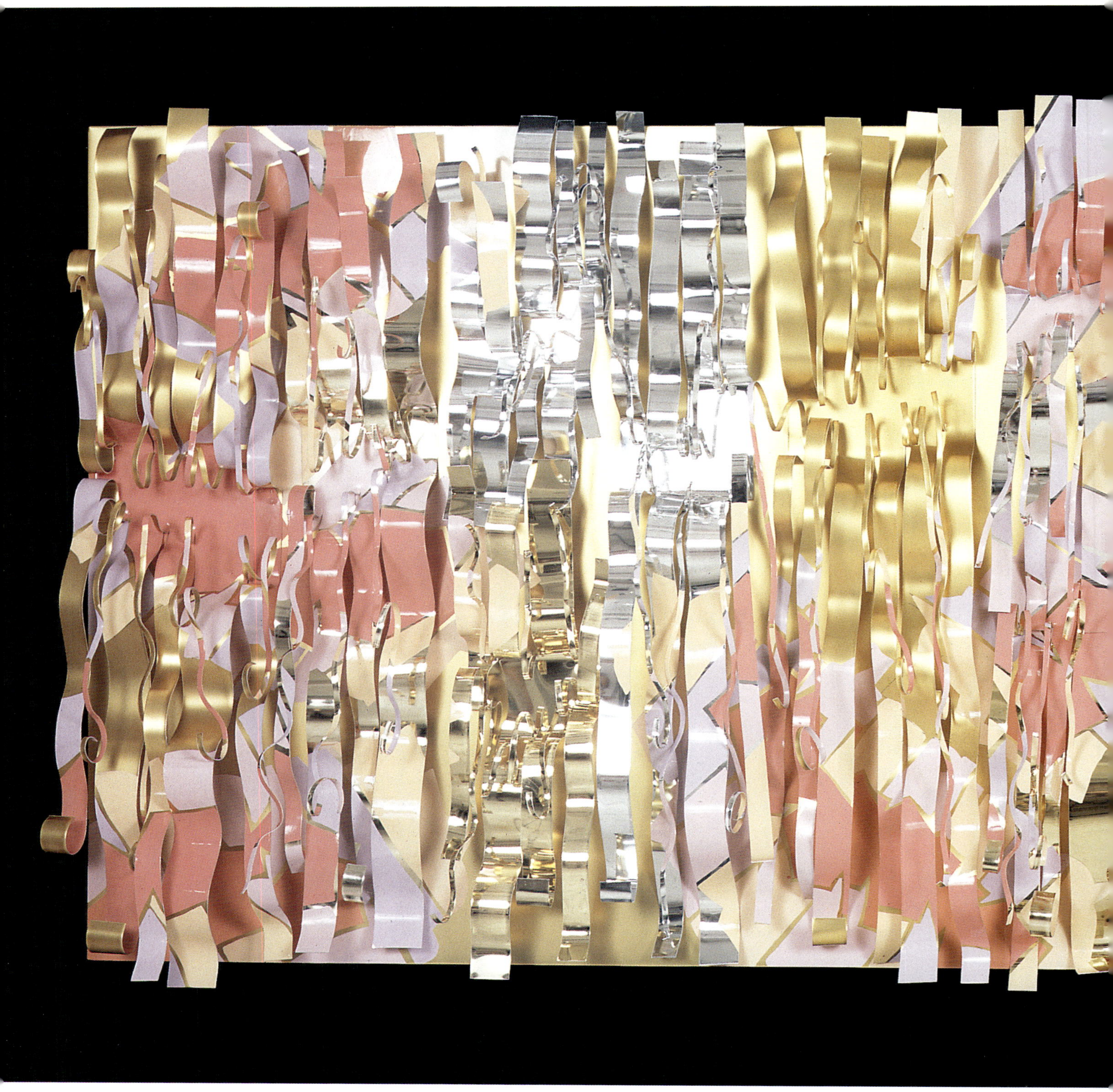

Royal Concerto, 1990, enamel on aluminum, 34" x 80" x 7"

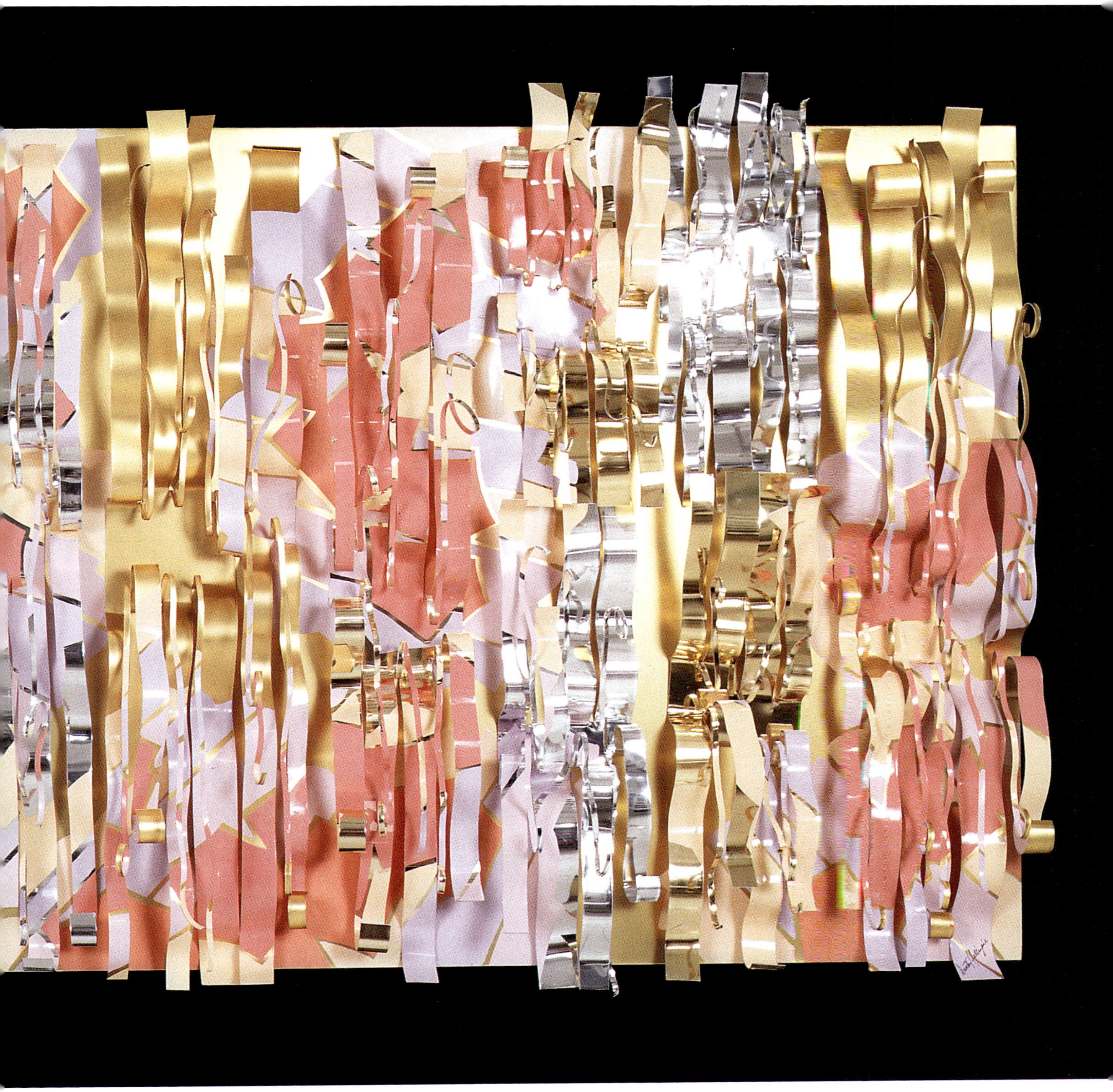

Royal Tribute, 1990, enamel on aluminum, 108" x 62" x 12"

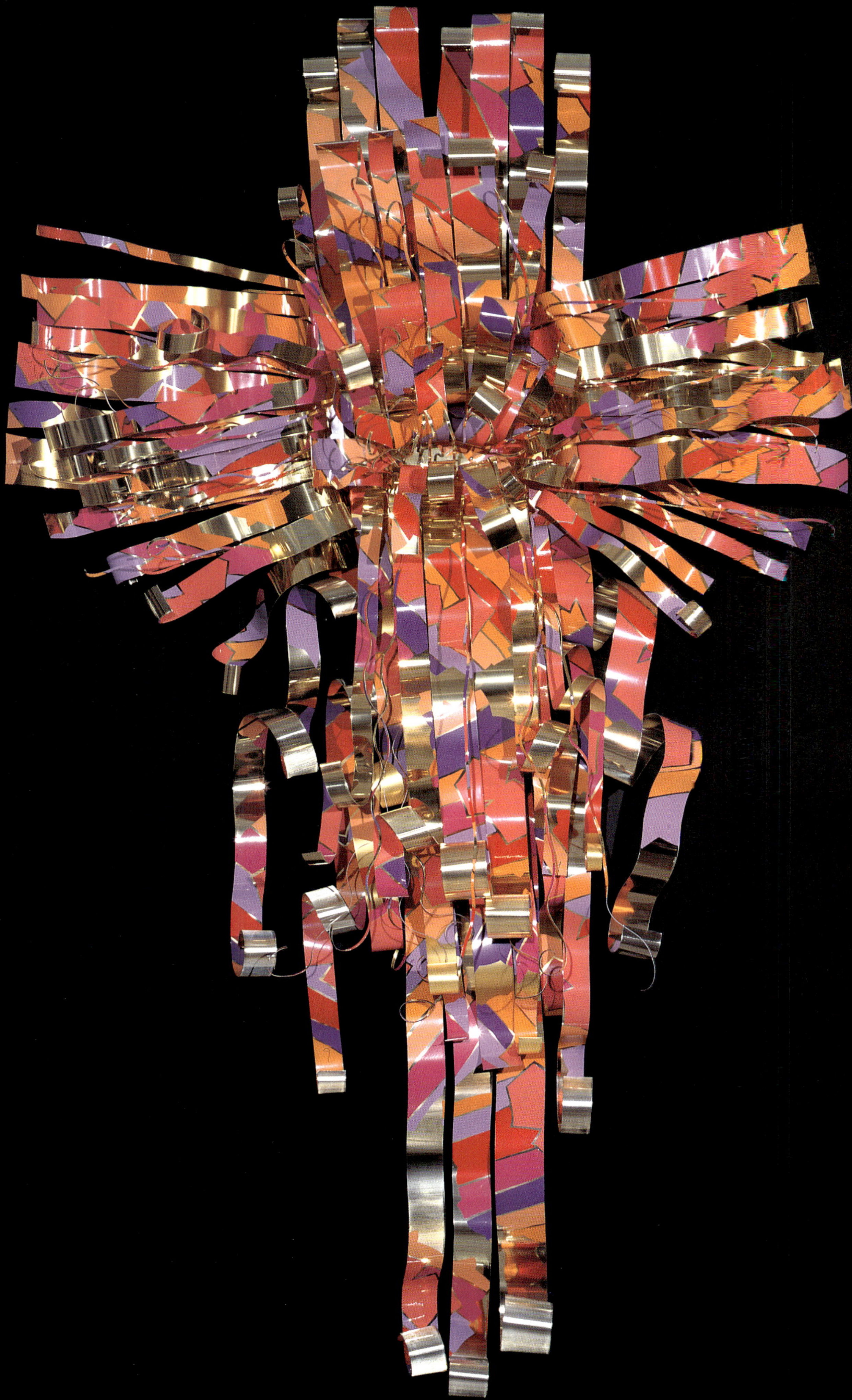

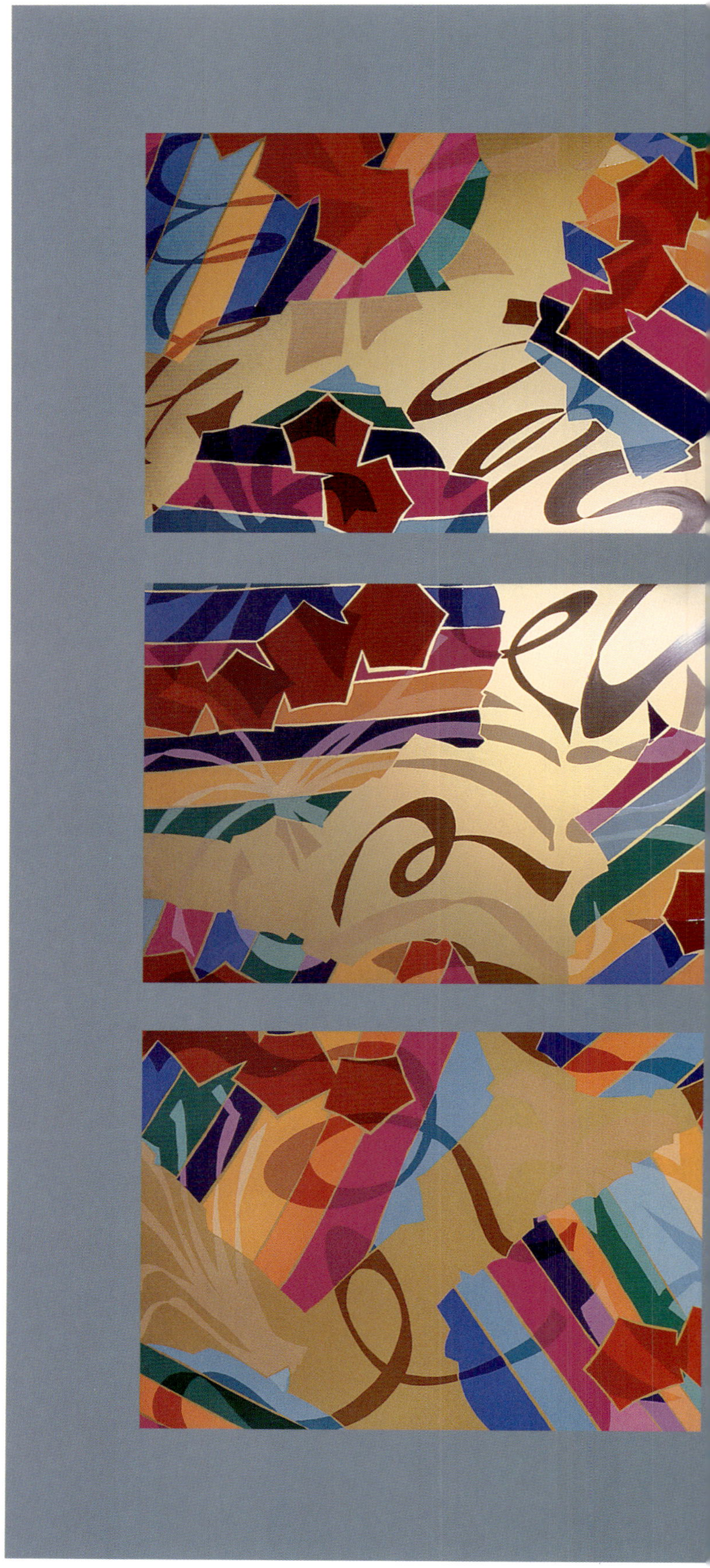

Shadows in the Royal Garden, 1991, enamel on aluminum, 90" x 117" x 1½"

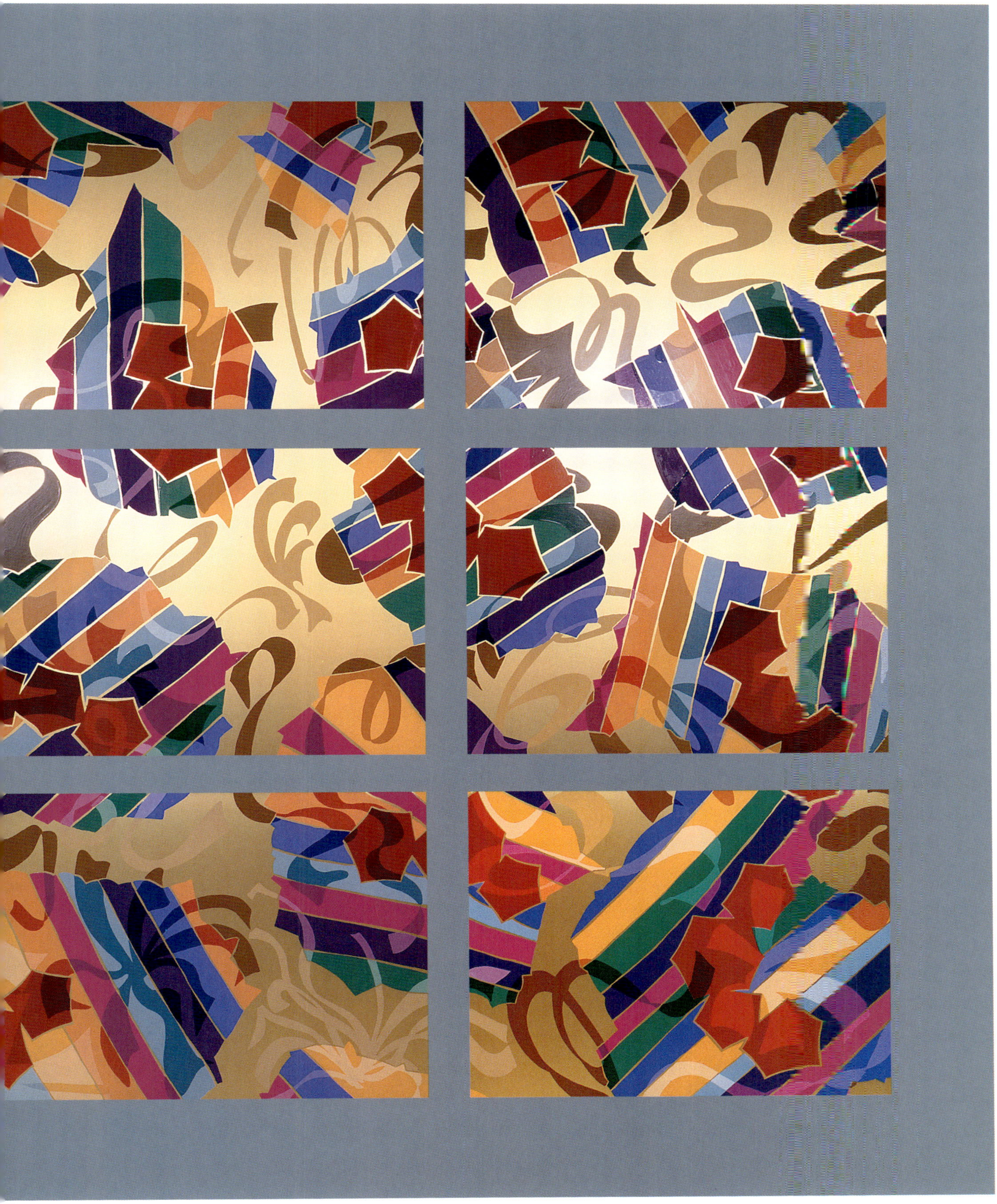

Changing Shadows, 1991, enamel on aluminum, 12' x 8' x 1 1/2"

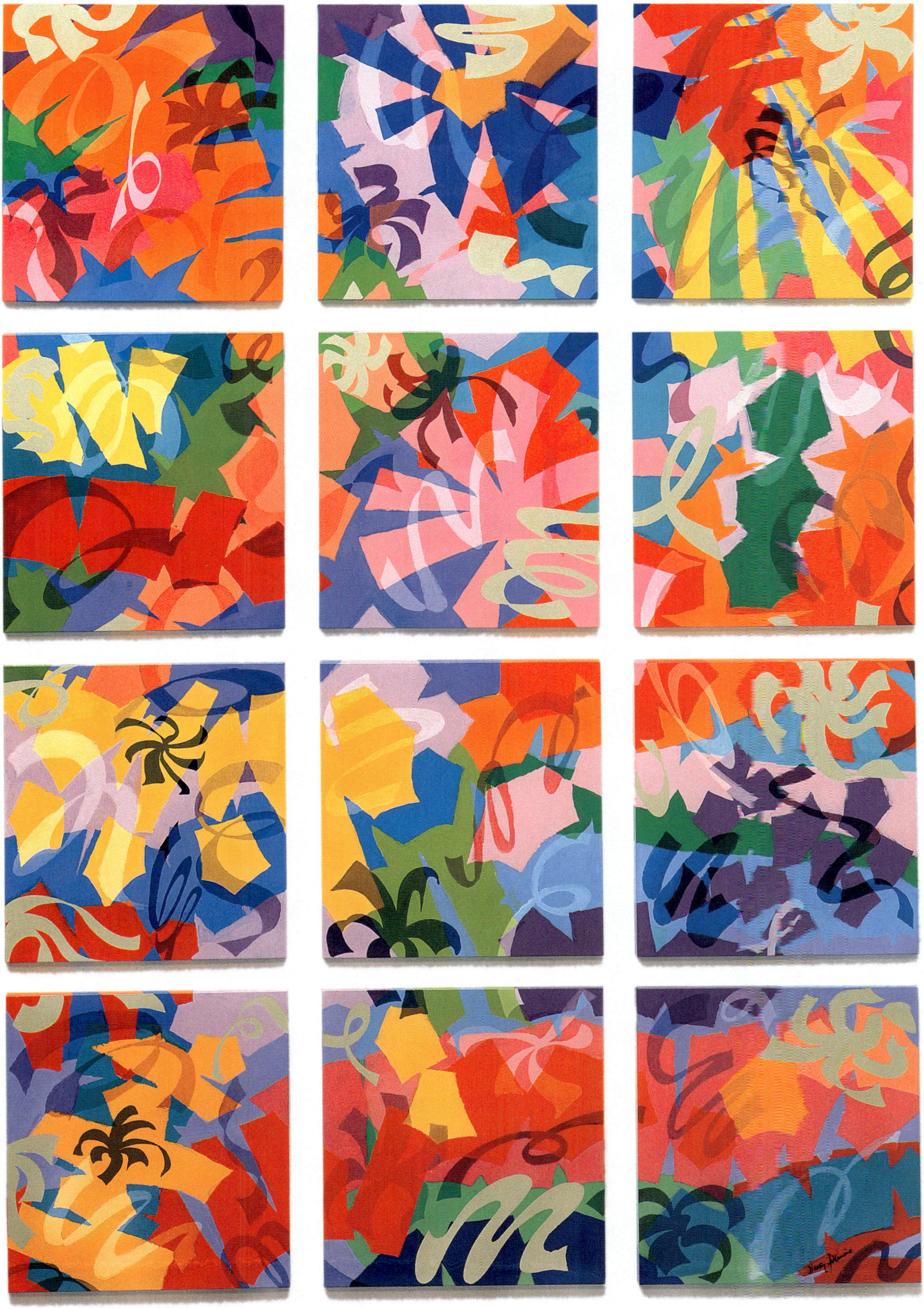

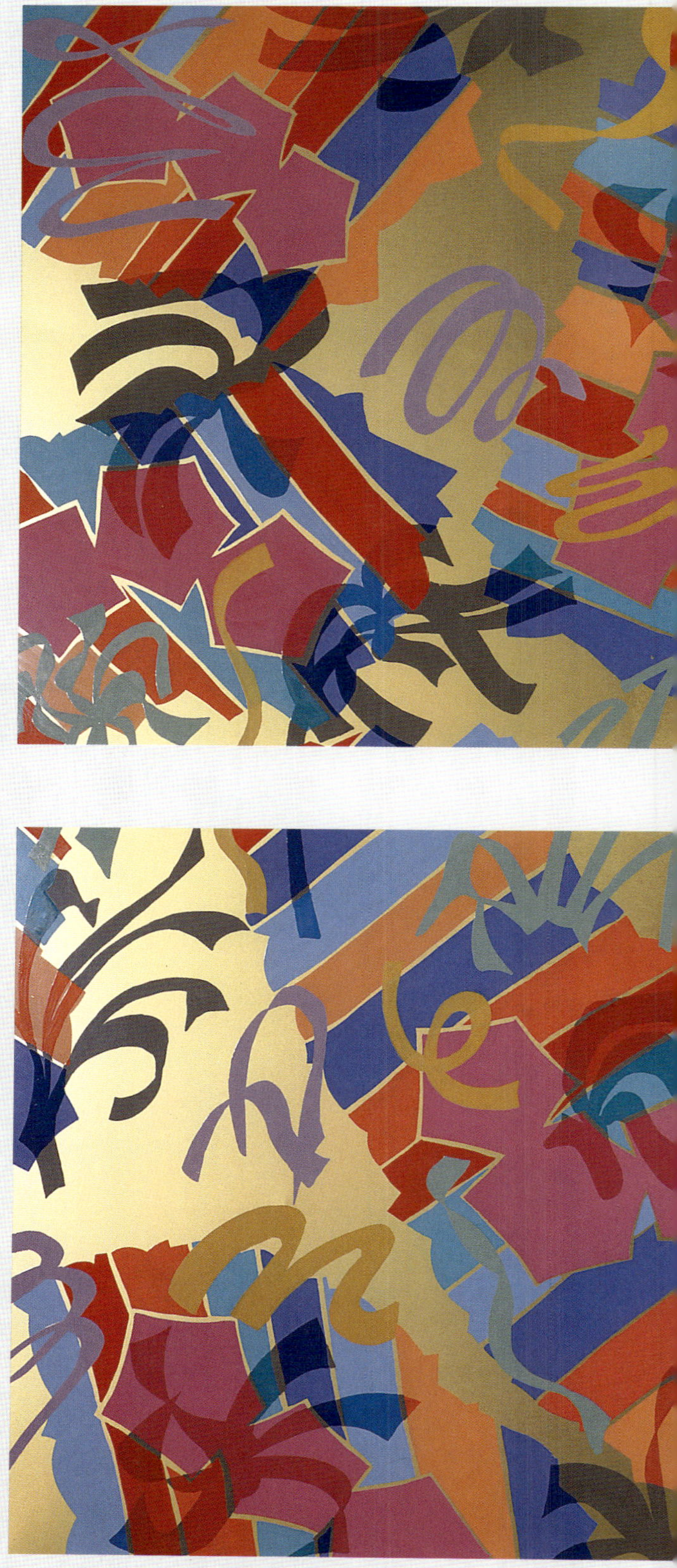

Shadow Tapestry, 1991, enamel on aluminum, 67" x 90" x 1 1/2"

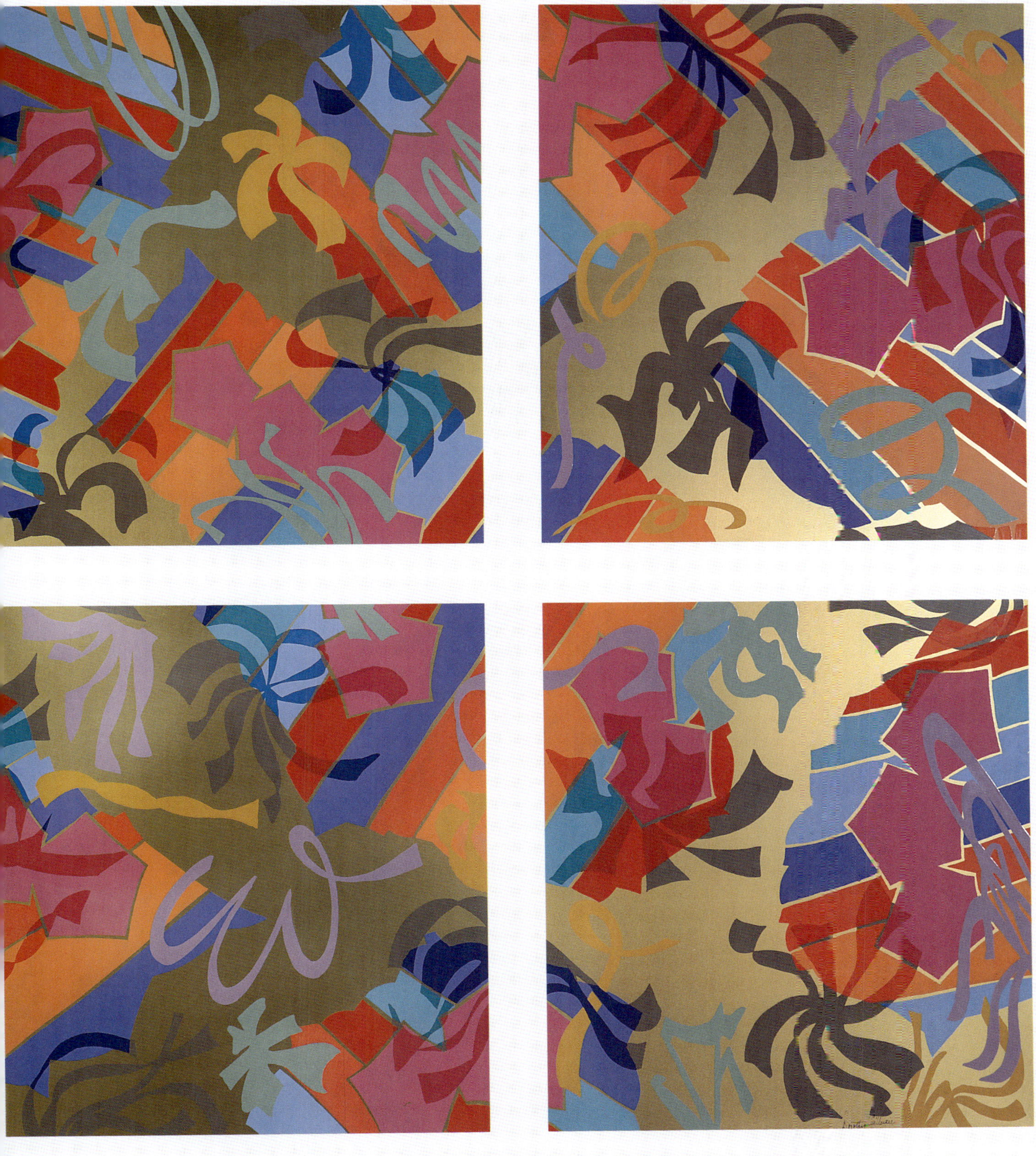

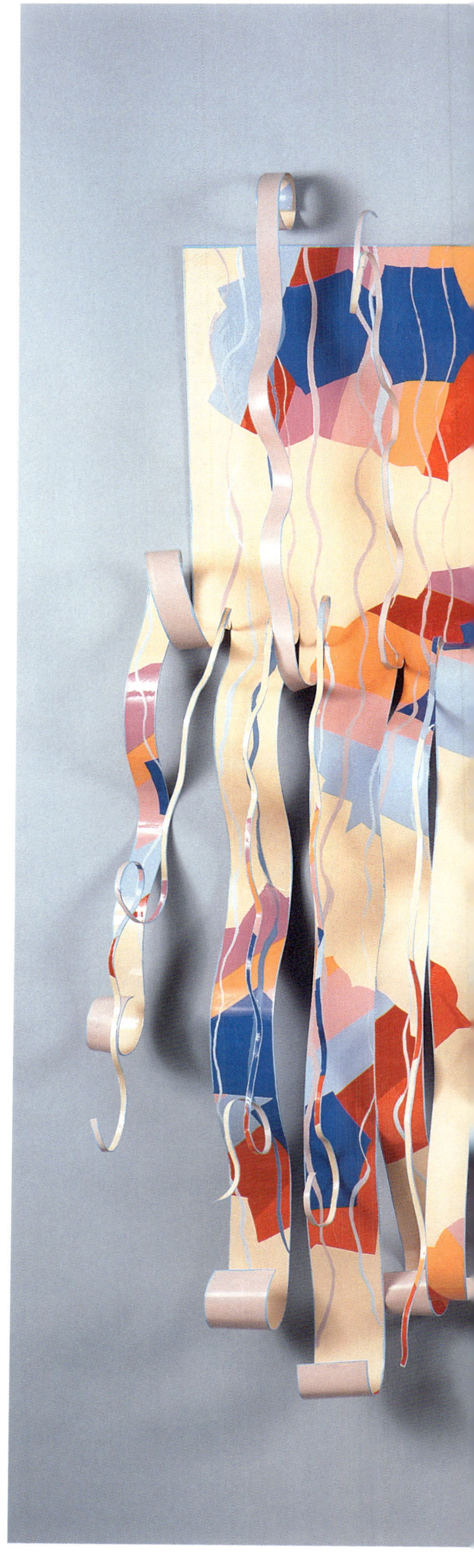

Colorfall: Mardi Gras, 1991, enamel on aluminum, 48" x 56" x 8"

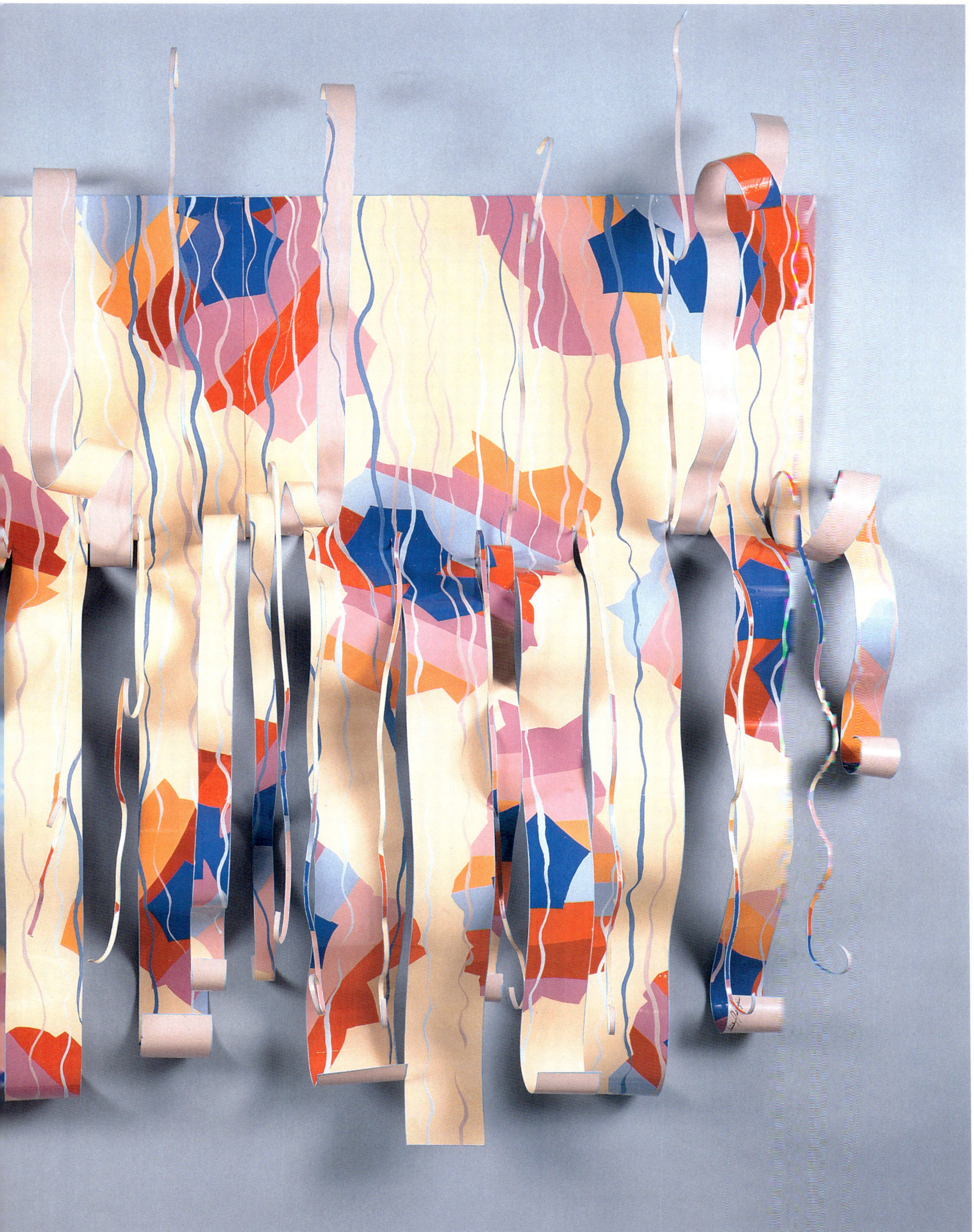

Shaman III, 1991, enamel on aluminum, 84" x 20" x 15"

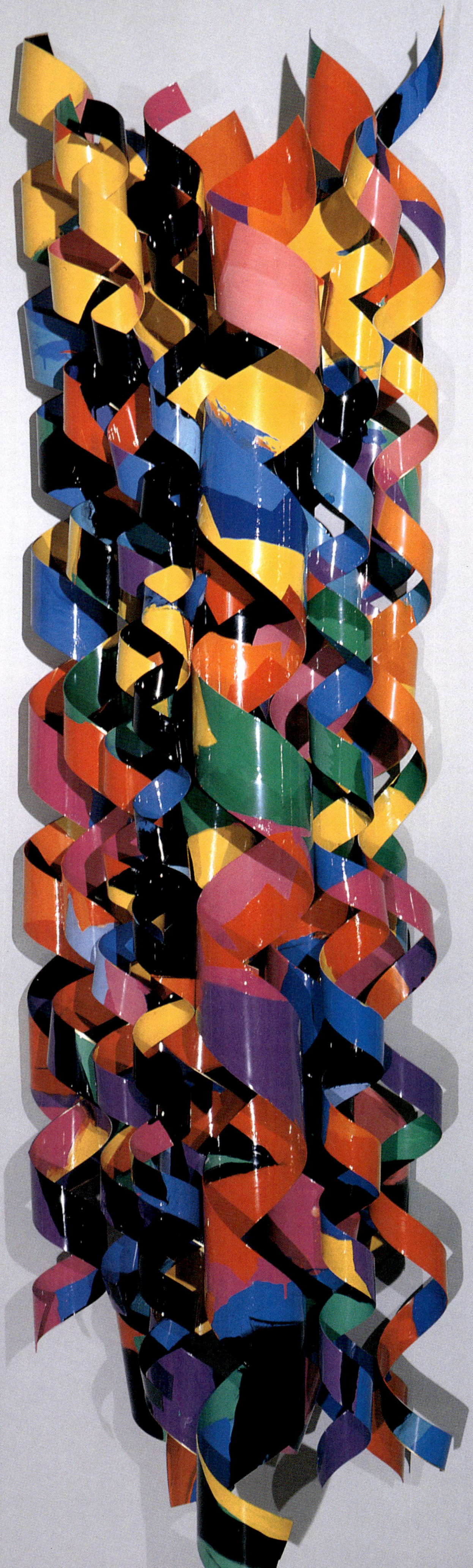

Bulrushes, 1993, enamel on aluminum, 30" x 30" x 30"

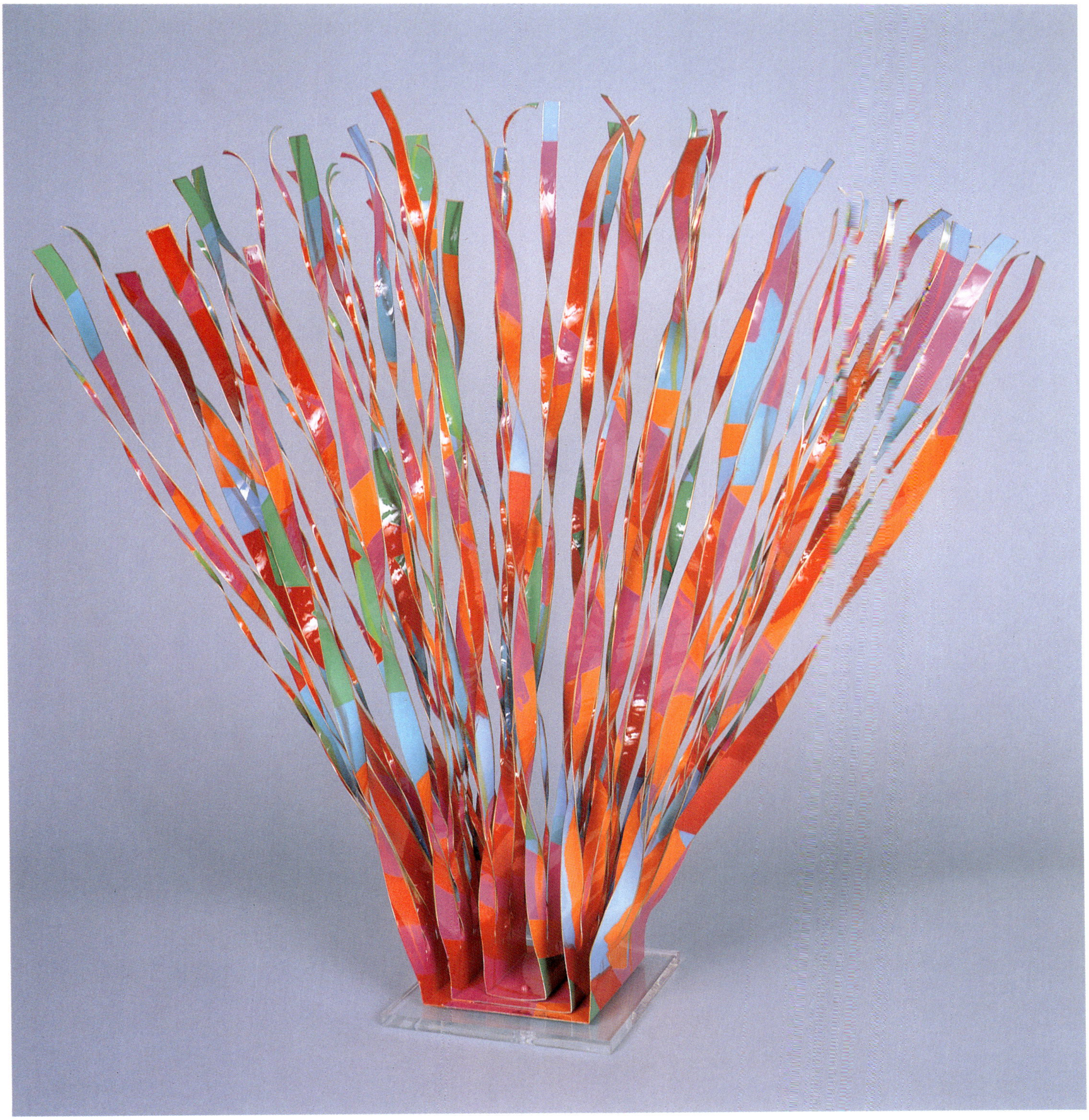

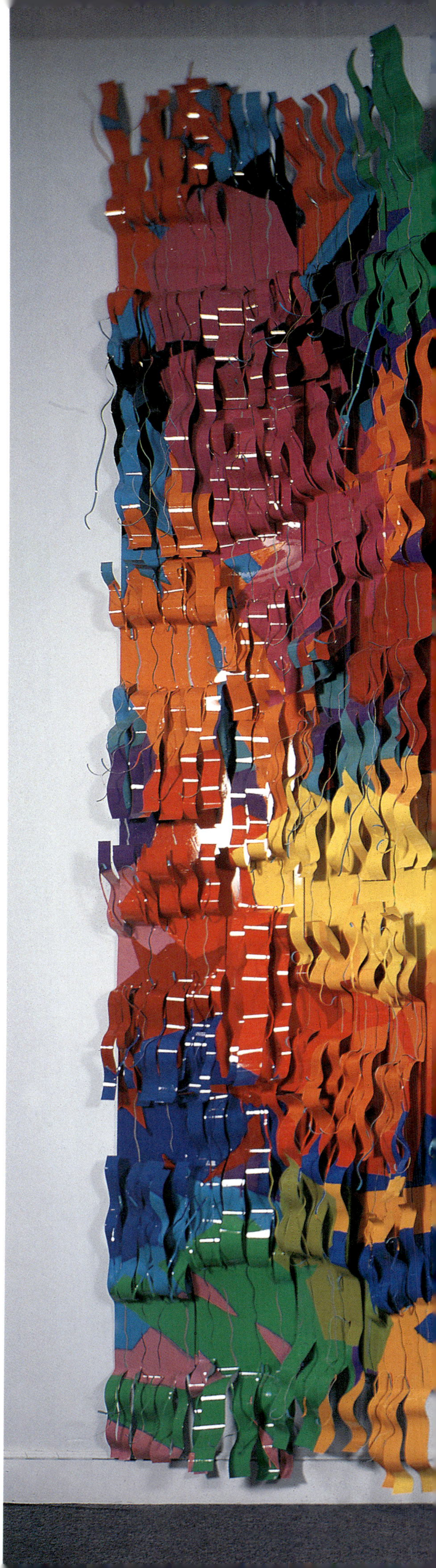

Colorfalls, 1992, enamel on aluminum, 14' x 15'4" x 14"

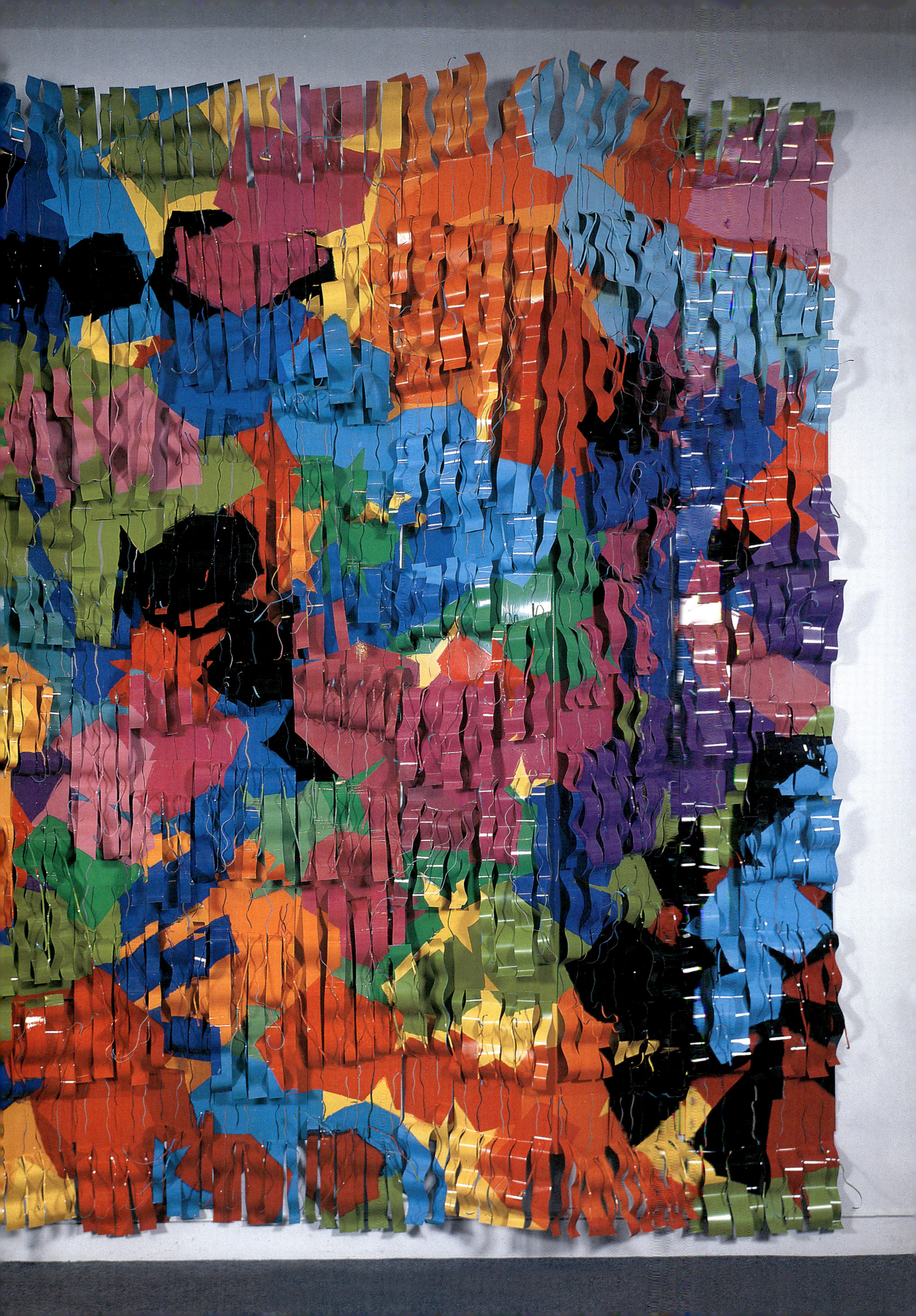

Entrance to the Enchanted Castle, 1993, 14'7" x 15' x 30"

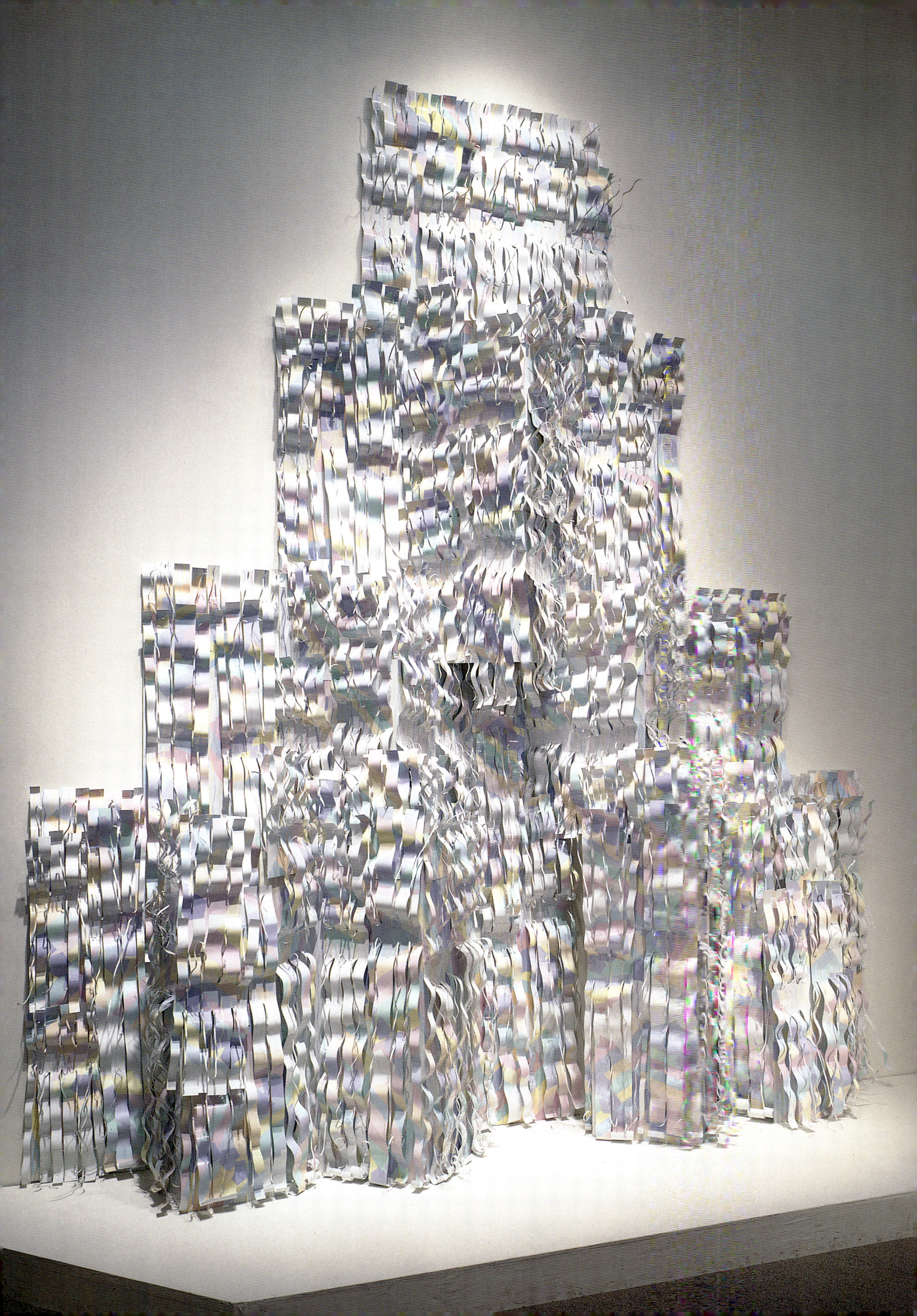

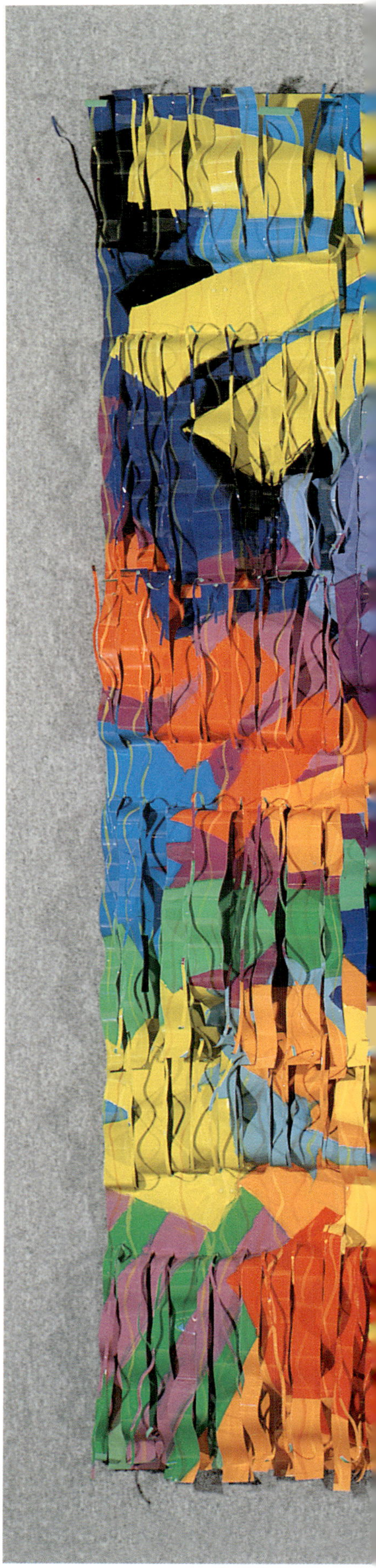

Landscape Memory, 1993, enamel on aluminum, 96" x 100" x 6"

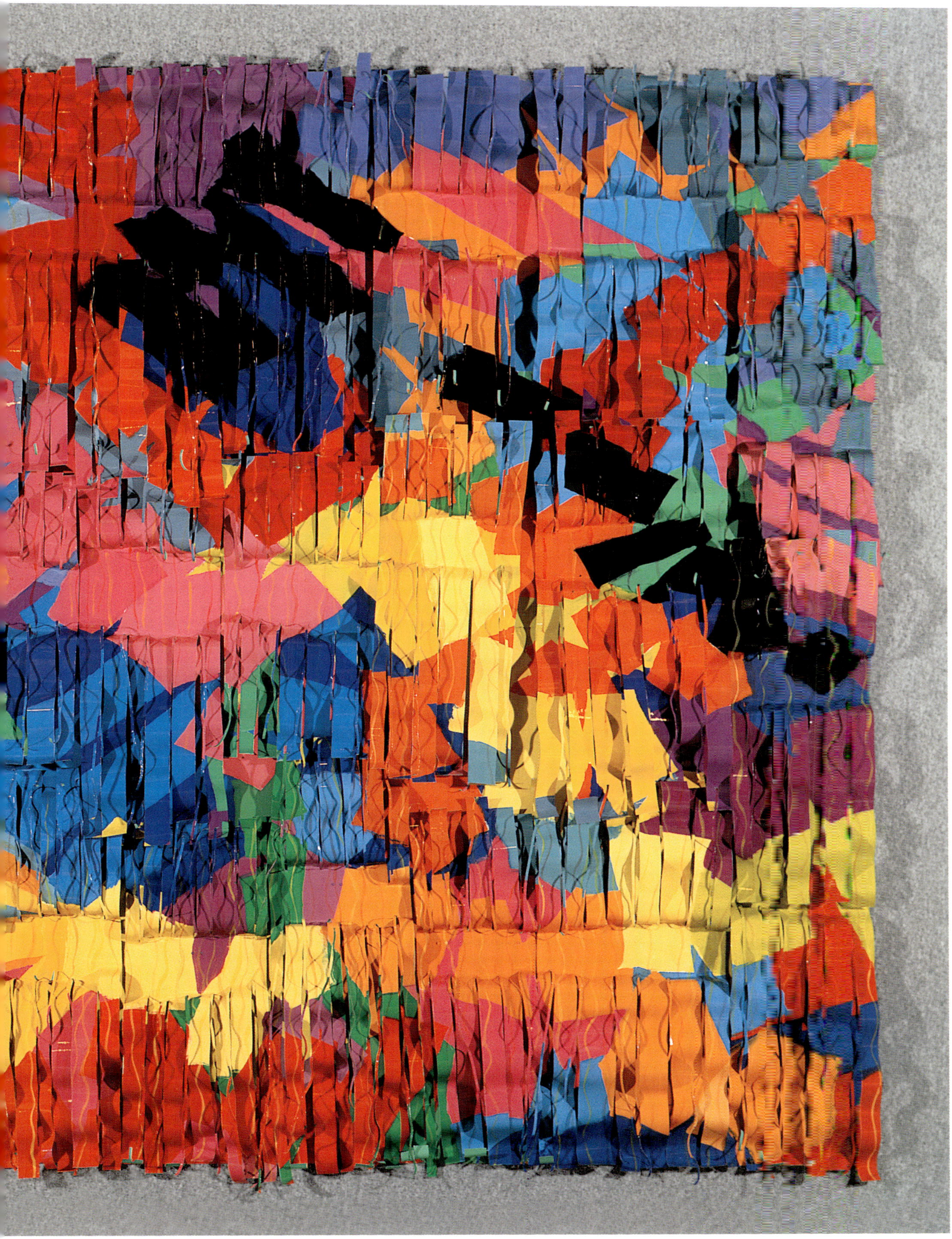

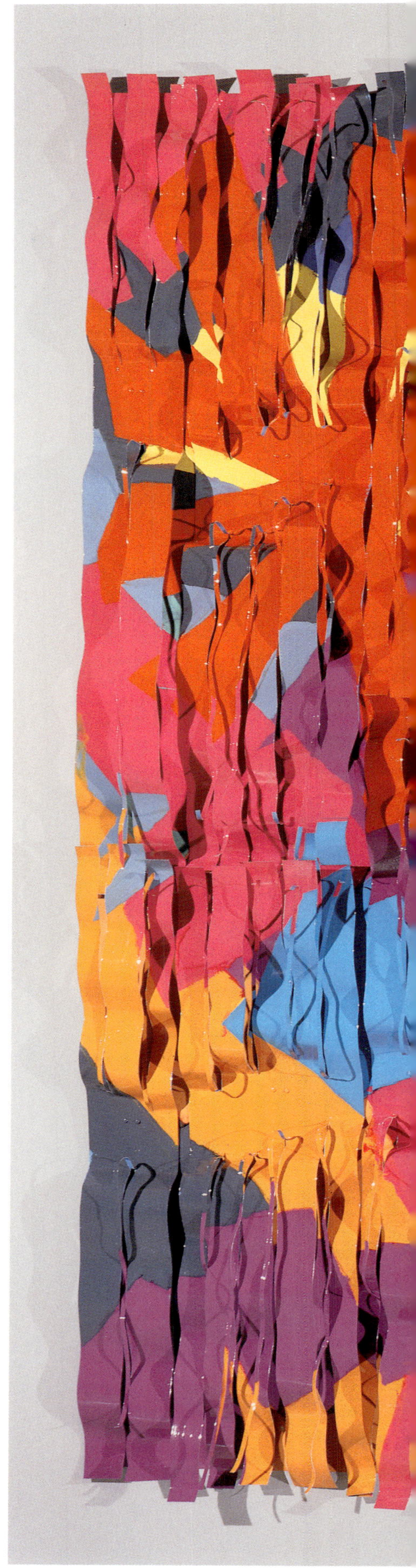

Colorfall: Garden, 1993, enamel on aluminum, 73" x 80" x 4"

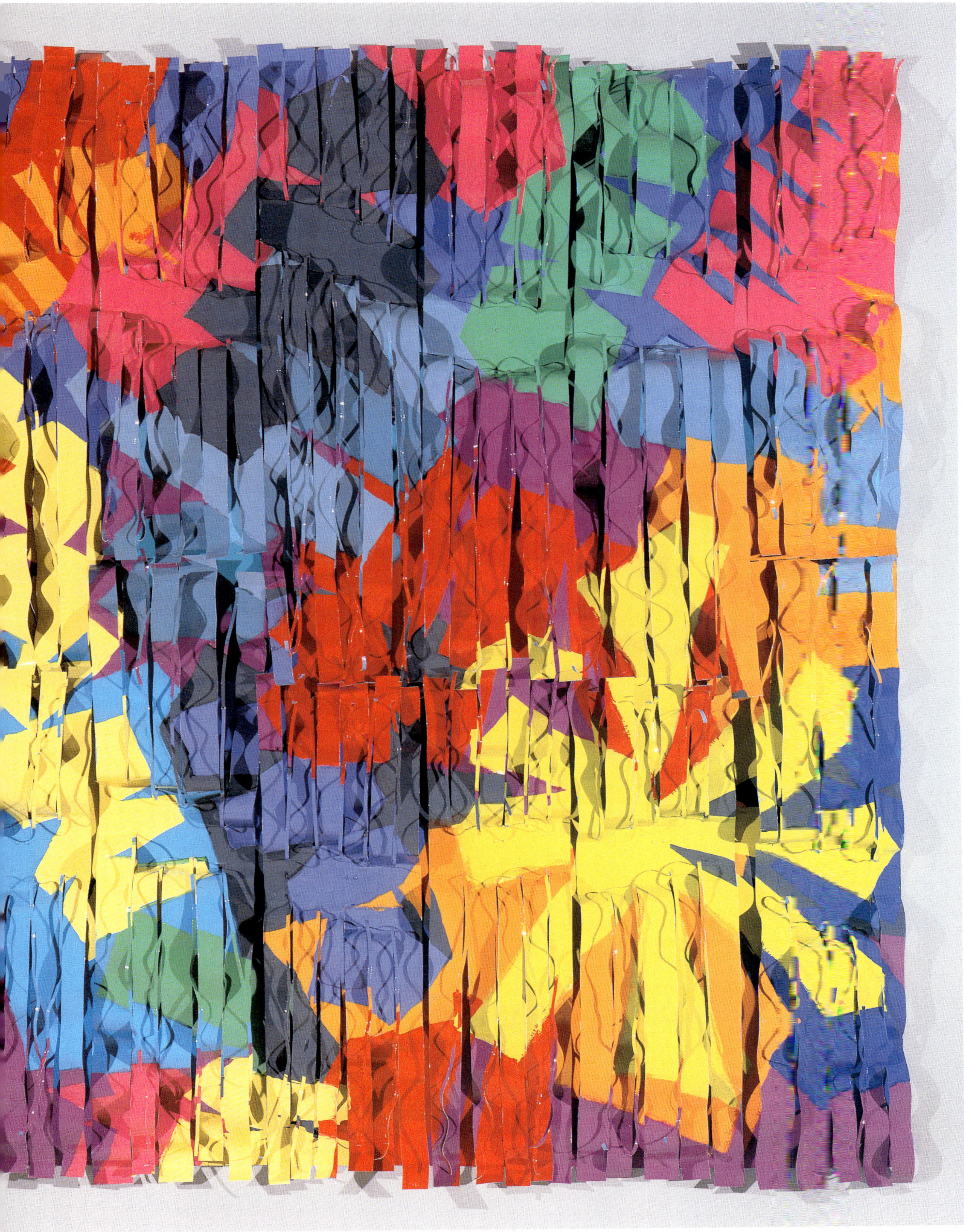

Triangled Celebration, 1985 – reinstalled 1993, enamel on aluminum, 120" x 40" x 42", 120" x 40" x 42", 120" x 48" x 48"

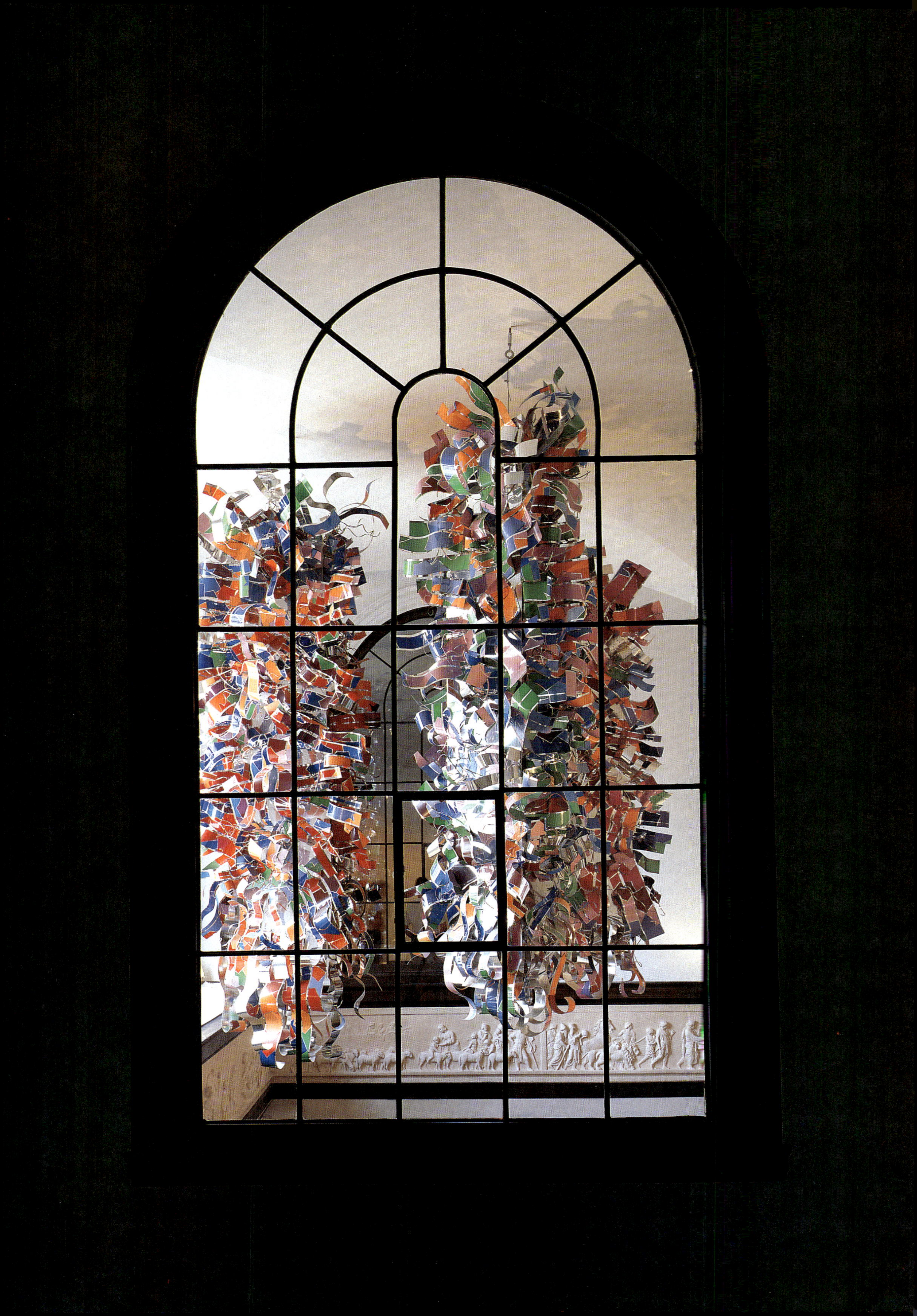

Celestial Celebration, 1994, ink and paint on plastic, 108½" x 76"

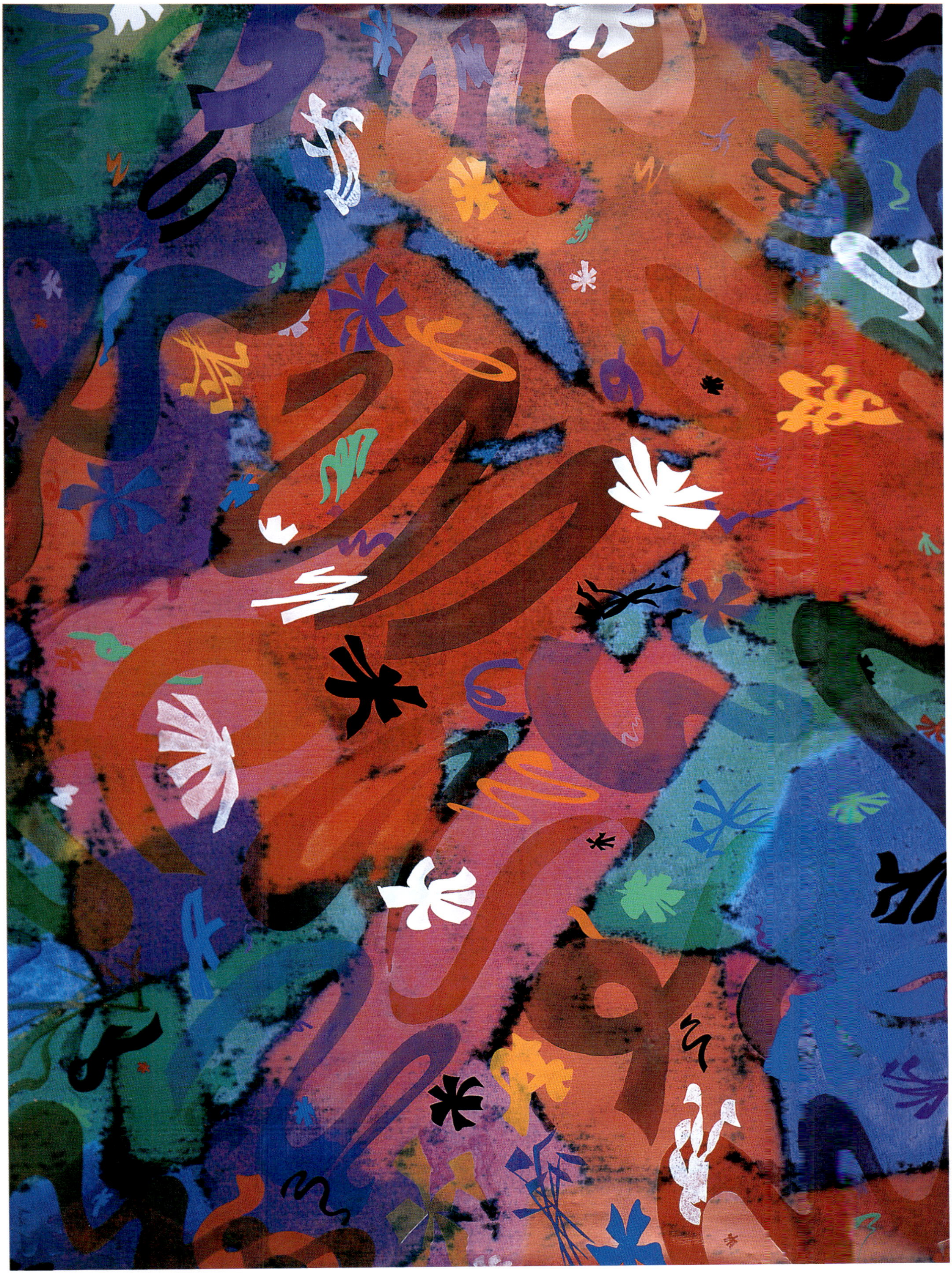

Magic Carpet Slides V, 1994, enamel on aluminum, 55" x 34" x 5"

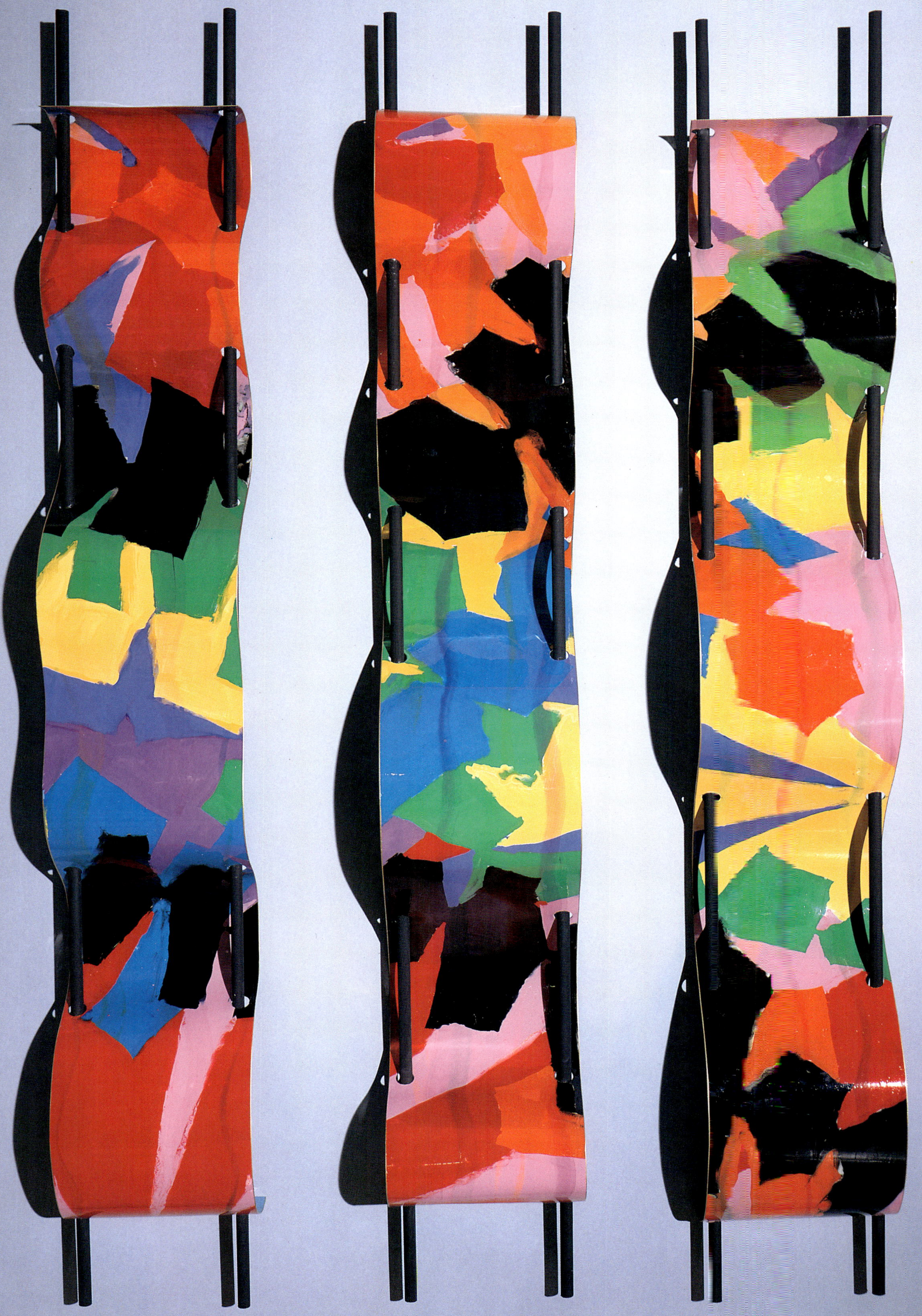

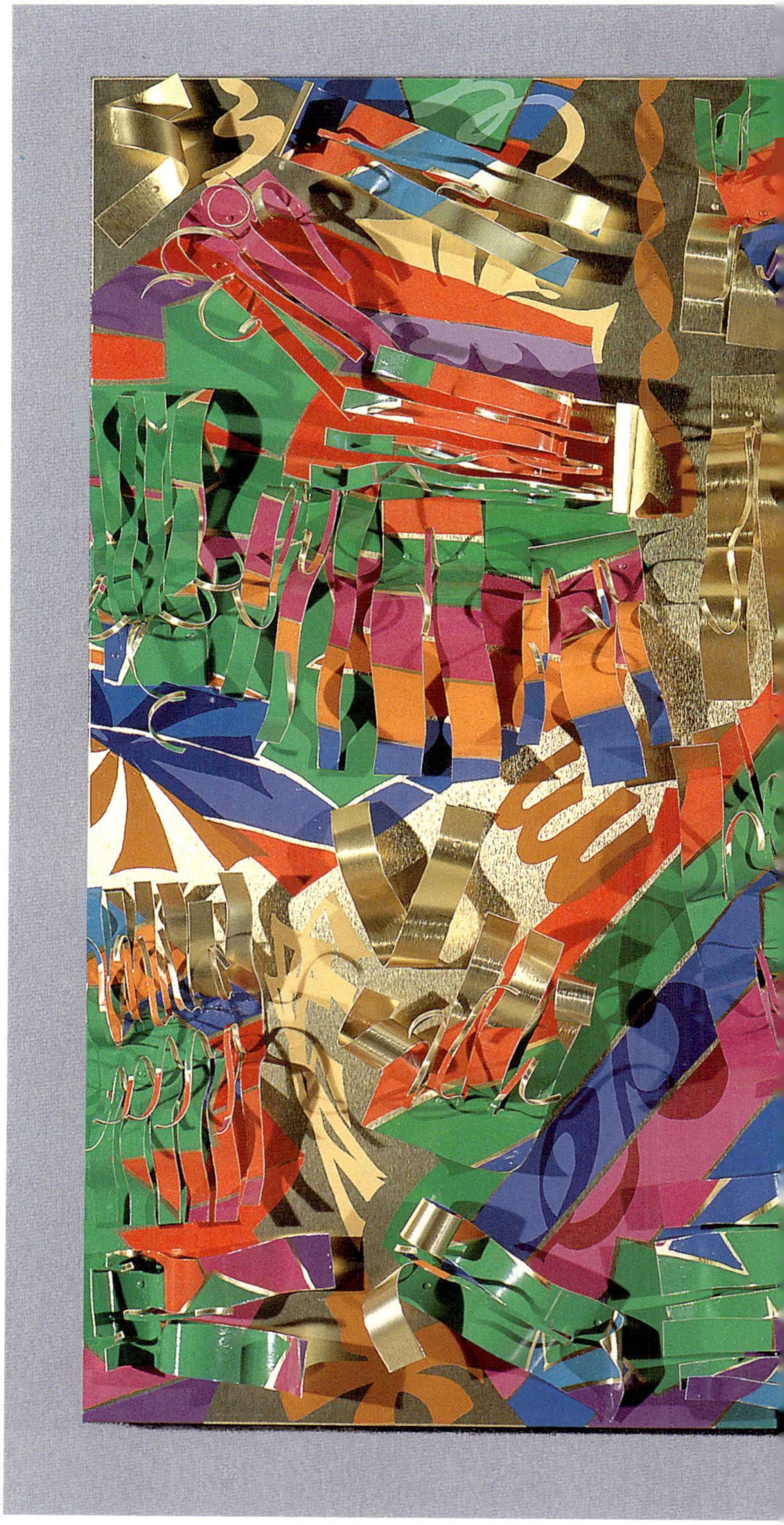

Royal Mardi Gras Encounter, 1995, enamel on aluminum, 48" x 72" x 7"

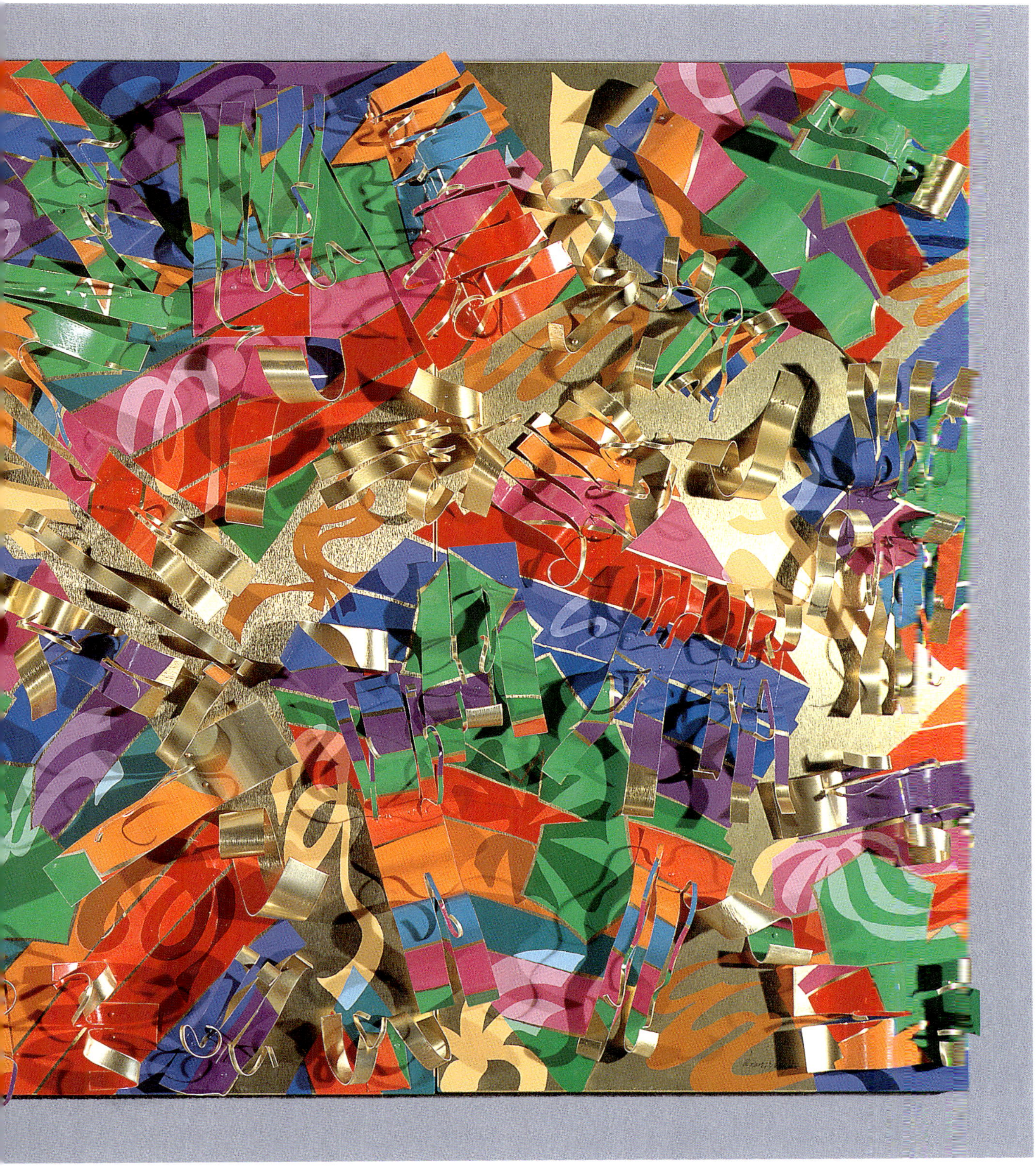

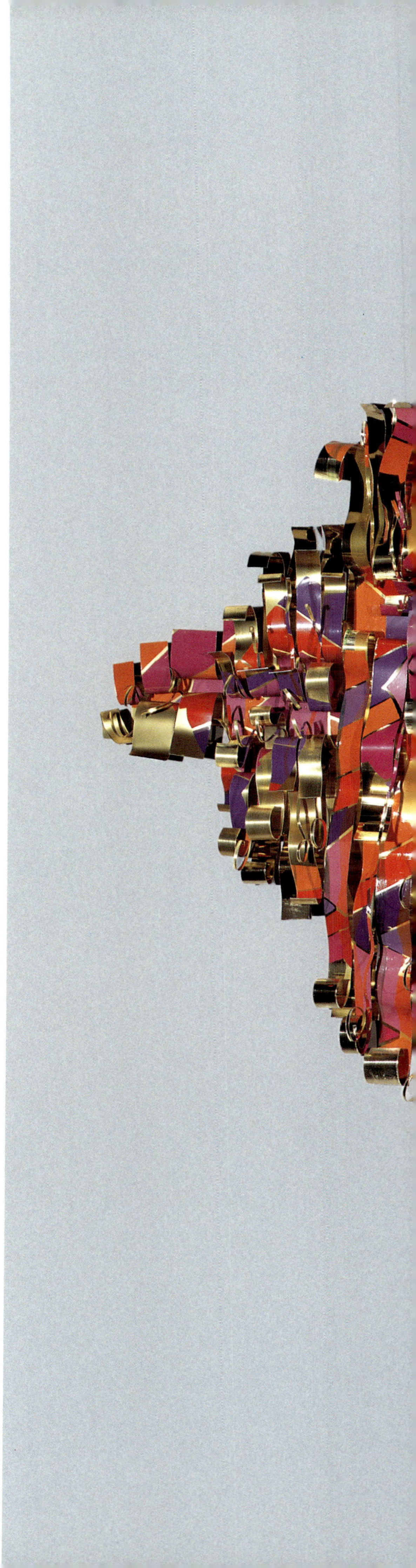

Wings of Song, 1995, enamel on aluminum, 85" x 88" x 9"

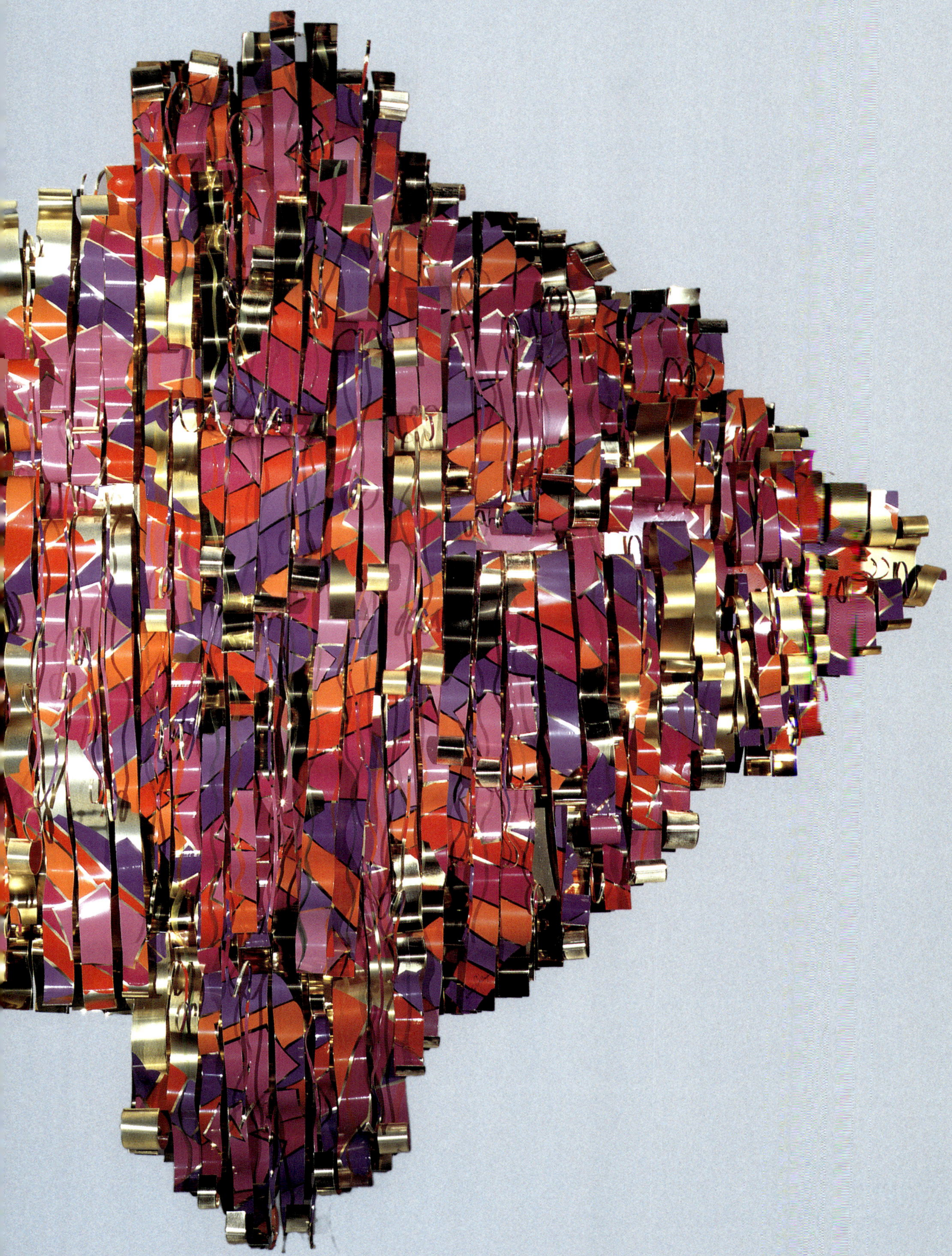

Ribboned Image I, 1996, enamel on aluminum, 54" x 24" x 28"

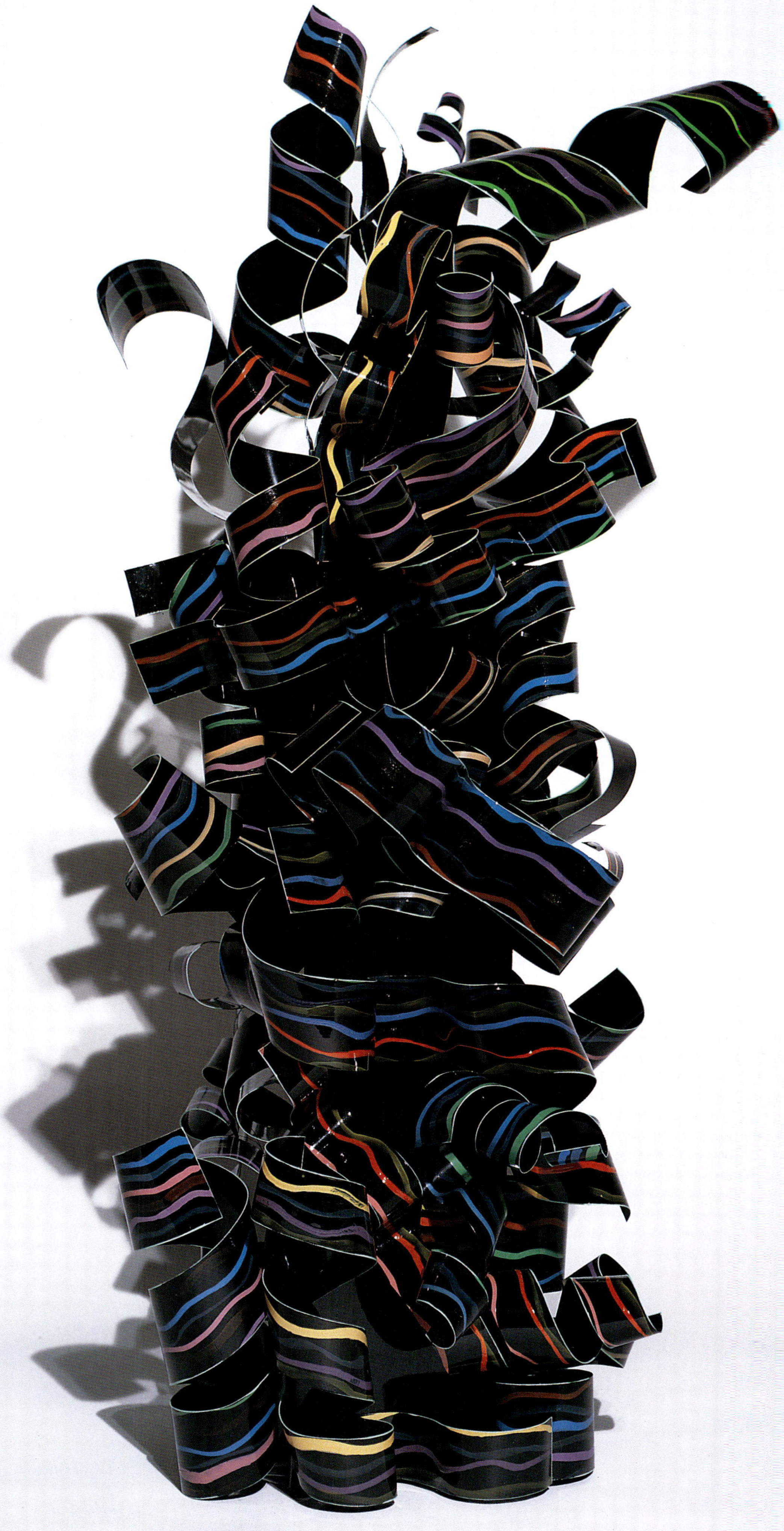

Lower section of *Encounter at the Winter Palace* (page 147), 1997, enamel on aluminum, 19'10" x 7'11" x 8"

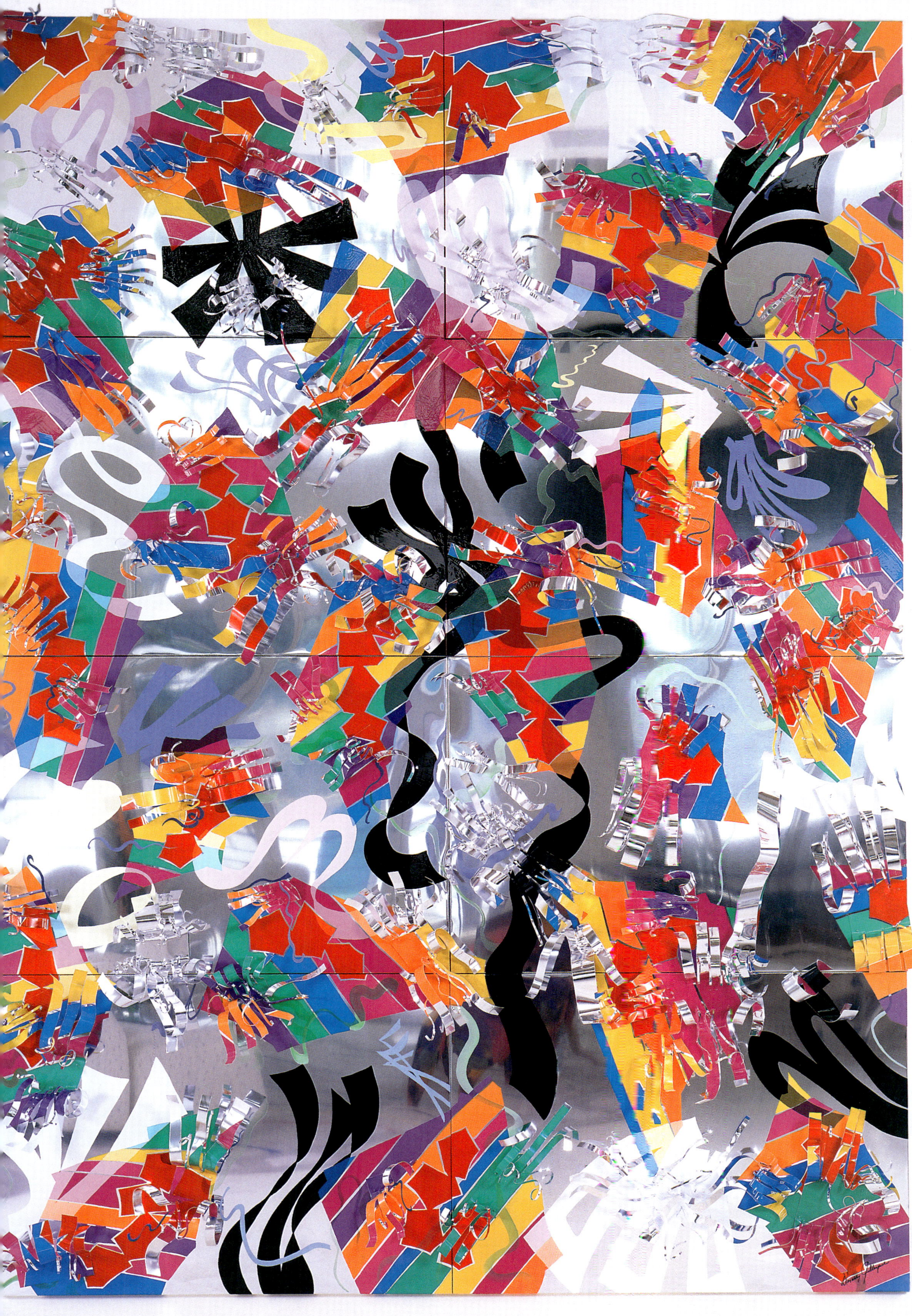

Dorothy Gillespie was born in 1920 in Roanoke, Virginia, where an early affinity for art (at school she was always the classroom artist) was encouraged by her parents – until she declared her intention to go to an art college. "Nice" girls did not go to art school. The family hope was that she would study at nearby Radford University and become a schoolteacher. Her wish was sanctioned by the fortuitous family visit of a minister who declared that Dorothy's was a God-given gift. She was duly enrolled at the Maryland Institute, College of Art, in Baltimore. There, the director, Hans Schuler, guided her away from only commercial art – with which she later supported herself for several years – and into fine art.

Having traveled from the South to Baltimore, Gillespie set her sights on the roistering art scene of New York City, where she arrived on June 5, 1943 (she memorized the date) at age twenty-three. To support herself, she took a job as assistant art director at the B. Altman department store, and promptly entered the Art Students League, a hotbed of eager students sharing ideas on technique, materials, and marketing one's work. At Atelier 17, the printmaking studio then recently relocated from Paris to Greenwich Village, experimentation was a keynote; Gillespie was encouraged to seek and produce her own ideas and images.

In 1946 Gillespie married Bernard Israel and soon bore their first two children, Dorien and Gary, which forced her to set aside her twelve-hour studio days. By the time their third child, Richard, arrived in 1957, Gillespie succumbed to her need to make art, however circumscribed the hours might prove to be. The family traveled extensively; in Peru and England Gillespie explored an interest in archaeology that affected her later work, with its elements of buried memory and discovery. Beginning in the mid-1950s the family spent eight years in Miami, Florida. By then Gillespie was moving away from the realism that had marked her work to establish herself as an abstract painter. She worked ferociously in a studio in Coconut Grove, showed locally and internationally, and founded a group called Six South Florida Abstract Artists.

In 1963 at age forty-three Gillespie returned to New York and full-time creative work. She also determinedly lent herself to the city's roiling art scene, its Happenings and loft events. Her gentility and lack of pretension notwithstanding, she fought fervently through the 1970s to rectify the plight of women in art, picketing the Whitney Museum, helping to form the Women's Interart Center and other organizations, curating women's art exhibitions, and authoring consciousness-raising articles.

By the 1980s Gillespie's work was well known and displayed internationally. Successive, sometimes overlapping commissions rolled in for works in public spaces, especially pleasing to Gillespie, who feels that art should be accessible to a broad audience. This sense of outreach brought her to teaching and coaching young artists, as a Woodrow Wilson Visiting Fellow since 1986, at Lehigh University and, in a mellow return to her roots, at Radford University, where she is Distinguished Professor of Art. The association with Radford began when, with a deposit of her own work, she helped start the university's permanent art collection. Today Gillespie's joie de vivre is still manifest, in her continuing travels to exotic locales and in her continuing curiosity about what sundry mediums can produce: painting, sculpture, editions, and most recently jewelry to wear or display.

Underlying the nostalgic appeal of Gillespie's art is an expertise developed over more than five decades of daily application in the studio. Since her work assumed its abstract character in the 1950s, it has moved from easel to wall to space, without denying its origin in the plane. Her higher education included drawing from casts and life as an introduction, and then moving to color – pastels and watercolor followed eventually by oils – for which she had a natural facility. Her style was a direct, unembellished form of realism, centered around portraiture (which she revived in the early 1980s). As with most art students and artists of the time, she was aware of the developments in modern art in Europe and the United States that led to abstractionism. She began the move in that direction as she turned to more and more ephemeral subjects.

From the beginning, Gillespie found correspondences between her abstract and realistic styles. She saw that patches of color in the shadows placed on skin areas in her portraits were the same irregular shapes that she employed in her abstract inventions. In the realistic paintings these shapes were subdued in color, elided and fused by her painterly style, and as often revealed from beneath the surface as imposed upon it. Similarly polygonal in contour, such shapes in her abstracted paintings sometimes joined, sometimes separated, but always functioned responsively with one another and the spaces between them. As Gillespie's works became undeniably abstract, she simply clarified the contours of the shapes and heightened them in hue. An additional element relating her late to her early style is an outstanding sense of imminent movement.

To Gillespie the full shift into abstraction was a real breakthrough, and like other abstractionists she projected a very individual style. She is proud that her autographic imagery came not by influence from others but from inner imperative (which is why she never wished to study with famous artists). All along, the entities with which she worked had become stronger and the ground more interactive, but it soon occurred to her that virtual space was not enough. A desire to incorporate actual movement and dimension inspired her to bring her paintings into the viewers' space and let the spectators move around them. She did this first by placing three or four canvases together in boxlike shapes, sometimes suspended from the center of a ceiling at eye level, so that viewers had to walk around or among them to see all their facets.

Gillespie's move toward compositional variation came when she turned directly to wooden cubes, with each side painted like one of her canvasses to be complete in itself, but also to coordinate with other sides when the cubes were stacked or arranged according to their multiple possibilities. Her standard number of cubes for a composition was nine, since this grouping could be logically stacked together as well as built into arches or squares. The next step was to regularize their arrangement by providing a setting for the cubes consisting of a base with a back attached at an upright angle that would ostensibly hold nine cubes; but now there were only four, which allowed the remaining ones to interact with the empty spaces and to project a patterning across several surfaces in any possible arrangement. She said that the shapes on the form as well as the form itself could be accommodated by the "mobile eye," but until this time she had depended on the spectators' mobility to give the needed animation. Now, she began to look for ways to make her work have a vivacity of its own.

The means presented itself in the 1960s when she discovered Mylar, a new plastic material, lighter than cellophane and stronger than steel of its own thickness. She first used it on flat surfaces, so that its mirrored finish left unpainted would reflect the spectators, thus drawing them into interaction with the painting. A watershed came around 1972, when she covered cardboard with Mylar and made a construction consisting of eight cylindrical pieces. This was when she started to do "paper things," as she calls them. The cylinders got larger and she then placed them in contact with paper that hung on the wall or fell to the floor so that they appeared to unroll. The next step was to let the paper actually unroll and fold back onto itself as it spread across the floor, eventually opening the way for all sorts of forays including increasingly larger paper strips going up steps or along walls.

Over the years Gillespie turned more and more to metal, backing Mylar with galvanized steel and paper with polished aluminum, before using these metals in their own right for works that are as flexible as paper yet able to stand alone. Being impervious to wear and weather, such materials offered perfect opportunities to carry outside what she was doing indoors. Two of her early exterior metal pieces were paradigmatic: one shot up a ten-and-a-half-foot head above a forty-three-foot-long body; the other was a ten-piece group of bowing and swaying "ribbons." The complex movement of these and similar pieces, which stand on one end and extend the other in vertical arabesques, caused art critic David Shirey to dub them "pictorial semiquavers," from which Gillespie adopted the name "quaver" to refer to any of them. Another outstanding variation on her metal works was a relief, consisting of a large rectangle from which strips of metal extrude in all directions before turning back toward the surface in what she calls a "peeled paint" effect. Whereas she had formerly superimposed her more muted shapes on a white space, here she painted them with pure-hued colors and continuously interlocked them so that the colors became "Fauvish."

As Gillespie's works became more multidimensional, she equivocated about calling them paintings or sculptures. The question was resolved when she saw the 1979 exhibition at the Guggenheim Museum called The Planar Dimension. Curator Margit Rowell explained the titular phrase in her catalogue: "'The Planar Dimension' is the painter's dimension. Yet, to the generations which came of age in the 1960s and 1970s planar is synonymous with sculpture and planar sculpture synonymous with one aspect of modernism."

This idea applied to Gillespie and others who brought their sculptures completely into space, but who kept them (in Rowell's words) "pictorial through the use of color, planes, and a strongly graphic articulation." In the fluidity and mutability of her art, Gillespie was extending the scope and scale of Modernism. It was once pointed out by Arnold Glimcher that the only thing about Modernism that did not still exist was its dogma: "The only rule is to break all the rules. . . . The only way to find the next step is to examine the last. Sometimes a break is the next step; you can take it by making something the most unlike as well as the most like the last. What is Post-Modernism but a break that is a continuation of Modernism?"

Gillespie's work grows out of the object-orientation of Modernism, at the same time representing the "break that is a continuation of Modernism." Respecting the past, she knows that participating in her own era does not remove individuality, especially in a period of pluralism. Currently, she has assumed a baroque stance, with more movement, more color, and more variety than ever. She continues to exhibit constantly and to sell her work, but there is a great deal of it left over to inhabit her magical studio, which looks to some like a "sculptural botanical garden."

In the essays that follow, Dorothy Gillespie's work is examined in all its diverse forms by Kyra Belán, professor of art and art history at Broward College in Florida; George S. Bolge, executive director of the Boca Raton Museum of Art; art critic and author Marcia Corbino; Francis Martin, Jr., professor of art history at the University of Central Florida; and Richard Martin, curator of the Costume Institute of the Metropolitan Museum of Art.

Francis Martin, Jr., concentrates on paper as having inspired all of the sculptural work. He surveys Gillespie's development in the medium, which began in the usual way with drawings, pastels, and watercolors; next for printmaking; and then in her unorthodox, monumental uses of paper.

George S. Bolge sees Gillespie's paintings as closest to her intent to communicate with directness and immediacy. Her notion that size could be associated with the environment led to the large-scale sculpture, but the gestural quality of the two-dimensional work so close to Gillespie's artistic personality remains the aesthetic heart of all her work.

Marcia Corbino's first essay addresses the radical social changes that erupted in the 1960s and the concomitant new forms in art, Environments and Happenings, in which Gillespie was a pioneer. A second essay chronicles the Women's Art Movement and Gillespie's tireless work on behalf of women artists – encouraging them to uphold the highest standards in education and in their art as well as to take political action – always with herself in the vanguard as exemplar.

Kyra Belán offers a thoroughgoing survey of Gillespie's site-specific projects. These difficult-to-categorize pieces are formal crossovers: artisanal, painterly, and sculptural. They are meant to enhance, to play with and against, the places in which they are set – attached to walls, freestanding in gardens and fields, suspended from ceilings, even inhabiting the ballet stage.

Richard Martin, in his essay on the sculptures of Gillespie's mature style, selects and provides a close analysis of seminal works from the past two decades. Behind the surface exuberance and technical mastery of these abstract constructs, he finds a persistent, nondogmatic statement of a specifically woman's art.

Of her consuming love of art, her productivity, and that of the very few like herself, Gillespie says: "There must be some reason why we make art, why it becomes priceless; the question has almost nothing to do with analysis – why some art is bigger than life and lasts longer than individual life. The artists I know with this respect for art had the feeling they wanted to do something terribly important and were willing to sacrifice everything for it."

Perhaps one explanation lies in the statement with which she ended the 1983 commencement address at the Maryland Institute: "The dedication of a life to producing works which have no practical purpose, which may or may not be preserved, which may or may not be sold, which may or may not be exhibited, and which may or may not be worth the original costs of materials, is a curious phenomenon that has existed in all civilizations. The creative artist is truly the great adventurer of all times."

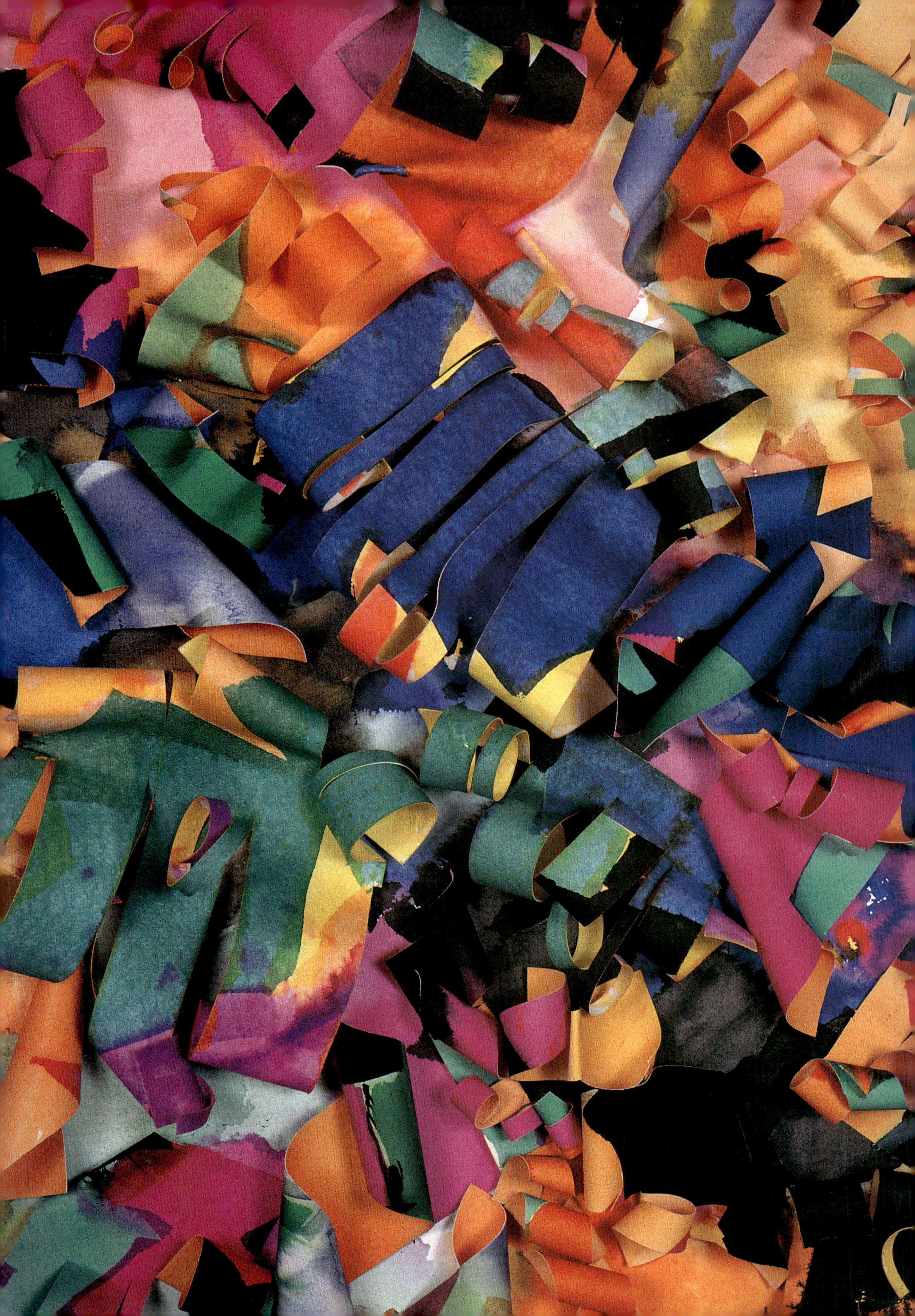

Dorothy Gillespie *loves* paper. It represents a passion rooted in childhood: her fascination with art. As a five-year-old, she worked a good deal with paper, cutting out strange and wonderful forms and, yes, paper dolls to which she applied transparent layers of succulent water-color. She still works with paper, but paper beyond anyone's expectations. It overflows from closets and storage bins, making the decor of her New York and Florida studios resemble paper warehouses during an after-Christmas sale.

But there is a difference between her love of paper and that of other paper addicts: for Gillespie, paper is spiritual, and its receptiveness, freedom, and flexibility are metaphors for her role as artist. She is paper and paper is Gillespie. Without the special blend that exists between the two, her work, as it is known, would not exist. "Without paper, I would never have realized or produced the metal sculptures I do today," she says. But while her sculptures owe their form to paper, paper is more than a rehearsal for her metal sculptures: it has its own raison d'être. It is both the core and the scaffolding of her art. She cuts it, she unwinds it, she stains it, all the while performing her magic as she physically moves in and around this material she imbues with life.

Gillespie has never designed for the faint of heart or for the art fogies of this world. Her patrons, too, are unfazed that her paper flies through space and dips into pools of resplendent hues. "Paper should be fun," she says. "It should be accessible, too. And if you are too conscious of its more traditional functions (framed and hung against the wall), you can't be spontaneous. Paper can lose its whimsy, and for me that's its charm."

Although she began her career as a painter, at the age of eleven Gillespie had won her first award with a colorful pastel design on paper. The significance of this is not lost on her today: "The award exhilarated me and cemented my interest in paper." Once in New York City and working at Stanley William Hayter's printmaking shop, Atelier 17, she explored and discovered new qualities of paper. "It was a terrific experience, but I always thought how strange that in the same building as this avant-garde artist there was an all-male art club that very definitely admitted no women artists."

As a Hayter protégée, she is not concerned with copper plates or massive litho stones for printmaking. Yet she still is close to what he stood for: an art that was self-justifying, that accounted to no one. "My work has no hidden stuff that needs to be explained. It simply is – clever or otherwise." Hayter's philosophy, "to subordinate ideas about art" to "the process of making it," took root in Gillespie. So did his insistence that painters – and she was a painter – learn the craft of printmaking from beginning to end.

During the war years artists were short of paper. "We worked on a smaller scale during those years," she says. Hayter's idiom was the print, and he gave free play to any technical innovations devised by artists. "I very much liked his emphasis on experimenting and learning. But while he himself used some color he encouraged his students to work only in black and white." Gillespie was a printmaker who longed for color, and after Atelier 17 her prints would in fact bloom with luxuriant color. She has always had a particular fondness for the intense color of the silkscreen medium. Whether a screenprint or poster, her graphic work typically reproduces abstract fields of luminous, glowing color, often incorporating gold or silver foil in designs of Byzantine richness. For example, *Scattered Forms* (26" x 39"), a colored silkscreen on gold-colored foil board published as a signed, limited edition in 1986; or the extraordinary poster (4[illegible]" x 32") she created in 1989 for Lincoln Center for the Performing Arts. The poster medium maintains a special meaning for her: over the years she has produced many in conjunction with her exhibitions.

Following her student days in Baltimore and New York, Gillespie developed her career as a painter, but she never set aside her love of paper. For the art world, 1971 was the beginning of another decade; for her it was the decade of a new beginning. In that year she began to paint on paper – enormous sheets of paper – for *Rituals '71*, a Happening that lasted for just three hours on a Sunday afternoon. If some viewers were amazed at the theme and ambitious scope of the project, no one seemed taken aback by the use of paper, except perhaps Gillespie herself. "It was at this event," she is quick to point out, "that I discovered that not only could I paint on paper, but I could paint on massive sheets of paper."

Since then, whatever the material – pliant aluminum or paper – she relishes grand scale and dimensions; when she thinks paper, she thinks big. It is not unusual for her

← *Phantom: Opera*, 1990, ink on paper, 31" x 23½" x 3"

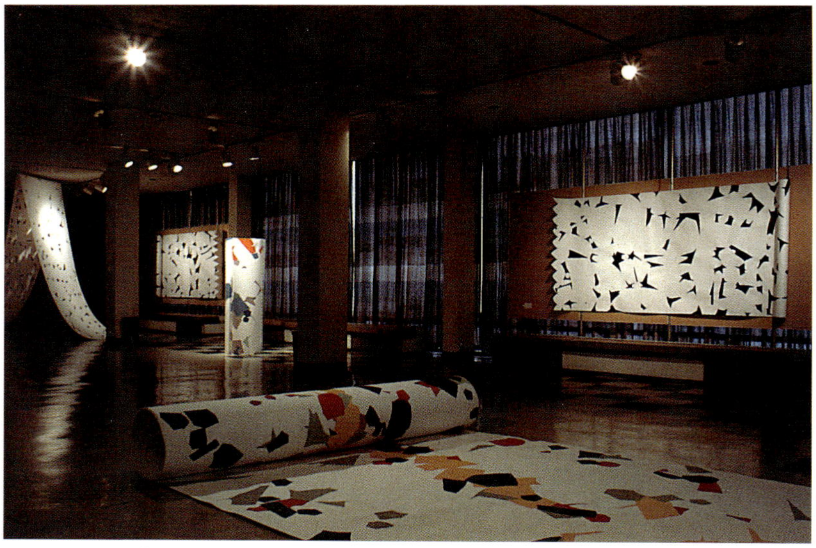

Paper Works, 1976, New York University

work to span 150 feet or more, up a wall or into a room. She sees not only the walls but also the space between them: "Distinctive spaces are truly wonderful, they invite use." Space is as much her concern as the objects she places in it. She likes to send paper soaring into space. The work may hang on the wall, be suspended from the ceiling, or spill, cascade, plunge, and thrust assertively into the surrounding space.

In her 1977 exhibition at the Jersey City Museum, Gillespie installed four paper pieces, 18 inches wide and 150 feet long, suspended in the staircase. Paper seemed to stretch and yawn for miles, as it rolled into the exhibition space below. Reaching across space, into many directions, her paper soared unfettered. It confronted the spectator with unconventional postures and luminous oil-stained configurations. As David Shirey, critic for the *New York Times*, pointed out, one gets the feeling that, if she had the time, she would take over the entire building – perhaps the surrounding areas, too – with her "art." He might better have said "paper."

Size, she feels, contributes its own statement: "Without a doubt, today, size is significant in determining the acceptance of a paper work. Often a small paper piece is much less acceptable, less marketable, especially for large interior spaces." She does realize that size can be immaterial, even misused, but points out that her own involvement with large-scale formats is necessary, as her art is often destined for spacious interiors. "Obviously, the work in question must be strong, creating a firm impact but, at the same time, it must be able to successfully compete with its environment."

To that end she also follows through with the installation of her work. While she may use a conventional mode for small pieces attached to a wall, suspending large paper pieces requires a degree of inventiveness (as well as effort). For this purpose she uses thin wire, which is never seen. With no visible means of support, the result – forms levitating in space – is magical. In other instances heavy paper rolls may provide support, but again the method of attachment is invisible. The success of the installation determines the success of the illusion: large paper forms that are self-supporting, free of the wall.

In addition to what she does with paper, Gillespie is concerned with the quality of her paper. Whatever the purpose, she buys a high-quality acid-free paper. While she realizes the perishable nature of the medium, she also is aware of paper's strength and variety. All types of paper – stiff, coarse, smooth, textured – are used, the type depending on the project. Paper may also be recycled. After some handling, a piece of paper that is 10 feet wide by 20 feet long, becomes dogeared and may need to have its scarred edges trimmed off: "I often end up with a much smaller sheet of paper."

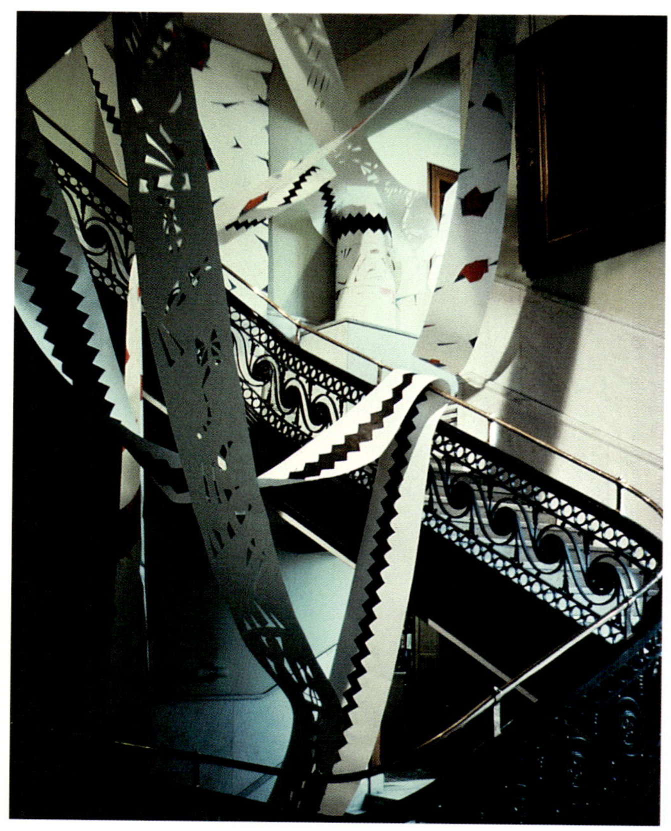

Paper Works, 1977, Jersey City Museum

She is also sensitive to how the paper will receive her color. "Water-based paint tends to pucker the paper, oil paint does not. Therefore, for the big constructions I use an oil paint applied with a brush to stain the paper and then I rub the color in with my hand or a cloth." She applies splashes of bright color to yards of paper, which may subsequently be rolled, crimped, pinched, or simply allowed to flow smoothly.

Action is essential in Gillespie's art. Her imagery flows as well, although it is difficult to describe: abstract shapes that suggest all sorts of unclassified zoomorphic or biomorphic forms. Whatever they are, they exist in a pulse of electric blues, oranges, reds, greens, purples, shimmering mauves, and even virulent magentas and chartreuses – all set against a nourishing and crisp white background. While color has a definite role to play in her art, it is paper that carries the work. In fact, the properties of paper determine the shape of her paper sculptures: "The paper itself dictates what I do. It is the paper that forms the the art." Whether rolled, cut out geometically, arranged in groups, painted both inside and outside, or cylindrical, flat, or curved in shape, paper is the show. It certainly was so in her 1985 exhibition at the Maryland Institute, College of Art.

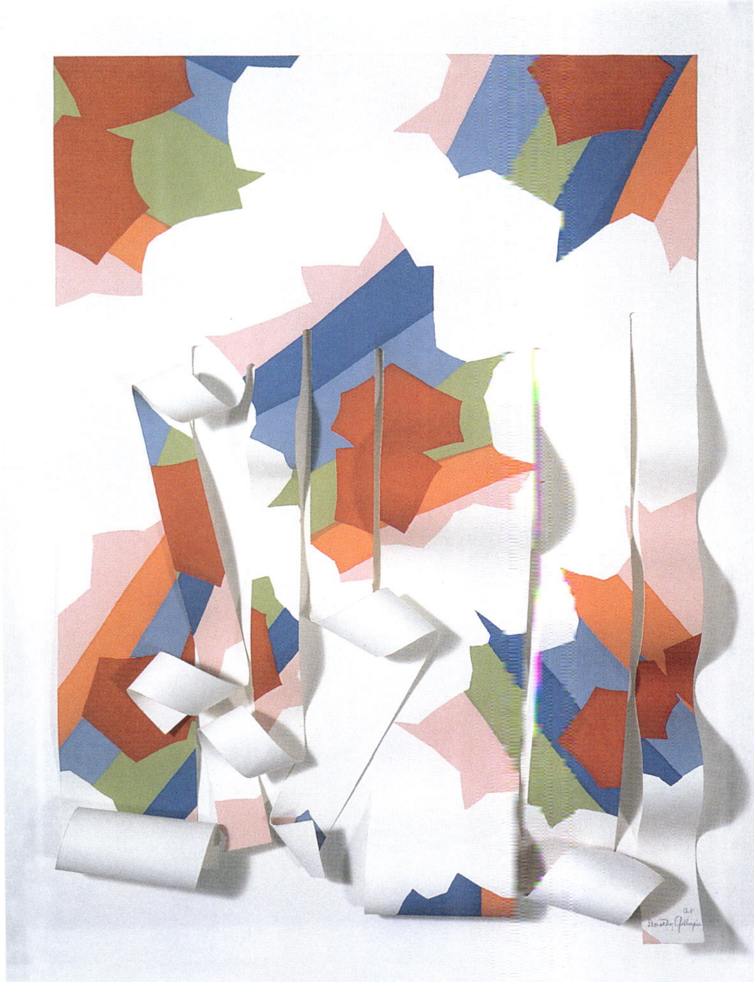

Lantern Festival, 1981, silkscreen on paper, 29" x 22" x 3"

For the Institute, Gillespie produced one of her most spectacular paper works. The Institute has a policy of inviting recognized artists to install temporary projects whenever a new building nears completion and before the occupants move in. Gillespie was invited as guest artist and given complete freedom. She undertook a project of extraordinary scope and dimensions: to face the glass facade of a building 28 feet high and 36 feet wide. Not only that, but she also transformed the interior and exterior glass wall, making paper perform, to tremendous popular and critical success.

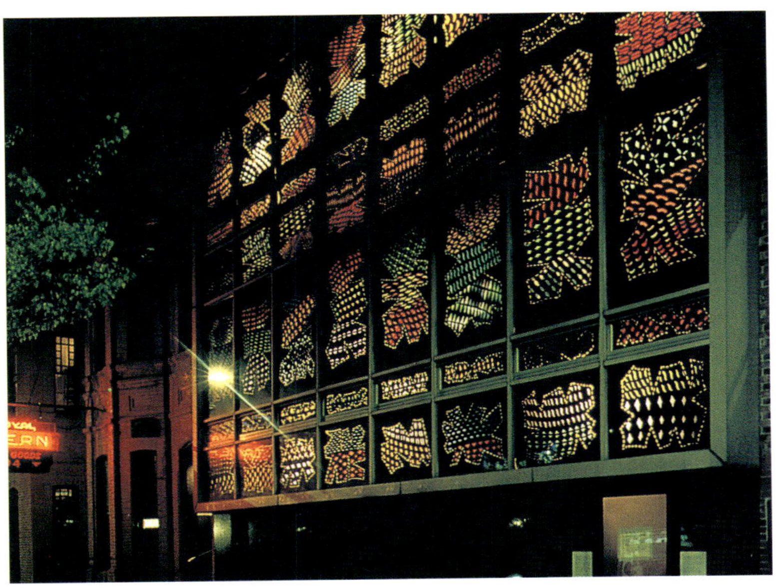

Maryland Institute, College of Art, Facade, 1985

The building's facade consists of eight window panels across, and six panels from top to bottom. The rectangular windows are 7 feet high and 2 feet wide, and some are subdivided into two smaller sections. Seeing the building, she knew immediately what she wanted to do: a form of point coupé (cutwork) in which spaces cut from a ground material are filled with decorative elements. Using large sheets of photographer's black background paper for her forms, she carefully cut out with an X-acto knife a myriad of large and small negative shapes – round, oval, star-like, and patterns of two, four, or more shapes. It was exhausting work, but exhilarating. The only thing missing was the color. But not for long.

Like a child's Lite Bright set waiting for its colored pegs, Gillespie filled all the cutout shapes in her black paper with dyed nylon fabric. Each opening came alive with color; colored shapes danced everywhere against the black background. To bring unity to the design she incorporated a yellow border around each modular form, in an effect reminiscent of the stained-glass windows in Gothic cathedrals. During the day, colored light illuminated the inside of the building. The reverse took place in the evening, when the facade took on a sense of mystery. Like Japanese lanterns in the night, color reached through blackness to illuminate the darkness outside. It was startling: a gigantic spectacle of color and abstract patterns.

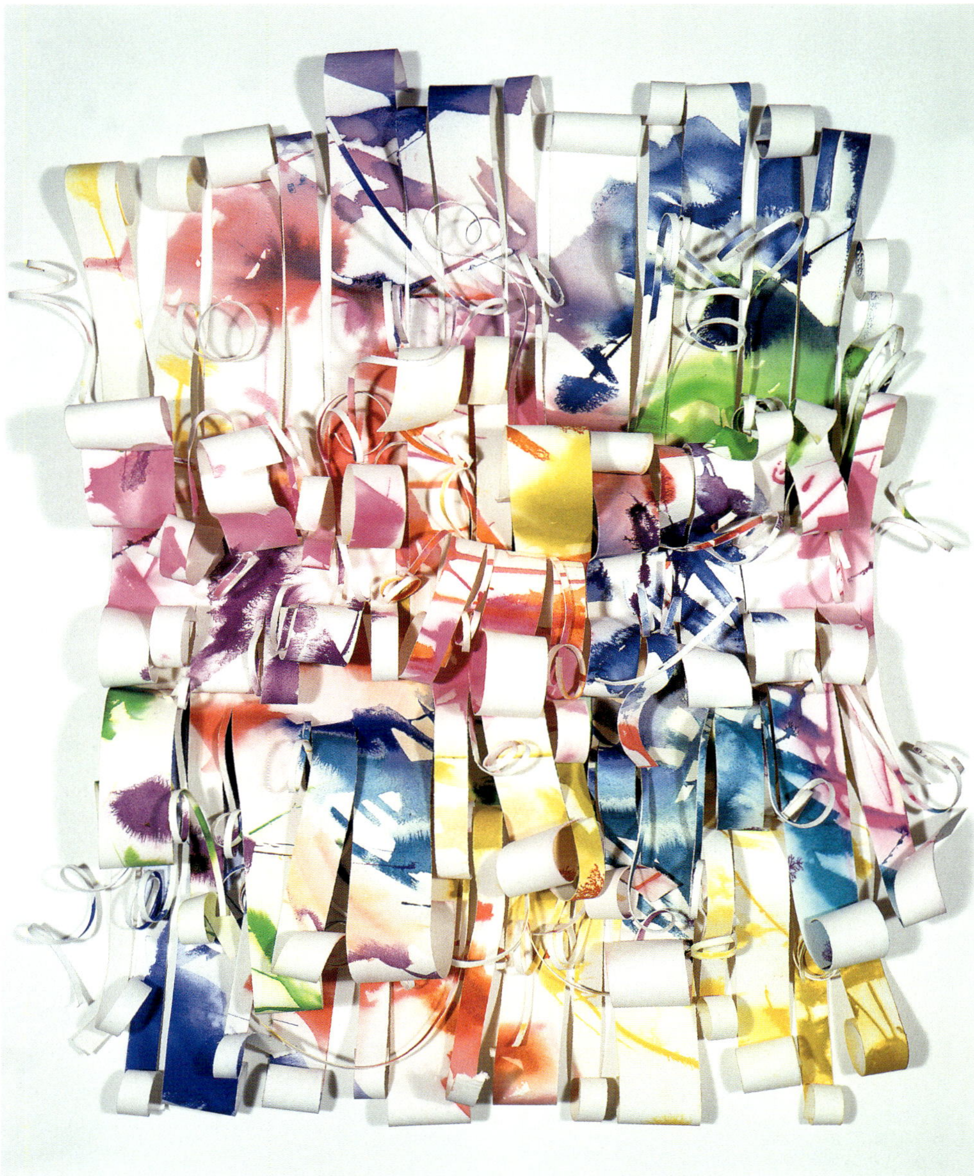

Fantasy Garden, 1986, ink on paper, 40" x 32" x 5"

Gillespie did not have cathedrals or paper lanterns on her mind when she designed the Maryland project. She was thinking of the women she had known who spent hours in the privacy of their homes doing fancywork, such as quilting, tatting, crocheting, knitting, embroidery. Women in art were realizing that much of what was considered just "women's work" was, in fact, art, and Gillespie had taken the idea of women's traditional handiwork and transformed it on a monumental scale.

In the years that followed, Gillespie continued to develop her interest in paper and to expand the stylistic parameters she had first established in the 1970s. An artist of rare innate ability, she has pushed her paper art to its highest fulfillment during the past two decades. And she has received a good deal of critical acclaim for her work in the medium.

In 1986 she had a solo exhibition at Gallery West in Los Angeles. One of the most memorable works shown was a colored ink-on-paper collage, *Fantasy Garden*. It is a symphony of exquisitely constructed, superbly orchestrated paper curls overlayed with dazzling hues of many shades – everything to delight the spectator's eye. How could simple paper and colored ink create such an extraordinary sense of the beautiful?

In 1990, she produced her *Phantom: Opera*, a work measuring 31 by 23½ by 3 inches and now in the Castellani Museum at Niagara University in western New York state. The *Phantom* series is a demonstration of her best efforts,

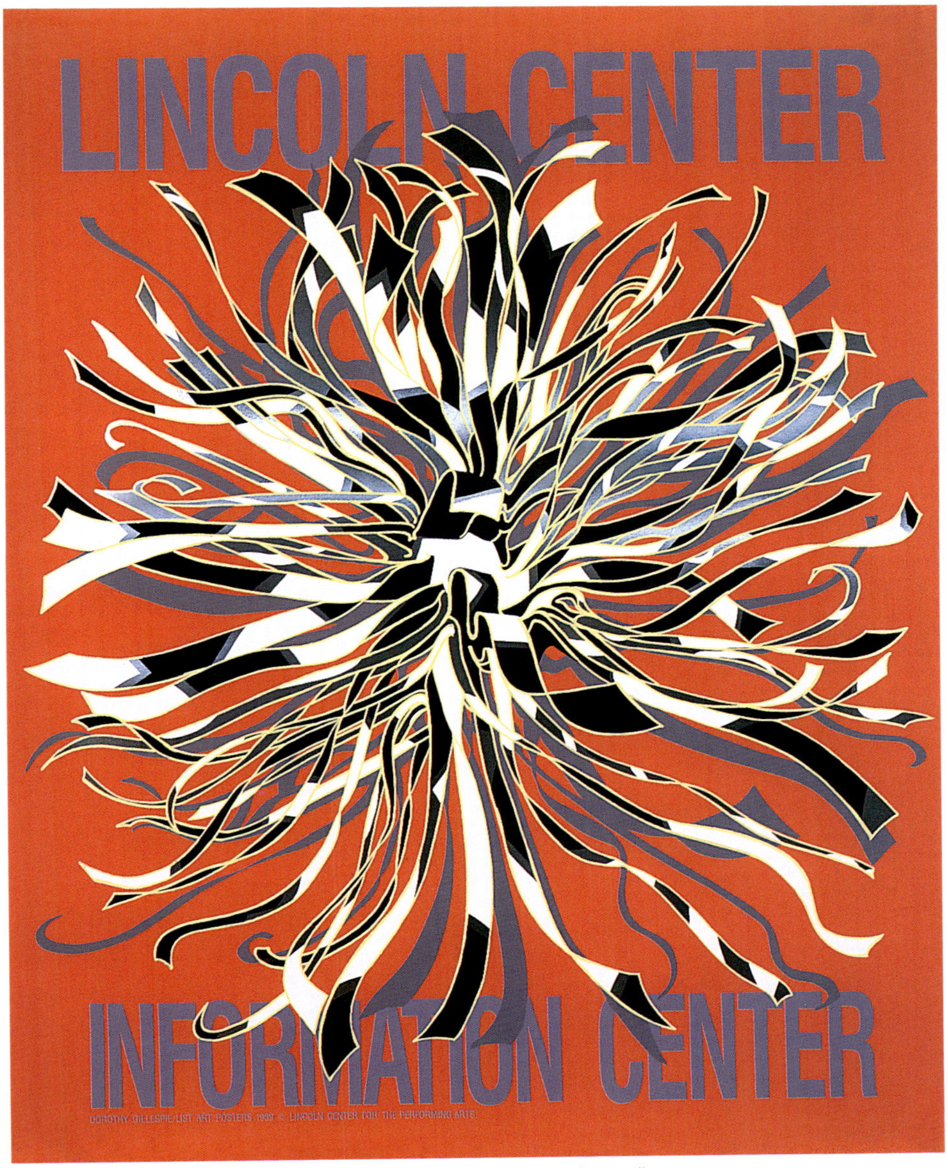

Lincoln Center Poster, 1989, silkscreen on paper, 40" x 32"

as well as showing a new and expressive direction in the use of form and color. Unlike *Fantasy Garden,* where multiple shades of delicate hues act like a veneer on white paper, in the *Phantom* series color completely dominates the paper. The delicate and translucent colors seen in the earlier works have been replaced with deep russets, purples, burnt oranges, dark greens. Instead of unfolding in tinted steam, Gillespie's flowers now close in opaque pools of color. In addition to new color, there is a different approach to forms. The energetic curls and twists of *Fantasy Garden,* for example, are now tighter, more controlled, as if they are constricted by maturity. While something of the organic and spontaneous quality is lost, the forms maintain a baroque richness and exuberance.

What a wonderful sense of the macroscopic as well as the microscopic Gillespie possesses: "Sometimes I feel like working big, sometimes little, sometimes average size." Large or small, her paper pieces sing. There is paper under Plexiglas, and there are simple, straightforward paper works in watercolor and ink that are no larger than a few inches, like oversized stamps or undersized postcards. There is a gentleness and a wonderful preciosity about these smaller works. Although they are reminiscent of hand-painted miniatures from some medieval monastery, close inspection proves they are not; they are small paper worlds that whet one's visual appetite.

Then there are the wove paper sketchbooks, her "little creatures," as she calls them. These are universes filled with the sights and sounds of her fantasies and observations. Whenever she travels, they travel with her; and in them she compulsively records new images and fresh ideas.

If twentieth-century art unframed paintings and removed them from the sacrosanct wall of the museum in order to integrate wall area and room space, then clearly Gillespie's releasing of paper from its traditional uses and restrictions is a singularly important contribution. Now that critics are beginning to grasp the role that paper has played in her work, they acclaim her use of it, particularly in the large sculptures, with lyrical phrases such as "divinely imaginative, radiant like visual music." But they somewhat miss the point, not explaining *why* she uses paper. To answer this question, one must turn to the artist herself: "I find it full of energy, full of promise. It has a feeling all its own, a life all its own. For me, it is unblemished, like youth – a world of magic."

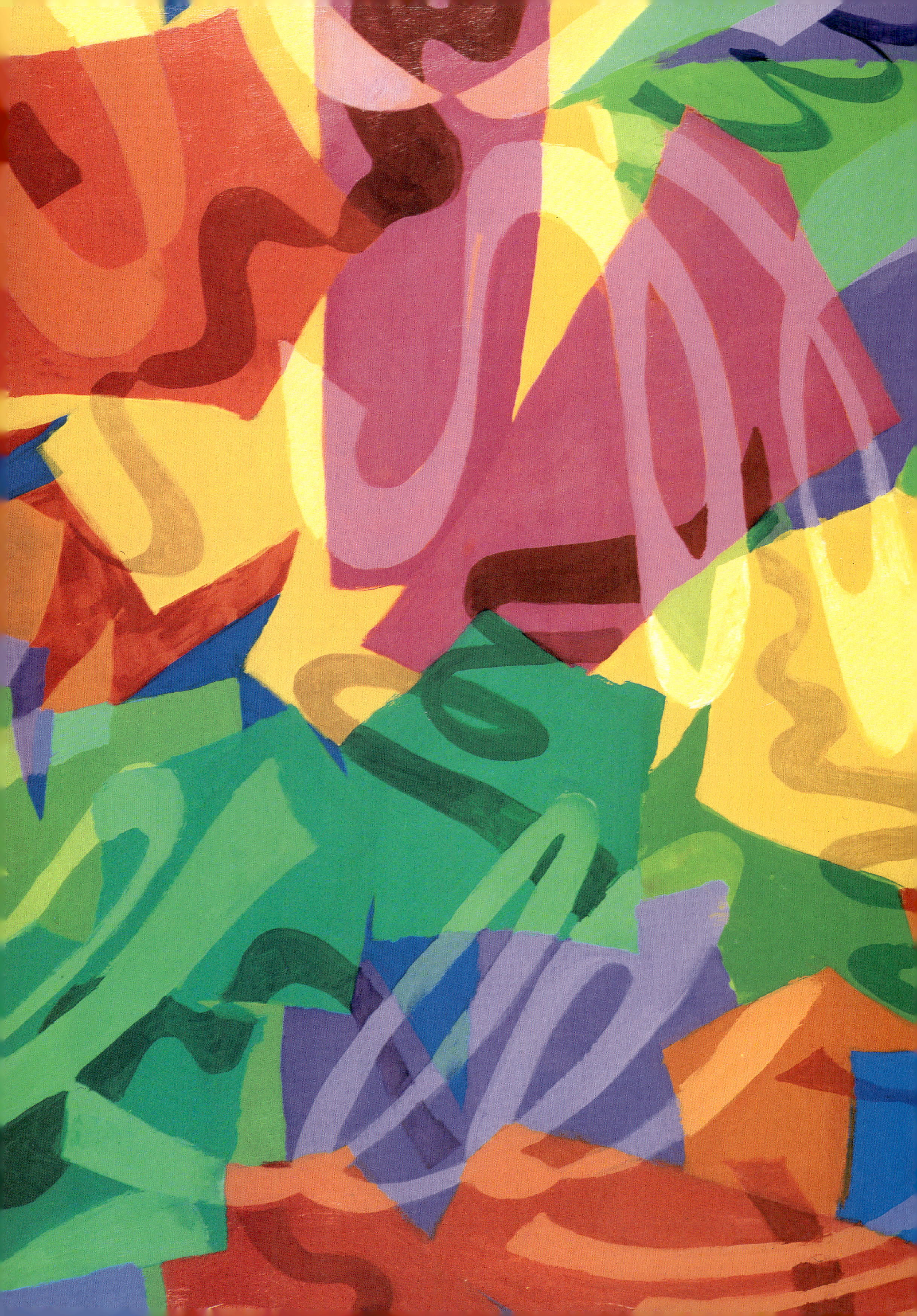

George S. Bolge

Centuries of thought and impassioned argument have not yet succeeded in explaining why it is that *homo faber* must make things, and neither has the key to the impulse to use matter to recreate experience been discovered. The one fact we can confidently proffer is that throughout human history there have been individuals driven to shape matter in ways that we have come to call artistic. Dorothy Gillespie belongs to one of the many Heraclitan currents flowing through the history of art, the current that carries the need to express, through the shaping of matter, the strongest and often deepest emotions common to human beings. Such artists obey a compelling command from within, grabbing at earth, metal, paint, or anything that is congealed matter to shape some analogue to what they feel. Emotions are at their fingertips. There have been many attempts to classify this particular stream in the history of art with labels such as romantic, primitive, and expressionist. Whatever we call it, the need to communicate a strong response to experience in the most direct way presupposes an instinctive faith in what modern philosophers call transsubjectivity. In making a painting, or looking at one, we want to have our own experiences universally confirmed.

As an artist, Gillespie allows her imagination and sensibilities free reign to wander where and how they will. Seemingly without conscious control, colors call to and respond to other colors, lines interact upon shapes, textures erupt out of smooth surfaces. Only when sensibility and intuition are blocked will she allow experience and skill to see what can be done to resolve matters. She is a consummate master of this method of working. She understands that trust in one's intuitions and sensibilities can result in as consistent a creative method as can tight and rigid control over every step of the creative process. All that is required is an alertness to whatever happens on the canvas and the ability and willingness to follow through. In order to do so, however, she has to be in step with the rhythms and patterns of growth, and she has to be able to prod along gently the pictorial image, much as the sun and rain incite the growth of delicate, living things.

Compared with the glories of Michelangelo's Sistine ceiling or Rembrandt's studies of humanity, this skill and talent may not seem extraordinary. However, very few artists have this gift. Gillespie is one of the few who does, and one of the very few able to bring it to life in others, both by example and through teaching.

Gillespie made her stylistic breakthrough in the 1950s, but her roots were in the discontents of the 1940s. American museums and galleries were backing American Scene painting, those nostalgic, rural idylls epitomized by the productions of Thomas Hart Benton, Grant Wood, and John Steuart Curry. They were also espousing Social Realism, which recorded the human cost of hard times but frequently sacrificed aesthetic control in order to score a simplistic political point. For Gillespie, those approaches to subject matter were artistically bankrupt: they did not take into consideration the achievements of European giants such as Picasso, Matisse, and Miró. Furthermore, provincial modes were inadequate for suggesting the tenor of the times. Her solution was to burrow inward.

What she sought to explore and affirm on canvas in paintings such as *Dancers* (1944) were states of feeling: an intense psychological moment, a religious or mystical experience, a deeply subjective reaction to a person, place, or occasion. Inner necessity, and nothing but inner necessity – as father-of-abstract-art Wassily Kandinsky put it – was to decide line, form, color, design, and rhythm. A painting equivalent of such inner states had to be invented. Since fears, obsessions, and the like do not have concrete, objective forms, it would be misleading to illustrate them as landscapes or still lifes. In Gillespie's view, therefore, a picture could be composed of shapes representing nothing in nature, yet it could be of great emotional and formal significance. As Robert Motherwell has noted, "States of feeling, when generalizing, become questions of light, color, weight, solidity, airiness, lyricism, somberness, heaviness, and strength."*

After a period of flirtation, Gillespie put aside the literal, clearly recognizable image. In the composition entitled *Winged Flight* (1957), the size, paths, and autographic quality of the individual brushstroke became of profound concern to her because of the emphasis placed on process and the signs of the artist's active presence in the work. The enlargement of the physical dimensions of the canvas assumed a similar urgency. She wanted viewers to be pulled into paintings like *Celebration* (1960) and to respond to them as an environment. Deep space, mass, and blinding bursts of light were seemingly hewn from the picture plane. These early paintings were given reso-

← Detail of *Kaleidoscope*, 1993, acrylic on canvas, 48" x 60"

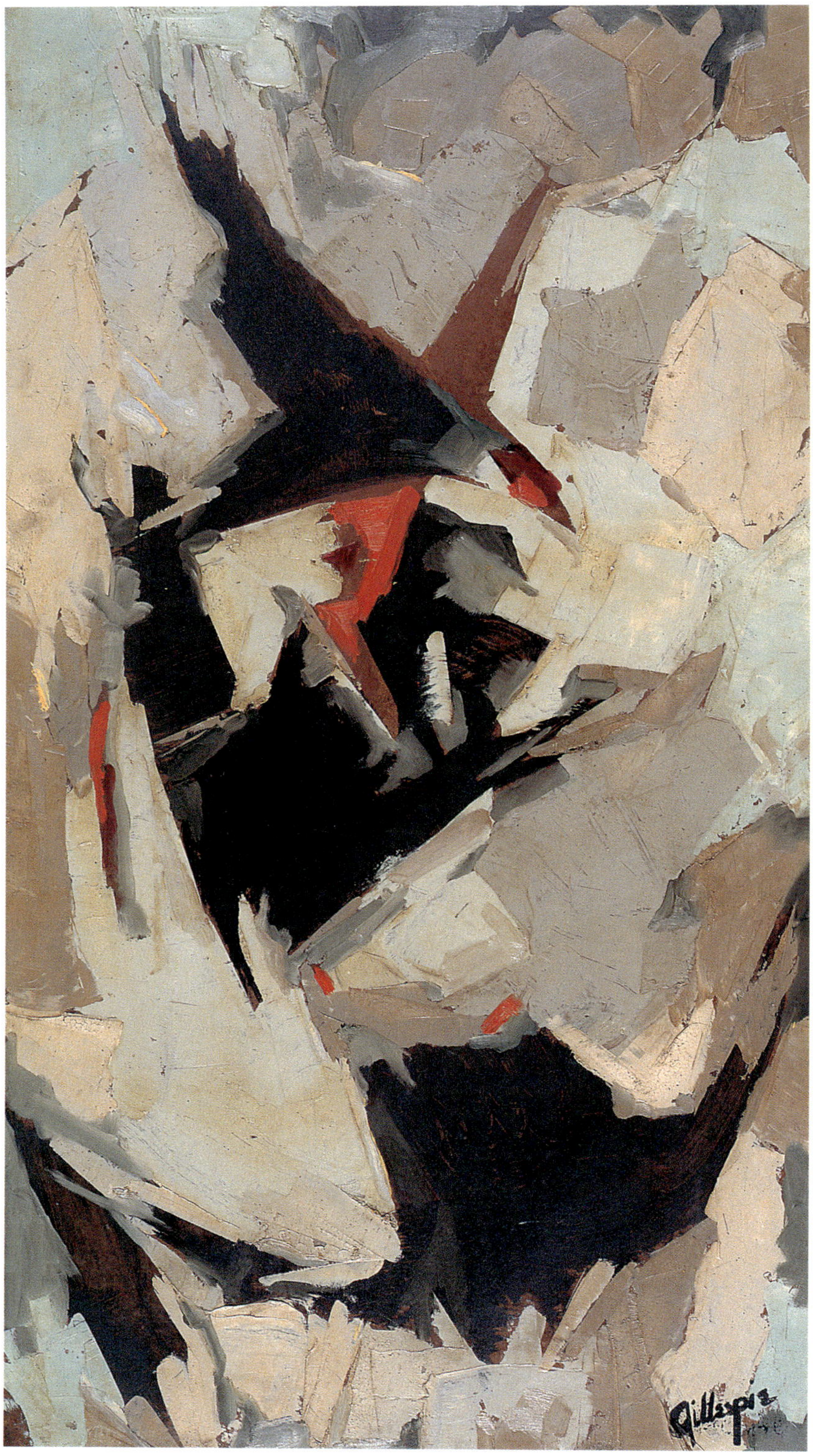

Winged Flight, 1957, oil on canvas, 40" x 22"

nance by the range of poetic and metaphysical speculation she was able to bring to bear on her subjects.

Achieving a specific, visual reality has been the goal of abstract painters during the last decade. It is not, and cannot be, their only goal, yet abstraction focuses on this problem in a singular manner. Yet once achieved, reality, whether in art or in life, has a way of evaporating, of becoming shopworn and less immediate, and of being replaced by a new reality. The form of abstraction presented in Gillespie's early paintings indicates both the speed and seriousness of this process. One of the greatest problems in approaching abstract painting, as exemplified in the painting titled *Primitive Theme* (1961), is to find ways in which abstract forms and paint handling may convey meaning. Consequently, this painting is not so much a demonstration of some "action" principle as it is a luminous sign of moments of consciousness, moments that have their source in great depths and bear their own mysterious charge of poetry.

A close examination of her work in the early 1970s reveals particularly important aspects of her creative contribution to this field of expression. In paintings such as *Forms in Space #8* (1973) and *Motion and Space #10* (1973) we can retrace the complex synthesis of her symbolic naturalism to its constituent parts, often subconsciously assembled by the artist. She seems to be interested in how to present an inner, emotional state in abstraction but related to nature. This artist believes strongly in her power of subconscious association; she arrests the process of painting at the moment when what she was seeking flashes into view. Her canvases contain layers of "colored mistakes" buried in them, layers of consciousness, of willing. The images in earlier paintings such as *Voyage* (1975) and *Displaced Journey* (1976) are intended to strike something that is an emotional involvement and that has to do with the human personality and all the mysteries of life, not simply colors or abstract balances. What happens on the canvas is surprising and unpredictable, for to her the act of painting becomes the experience.

Gillespie's work from the late 1970s, as exemplified by *After the Storm* (1976) and *The Promise of the Hidden Sun* (1978), is occupied with breaking through the linear continuum by isolating forms of a shape that would repel each other, then relating them to a slightly felt scaffolding and an irrational, meandering line. The adjustments of opposites in the painting constitute the core of her art: closed form versus open line, clear definition versus ambiguity, and, most significantly, chance versus deliberate manipulation.

The earlier pieces achieve a new synthesis of formal elements and content, thus making more explicit Gillespie's conviction of the interaction among life, nature, and abstract art. Her use of the expressive potential of the large painted canvas propels her toward a content that is both powerful and emotional. In *Shadow of the Evening Clouds* (1979), the animated surface of the painting conveys a sense of endless, harmonic rhythm extending beyond the confines of the picture's actual edges. The canvas becomes a large enough arena in which to lose oneself. Her paintings exist as a gestural record of the aesthetic process at a particular instant, regardless of how long it takes actually to complete the pictures. In effect, her painting is painting about the act of painting.

In *Mythical Summer Day in the Hidden Valley* (1983), there is an interplay between the picture plane and the background areas of the canvas that creates a shifting, changing space in which the forms appear to be in a state of flux: matter becomes energy. Within this evolving space, the eternal tensions between man and nature, land and sea, surface and depth, toughness and sweetness, emotion and reason create infinitely complex structures. The restless quality exuded by these shifting relationships gives the work a tension and complexity that is challenging.

Gillespie's work continued to grow, becoming stronger

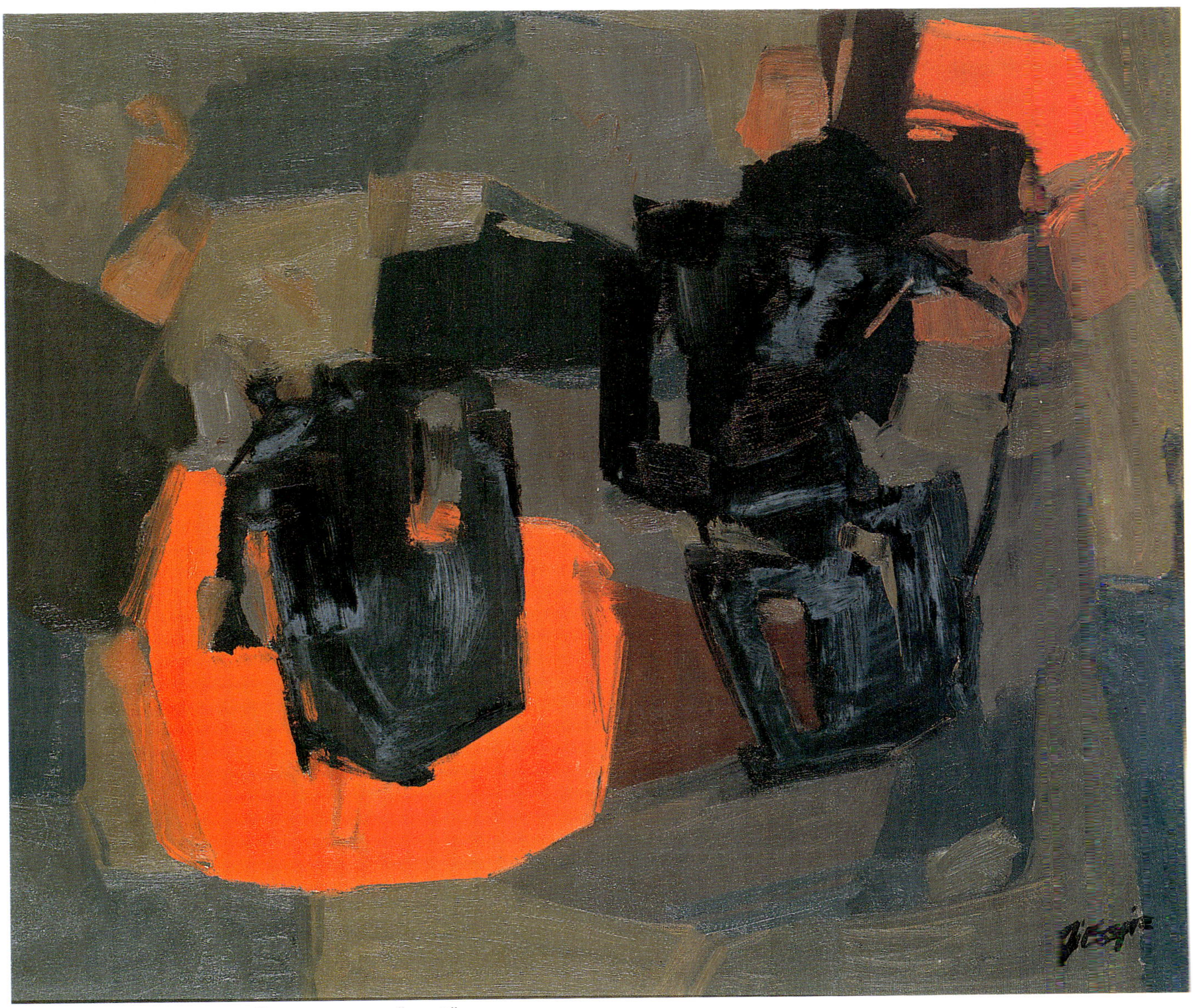

Primitive Theme, 1961, oil on canvas, 40" x 48"

each year. By withdrawing into her own world as an artist, she won through to an even surer, freer, and more complete understanding of her complex vision of man and nature. What Gillespie does is this: she meditates; she connects her hand and paintbrush to the deeper, quieter, more mysterious parts of her mind, and she paints pictures of what she sees and feels in there.

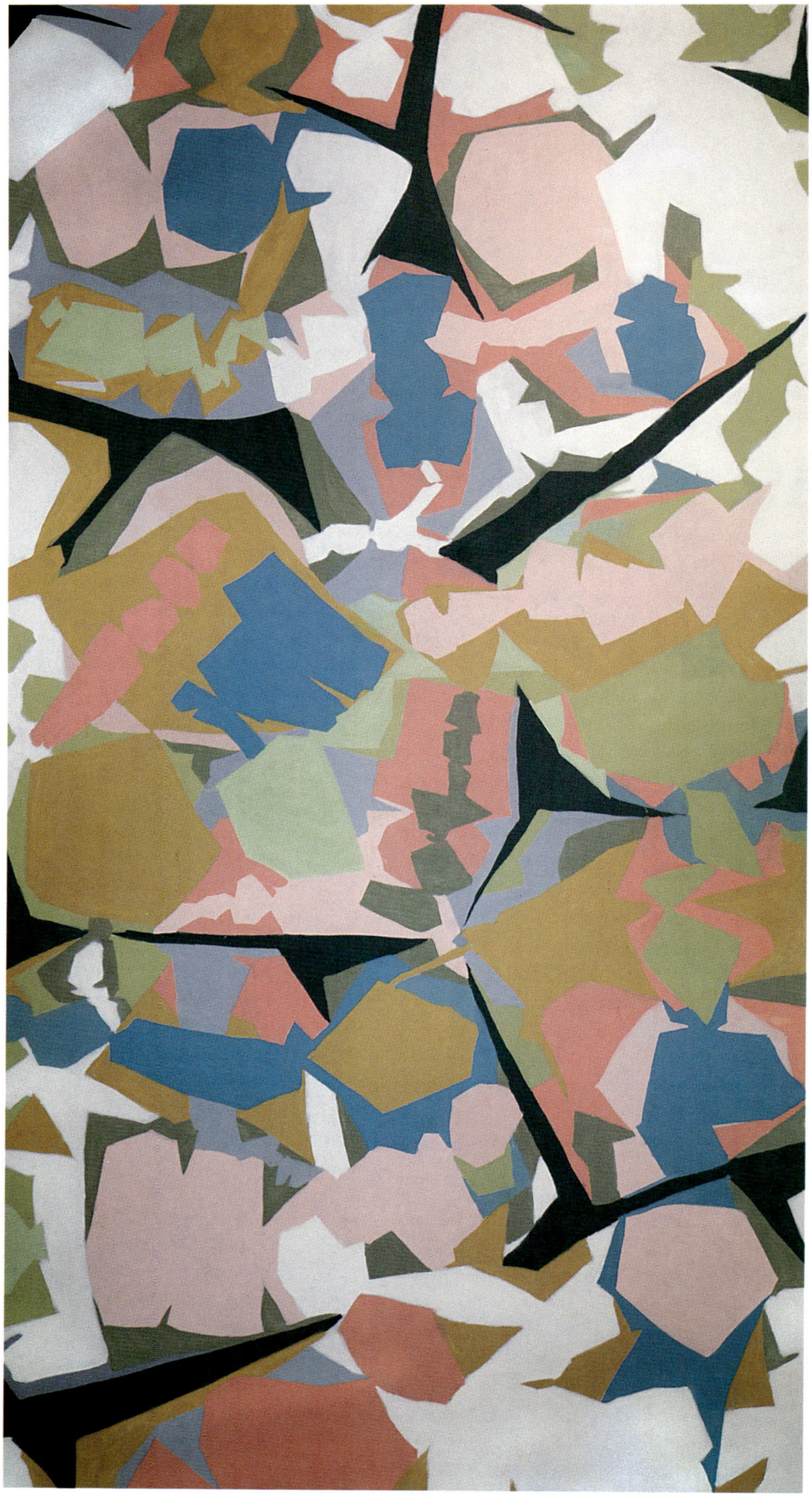

Motion and Space #10, 1973, oil on canvas, 98" x 48"

Gillespie's later paintings can be linked to landscape themes. The association depends primarily on scale. Large, grid-formatted works such as *Through the Looking Glass* (1988), page 140, or *Changing Shadows* (1991), page 85, signify her rejection of preciousness. They repudiate the viewer-connoisseur and solicit a situation in which the power of the work reaches everyone in its vicinity. Her paintings look as big as all outdoors; evoking the grandeur of nature itself, they aim to present overwhelming forces. The scale of these "painterly grids" affects aesthetic elements differently. The biggest changes relate to color, where a really large area can change our sense of the total amount and quality of light around us, and to line, where kinetic force increases geometrically with the amount of the visual field it covers.

The marks Gillespie makes on a canvas or sheet of metal and the way the picture surface retains or absorbs the evidence of that marking are crucial elements of the experience the picture provides. This process produces images recognizable as uniquely her own. Her images are as individual as speech patterns and physical gestures, both biologically and temperamentally. But the personal identifiability of her pictures is not the point; it merely testifies to the authenticity of their "statements." In her work, both the objective world and the subjective self are supposed to be consumed in the fiery experience of encounter. Exactly that fusion of the separate parties is a quasi-existential encounter in

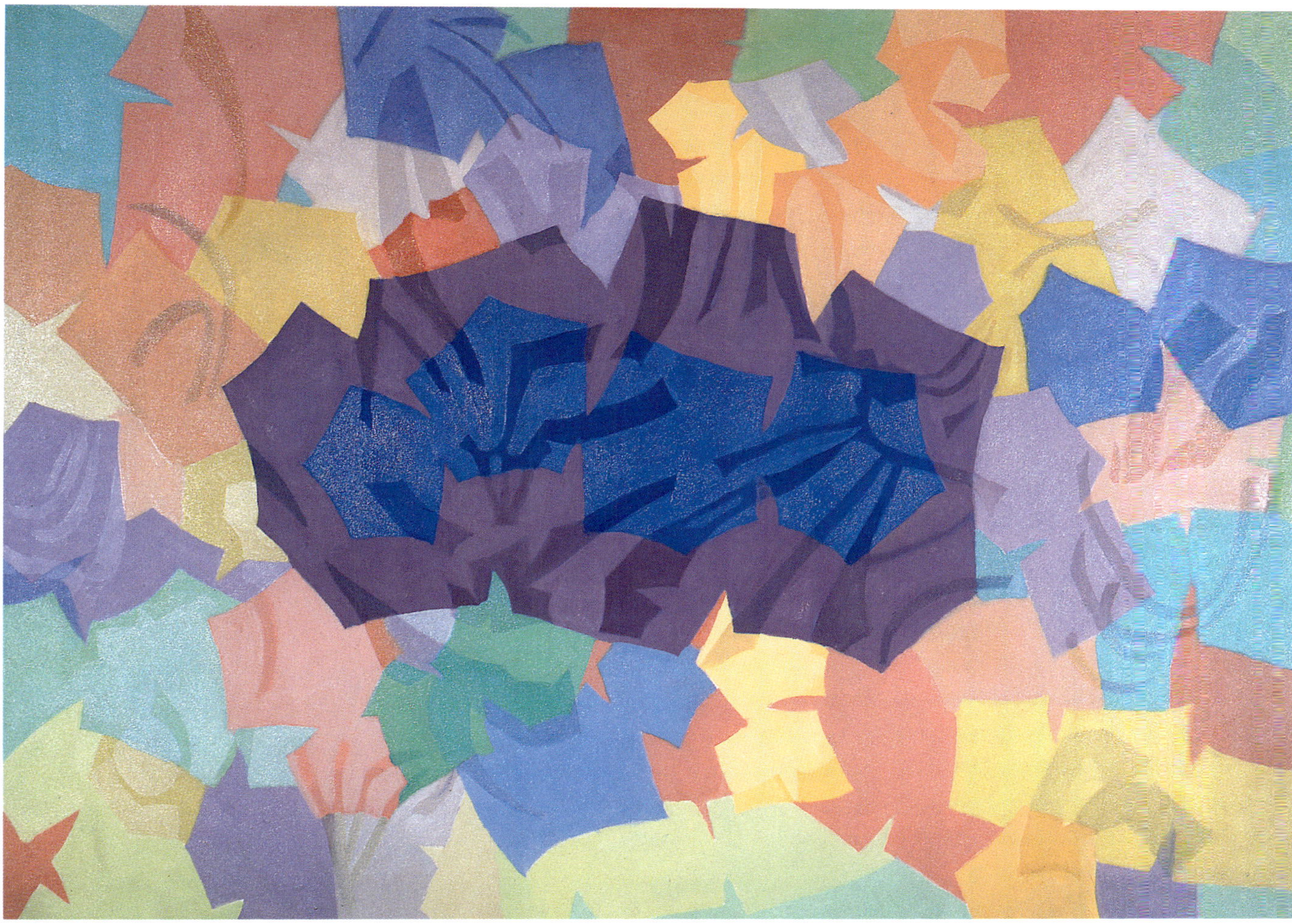

Mythical Summer Day in the Hidden Valley, 1983, oil on canvas, 30" x 42"

what sets them apart. It is also what her viewers are meant to achieve. The aim is a contagion of ecstasy that results from a passionate absorption in the painter's immediate, contingent situation.

Gillespie tries to abandon intention and to reach a "no man's land" where the ephemeral and the eternal become one. The names of her paintings specify her recognition of what has emerged, and the titles she gives the works become something like T. S. Eliot's objective correlative. They are verbal clusters that correspond to nonverbal complexes, parallel inventions that imply no logical or causal relation to the first creation. Landscape imagery is, for her, an ever-present but passing reference in a perennial experience of transformation and flux. She achieves complexity of meaning in her recent work, *Kaleidoscope* (1993), detail on page 126, for example, by multiplying allusions and associations. Her style continues to assert the possibility of shared meaning in a world where the units of meaning have become stale and frayed. She is an expresser of adoration for a world that has colors, shapes, and spaces that may manifest the human spirit as it moves and has its being.

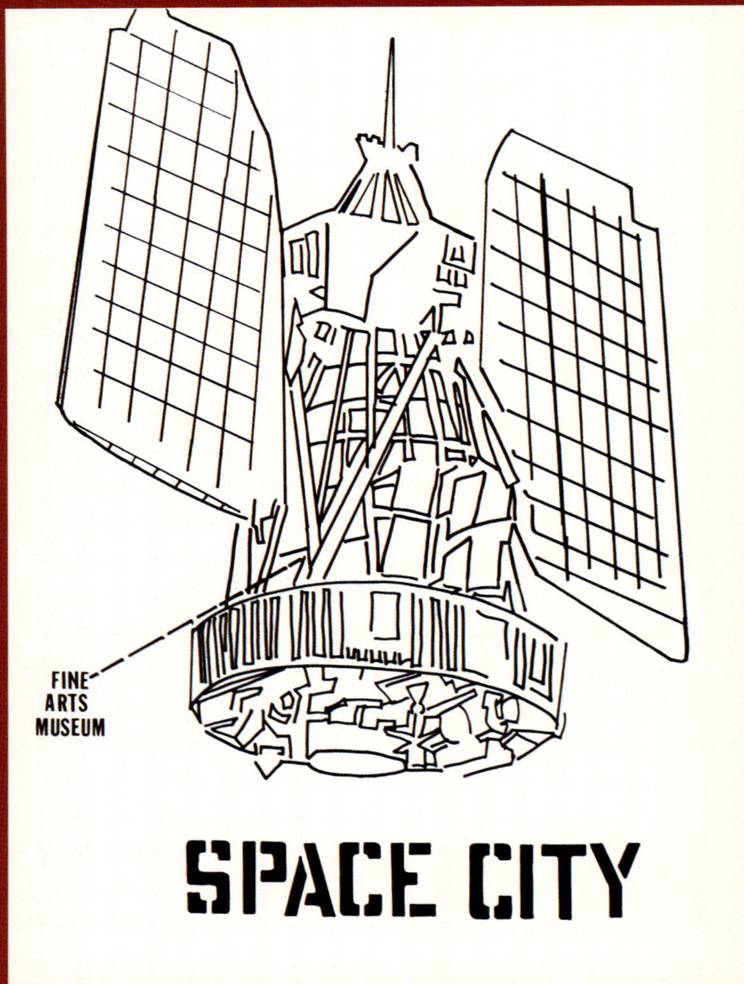
FINE ARTS MUSEUM
SPACE CITY

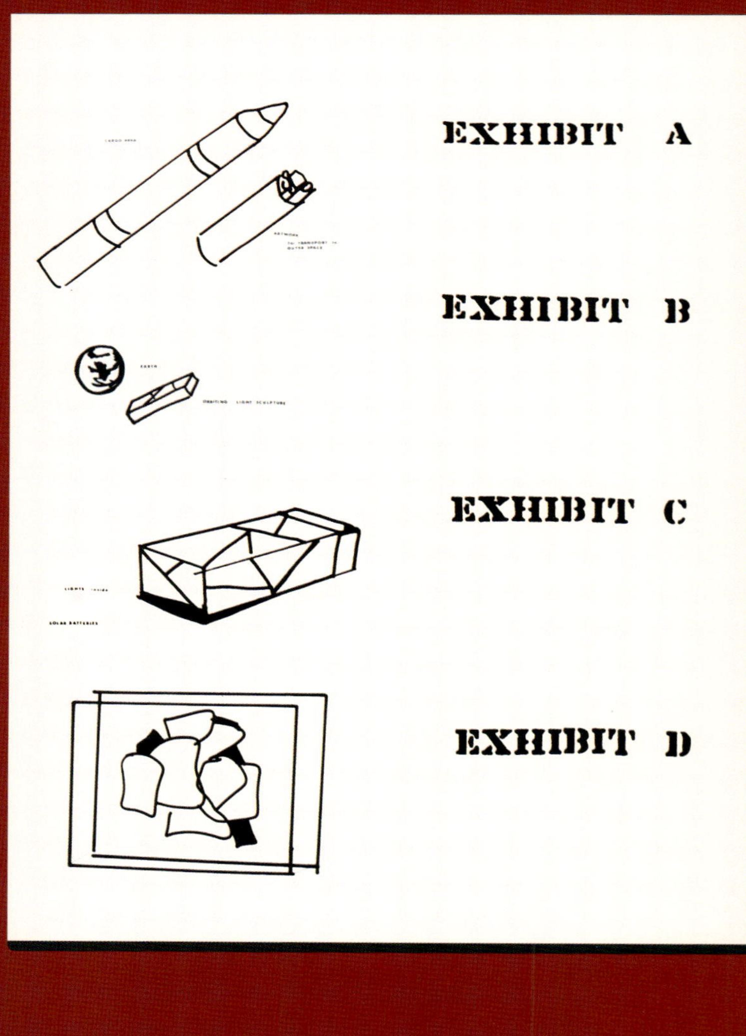
EXHIBIT A
EXHIBIT B
EXHIBIT C
EXHIBIT D

During the social and political turmoil of the 1960s there was a vanguard of underground artists, such Allan Kaprow, Red Grooms, and Claes Oldenburg, who rejected the consumer-oriented marketplace of the art establishment. They advocated a dramatic and revolutionary new medium – real objects and real people gathered together in Environments and Happenings. There were also new collaborative groups such as Fluxus in Europe and the No!Artists in New York's East Village, a group whose history has been documented in an anthology, *No!Art*, published in Germany in 1988.

Dorothy Gillespie quickly became a major force in the avant-garde scene with her first Environment, *The American Way of Death*. Her friend and collaborator in this exposé of consumerism was No!Artists leader Sam Goodman, who was described at the time by Tom Wolfe as "short, plump, shaggy, rumpled up, 45 and never too old for the life of Artist in Protest. He and his friend Boris Lurie have been working for the last seven years down on the Lower East Side in the general field of shocking the bourgeoisie and revolting against the establishment."

Gillespie's first Environment was motivated by an intensely personal experience – the sudden death of her father. While arranging his funeral she unexpectedly became entangled in a labyrinth of exploitative and expensive scams devised by the funeral industry. In the transition from real life to art event she and Goodman visited funeral parlors throughout the city, where they were appalled to discover that death was a big, big business in America. As the directors of funeral homes began to refuse their requests for information, they realized that there were many suspect practices that should be exposed to the public as fraudulent if not criminal.

The "Unveiling of an Exhibit dedicated to *The American Way of Death*," was held on April 8, 1964, at the Champagne Gallery in Greenwich Village. The show was described by Lurie in *No!Art* as a "realistic environment of a funeral parlor with coffins, burial-lot plans, burial accessories, all faithfully realistically reproduced, scrupulously marked out with payment plans, prices and attractive sales descriptions – precursor of present sociological art. Coffins with the deceased on display as well: Sam Goodman horribly prophetic here, this was next to his last show – a few years later only he died himself in anger to the last."

The two garish open coffins, designated His and Hers, were heavy with satire and the meaninglessness of typically American burial rituals. His coffin was lined with artificial grass, and a set of golf clubs shared his final resting place. On the lid was a painting of a putting green at the 18th hole with real golf balls forming a design. Her coffin featured the latest decorator colors in satin fabrics and metallic paper. A white kitten and the newly marketed Princess telephone were placed inside the coffin. There was a mirror on the lid so that the deceased, represented by a manikin, could see herself when the lid was closed. A light was installed in the event she was afraid of the dark.

Banners of pretense denying death, printed with "Just Resting" and "Peace at Last" in gold letters, were hung so low that they brushed against people as they walked through the Environment. A sculpture was created of samples of wood the mortician deemed suitable for cremation, as a coffin was required by law to burn with the body. A profusion of dusty plastic flowers with a projected lifespan longer than the corpse adorned both coffins and tombstones. Prophetic signs announced the acceptance of credit cards and the dispensing of green stamps, sales tools later adopted by the funeral industry. A money box was provided for those who "want to take it with them." The musical background was a recording of Gregorian chants played backward to dispel any aura of reality. Viewers, who included celebrities like Allen Ginsburg, were served black champagne. Al Valentine filmed the show as a black comedy, with Gillespie and Goodman as performers and the gallery visitors who appear as unwitting mourners. Gillespie's interest in film as an art form was initiated by this experience, and she purchased a camera for the purpose of shooting her own films in the future.

Made in the USA, described on its poster as "A Critical Environment" and also devoted to consumerism, opened in early 1965 at the Champagne Gallery. A Gillespie catalogue published later by the Gertrude Stein Gallery, which had sponsored *Made in the USA*, described it succinctly: "It consisted of blinking lights, peep holes, mirrors, revolving figures, three-dimensional shadow boxes which utilized theatrical gauze, plastic and aluminum to depict the stereotypes on the American scene. Colored lights rotating continually created a startling psychedelic effect heightened by stereo tape recordings of street sounds,

← Detail of a panel for *The First Museum in Outer Space*, 1974 music, news, speeches and sirens – all combining to give the viewer, who was also a participant, a feeling of unreality while seeing, hearing, touching, smelling and tasting the familiar."

Gillespie built huge shadow boxes with scrim tacked to the open side. When the light went on a life-size painted silhouette inside the box was illuminated. Each shadow box was a satire devoted to a current fad. Dieting was represented by a thin silhouette inside the shadow box along with pictures of low-calorie foods and words such as "thin." In contrast, the silhouette painted on the outside was a fat female body. Some of the figures were also reproduced in the center of the room as metal cutouts that would swing and twirl; the obese woman, for example, was flesh-colored on one side and painted with red and white stripes suggesting a flag on the reverse.

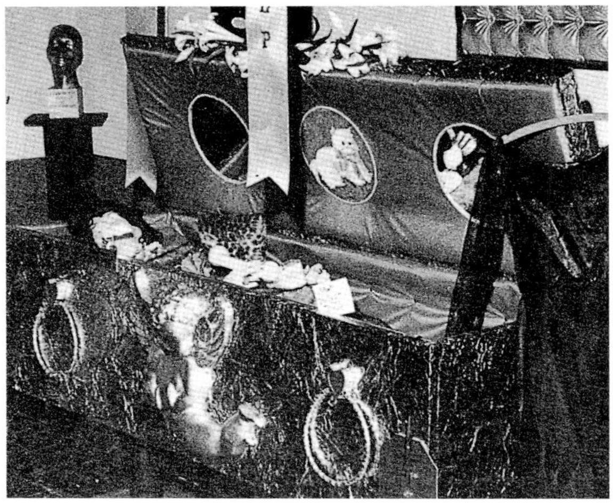

The American Way of Death, with Sam Goodman, 1964, mixed media

As peopled entered the space, they were disoriented by the rotating colored lights and hanging figures. The scent of newly developed deodorant sprays filled the air, while a television set played a looped tape showing an ominous mushroom cloud rising from the explosion of an atomic bomb. Sounds and music recorded on stereo tape competed with a beeping, blinking computer. The sense of unreality was so pervasive that viewers assumed that the real dollar bills scattered on the floor along with play money were also fake. An eight-minute film was shot documenting Gillespie installing the exhibition and showing guests arriving at the opening reception. There is a spooky feeling to the film as the revolving lights give the effect of darkness alternating with an eerie burned-out white light. The figures swinging from the ceiling and the real people wandering through the gallery seem to materialize and evanesce like phantoms. Perhaps in reaction to *The American Way of Death* and *Made in the USA*, Gillespie mounted a solo exhibition the following year titled *Light and Motion* that intentionally used the energy and activity she felt emanating from her beloved city of New York.

Film became an integral component for her next Environment, *U. S.* She spent months shooting her own footage on trips throughout the city or along its highways. Sam Goodman sometimes went along and one scene features him eating a hot dog at Coney Island. The multitude of ideas and images in this film represents the creativity and energy of an artist who is intimately engaged by diverse activities. Yet the scenes are all shot through or contain some version of the American flag. The film opens with stars twirling on the screen followed by stripes in a circle swirling about. Sometimes the flag is a scrim with images such as newspaper headlines, space capsules, or children visible through the stars and stripes. As there was no live soundtrack for the film, a radio tuned to a news station was concealed behind the screen. The film was shown continually as part of the Environment and again in 1974 during a film festival at the Women's Interart Center.

Gillespie's *U. S.* Environment opened to critical acclaim on September 27, 1966, at the Gertrude Stein Gallery. A *New York Times* headline proclaimed, "Flag is Subject of an Art Show." The Sunday review by Alfred E. Clark said, "A modern-day Betsy Ross, named Dorothy Gillespie, figured last week that she had cut, snipped, shaped and painted about 3,500 stars of mylar, aluminum, plastic and sundry materials for her one-woman show devoted to representations of the American flag.

"Miss Gillespie, a onetime abstract artist whose works hang in museums from Tel Aviv to Miami Beach, said she could not estimate the number of yards of red and white ribbons she had created. The stars and ribbons glittered from paintings, collages and sculptures in her exhibition, which she described 'as an extension of pop and op art.' Walls and ceilings of the Gallery Gertrude Stein . . . were festooned with the cut-outs that rippled as mobiles . . . .

"Asked what she was seeking to achieve in her show, she replied: 'My basic idea is to involve the viewers in all of their five senses.'. . . In the main room about two dozen representations of the American flag, mostly fragments of the white stars and blue background or sections of the stripes, hung from the walls. Some were paintings, several mobile sculptures and collages made of various materials. In her sculptures, Miss Gillespie said she sought to obtain a 'third-dimension feeling' by creating the forms out of clear plastics on stands that could be revolved. The spectator can see through the stripes as it turns and can experience a symbolic rendition of the flag. 'What I am trying to do is to make people think of what we have here. Not everything is right, but we are living in the most wonderful time in the world and I think most of us take too much of it for granted.' At the opening, Miss Gillespie satisfied the sense of taste by providing Scotch whisky in which she used a food-coloring additive to change it to a vivid red color. The bourbon was turned blue, and the gin remained clear."

There were a number of aesthetic breakthroughs for Gillespie in this exhibition, as she expanded her artistic dimension from painting on a flat surface to combinations of media such as film, collage, and sculpture. Perhaps most important was her discovery and use of reflective materials, which are now such an integral part of her work. She had used aluminum foil in the past but was always searching for a more flexible material that could be manipulated visually as well as physically. For the first time she used Mylar, a new material that Gillespie had first seen at the New York World's Fair. Over enormous wood frames she stretched thin panels of silvered Mylar, which shimmered and quivered like fun-house mirrors. The walls of the first room were covered with these panels so that viewers saw themselves reflected grotesquely as a stage light revolved, flashing different colors. The critic for *Art News*, writing for the section of double-liner reviews in the November 1966 issue, concluded, "Dorothy Gillespie likes to make use of slapstick, puns and the absurd. She does so with the aid of movie news and flashing lights surrounded by American Flag reproductions that reflect it all endlessly."

One of Gillespie's most prestigious exhibitions of the time was for the New York University series Sundays at Three. Many avant-garde artists, such as John Cage, had been honored with an invitation to prepare or perform one of these coveted Sunday-afternoon events. With her undaunted energy and exactitude, Gillespie worked full time for one year on this exhibition – which would last only three hours. *Ritual '71*, as she called it, went beyond an Environment to a Happening in which viewers participated. Gillespie and her children installed the complicated exhibition in the Eisner and Lubin Auditorium at the Loeb Student Center in May 1971.

The theme was an extension of Gillespie's investigations into the influence of rituals – such as death and the flag – on American culture. She determined that the most popular contemporary ritual in the United States was the Super Bowl; statistics confirmed that on that Sunday every year almost everyone in America is in front of a television set watching football. To avoid the simplistic, Gillespie decided to present a historical perspective of rituals culminating in the Super Bowl. For research she enrolled in a course on witchcraft at NYU, and for six months she delved into the shadowy world of magic and the occult.

To announce this "Special Event" a handbill was printed with a drawing of a wheel of fortune surrounded by the words Astrology, Palmistry, Tarot Cards, Numerology, Fortune Wheel, Magic Disc, Handwriting, and Voodoo. Inside the circle were the words Touch, Smell, Hear, See, and Taste. Admission was listed as one dollar. All the seats were removed from the auditorium and the walls were draped in black to create a dark and supernatural ambience. Enormous paintings of various occult symbols were hung on the walls. Passageways led to separate booths where each ritual was staffed by a person dressed in an appropriate costume. As viewers were guided from booth to booth, they heard Gillespie's voice on a tape recorded by George Jacobs, discussing and explaining each ritual. Music ranging from Indian chants to the dances of voodoo ended with the crashing sound of thunder.

The most popular exhibit was a display of fertility rituals from the past and present. Gillespie had discovered that in some primitive cultures women ate ginger-

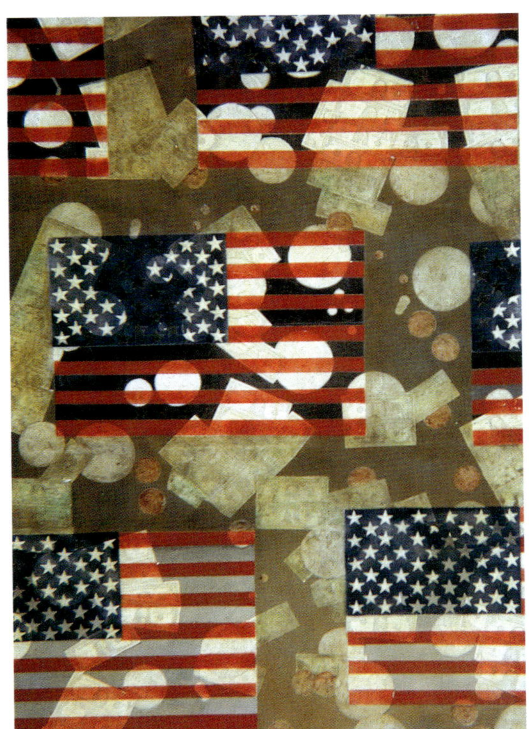

Flag Show Collage, 1966, paper, aluminum and paint

bread men to encourage pregnancy. She and her children baked hundreds of gingerbread men, served alongside M&M's candies that represented birth-control pills. Viewers were encouraged to make an ideological choice by eating a gingerbread man or taking the contoversial "pill."

A booth with a jungle setting featured voodoo dolls that Gillespie had made by hand. The 14-inch dolls were fashioned of black cloth and had faces painted on them to represent real people, such as Mohammed Ali, Ted Kennedy, J. Edgar Hoover, or Nelson Rockefeller. One doll had a question mark instead of a face, so that viewers could visualize their own victim. Colored pins were available, encouraging viewers to put a curse on a person of choice. By the end of the afternoon all of the dolls, except Kennedy's, were pierced by pins. Gillespie's daughter Dorien, now a well-known channeler, was in charge of the booth.

The route through the Happening was leisurely, as viewers lingered to consult astrologists, numerologists, palmists, or ouija boards. The final installation, the ritual of 1971, was assembled like a theatrical set on the stage of the auditorium. A man, seen from the back, was sitting in an overstuffed chair watching the game on a television screen. As videotape was not yet commonly available, an audiotape of the most recent Super Bowl was playing. Gillespie's husband, Bernard Israel, always supportive of her work, assumed the role of sports fan for the three-hour event, beer and pretzels by his side.

Ritual '71 was a great success and cemented Gillespie's relationship with New York University, where she subsequently mounted a number of exhibitions and organized seminars. At the time Environments and Happenings received scant coverage from the art press, which tended to dismiss the whole movement as a rejection of traditional aesthetic values and commercial requirements. But idealistic and committed artists like Gillespie felt they had nothing to lose by using nonaesthetic materials to create alternative exhibitions in which there was nothing to sell. Today, every group show throughout the country includes "Installations" and "Performance Art," the contemporary sequels to the pioneering Environments and Happenings of the 1960s.

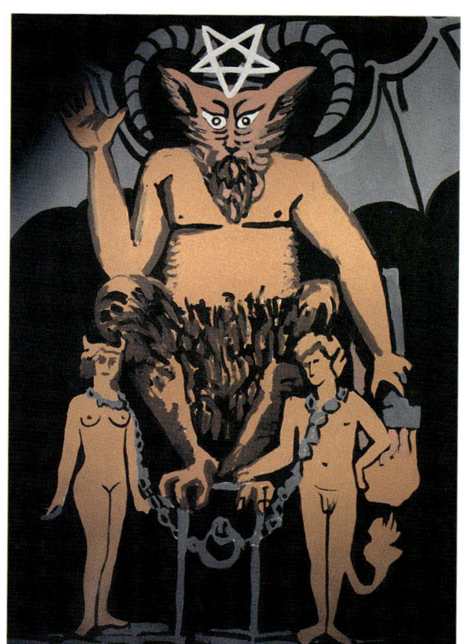

Devil, 1971, acrylic on paper, 75" x 60"

Women's Movement

During the 1960s women began to confront the primeval ritual of male domination. Activists united to form organizations to challenge the perception of women as economically, socially, and culturally inferior to men. In the art world the inequality between men and women was particularly obvious. Men controlled exhibitions, denying access and visibility to women artists. The discrimination actually began in art schools, where female students were not taken seriously and not encouraged to become professional artists. The bias followed women beyond the campus and was reinforced if they married and had children.

But for Dorothy Gillespie, the joy of making art had always taken precedence over the mythic promise of fame and fortune. This objectivity has given her life an enviable satisfaction and status, which is obvious to anyone who meets her. Deep within herself is an awareness that is more significant and valuable than any of the external symbols of success. When she attended the second meeting of the newly organized Women in the Arts, she felt that she was "too naive" to understand the intensity of anger dominating the room. Her independence and involvement in her own work had protected her from many of the injustices suffered by other women artists whose work was ignored by museums, galleries, and collectors. She had had more than twenty-three solo exhibitions and her work was in museum collections throughout the world.

Gillespie's involvement in the Women's Art Movement became more than simply a membership in a clique of angry women artists. Although many competent groups were forming to protest inequalities in the art world, Gillespie chose her affiliations carefully. In retrospect she recalls that a psychic impulse seemed to activate her commitment to the movement, compelling her to assume a role of leadership despite her reluctance to become involved in the disputes and quarrels that inevitably surface in such a collective endeavor.

Although Gillespie admits that she had some early reservations about participating in public demonstrations, she was on the picket line when Women in the Arts and other feminist groups protested at the Whitney Museum in 1970, demanding that the curators choose more women artists for their "Annual" exhibitions. She still recalls the feeling of exhilaration that swept through the crowd of protesters. Although the Whitney Museum did include a few more women in the next Annual, the protest organizers felt that too little progress was made. Subsequently, Women in the Arts decided to sponsor their own exhibitions devoted solely women's art.

One of the first shows in which Gillespie participated was Unmanly Art at the Suffolk Museum in Stony Brook, Long Island, in October 1972. For the first time she exploited one of the channels opened by the Women's Movement by creating imagery specifically related to women. She constructed an Environment of tubes that were similar to the shape of bolts of fabric or rolled-up rugs. The cylinders were covered in silver Mylar and painted in her colorful abstract expressionist style to incorporate the Mylar as a random reflective background. The tubes were suspended from the ceiling in groups of eight and were continually in motion, so that the reflected colors were continually shifting. Gillespie continued her interest in feminist issues with her first sexually oriented imagery created for the Women in the Arts exhibition at the C. W. Post Campus of Long Island University in the summer of 1973. Her Environment, *The People Factory*, highlighted themes of aggression and domination. She constructed female body parts, such as arms and hands, that were hung from the ceiling with signs reading "For Rent" or "On Loan."

In 1973 a landmark show, Women Choose Women, at the New York Cultural Center, presented the work of one hundred artists selected by members of Women in the Arts from seven hundred slides submitted anonymously. *Artforum* magazine (March 1973) published a major article by April Kingsley that described the exhibition as "a pioneering enterprise with repercussions for the entire art-institutional structure. It is the first example of a large-scale exhibition held in a major art museum and organized entirely by the members of a minority group within the art community. We have often heard in the past few years, since women artists have been forming politically active groups, that hundreds of talented women artists are working without recognition. This is our first opportunity to see what a large body of their work is like, and its quality more than justifies the rhetoric."

Despite the critical success of the exhibition, Gillespie felt that Women in the Arts was losing its focus as a group dedicated to political activism. In order to reestablish a powerful political voice, Gillespie and Joyce Weinstein founded a new group called New York Professional Women Artists. The fourteen members lectured at universities and wrote articles to encourage women artists. Artistic quality was the emphasis of their exhibitions. In 1974 Gillespie organized an innovative outdoor exhibition, Walk Through Art, that was mounted in New York in Central Park, Battery Park, and Rockefeller Center, and then traveled to fifty colleges, universities, and street fairs around the country. Always compelled to involve viewers in her work, she created triangles more than 7 feet in height, assembled so that people could walk through the sculpture.

In 1972 Gillespie was asked by Ruth Van Doren, director of the Human Relations Center at New York's New School for Social Research, to originate a course that would enlighten and educate women in the visual arts. The intent of this pioneering class, "Functioning in the Art World," was to prepare women for a new, more aggressive role in that world. As Gillespie already had a heavy schedule of painting, traveling, and lecturing, she asked artist Alice Baber to share the task of revealing and interpreting the "system" that drives the New York art world. Following Baber's untimely death, Richard Martin taught the course with Gillespie. The emphasis of the course was to "get your bearings" in the art world and then work from a solid base of acquired knowledge to attain your goals. She was brutally honest with her students regarding the difficulties of succeeding in New York City, stressing that the person who works the hardest gains the most. From 1977 to 1983 Gillespie was also the director of the Art and Community Institute at the New School for Social Research. Once a year Gillespie organized an intensive five-day seminar which began with breakfast meetings and ended late at night in artists' studios.

One of the early achievements of the Women's Movement was the first national Conference for Women in the

Visual Arts held in April 1972 at the Corcoran Gallery of Art in Washington, D. C. The Corcoran had been picketed by faculty members of its own art school for not including any women in its Biennial, and in a conciliatory gesture the director agreed to host a conference devoted to the marginalization of women. Cindy Nemser, writing in *Art in America*, described the two-day conference as "one of the most stimulating, irritating, exciting, disturbing, debilitating, tension-filled, thought-provoking, sleep-stealing experiences of my life. . . . Over 350 women involved in the visual arts came from all over the country, each bringing her own needs, hopes, desires, frustrations. . . . As Dorothy Gillespie, a New York painter, later told me, she couldn't put her finger on what exactly set the audience off, but . . . things really started to erupt. . . . It seemed to me that the basic antagonism, the love-hate relationship between the artist, the critic and the curator, was undermining our common ground as women that had brought us to the conference."

Gillespie, who had been asked to report on the conference to the Women's Interart Center, recognized that the confrontation between the powerless women artists and the powerful women critics and curators – who were ignoring their work – threatened to obliterate the goals of the meeting and movement. But she saw the attack by the women artists as an act of courage that served to emphasize the interdependence of women's roles in the art world. Gillespie was elected co-coordinator of the Women's Interart Center, a position she held from 1973 to 1976. She was directly involved with its program of exhibitions, fund-raising, and workshops. She founded the Women Artists Historical Archives, which includes film and taped interviews with leading artists. The Center, which is devoted to the advancement of women artists of all disciplines, is located in a converted warehouse on the west side of midtown Manhattan; since 1972 Gillespie has been its Artist in Residence, establishing her studio in a vacant space she discovered one night while walking down the stairs when the elevator was broken.

Gillespie's only foray into hard-core feminism was her participation in the Women's Interart Center's 1973 exhibition Erotic Garden. Described as "a sensual environment," featuring the work of twelve women, the exhibition was further defined as "an act of liberation – liberation from the traditional taboos that have prevented women from publicly expressing their sensual or erotic feelings and sensibility." Gillespie, who admits that she is not and has never been an erotic artist, created a survey, the final presentation at the end of the tour through giant panting flowers, penis pillows, walls of breasts, a vagina hammock, and a womb-dome. Her portion of the exhibit was separated by a black curtain from the preceding displays of erotica, so that viewers could answer questions about various objects and images Gillespie had arranged on tables and panels. The exhibition was reviewed in Ms. magazine by Harriet Lyons under the headline "One Man's Cucumber is Another Woman's Tomato." The text read in part, "Raisins or Cheerios – which are more erotic? This was just one of the questions raised by a recent art exhibit . . . a kind of erotic rezoning designed to arouse all the senses. . . . Dorothy Gillespie dished up 20 touch-taste-smell-feel exhibits and a questionnaire – the answers to which indicated that women found tomatoes the most erotic vegetable, while men chose cucumbers."

For a 1974 exhibition at the Center called Works in Progress, Gillespie built on her previous work with tubes, creating a small three-dimensional construction. *The First Museum in Outer Space* was a humorous work, which included small abstract expressionist paintings rolled into cylinders and packed into rockets for the journey to outer space. Inside the museum, tiny people could be seen floating upside down looking at the paintings. In a review in the May 1974 *Arts Magazine*, Jane Bell devoted almost half her text to Gillespie: "Certainly one of the most charming, stimulating 'works in progress' . . . was Dorothy Gillespie's conception of the place of art in the near future. She has conceived a space city, in which a new museum displays an ever-changing light sculpture, operating on self-sufficient solar energy. . . . Gillespie's statement was the most arresting in a show overflowing with statements: 'Art in outer space will be viewed from all angles. . . . The viewer will become part of art itself.'"

Ms. en Scene, a program of films by women filmmakers was held at the Women's Interart Center in 1974. Gillespie showed two of her films: *U. S.*, the short film made for her eponymous 1966 Environment, and *The Pope*, shot in St. Peter's Square with zooming, spinning, and floating images of religious banners and portraits of the Pope. Gillespie and her work were featured in three work-in-progress films, *Color*, *Logo*, and *Silkscreen*. At the time Gillespie was shooting experimental pieces she called "Scratch Films," using a number of chance techniques such as abrading the surface of the film before or after processing and dyeing the footage with food coloring.

The following year she collaborated with filmmaker Rikki Ripp to make a biographical video for the United Nation's International Year of the Woman. Called *Dorothy Gillespie in Her Studio*, it is a seventeen-minute black-and-white documentary in which Gillespie describes the feeling for life, both joy and frustration, that motivates her work. She demonstrates how her paintings gradually began to come off the wall to become free-standing sculptures, a transitional accomplishment that was changing the direction of her career as an artist.

For the International Year of the Woman, the Women's Interart Center inaugurated the festivities with a special exhibition curated by Gillespie. Women Artists/Games opened on December 17, 1974, and included thirty women artists whose work ranged from Photo-Realism to

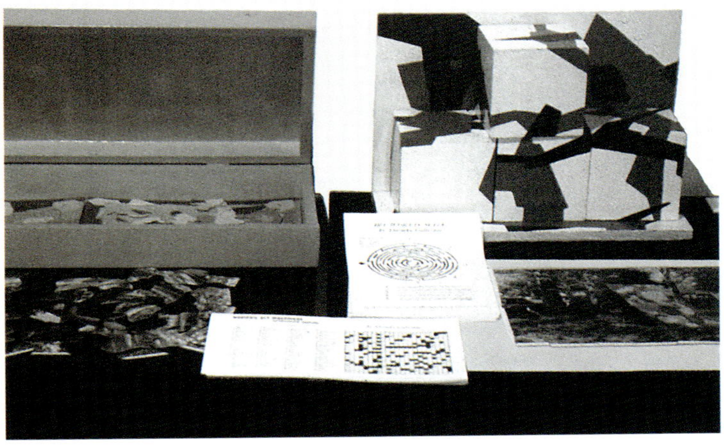

Women's Art Crossword Puzzle, *Art World Maze*, and other objects from Women Artists/Games, 1974

Conceptualism. For an exhibition called Works on Paper – Women's Art, sponsored by Women in the Arts, Gillespie changed her art medium from acrylic to pastel. She used it because pastel had always been denigrated as a woman's art medium, seen as weak and unacceptable for serious work. Gillespie's piece for the show was an assertive rediscovery of pastel's pure color and variable texture.

In 1975 Gillespie mounted her third solo exhibition, Paintings, at New York University. The miniature rolled canvases from her construction *The First Museum in Outer Space* were enlarged to cylinders, which she described as "pick-up sticks." The outsides of the cylinders were similar in color composition to her abstract paintings, while the insides were painted a single color. Spotlights gave the works an illusion of transparency. She persuaded the university to sponsor ten days of panel discussions, slide shows, and films by women artists to commemorate the International Year of the Woman. Posters and flyers announced the event and every woman's art group in New York was invited to participate. She also arranged for the university to tape record twelve women artists discussing their thoughts on the future of the Women's Movement.

An additional event proposed by the United Nations was an International Women's Art Festival. Gillespie was a member of the Fine Arts Committee, assigned to organize the first worldwide exhibition of art by women. As the projected costs of a global exhibition spiraled into the hundreds of thousands of dollars, Gillespie suggested a slide exhibition, which would give visibility to the largest number of women artists and could travel to countries throughout the world. To inaugurate the slide show, a prestigious ceremony was arranged, with Gillespie presenting awards to twelve living women artists born before 1900. She also assisted her friend Alice Baber in curating Color, Light and Image, which opened in November 1975 at the Women's Interart Center. The exhibition included the work of 115 women from the Americas, Europe, Africa, and Asia. A six-page review in *Art International* concluded, "In its overall impact, the show was an esthetic-political event evidencing high esthetic value directly while political importance remained implicit. . . . Baber and Gillespie were able to mount an exhibit that was impressive apart from feminist concerns while it advanced the cause of women in art with an admirable openness and evenhandedness."

Gillespie continued to conceive and curate exhibitions featuring women, such as Women Artists' Sketch Books drawn from the historical archives of the Center and Women Artists Paint Women Artists, which traveled to galleries in Florida and Virginia. She wrote a number of essays, including "Professionalism and the Woman Artist," which was included by Judith Loeb in *Feminist Collage*, published by Teachers College at Columbia University. Another text, "Overcoming Barriers: Special Problems of the Woman Artist in the South," was printed in the *Southern Quarterly*.

Gillespie is still a role model for women artists because she seems to have had it all: a successful career, a happy marriage with children, and a sense of purpose concerning the inequalities endured by women artists. She feels that the most important accomplishment of the Women's Movement was that the women artists got to know each other, which eased a terrible feeling of isolation. Today she says simply, "The Women's Movement was an exhilarating time."

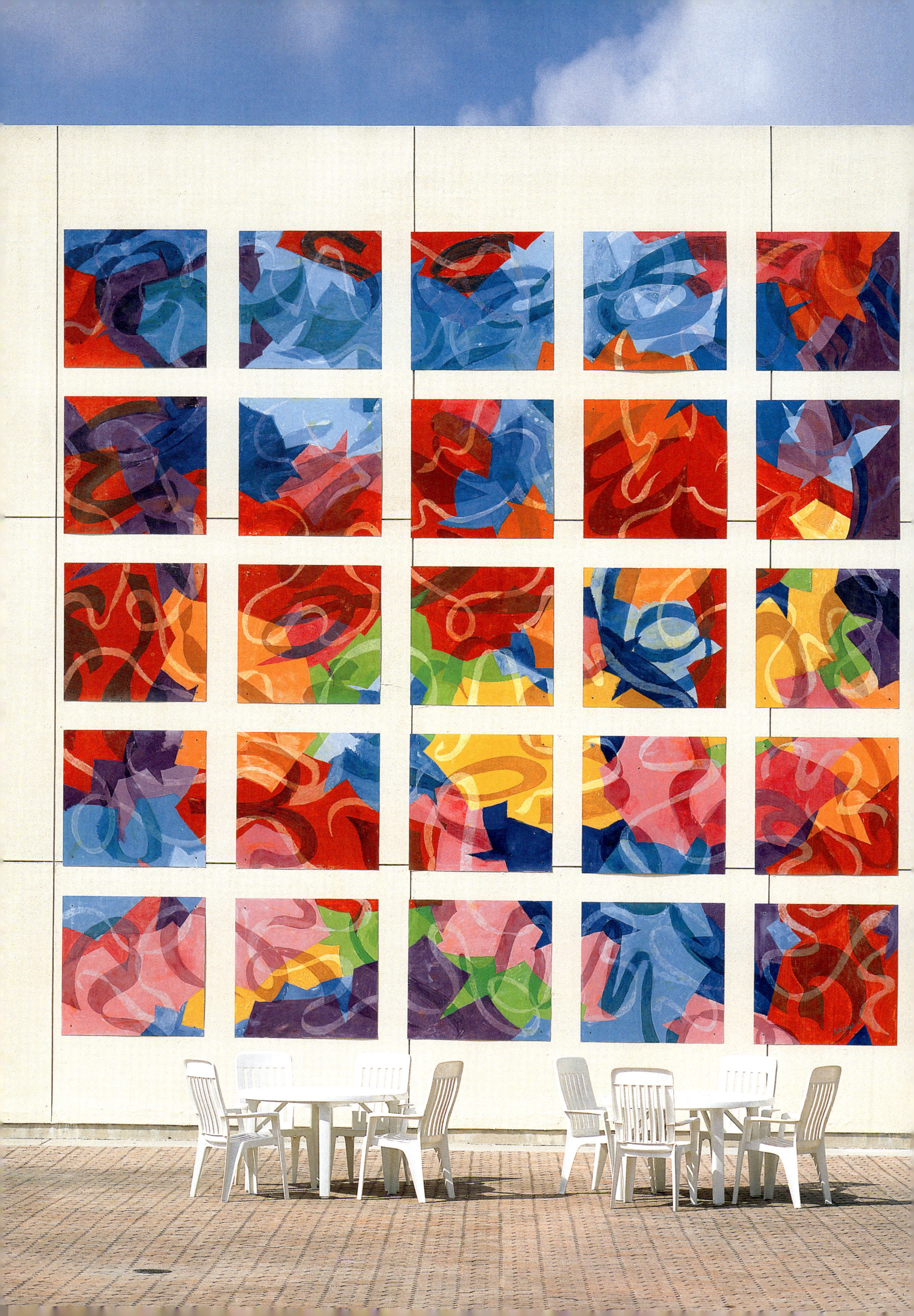

Dorothy Gillespie remembers clearly just when her personal artistic expression took form in the 1950s. She was painting a Gothic cathedral and kept abstracting the form by taking out more and more detail. Then, while working on the steps that led to the front portal, she realized that she "did not want to tell anyone how many steps they had to walk up"; instead, she "wanted to paint what they felt entering their house of worship." At that moment, she "was ready to paint abstract art." She suddenly became aware that, for her, completely abstract or nonobjective painting was not the result of a "natural progression from realism to total abstraction; rather it is a 'mental thing' at which you arrive through a quantum leap of sorts."

Then through a deep commitment to the Environments and Happenings of the 1960s, she embarked on the creation of site-specific projects beginning in the next decade. In 1975 Gillespie made her first major, public, site-specific work. Called *New York City Wall*, the giant mural, measuring 53 feet by 90 feet, has a horizontal composition. The location that Gillespie selected offered her work great visibility owing to its location on the corner building that faces north on Houston Street at Mercer Street. Pedestrians, passing traffic, and aircraft passengers are able to view the work. (Gillespie herself has seen it from the air on more than one occasion.) She carefully mixed the cool and delicate tints for the mural out of exterior flat house paints. Her configuration of nonobjective forms, in predominantly light violet and gray-blue muted tints and shades, joyfully contrasts with the drab colors of the building.

Gillespie's ability to integrate a variety of spatial configurations into an art work is clearly evident in *Paper Works*, her Environment shown at New York University in 1976. Paper as her primary material allowed Gillespie to maximize experimentation within numerous environmental and site-specific locations. By having an abundance of material, she could create a variety of positive and negative spatial relationships. Gillespie was involved with the extensive expanse of horizontal space, while also venturing into the exploration and the permutations of vertical space. This thorough engrossment into the surrounding space allowed her to develop a special sensitivity to the challenges of the spatial configurations in which her abstract two- and three-dimensional forms took residence.

The *Paper Works* installations consisted of groupings of cylindrical shapes, painted both inside and outside, and of various flat and curved shapes, painted with colorful abstract designs. Additional dimensionality was generated by shadows and reflections, producing an integrated universe of forms. Self-contained within its confinements, this was a universe of playful wonder. This playfulness of "moving" forms seems to be Gillespie's artistic signature and her major contribution to the art of the twentieth century. Although we may trace the origins of this playful, joyous element to some of her modern forerunners, such as Miró, Klee, or O'Keeffe, it was not isolated with such crystalline purity in their works, in which somber, ambiguous, or sexual overtones can be detected. Gillespie, however, wishes to explore the feeling of joy: pure, distilled, and totally abstracted.

In 1979, Gillespie's *Roanoke Wall*, a 50-by-50-foot mural on the Court House Square Building, was financed by Ann Lee, a developer in Roanoke, Virginia. The mural provides visual relief within the urban environment. Its effect of a "moving" pattern or group of forms infuses a burst of joyful energy into the otherwise routine street life of a city.

The following year nature became an integral part in Gillespie's outdoor site-specific work *Sentrees*, which is located at a private residence in Londonderry, Vermont. It consists of three vertical aluminum structures, each 12½ feet high. These units are painted with automotive lacquer in order to prevent discoloration from the drastic weather conditions in the area. The white totemic and curving aluminum shapes are covered with colorful geometric designs in brilliant reds, yellows, blues, and violets. The friendly but powerful forms seem to overlook the surrounding landscape that generates their negative shapes. In summer, the dominant greens of the foliage create textures that converge with the shimmering water of a lake, which also mirrors the sculpture. Reminiscent of three totem/toys, the forms are designed to interact differently with the same environment during the winter season. The usually abundant snowfalls submerge part of the sculpture – up to six feet – under the white mass, allowing spectators to view the triple structure from a different vantage point. This phenomenon occurs six months out of a year; the area is part of a cross-country ski trail, bringing viewers throughout the winter.

Summerscape, designed in 1982 for the Cleveland Ballet, might be considered Gillespie's *magnum opus*. This

← *Through the Looking Glass*, 1988, enamel on aluminum, 23' x 23', Museum of Art, Fort Lauderdale, Florida work was not only sculpted for a particular space, but also came into existence in order for another work of art to be born: a ballet by Dennis Nahat choreographed to Dmitri Shostakovich's Concerto No. 2 in F. Collaborations among sculptors, painters, choreographers, and composers have a long tradition in Western art, especially in this century, with artists such as Salvador Dali, Alexandra Exter, Natalia Goncharova, Pablo Picasso, Sonia Delaunay, Andy Warhol, and Isamu Noguchi preceding Gillespie. *Summerscape* may be the first time, however, that a visual artist's work initiated the planning. The series of ten sculptures of enameled aluminum she created for the stage space range in size from 4 to 7 feet in diameter. The undulating ribbons that form the celestial configurations are reminiscent of starbursts, colorful suns, or even flowers. A playful mixture of cosmic energy and joyful toys, they reminded the choreographer of the exuberance of youthful happiness and enthusiasm. This youthful energy established the mood for the ballet, enhanced by Nahat's selection of appropriately youthful music: the concerto Shostakovich wrote for his son's nineteenth birthday. The costume designer for the ballet, David Guthrie, based his color scheme on Gillespie's sculpture.

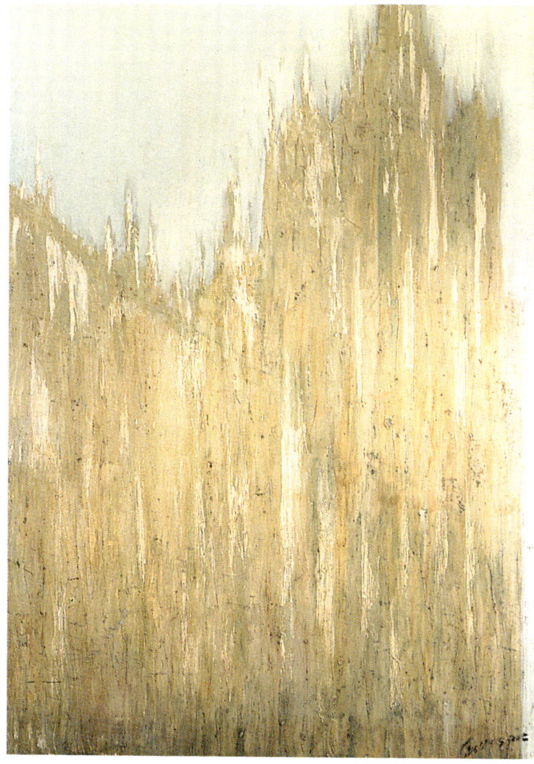

Cathedral, 1956, oil on masonite, 72" x 48"

The ten units of this environmental sculpture radiate their ribbons/rays from the central core outward. The feeling of motion is established by the starbursts executing their own ballet at the beginning of each performance. After the curtain is up, the starbursts are located a few inches above the floor. They gradually rise, ending their journey in exactly designated locations. The shadows that are cast by each unit increase in size during the upward trajectory. Then, the motion of the sculptures ceases and the motion of the dancers begins, while the starbursts continue to contribute subtly to the movement by casting their shadows and dispensing shimmering reflections into the surrounding stage space. Nahat was also inspired by the directions of the starbursts' tentacles. The movements of individual dancers and the groupings of dancers were in part determined by the shapes and locations of the rising/raised starbursts. The interaction between the vibrant bodies of the dancers and the inanimate forms above proved emotional and sensual.

Another project by Gillespie emerged as a result of this collaboration. Nahat, aware of the emotional benefits that the dancers derived from the presence of the sculptures during the performances, decided to extend this benefit into the classroom. He asked Gillespie to create an environmental work for the dancers' rehearsal space. This work, completed in 1984, was named *Cleveland Ballet Rehearsal Studio*. The sculpture, located on the upper half of the entire wall space, consists of multiple interconnecting ribboned forms of enameled aluminum. The forms are rhythmic and musical, suggesting motion and bursts of energy. The colors are a mixture of muted lavenders, golds, reds,

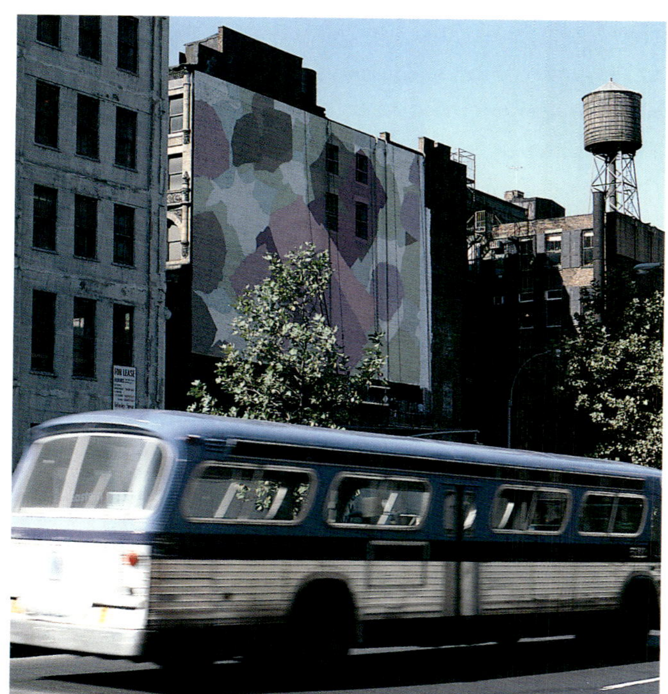

New York City Wall, 1975, 56' x 93'

and blues. The shapes cast shadows and generate reflections of light, enhancing the feeling of motion and evoking a fantastic musical forest. The effect on the dancers is energizing and uplifting.

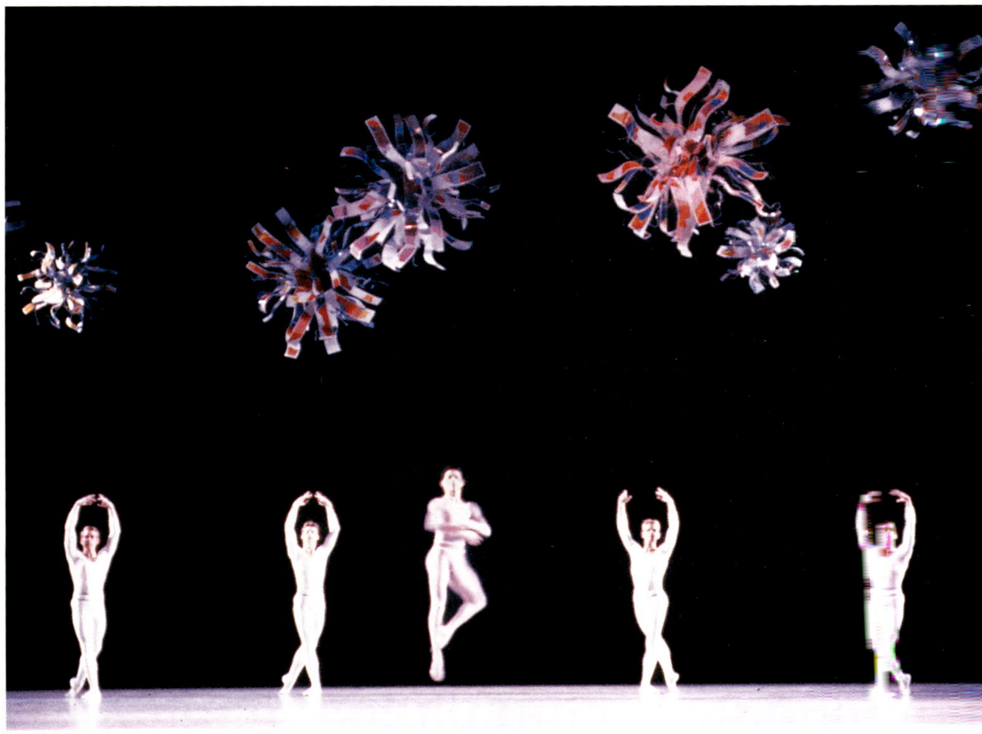

Summerscape, 1982, for Cleveland Ballet, enamel on aluminum, 10 units 4' to 7' diameter

In 1985 Gillespie completed a site-specific project for the main lobby of the South Square Corporate Center in Durham, North Carolina. The large work, *Triangled Celebration*, was shipped flat and then finished by her on the site. The 880 feet of flat, enameled aluminum were transformed into three 16-foot-high totemic forms. All possessed triangular silver cores, to which ribbons of metal, ranging from 6 inches to less than 1/4 inch, were bolted. The brightly multicolored free-form shapes were painted over a silver background with gloss enamel. The giant assemblage's ribbons bent, twisted, and spiraled outward, radiating color, energy, and movement caused by the flow of air from passing crowds, who could view the work from two levels. The project remained in the lobby for more than seven years. Life often presents interesting and surprising twists of fate; *Triangled Celebration* became part of a synchronistic event when, in 1993, it was acquired by the Asheville (North Carolina) Museum of Art, page 103. Gillespie redesigned the work for its new space. The three totems now hang from the ceiling of the atrium of the museum. Three arched windows allow them to be viewed from the exterior space in front of the atrium, and they are also visible from various vantage points within the museum. The powerful forms are reminiscent of the lush tropical trees from a child's fantasy of a planet of happiness, or the magnificent elongated garments of the Native American matriarch, the Buffalo Woman.

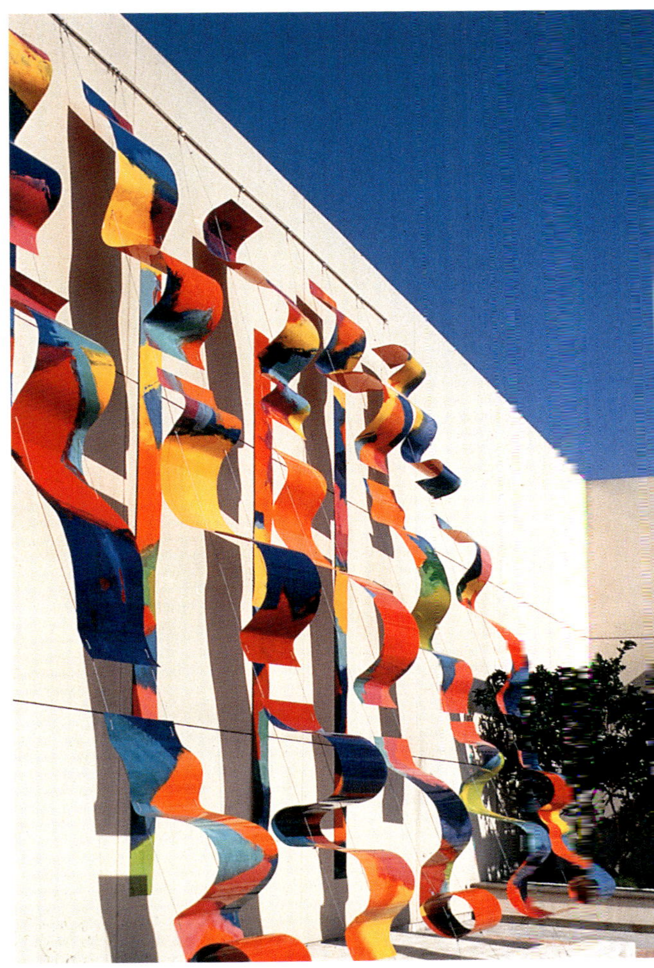

Magic Carpet Slides, 1986, enamel on aluminum, [illegible] x 26' x 8', Museum of Art, Fort Lauderdale, Florida

A commission from Indiana's Greater Lafayette Museum of Art for an outdoor environmental sculpture presented Gillespie with a special challenge: to harness the forces of technology by transforming space-age materials into a work of art, which she completed in 1985. This project, *Launched Ribbon*, was sponsored in part by the Indi-

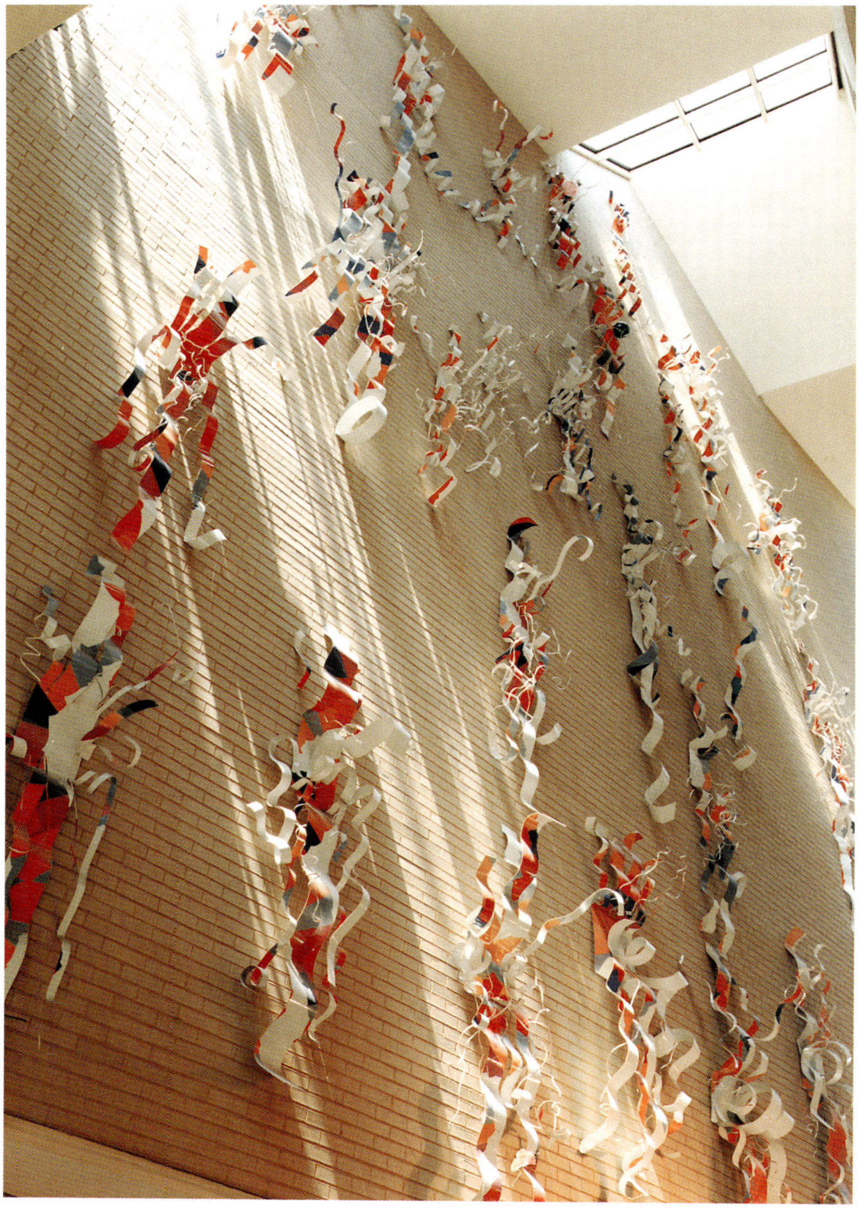

Centered Celebration, 1985, enamel on aluminum, 60' x 50', Center in the Square, Roanoke, Virginia

ana Arts Commission, The National Endowment for the Arts, and the Alcoa Foundation, which supplied the material for the sculpture – mirrored airplane aluminum. This thick aluminum sheet cannot be permanently bent or twisted, but bounces back to its original flat state. Gillespie had to devise new methods to deal with this high-tech material, resulting in a new basic unit for her sculptures – the loop. She riveted each section of the sculpture together in order to force it to hold a curve permanently. She also had to paint its abstract design on separate, thin aluminum (airplane aluminum does not accept paint) and then cut out and bolt it to the mirrored surfaces of the loops. Gillespie is convinced that "in the high-tech age, using the hands is even more important than ever. If something is all high-tech, it seems foreign, removed from human beings, and they can't relate to it."

Launched Ribbon is a sculpture with its highest point at 15 feet. Its composition allows it to cast strong shadows on the background wall, while also breaking into the sky above. Serpentine and vertical, the sculpture seems to have the countenance of a benevolent guardian or a toy dragon. This playful "dragon" has bright, free-form blotches of color over its "body," painted in red, orange, yellow, and blue. The background color of the ribbons is the mirrored silver surface that reflects into itself the surrounding environment, becoming a part of the site; it also reflects the sky, the clouds, and the spectators. These reflective properties generate an interconnectedness among the artist (who can also enter her sculpture via reflection), her art work, and the environment.

The year 1985 was prolific for Gillespie's site-specific projects. Among them was a five-story-high environmental art work she designed as a personal tribute to the city of Roanoke, her place of birth. The monumental work, *Centered Celebration*, was created in her studio out of sheets of aluminum, painted and partially cut into shapes. Subsequently, they were shipped to Roanoke and installed at the Center in the Square, a cultural complex that consists of the Roanoke Museum of Fine Arts, the Mill Mountain Theatre, the Roanoke Valley Historical Society, the Roanoke Valley Science Museum, and the Roanoke Valley Arts Council. The extensive wall space serves as the negative space for the installation of more than forty multiple units, which can be observed from different levels and angles as well as from the glass wall of the adjacent high-rise building. The three-dimensional units of ribbons, enamating from their centers, often touch each other and intertwine. The brightly colored free-form shapes are painted on the metal over the original white finish. The smooth, gleaming surfaces contrast against the textures of the brick wall. The effect is multidimensional and multifaceted: the subtle motion of the ribboned forms and the change in light as the day passes create numerous permutations of glints and shadows. The shapes produce an illusion of a paradise of exotic vegetation.

Gillespie designed an environmental sculpture for the Museum of Art in Fort Lauderdale, Florida, in 1986. The installation (28' x 26'8"), commissioned by the Cypress Savings and Loan Association for the museum, consists of nine sections of painted aluminum, with alternating ribbons that are either attached to the wall or suspended by cables to float over the wall surface in a vertical configuration. The floating shapes are three-dimensional, curling and curving as if in a process of upward ascension. Called *Magic Carpet Slides*, the sculpture suggests the world of fairy tales and a promise of a happy skyride on these ascending "magic carpets." Gillespie used cables to secure the floating carpets/magic serpents, allowing them to sway gently and to produce their own sound as wind currents touch the ribbons. The wall is the tallest of the three that enclose the sculpture garden, located on the second floor of the museum. Both the height of the wall and the size of the sculpture force the spectator's eyes to glide over *Magic Carpet Slides*, past the wall, and into the Florida sky, causing a perception of the possibility of a flight into the realm of spirituality.

Three years later the Art in Public Places of Broward County, Florida, commissioned Gillespie to create a mural suggesting the theme of flight. She completed it in 1989, and it was installed in the Delta Air Lines terminal of the Fort Lauderdale/Hollywood International Airport, inside the escalator well on the left side. *Color and Forms in Flight*, page 58–59, consists of forty rectangular units of enameled aluminum, 12 feet 2 inches by 22 feet 2 inches. Each square is surrounded by negative space that forms a framed grid. Although the surface is two-dimensional, the multitude of colors – more than 130 hues, tints, and shades – generates a spectacular view for the thousands of returning passengers who use the escalator. The moving staircase, by gradually bringing the viewer closer and closer to the work's surface, adds to the participatory effect, allowing the viewer to become briefly but intensely absorbed into Gillespie's world, a world that may be perceived as a tropical forest, viewed from a descending aircraft.

Another commission brought Gillespie to Wilmington, North Carolina, in 1989. *Colorfalls*, a 42 feet high by 11 feet wide sculpture, detail on pages 54–55, is located in the center of city life, Thalian Hall. Its fifteen-foot-wide atrium is four stories high. The staircase and balconies allow the sculpture to be viewed in its entirety from every level. A skylight in the atrium's ceiling provides the nuances of changing illumination at different times of the day. Gillespie created the painted aluminum work section by section in her studio in New York for "Artluminium," an in-

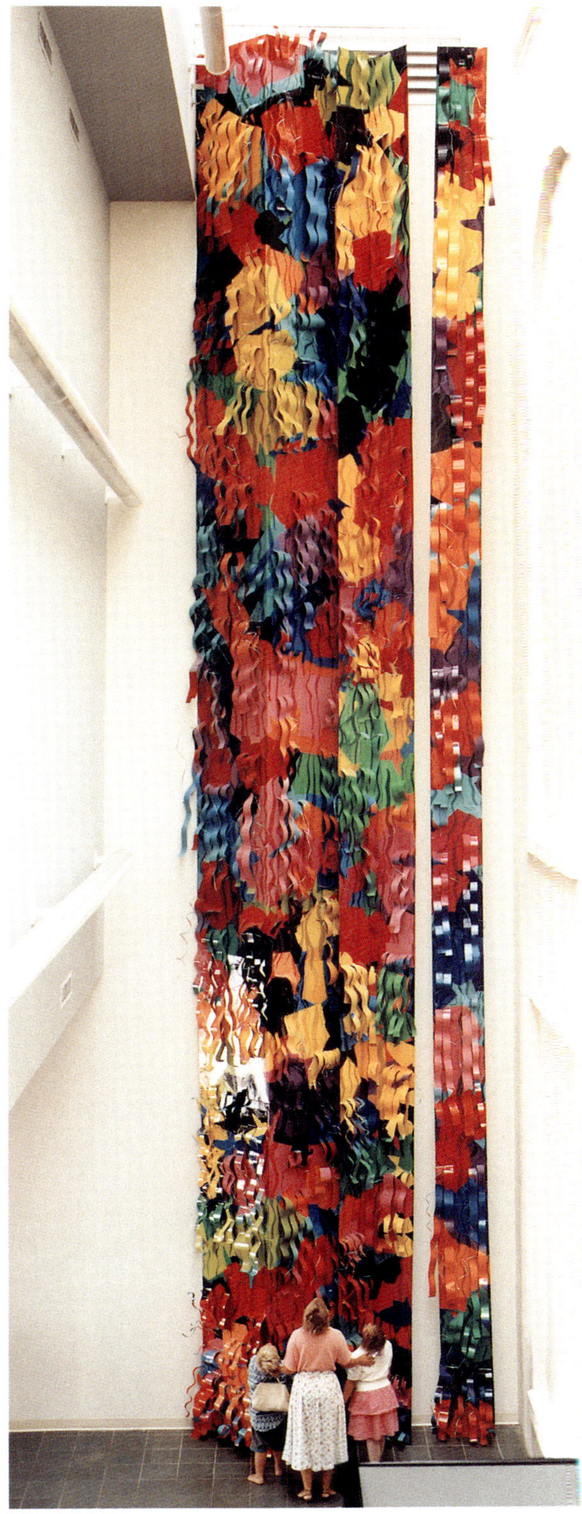

Colorfalls, 1989, enamel on aluminum, 42' x 11' x 3',
Thalian Hall, Wilmington, North Carolina

vitational exhibition in Montreal, Canada, sponsored by Alcan. Much of the final shaping of the cascading, waving, and curling ribbons, however, was done by her on the Canadian site. The top of the sculpture was designed to fit within the Wilmington atrium, gracefully hugging a cylindrical fixture, with several tendrils stretching in the direction of the skylight.

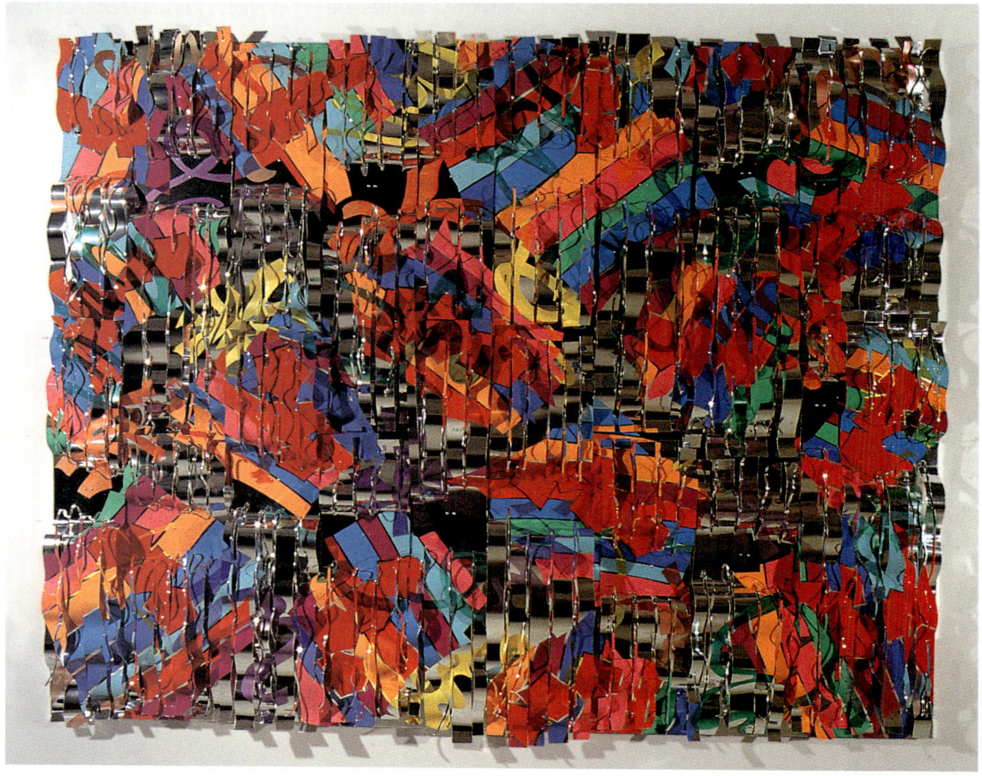

Winter Palace Concerto, 1993, enamel on aluminum, 74" x 90" x 4", Buena Vista Palace Hotel, Disney World, Orlando, Florida

Colorfalls consists of two sections of uneven proportions, thus generating a negative space that provides the illusion of depth. The sculpture cascades down – its "waves" spilling and getting wider as they reach the floor – a monumental splash of vivid reds, pinks, oranges, yellows, greens, blues, and violets, with a touch of black. The sculpture forms a fantastic waterfall of imposing proportions.

Two sculptures were created by Gillespie for Broward Community College in Pembroke Pines, Florida, in the 1990s. *Royal Crest*, a work of enameled aluminum, is located indoors, where it is attached to the wall, extending from the window on the building's north side to the second-floor balcony, and from the ceiling to the upper level of the first floor. The sculpture consists of ribbons radiating from one center, a sunburst configuration also reminiscent of an elaborate bow on a gift package. The background color is gold, possessing a high degree of luminosity and reflectability. The free-form shapes that Gillespie painted over the gold metal surface are in reds, oranges, greens, and blues. The undulating tendrils twist and curl, as if the mass that they form is imbued with the exuberant life-force of youth. The work can be viewed from several levels: the first floor, the steps leading up to the second floor, and the second floor itself. The shadows and the reflections on the white wall change throughout the day, since the lighting is both natural and artificial. The golden glow of the metal surface contrasts with the bright colors.

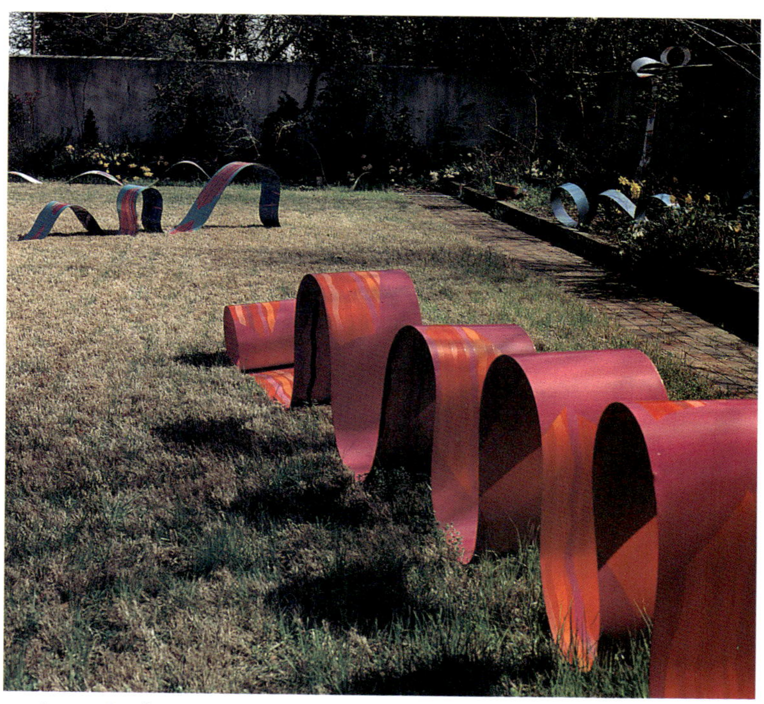

Lawn Sculpture, St. John's Museum, Wilmington, North Carolina, 1993

The second sculpture, *Color Clouds and Ribboned Currents*, pages 70–71, is an outdoor piece located on the east wall of the lecture hall, opposite the art gallery. When planning the work, Gillespie kept in mind the amount of pedestrian traffic in the area, the shapes and colors of the surrounding architecture, and the environment. The sculpture occupies nearly two-thirds of the upper level of the wall. It can be seen from several vantage points outside the campus, especially by motorists and by people in the low-flying aircraft of adjacent Hollywood Airport.

The work consists of seventeen aluminum ribbons, nine of which are wide and wavy, and eight of which are flat and firmly attached to the wall. The nine wavy strips of painted aluminum curl away from the wall on both the top and the bottom. The background color of all the ribbons is white, and the geometric free-form shapes are painted in reds, yellows, blue-greens, blue-grays, blues,

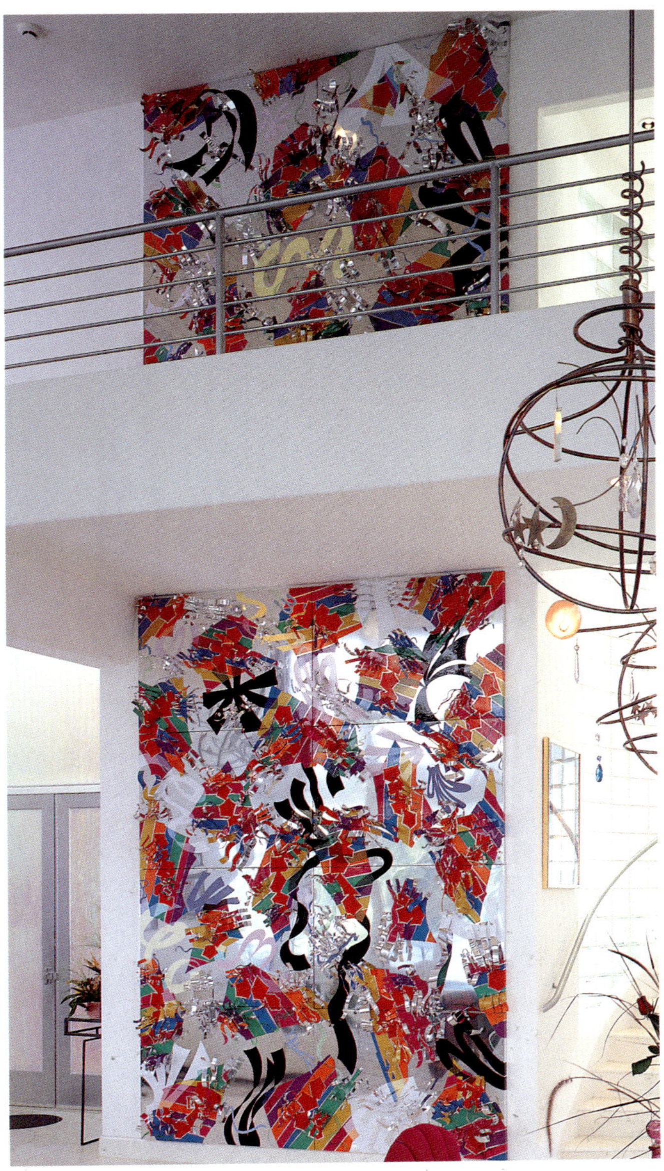

Encounter at the Winter Palace, 1997, enamel on aluminum, 19'10" x 7'11" x 8"

and shades of violet. These forms seem to travel through the ribbons themselves and are connected by serpentine shapes in a variety of blue and gray colors, from light to dark. The seventeen ribbons are all visually interconnected by the rhythm of their own floating patterns. The ever-changing shadows of the nine undulating ribbons elongate with the sun. This work's connection with the continuum of the passage of time as well as its majestic verticality force the spectator to glance heavenward, particularly during sunsets.

It seems very natural that Gillespie's next work found a home where fantasy is reality. *Winter Palace Concerto* was installed at the Buena Vista Palace Hotel at Disney World in Orlando, Florida, in 1993. Gillespie used a neutral white wall as the background for a rectangular, enamel-painted aluminum sculpture of some 7 feet by 8 feet. The metal ribbons are arranged vertically in a flow of wavy configurations in exuberant colors: brilliant reds, oranges, pinks, violets, and yellows. The silver background of the serpentine and curling ribbons shimmers and reflects both the colors present in the sculpture and the glow of the surrounding lighting. The ribbons break out of the rectangular shape and into the wall space, creating a variety of subtle shadows that surround the work like a halo. The spectator is presented with a feast of real and illusional three-dimensionality, accented by the rhythmic groupings of the colors themselves.

The examination of Gillespie's site-specific art makes clear that her creative manipulation of natural, urban, and interior space transcends that of her predecessors and establishes her major place within postmodernist art. Clearly, other artists have used these aspects in a similar way, such as Alexander Calder, who painted and bolted together metal constructs and played with the concept of real or implied motion, or Chryssa, who is interested in shadows and in actual and reflected lights. But it is only in Gillespie's art that the interplay and layering of shape, shadow, light, motion, and the illusion of motion are thoroughly explored, reinvented, and constructed into a new art form, in which the art of painting and sculpture become one and external space is integrated into the work itself. In the hands of Dorothy Gillespie, the arts of painting and sculpture become one with the environment that they occupy. She is able to transmit to the viewer the emotional impact of her art: the pure essence of joy, energy, and spirituality. Gillespie may be the current artist who best prophesies the art of tomorrow: the sibyl of site-specific art.

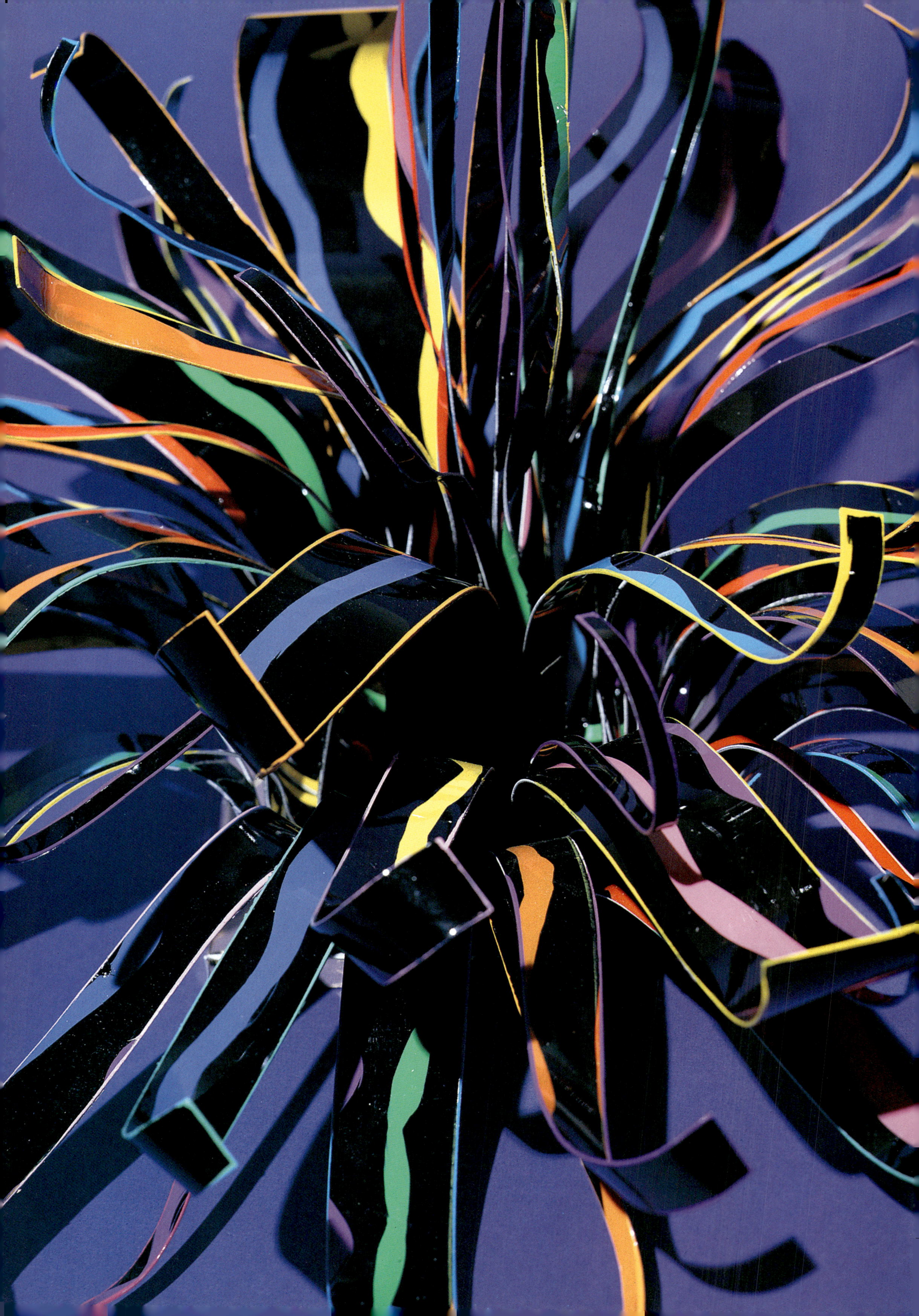

The magic and the energy of the pinwheel are the only explanation or metaphor sufficient to Dorothy Gillespie's sculptures. Long compelled by the enchanted and spiritual elements seized from the mundane in her performance art, Gillespie developed her exceptional sculptural vocabulary from a like innocence and a like mysticism.

Indicative of the magical matrix is her *Rain Dance to the Sun II* (1990) and the *Rain Dance* series dating back to the mid-1980s (pages 32–37). A cascade erupts from a fundament of the aluminum base, barely discernible toward the top. But both above and below, the flat plane is twirled and twisted into new shapes and given all the kinetic powers of rushing water, the still plane of the placid pond reengineered in a short passage to the turbulent and three-dimensional. As a river's run can give dimension and tint to the plain and planar pond, Gillespie discovers both color and energy in her torrent into three-dimensionality. Gillespie, in this title and many others, acknowledges that the inspiration and reference are in the motion and commotion of natural phenomena, not a formal process alone. In all the permutations of her sculptural ideal, Gillespie never succumbs to mere formalism, always shaping ideas as significant as the form itself. Thus, the concept of a rain dance, suggesting plumed Native Americans and the mystery and striving for mastery over nature, are the inexorable elements of thinking that accompany Gillespie's forming and looking. What does the rain dance try to do, but to give human beings a dominion over (or, at least, a negotiation with) the immense power of nature?

Thus, *Rain Dance to the Sun II* is the mediation of human dance upon the authority of the world as a given. Such interpretation demonstrates the connection between Gillespie's sculpture of the 1980s and 1990s and the earlier work. The sculptures that burst from the wall or plunge from heights are not discontinuous with Gillespie's sensitive earlier work. On the contrary, these sculptures sustain Gillespie's deep involvement with the real world and her will to transfigure that world in the mystical powers of art. Her "rain dance" precipitates torrents; her sculpture gives us every reason to believe in the supernatural power of a work of art. In *Rain Dance to the Sun II*, the colors that remain more or less unfulfilled on the plane are made into curls of energy as they lash into space, letting the spectator realize the unleashed, unlacing dynamic of a sculptural line that truly functions in the three dimensions. Color becomes released and liberated when it is not confined by the plane. Further, for Gillespie, the eccentricity of shape, allowing tendrils and extensions, shaggy edges, and frothy elongations, defies any parameter. She believes in the self-defined shape that defies the rectangle or any other given geometry. One of the reasons why her work feels so organic is that she resists the easy solution of form gathered, ungathered, and then gathered again. Gillespie genuinely lets forms seem to go awry, even as she so often works on the large scale. In *Rain Dance to the Sun II* the general shape is hard to define: it is not quite ovoid or any other demarcated form.

Inchoate, self-determined form is an abiding characteristic of Gillespie's work. Even the public and commissioned works do not regularly fill the wall or the space offered, but are much more likely to situate themselves on the site as if they had grown there, subject to the perverse rules of nature, not the standardizing segments of human geometries. Like the artist's age-old investigation of the water-stain on the wall as a grail for bestowing form and defying absolutism, Gillespie's search for form inspires every spectator to a similar scrutiny toward art. As impulsive and as unplanned as primal dance the configuration Gillespie causes is sublimely organic, suggesting the spontaneous and free.

Gillespie creates the tempest. The "rain dance" has manifestly succeeded as color surges down the wall as if leaping along river cataracts or plummeting from the skies. A supernatural magic has been wholly invoked in the properties of sculptures to be observed and enjoyed as form and as wizardry subduing nature, defying expectations.

Likewise, three of Gillespie's early stalagmites testify to the same fusion of the formal and the occult. *Conjured Image #1, #2, #3* (1982), page 19, are three related sculptures seminal in Gillespie's work. Their impact is primary; their colors are the optic primaries of red, yellow, and blue, but their "conjured" impressions are even more than color alone. These are bewitched sculptures as startling in their presences in our physical world as anything dreamt up in Hollywood's alien-happy history. Yet, as impressive as anything Steven Spielberg could create, Gillespie's standing free-form figures are both of art's world and of human reference. After all, each of these is larger-

← Detail of *Night Song*, 1997, enamel on aluminum, 20" x 20" x 21" than-life, standing just above 6 feet, stretching out with outlandish and exotic curls, ringlets, and swirls, their corkscrew animation suggesting something a little bit out of Uncle Remus's tar baby, but something equally out of the contemporary alien. These are space invaders of the most basic kind in their relative congruity to human beings, but also in their spiny foreignness. Gillespie had set out, as early as 1982, to describe a sculptural form pertinent to the human body, primary in its shapes yet inexorably new and different. Her images are not merely made in the twisting and manipulating of three-dimensional space, though there they are crafted and innovative. Gillespie's images are conjured: summoned up in pure magic as well as in sculptural shape.

A similar floor-sited sculpture, *Royal Sentinel* (1984-88), page 45, is also a 6-foot-high sculpture as spiny as a cactus and as animated as a pirouetting dancer. While Gillespie tends to explicit reference rather than wordplay, it is hard to imagine that she has not thought of the sentinel as one who is sentient and alert in feeling as well as a watch-person. *Penelope's Tree* (1987), page 39, glitters with resplendent light. Penelope is, of course, the woman who weaves in order to fend off her suitors. By assuring such suitors that she cannot meet with them until she finishes a funeral garment for her father-in-law, Laertes, the faithful wife to Odysseus connives not only to weave, but also each night to rip apart the day's weaving so that the task is never achieved. What, then, is this tree dedicated to the weaver? It is the celebration of a traditional woman's craft and it is the implanting of that tedious craft into the grandiloquent aesthetic of sculpture, the medium aluminum and the scale 9 feet tall.

How did Gillespie arrive at this amalgamation of the physical and metaphysical as the nexus of her sculpture? The origin of her magic is, of course, her assimilated feminism, the impact of Mother Nature and such forms as rivers in their course, stalagmites in their free-standing assertion, and the amorphous aspects of forms familiar and forms invented. To be sure, there are other artists who have willfully shared art's invention with Mother Nature's and with the feminine form-giving property. Gillespie is no O'Keeffe; she does not yield to one recurrent metaphor, soon jejune. Gillespie is no Bourgeois; she does not answer Freud or Eliade. Gillespie is no Mendieta; she is not earthbound, though she is earth-referring and earth-enlarging. But Gillespie's sculpture, as her culminating achievement, effects the synthesis of agenda, fully assimilated into the work, and the exultation in form. We know how humanoid, how natural, even how wonderful Gillespie's sculptural forms are even while they enrapture us visually. It is the reconciliation of the formal and the mystical, physical energy and the delightful incorporeal feeling that is Gillespie's conjuring and image-making. Simply put, it is amazing grace, an intangible rendered palpably physical.

Knowing that we are drawn to the physical in Gillespie's sculptures but are inevitably taken into her metaphysical dimension, the erupting flowerlike sculptures of the mid-1980s constitute a major step for Gillespie. These sculptures, in particular, seem to explode off the wall with the effect of fireworks or confetti shooting all from multiple centers. In one example, that eruptive force is compared to a *Celestial Journey* (1987), page 41. The journey is an important simile for Gillespie. The cliché of life's journey is rendered profound in the complexity of Gillespie's artistic and personal life, her indomitable conviction in being an artist, and her will to advance her art, never letting it rest in one psychic place or formula.

Moreover, Gillespie employs a favorite description of a sky journey to recall her astonishment the first time she flew above the clouds in a plane. That upper zone – once heavenly, now visible and certain – is Gillespie's most frequent explanation of the amazements of a modern artistic and visual life. Therefore, when Gillespie depicts a celestial journey, it is based in her own experience in flight but no less the ambition of life as well. The white field of *Celestial Journey* is, of course, the "ground" of the clouds; the inflections of color above and the projectile spurs of aluminum lick into a three-dimensional space, but Gillespie's exploration of a formal space is always her sensibility for the astral and heavenly, not forgotten in her sculptural blast. As much as Gottlieb's bursts stirred not only canvas but also earth and bomb, Gillespie's explosions send us into an outer space of the mind and of life's journey as much as they articulate the circumscribed space of the wall.

The wall-rippling music series of the 1990s (especially *Royal Concerto*, pages 78–79, and *Royal Concerto II*, pages 4–5) are sculptures that cease the eruption and begin to orchestrate the plane. Color is more dramatic than ever; this is, after all, baroque music. But the convulsive rupture of the 1980s is replaced by rhythm in the 1990s. After all, Gillespie knows the tempered sculpture as much as the all-out burst. In a sense, the *Royal Concerto* sculptures are influenced by and most like her 1970s stewardship of artist quilts, understanding fields of color. Gentle fluctuation waves across the broad expanses of these sculptures, a mellow moment of musicality for Gillespie, whose relations to music and dance are recurrent throughout her art. Moreover, Gillespie's sculptural music had begun earlier in works such as *Festival Concerto* (1982), page 21, a germinal work in which twirl and curl begin to be more independent of the wall and the process of shredding is progressively more a process of knitting and suturing and twisting.

Among the musical subjects, Gillespie's *Winter Jazz* (1989), page 57, befits its name, recognizing the syncopation of the music in a burst form of large petals, augmented by a system of smaller tendrils. Jazz's natural form, without seeming to be unduly controlled, is a perfect counterpart to Gillespie's innate improvisations. As dauntless as ever, Gillespie set herself the double task of embodying music and of capturing the season in one sculpture. If music is, as Goethe imagined, an ultimate abstraction, the flickering white light of the sculpture is an abstraction but also a glimpse across a snowy winter landscape shimmering with color.

Gillespie captured another season the following year. *Rite of Spring* (1990), page 73, is again a musical refrain and a season's evocation. At first the shape and the colors suggest a Christmas tree, but Gillespie deftly leads us in the direction of spring as the yellow, chlorophyll green, and vermillion of her exuberant stele declare the colorful season. Ribbons of bright color, intensely conjoined, are like a spring garden of bounty and budding verdure, a spectacular feast for the eyes. Characteristically, Gillespie gives us Stravinsky, but reminds us of spring's first flowers as well. In another season, the music is unheard; *Autumn Beanstalk* (1990), page 69, narrates instead the sky-climbing story of Jack and his bean. Given that Gillespie is in virtuoso command of gravity in such sculptures, rippling them along a wall to which they cling with tenacity but never feel pressed, the aspiring beanstalk is an apt metaphor. Further, Gillespie is never afraid to express her sophisticated optimism in terms as fundamental as a child's story.

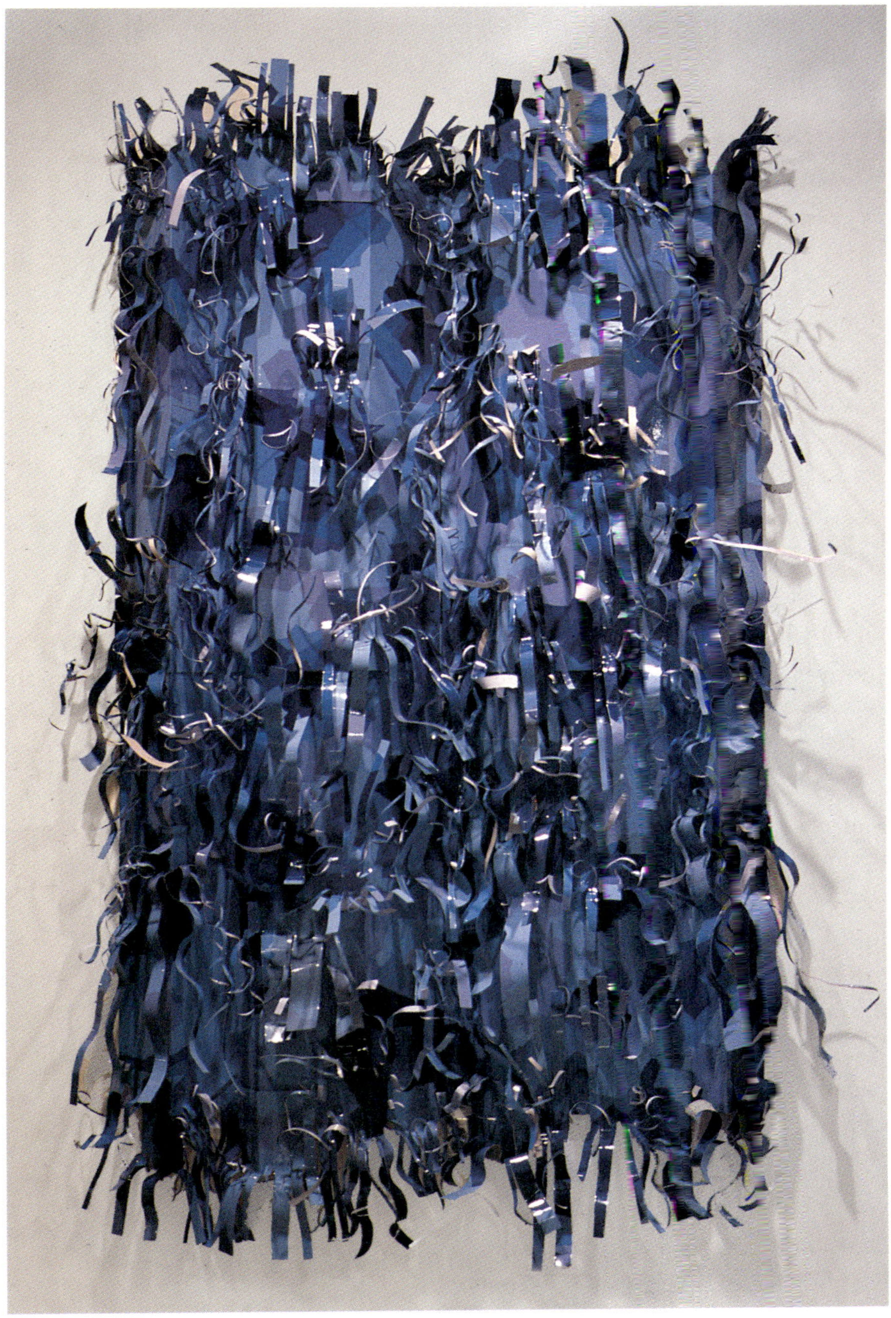

Ritual Grande, 1982-84, enamel on aluminum, 122" x 72" x 18"

Gillespie's abundant joy is evident in all her art. In *Crayolas* (1990), page 77, the artist takes from the child's crayon box, but laces and plaits with a special deliberation. The raveling forms take on the circles of parings, as if skinning an apple, sharpening a pencil, or (as every child does at one time) stripping the colored paper from a crayon. Of course, the crayon is color within as well as color outside. Gillespie offers a similar revelation: her peels, clumped together in cascade, rotate color exposed and color within in a continuous strip. The pigtail-like interlacing of *Crayolas* is merely reinforced in *Shaman II* (1990), page 75. The sweet memories of childhood are supplanted by bright colors and a mystical ideal of a shaman (magician, conjurer, healer). Gillespie's belief in this healer is apparent. The luscious colors make a ribbon candy of this mystical magician, but even more importantly Gillespie attributes to the shaman the dynamic of interlocked colors and twists. In fact, *Shaman II* defies the wall, seems to suspend gravity, and generates a spunky, shiny pointillism of colors lashed together.

By 1989-1990, Gillespie was so confidently in control of her legerdemain of the wall to begin a colorful series and to initiate a series on landscape, our references to the phenomena of nature. Great splotches of color, reminiscent of Jasper Johns's 1960s parodies of abstract painting, prevail in *Colorfall: Landscape* (1990), page 65; here, she definitely plays with words as well as the wall, concomitantly delighting in a waterfall of color and a colorful scene. Gillespie leads the eye of the viewer through the colors of her labyrinthine ribbons, letting us identify motion without ever being certain that we can follow one line. Waterfall, color, and landscape should perhaps conspire to deny sculpture and to affirm painting, but Gillespie is supremely the sculptor by 1990. *Landscape Memory* (1993), pages 98–99, even takes on the accustomed rectangle of modern painting, but insists on her ability to render even landscape as something fully sculptural. The massive *Colorfalls* (1989), pages 54–55 and 145, which had initiated this effort, renders the waterfall in the manner of a Matisse cut-out of the 1950s. Rich, juicy color abounds and pushes the falls toward an abstraction so intense that no natural kaleidoscope

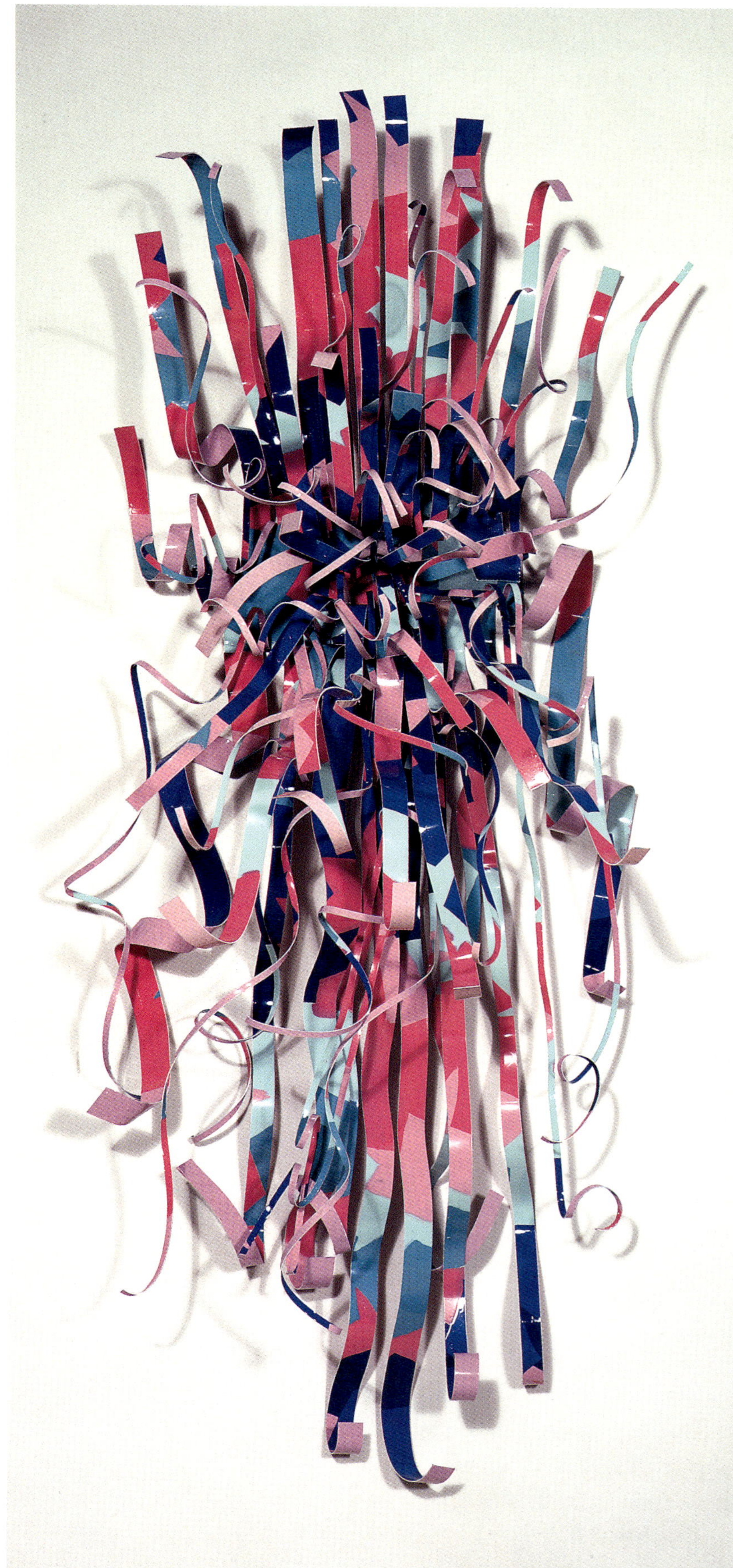

Rain Dance I, 1987, enamel on aluminum, 46" x 19" x 14"

could match its brilliance or its boldness. The irresistible sparkle of *Colorfalls* (1992), pages 94–95, functions in the same way: the intense painterly field is even heightened by the aluminum medium, made more vivid by the curling, twirling forms and their propensity to catch light at any angle, and the quiltlike intense field of the sculpture's giant rectangle. It is Wordsworthian nature rendered in neon-acute hyperbole, but with the passion we reserve to the cosmos.

In *Wings of Song* (1995), pages 110–111, Gillespie conveys her interest in the quilt's field of color under the impact of her constructed field into three dimensions. The shape is more or less a square, but, like Mondrian, Gillespie converts the square to a diamond, subverting our orderly flatness and directing our attention to the ribbons of color, concave and convex, flexing across its surface. Even when we discern the outline – a diamond, or is it Africa? – we see more clearly the rippling structure of the aluminum ribbons basted and puckered and plaited.

Gillespie, the great feminist, has thus insinuated another quiet revolution. Not with the declamation of Judy Chicago, but with her own quiet fortitude, Gillespie has placed sewing and weaving in a man's medium of metal and of sculpture. Her poetry of intentions, her lyricism of beauty, and her willingness as an architectural sculptor to collaborate with space are all signs of the feminine. But is the stitch – elsewhere, "the subversive stitch" – not the rippled replacement for the masculinized gesture of painting, or facture? Sculpture as something intractable has been replaced in Gillespie's sculpture by the bouncy, animated vivacity of color and improvised sculptural form.

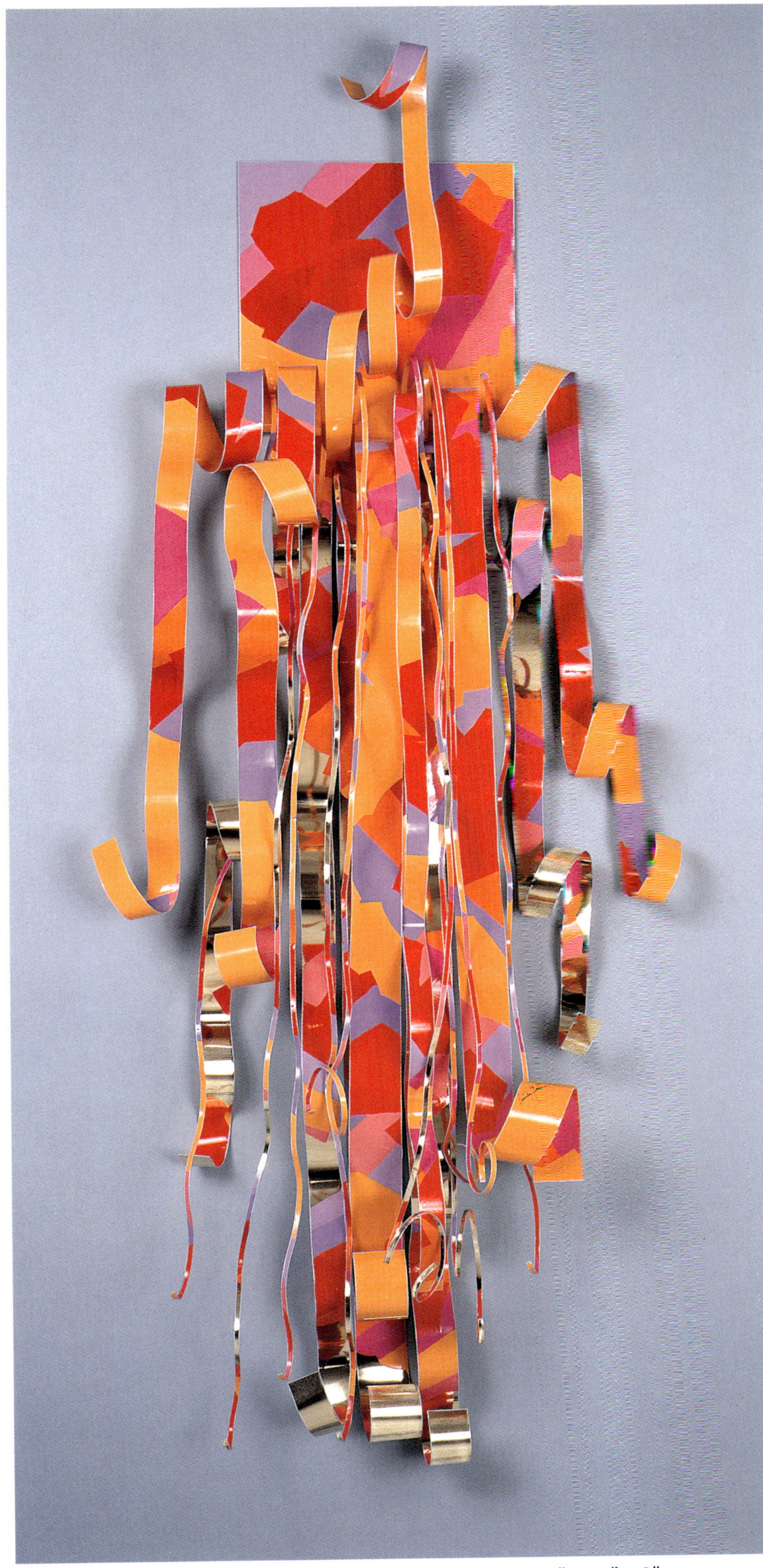

Rain Dance to the Sun II, 1990, enamel on aluminum, 59" x 24" x 3"

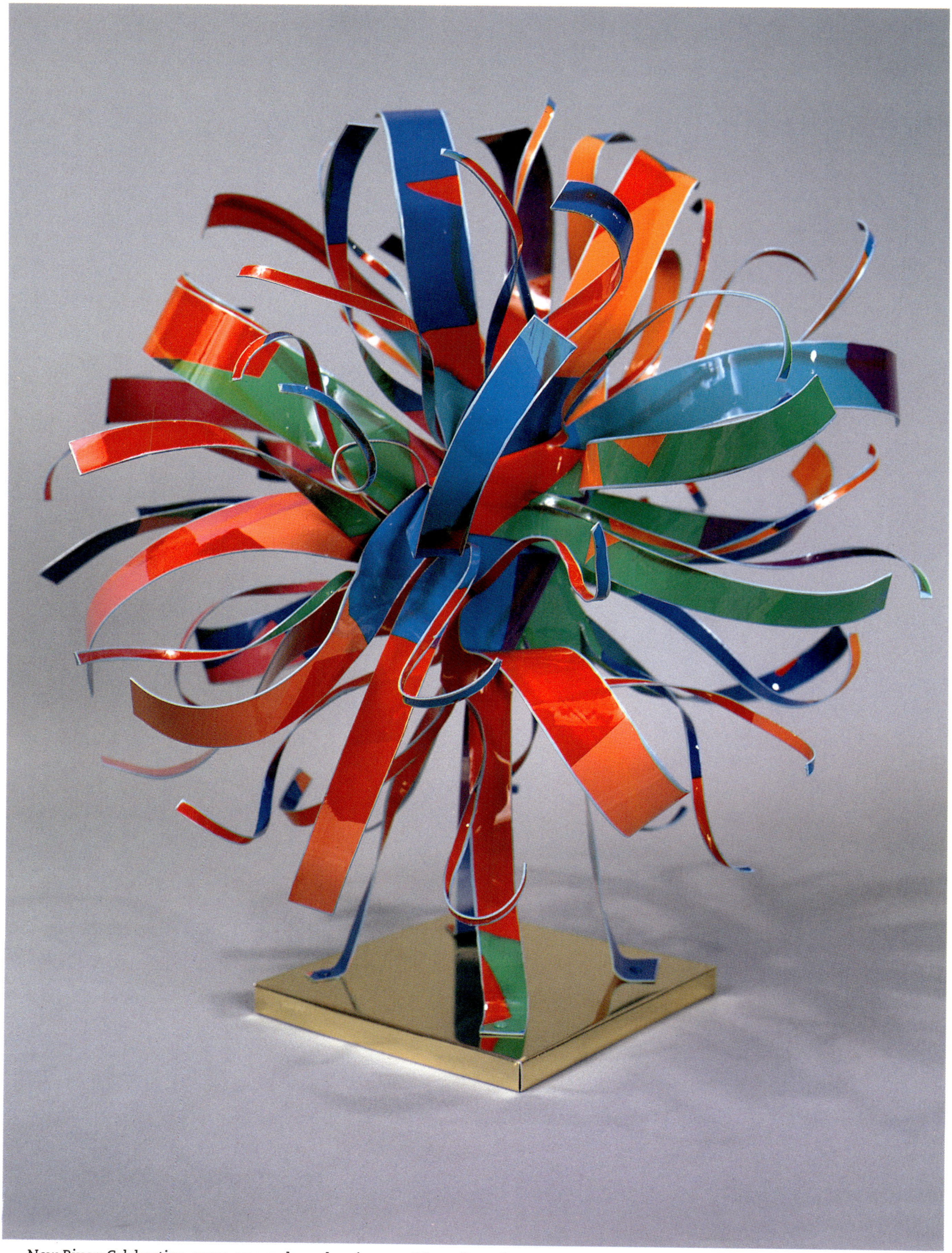

New River: Celebration, 1997, enamel on aluminum, 18" x 17" x 17"

Anncha Briggs
David Bromberg
Matt Bromberg
Trudy and Ralph Bromberg
Brooklyn Museum, New York
Deborah Brown
Debra and Chance Brown
Stuart Brown
Kathy and Richard Bruch
Marian and Hugh Bryan
Ann and Abe Buchman
Jennifer Buchman
Jonathan Buchman
Joyce and Joel Buchman
Wendy and Dennis Bullard
Caldwell College, New Jersey
Barbara Callaway
Pam and William Campbell
Edward Cantor
Gail and Alvin Capp
Mary and Gerald Caress
Castellani Museum, Niagara University, New York
Center in the Square, Roanoke, Virginia
Central Carolina Bank, Chapel Hill, North Carolina
Thad Chambliss
Roslyn and Edward Chudnofsky
Cleveland Ballet, Ohio
Fred Cohn
Dr. Michael Collard
Amy Fine Collins
Bradley I. Collins
Flora Collins
Debbie and Michael Corbino
Lee Corbino
Marcia Corbino
Corroon & Black, Washington, D. C.
Court House Square, Roanoke, Virginia
Beatrice Covington
Douglas Covington
Elizabeth Cox
John Cox
Lily Croom
John Paul Dalsimer
Edgar Daniels
Julia and Frank Daniels
Darmstadt Museum, Germany
Berte D'Arrigo
Delaware Museum, Wilmington, Delaware
Delta Air Lines Terminal, Fort Lauderdale Airport, Florida
Dr. James Denton
Cheryl Diamond
Eleanor Dickinson
Cler Doty
Mr. and Mrs. Mark Eddins
Penny Edelman
Judith and L. G. Edwards
Kathy Einhorn
Mark Epstein
Erda Erdos
Audra and Jerry Evert
Fabrice
Sherry Fabrikant
Roberta Feuerstein
Elsa Hoenig Fine
Erica Fine
Dr. Harold Fine
Lori Fine
Fine Arts Museum of Roanoke, Virginia
Jimmy Finney
R. B. Fitch
Dolly Fiterman
Fones & Mann, Durham, North Carolina, and New York
Fort Lauderdale Museum of Art, Florida
Fort Wayne Museum of Art, Indiana
Alice Fox
Frankfurt Museum, Germany
Jean Freedman
Irma Freudenreich
Molly Friedman
Fritz-Sessler Corporation, Dallas, Texas
Pat Frizzell
Kathleen Galop
Garren, New York
Julie Garrett
Lloyd Gathings
Ronnie Geist
Silvia Gelbum
Jean and Martin Gerstell
Gibbes Museum of Art, Charleston, South Carolina
Betty and E.V. Gillespie
Jackie Ginsberg
Karen and Michael Ginsberg
Regine and Reuben Ginsberg
Sandi Glaberson
Glaxo-Wellcome, Research Triangle Park, North Carolina
Irene Glenny
Betty Gold
Judith and Michael Goldman
Lauren Goodman
Arlene Gordon
Eric Green
Blue and Abe Greenberg
Grey Art Gallery, New York University, New York
Mr. and Mrs. James R. Griffith Sr.
Solomon R. Guggenheim Museum, New York
David Guthrie
Diana and Gene Haberman
Janet Hahn
Peter Haige
Lillian and Frank Hall
Margaret and Clay Hammer
Wally Harper
Anita Charney Harris
Hilda and Paul Harris
Stefan Hartman
Delmar Hendricks
Tressa and Bernard Herold
Tom Hicks
Mary and Watts Hill
Gloria and Harold Hoffman

Hollywood Federal Bank, Coral Gables, Florida
Inez and Sidney Horn
John Hornbaker, Jr.
Sheila Houlihan
Housing and Urban Development Corporation, North Miami, Florida
Mr. and Mrs. John Houston
Jack Hulen
Eric Hunter
Tim Huskins
Institute of Contemporary Arts, Lima, Peru
Andrew Israel
Beth and Gary Israel
Bruce Israel
Doris and Richard Israel
Elfie and Stuart Israel
Karen Israel
Madeline and Paul Israel
Sandra and Mardon Israel
Silvia and Dave Israel
Steven Israel
Victoria and Eric Israel
Izmo Productions, Inc., New York
Harry Jacobs
Ann Jaffe
Johnson Museum, Cornell University, Ithaca, New York
Diana and Arthur Jones
Mr. and Mrs. Myrl Jones
Ruth Julian
Constance Kane
Honni Kaufman
Terry and Sam Kaufman
Bernerd Kautz
Kenan Center
Kessel Museum, Germany
Mary Kilroy
Donald Knaub
Nancy Knox
Muriel and Marvin Kogod
John Kohler
Wally Kolodinski
Andrea Kramer
Edward Krumbhaar
Chuck Kugler
Judith and Harold Kulman
Linelle La Bonte
Lafayette Museum of Art, Indiana
Mary Ann Lambros
Sue and Zev Lapin
Barbara Lea
Mr. and Mrs. Don R. Learned
Doris and Bill Leopard
Joseph Levine
Eric Levy
Margot Lewitin
The Lighthouse, Inc., New York
Janet Liles
Rayford Liles
Lincoln Center for the Performing Arts, New York
Virginia and Robert Loftin
Midge Longley
Lowe Museum, University of Miami, Florida
Fran Luckoff
Henry Luckraft
Maitland Art Center, Florida
Francis Martin, Jr.
Maryland Institute, College of Art, Baltimore
Ann Masters
Mayo Clinic, Rochester, Minnesota
Karen and Jerry McCarthy
Romey McCoy
Mimi and Claude McKinney
Michael McLaughlin
Regina McLaughlin
Lois Mapes
Meadows Museum, Southern Methodist University, Dallas, Texas
Miami Public Library, Florida
Mitch Middell
Barry Miller
Scott Miller
Helen Mills
Beatrice and Alan Minion
Lynn and Loren Mintz
Edna and Leo Monger
Montebello University, Alabama
Kathy and Max Moore
Philip Morris, New York
Mr. and Mrs. A. L. Mueller
Charlotte Murdoch
Eileen and John Murphy
Esther and Ken Myer
Dennis Nahat
National Museum of Women in the Arts, Washington, D. C.
New School for Social Research, New York
Newark Museum of Art, New Jersey
Beatrice Arden Newman
North Carolina Central University, Durham
North Carolina Museum of Art, Raleigh
Norwest Bank, Rochester, Minnesota
Sheila Nussbaum
O'Conner, Maillory
Ohio Dominican College, Columbus
Jessica and Fred Olefson
The Palace Hotel, Orlando, Florida
Diana Parish
Sharon Crockett Peet
Jeffrey Penneys
Judy and John Perrone
Charles Perry
Lee Perry
Patty Perry
Peter Perry
Jane Peterson
Louise Peterson
M. G. Pharo
Frances and David Platzer
Georgia and Monty Pooley
Don Porcaro
Scott Powhatan
Dr. John Poyner
Lisa and Timothy Priano
Thom Priano
Radford University, Virginia
Michele Reekie
Virginia Rembert
Jenny and Bill Rhodes
F. D. Rich, Stamford, Connecticut
Elizabeth and Bill Richards
Sara and Dr. Henry Rittenberg
Tony Rivenbark
Diana M. B. Roberts

Marjorie and Shaler Roberts
Ann and Ike Robinson
Charlotte Robinson
Fred Rogers
Rollins College, Winter Park, Florida
Sheri Romanoff
Pat Rosenstein
Roslyn and Manny Rosenthal
Edward Ross
Charlotte and Harold Rotenberg
Janet Rothberg
Joe Rowand
Rowe Development Corporation, Research Triangle Park, North Carolina
Lucille and Walter Rubin
Ruth and Dr. Lester Rudy
St. Marks School, Dallas, Texas
Beverly and Alan Sanberg
Annette Schiff
Marian and Burt Schools
Rita and Joe Schwartz
Tremayne Selic
Mary and Jim Semans
Betsy and Dick Sesler
Jerry Shepp
Lisa and Martin Silver
Dorothy Silverman
Lois Simon
Elaine and Don Singer
Lauren Singer
Sandra and Carl Sloan
Diedra Smith
Monterey and Warren Smith
Willa Jean Smith
Smith College, Northampton, Massachusetts
Mary Smithe
Janet Solinger
Mr. and Mrs. Ron Sorrow
Rosanne Spear
Alan Spence
Coletta Sperling
Sprint, Inc., Wake Forest, North Carolina
Langston Stabler
Monty Stabler
Vastine Stabler
Stamford Harbor Park Sculpture Garden, Connecticut
Betsy and Bruce Stodola
Louise and Chuck Stone
Jill and Bill Strode
Beth Sullivan
Johanna and Richard Swanson
Systems Associates, Charlotte, North Carolina
Pat Taylor
Richard Taylor
Tel Aviv Museum, Israel
Thalian Hall for the Performing Arts, Wilmington, North Carolina
Sharon Theobald
Diane Thoenen
Jock Truman
Francene Turkin
Edna Tuttleman
Kelly Turner
Mary and Dan Udell
United States Mission to the United Nations, New York
University of Arkansas, Little Rock
University of North Carolina at Chapel Hill
Ruth Van Doren
Debra and Jaap van Opstal
Bill Vaughn
Leonard Verebay
Ron Vereen
Virginia Museum of Fine Arts, Richmond
Virginia State Theater, Abingdon
Mary and Norbert Vonnegut
Robert Votsmier
Jane Waites
Barbara Wallace
Max Wallace
Alice Warren
Warren Wilson College, Asheville, North Carolina
Sharon and David Watkins
Leslie Wayne
Charles Weatherby
Ann and Jack Weil
Ann and Sidney Weinstein
Bibi and Sid Wendroff
Jack Wheeler
Tiffany Wilcher
Karen Wilkerson
Lillian Wilkerson
Barbara Wisch
Charles A. Wood, Jr.
Woodrow Wilson Foundation, Princeton, New Jersey
Caroline Brown Woods
Jody Wycoff
Noel Wynn
Yale University Art Gallery, New Haven, Connecticut
Sabrina Yen
Martha Yielding

Acknowledgments

Thanks to:
Deborah Brown, Dale Carman, Don Daniels, Tom Hicks, Marvin Hoshino, Jeanne Johnson, Richard Martin, Barbara Palfy, Jason Taback, Charles A. Wood, Jr.

Photographers:
Fran Barkus *page* 143
Chris Burke 53
Joseph Caravel 143
Carin Drechsler-Marx 122, 142
Jon-Eric Eaton 17
Everett & Soule 115, 147
Theodore Flagg 87, 99, 109
Sam Goodman 134
Anne Gummerson 123
Don Hall 85, 95
Gerhard Heidersberger 129, 140
Tom Hicks 15, 19, 21, 23, 25, 29, 31, 33, 35, 37, 39, 41, 43, 45, 47, 49, 51, 55, 57, 61, 63, 65, 67, 69, 73, 75, 77, 79, 81, 83, 89, 91, 93, 101, 105, 107, 111, 113, 120, 123, 124, 125, 126, 128, 130, 131, 142, 148, 151, 152, 153, 154
Paul Jeremias 103
Michael Zirkle 97, 144, 145, 146

ISBN (cloth) 0-9633654-3-6
ISBN (paper) 0-9633654-4-4
First Edition
Printed in Hong Kong through Palace Press International
Typeset in ITC Officina and PMN Caecilia
Graphic Design by Marvin Hoshino

ideals®

MOTHER'S DAY

MARCH 2004

Dedicated to a celebration—through poetry and prose—of the American ideals of faith in God, loyalty to country, and love of family.

When God created Mother, He knew there could not be a greater symbol of His love expressed so perfectly.
—Wendy Wagner Tousignant

IDEALS Vol. 61 No. 2 March 2004 IDEALS (ISSN 0019-137X, USPS 256-240) is published six times a year: January, March, May, July, September, and November by IDEALS PUBLICATIONS, a division of Guideposts, 39 Seminary Hill Road, Carmel NY 10512. Title IDEALS registered U.S. Patent office. Printed and bound in USA by Quebecor Printing. Printed on Weyerhaeuser Husky. The paper used in this publication meets the minimum requirements of American National Standard for Information Sciences - Permanence of Paper for Printed Library Materials, ANSI Z39.48-1984. Periodicals Postage Paid at Carmel, New York, and additional mailing offices. Canadian mailed under Publications Mail Agreement Number 40010140. POSTMASTER: Send address changes to Ideals, 39 Seminary Hill Road, Carmel, NY 10512. CANADA POST: Send address changes to Guideposts PO Box 1051, Fort Erie ON L2A 6C7. For subscription or customer service questions, contact Ideals Publications, a division of Guideposts, 39 Seminary Hill Road, Carmel, NY 10512. Fax 845-228-2115. Reader Preference Service: We occasionally make our mailing lists available to other companies whose products or services might interest you. If you prefer not to be included, please write to Ideals Customer Service.

ISBN 0-8249-1231-4 GST 893989236

Visit the *Ideals* website at www.idealsbooks.com

Cover: Flowers tumble gracefully out of their confinement in a painting by Alfred Godchaux (1835-1895) entitled ROSES AND LILIES. Image from Fine Art Photographic Library, London/Art Resource, NY.

Inside front cover: A young girl shares a special moment with her mother in Edith Scannell's painting A GREAT SECRET. Image from Fine Art Photographic Library, Ltd., London/David Messum.

Inside Back Cover: Pastel roses make a lovely arrangement in Helen Cordelia Angell's painting entitled A VASE OF BEAUTIFUL ROSES. Image from Fine Art Photographic Library, Ltd., London/Kaye Michie Watercolours.

In This Issue

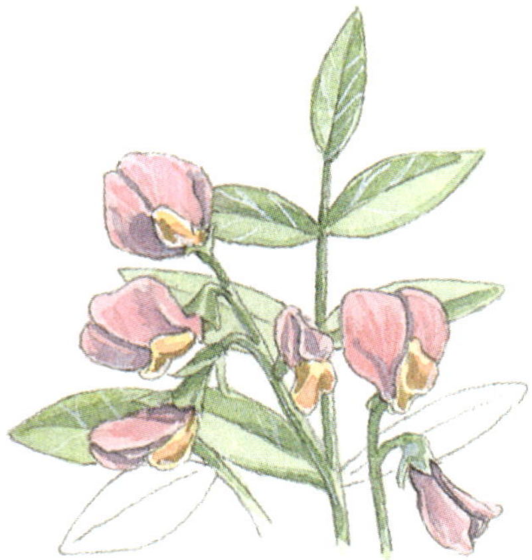

From

This Hill, This Valley

Hal Borland

May, which came in with daffodils and goes out with peonies ready to burst bud and lilacs fading, and in between almost all the flowers of spring. That's May for you, and you can count on it as on few months in the year. It may start cold or it may start late, but before it comes to its end, May has fulfilled its promises.

There is a cold certainty about January, and August is ripe as sweet corn. But May is all growth and flowering, from the last of the bloodroot to the first of the daisies and buttercups. May is new as a baby radish, prime as a scallion, sweet as a swamp violet. May is full of bird song, bee hum, flowing brooks. Here it is, and almost gone; and having lived with it again, having felt its pulse and exaltation, I know that any year with May in it is a year worth living.

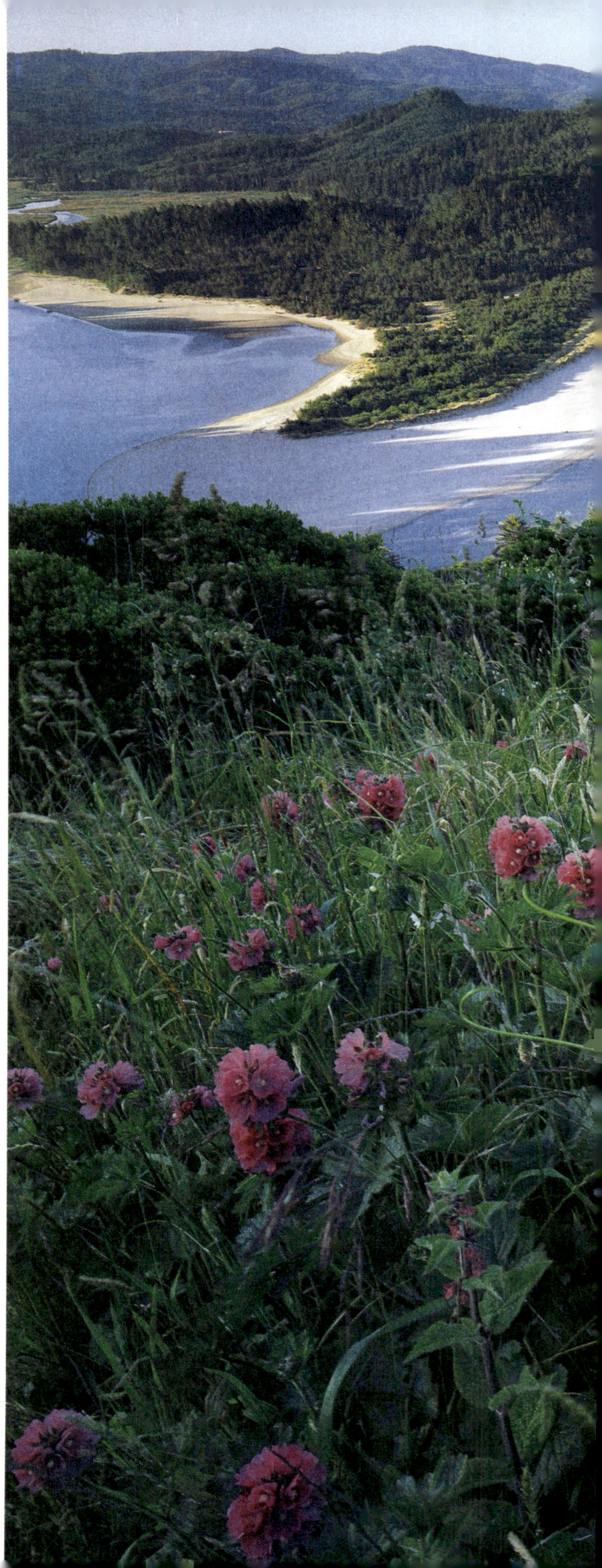

A prairie at Cascade Head, above the mouth of the Salmon River in Oregon, shelters beautiful wildflowers. Photograph by Terry Donnelly.

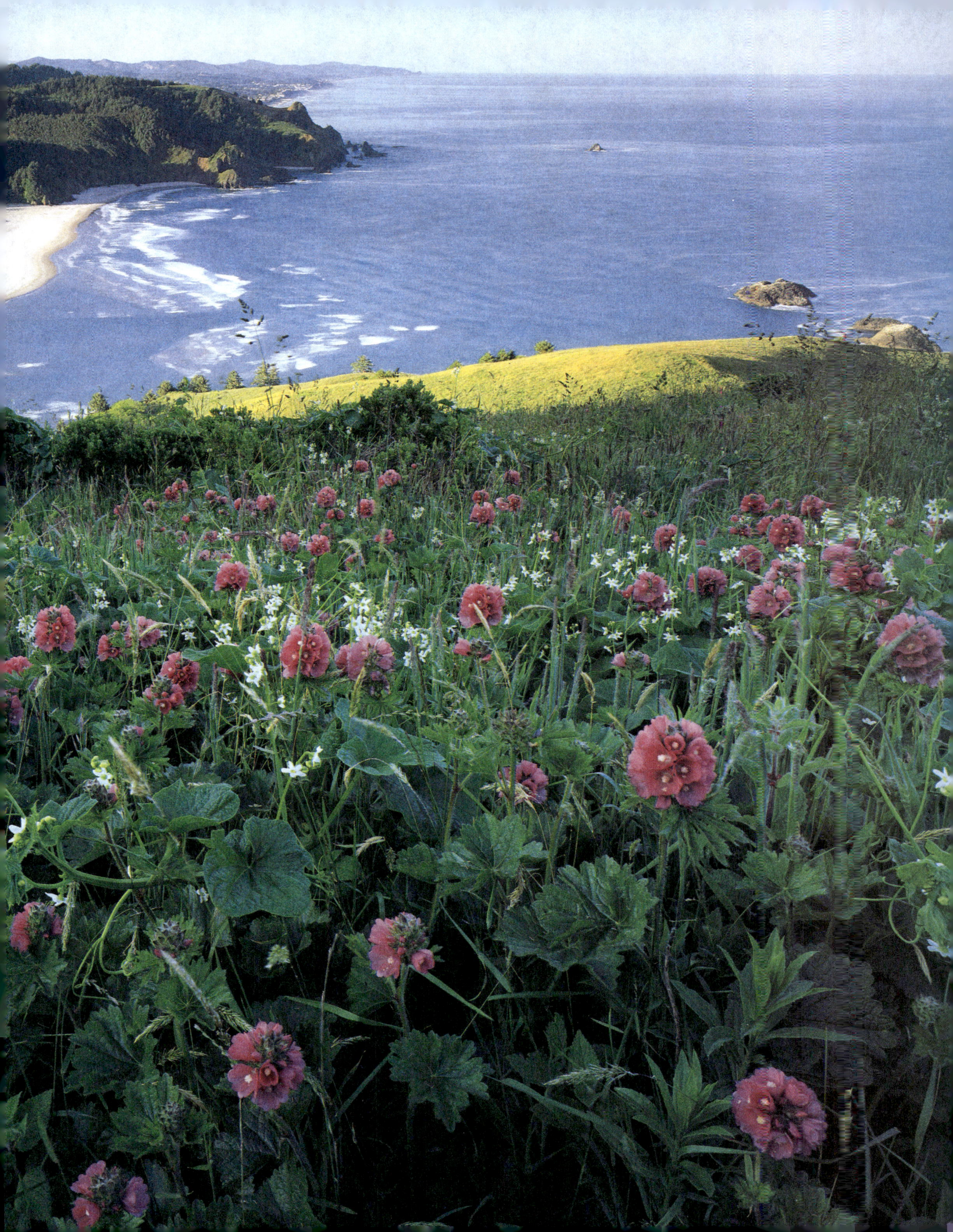

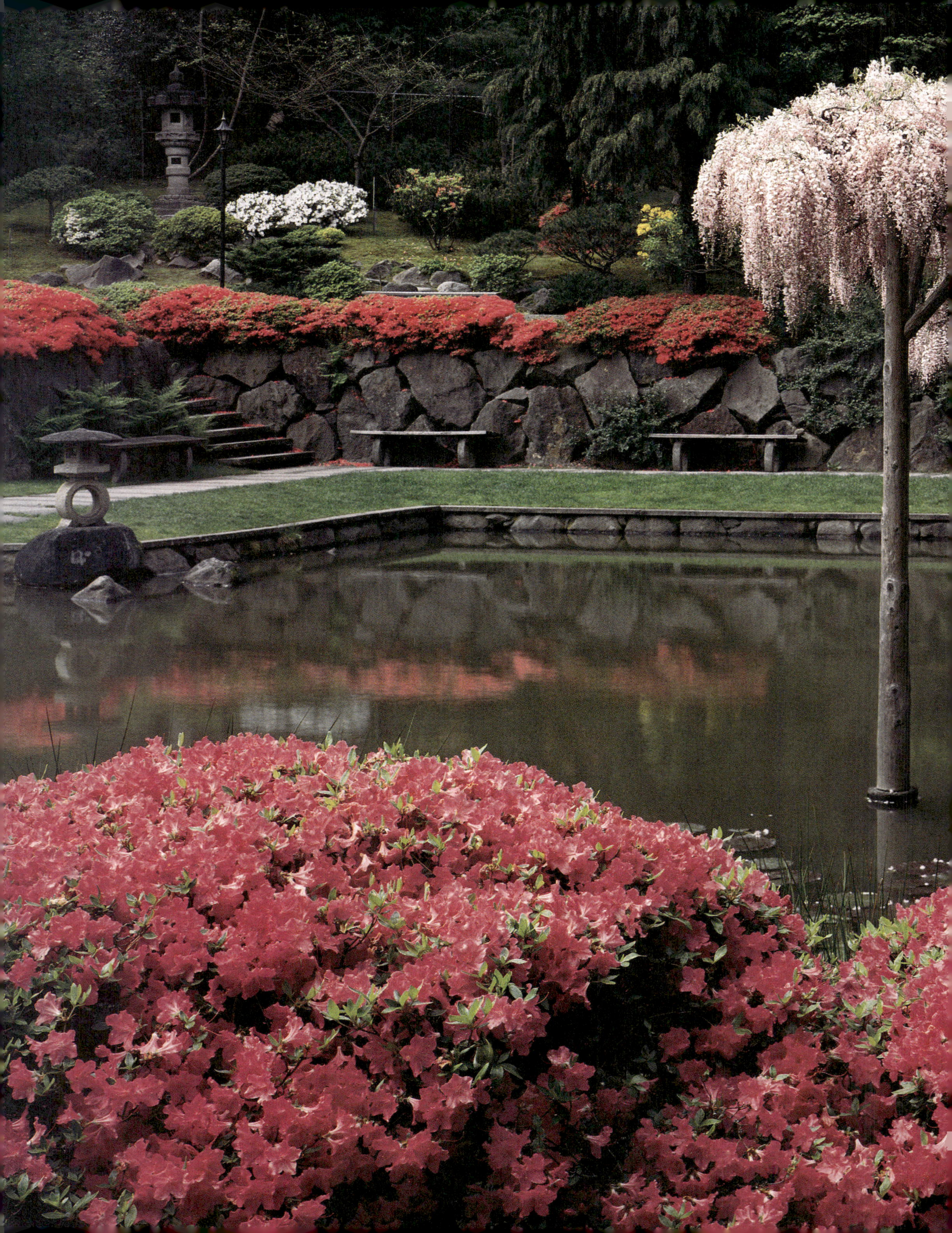

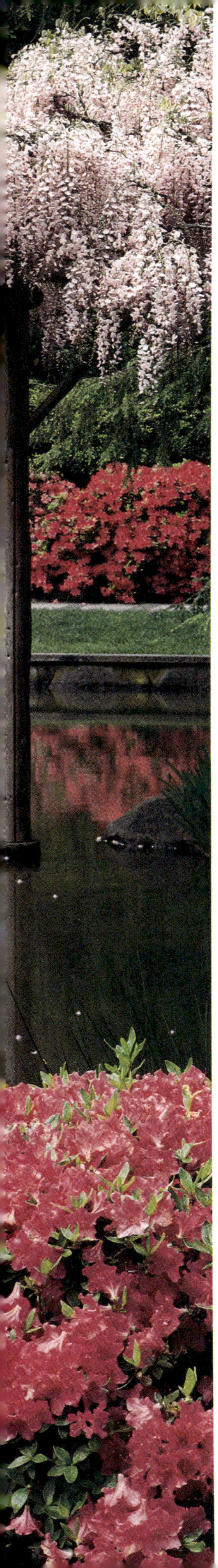

Enchanted Spring

Elisabeth Weaver Winstead

Through wind as clear as polished glass,
The wild spring geese go gliding past.
A clear chorus of peepers echoes in the night;
And ruffled plum trees wear halos of silvery white.

The rosebush gleams with fragrant flowers
Burning crimson through breezy, sunlit hours.
Exultant in splendor, they wave and fling
Bright blossoms of soft-burnished spring.

Glowing daffodils and sweet jasmine grow
By bluebells shining in satin row.
Bouquets delight with sky blue and gold—
All that my waiting arms can hold.

Cheery robins, attired in feathered fire,
Hold concerts from a low fence wire.
In sunlit glow, spring steals the scene,
An enchanted beauty in gossamer green.

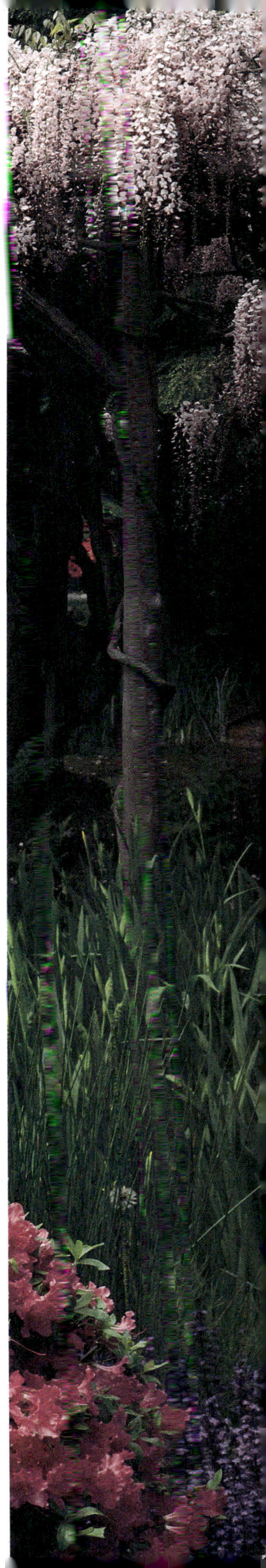

Flowering wisteria and azaleas dramatize the gardens of Japanese Garden Lake at Washington Park Arboretum, near Seattle, Washington. Photograph by Terry Donnelly.

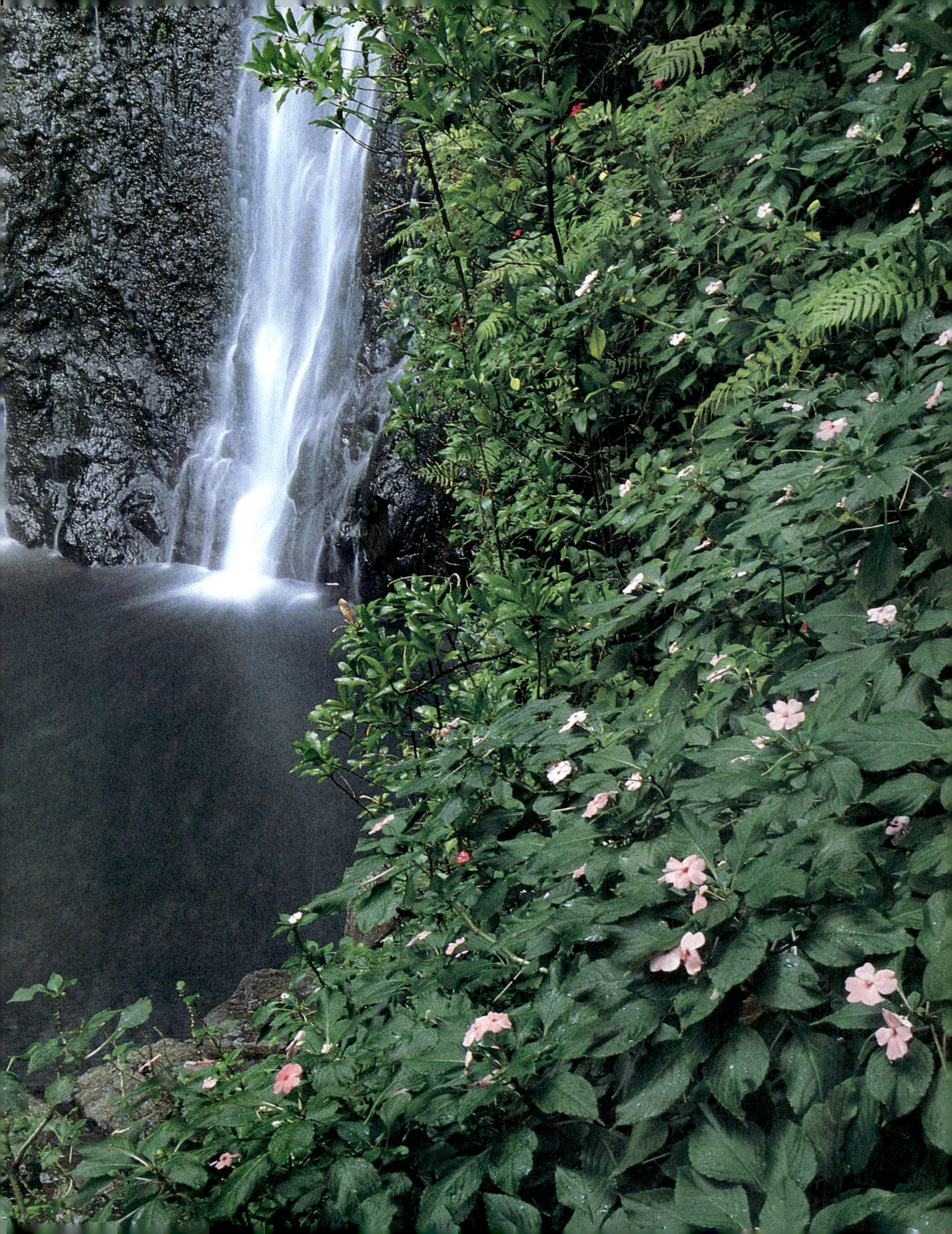

Petals

Amy Lowell

Life is a stream
On which we strew
Petal by petal the flower of our heart;
The end lost in dream,
They float past our view,
We only watch their glad, early start.

Freighted with hope,
Crimsoned with joy,
We scatter the leaves of our opening rose;
Their widening scope,
Their distant employ,
We never shall know. And the stream, as it flows,

Sweeps them away;
Each one is gone
Ever beyond into infinite ways.
We alone stay
While years hurry on,
The flower fared forth, though its fragrance still stays.

The Rose

Branch Allen

How lovely the rose
So gently to me speaks.
How lush its fragrance,
So powerful, yet meek.

Tender velvet petals,
Fragile, so full of grace,
Carry me away
To a heavenly place.

Why must this flower,
So beautifully adorned,
Be cursed with the wearing
Of so wicked a thorn?

In quiet supplication
We find its true appeal—
Without the barb,
It's just a posy in the field.

So we learn from this bloom
On this wicked stem borne,
We cannot truly love
And not accept the thorn.

Wailua Falls, on the Hana coast of Maui, is framed by lush tropical flowers.
Photograph by Gnass Photo Images/Jon Gnass.

Angels' Wings

Timothy L. Frank

Within my garden sweetly grows
A flower fairer than a rose,

With petals white as angels' wings,
Whose beauty heaven surely sings.

The morning air fills with perfume,
This tender fragrance from a dainty bloom.

A gardenia, delicate as lace,
Has blessed my garden with its grace.

Nature's Gentle Care

Alice Kennelly Roberts

No earthly baby ever knew
A crib more beautiful than you,
With roses just above your head,
Twined all about your leafy bed,
With honeysuckle climbing high;
And, over that, a turquoise sky,
The lullaby of lazy bees,
And breezes through a maze of trees,
A canopy of lacy net—
This is the robin's bassinet.

The fragile beauty of a gardenia in bloom invites the onlooker to savor its natural perfection. Photograph by Grant Heilman/Barry Runk.

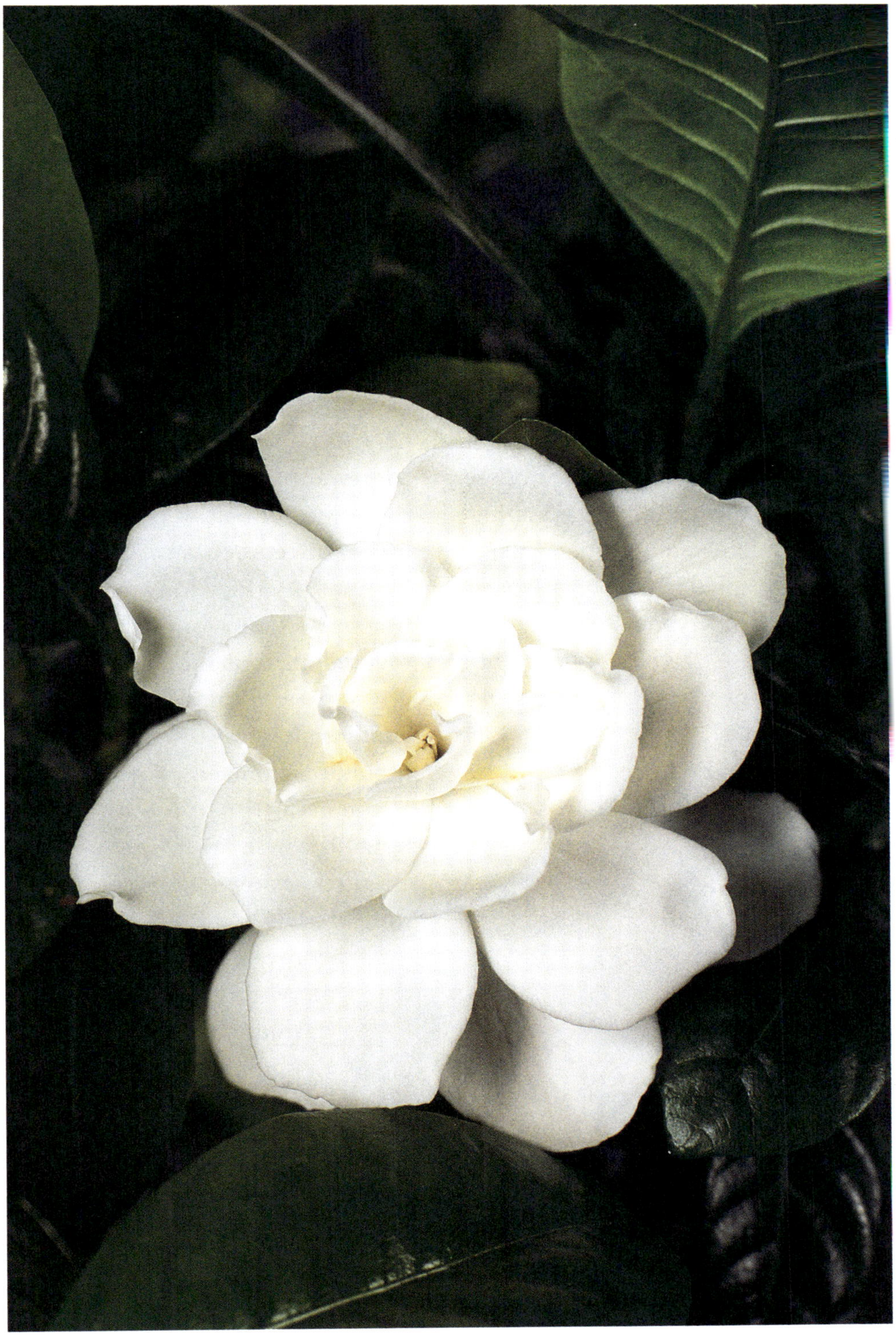

From My Garden Journal

Lisa Ragan

Peonies

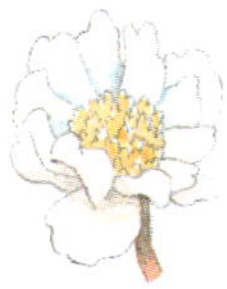

The women in my family have been gardening for generations. Conversations at our family gatherings always included discussions of what's blooming at Grandma's house or at Great-Aunt Lillian's house across the field. When Aunt Lillian died at age ninety-seven, my grandmother, my mother, and my aunts divided and transplanted many of her flowers before her house was sold. Everyone took a division of her beloved peony bushes. Today my mother treasures the two thriving peony bushes in her backyard as living heirlooms of a favorite aunt.

The peony's name can be traced back to the mythology of ancient Greece. The hero of this myth, *Paeon*, was the young pupil of *Asclepius*, the Greek god of medicine.

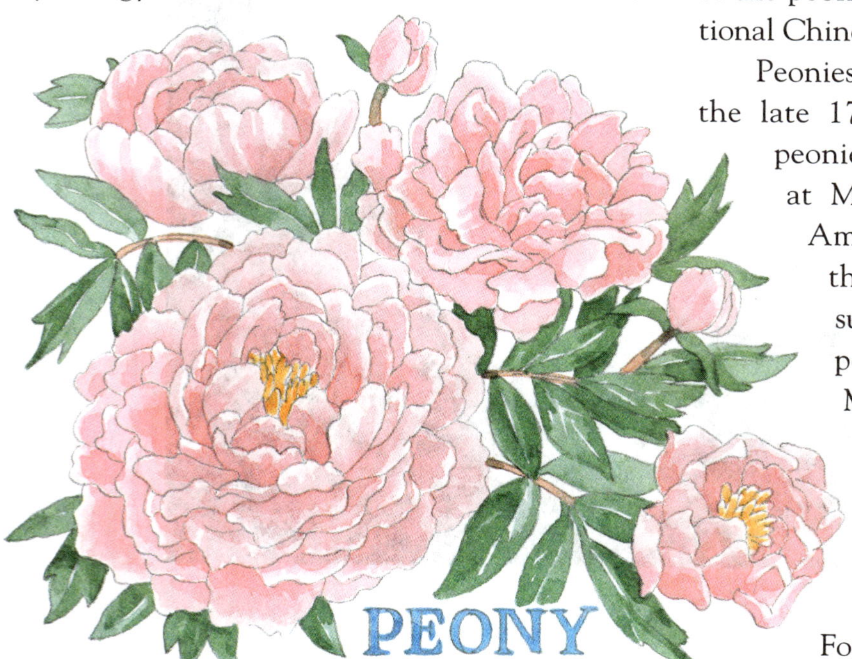

While ancient Greece may have given us the peony's name, it was ancient China that gave us the type of peony that has gone on to parent thousands of cultivars—*P. lactiflora*. As early as the sixth century, A.D., Chinese gardeners began cultivating the peony, particularly *P. lactiflora*, not only for its beauty, but also because they revered it as a medicinal herb. Even Roman philosopher Pliny the Elder wrote of the peony's medicinal power to cure a variety of afflictions, including stomach pains and jaundice. Extracts of the peony plant are still used today in traditional Chinese medicine.

Peonies traveled from Europe to America in the late 1700s; and Thomas Jefferson listed peonies in a list of hardy perennials grown at Monticello as early as 1771. Soon American nurseries were developing their own cultivars. One of the first successful American nurseries to breed peonies was that of Oliver Brand in Minnesota. The Brand nursery produced the American varieties Longfellow, Richard Carvel, and Myrtle Gentry, among others. The peony steadily gained in popularity through the years. Following the Civil War, the Memorial

Day peony, *P. officinalis* Rubra, became a popular choice to decorate the graves of fallen soldiers.

American gardeners today can choose from a wide range of peony cultivars, most of which can be traced back to the *P. lactiflora* of ancient China. Color options run the gamut from white, cream, and yellow to lavender, pink, red, and even burgundy and black. Blossoms can be seen in single, semi-double, double, and Japanese forms. The Japanese blossom features much larger outer petals. Foliage colors also vary and include bright grass-green, softer greens tinged with red, or even gray-green foliage. Sizes of peonies vary greatly as well; peonies can be found that reach as little as eighteen inches high or as tall as five feet and as large in circumference. The tree peony, a different species altogether, features woody stems that can stretch up to ten feet high.

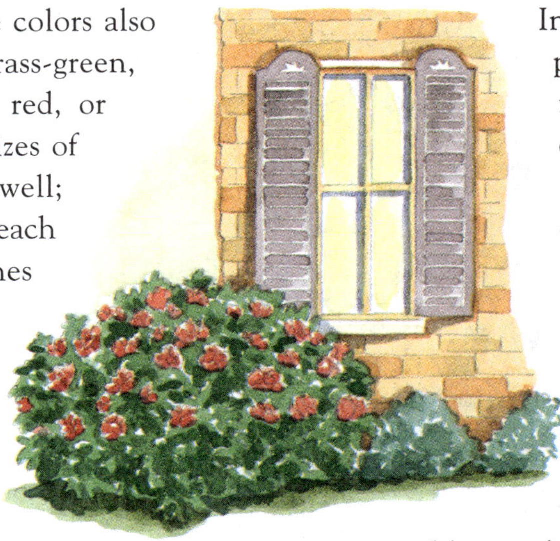

The herbaceous, perennial peony produces lush, green foliage that will remain neatly rounded all summer before dying back in autumn. A hardy plant that not only survives winters well but actually requires a winter period of dormant sleep, the peony produces spring shoots tinged with red or purple, which fade away as the plant grows. The typical blooming period is a mere two weeks but can be extended throughout the growing season by planting a variety of peonies that bloom in early season, mid-season, and late-season.

Peonies perform exceedingly well indoors as cut flowers. Since sunlight can bleach the color of peonies outdoors, color retention can be improved in cut flowers by selecting buds and allowing them to open indoors. Gently remove ants by washing them off with water. Peony blossoms also perform well as dried flowers. The darker-hued varieties retain the best color when dried.

Peonies can be grown from seeds, divisions, or their tuberous roots. Planting peony seeds requires patience, since the seedlings will not produce blooms for four to five years. Many gardeners plant the tuberous roots, which feature a crown of pinkish buds called *eyes*. In autumn, the roots should be planted in a location that receives full morning sun and dappled afternoon shade.

Aside from staking, the only maintenance these plants require is removing withered blossoms regularly and cutting the plant to just above ground level in autumn.

Few pests and diseases plague the hardy peony. Peonies are immune to nibbling rabbits and deer because their stems, foliage, and blossoms taste bitter. The Japanese beetle may actually be controlled by the presence of peonies in a garden. The nectar in the flowers attracts the beneficial spring tiphia wasp, a predatory insect that attacks Japanese beetles in their grub stage.

As far as I know, Aunt Lillian didn't do anything special to her peony bushes, other than provide them with a home in her garden. I can only hope that my mother's heirloom peonies from Aunt Lillian last another century to provide our family with living memories of generations of women who love beautiful flowers.

Lisa Ragan, with the help of her son, Trenton, tends to a small but mighty garden in Nashville, Tennessee.

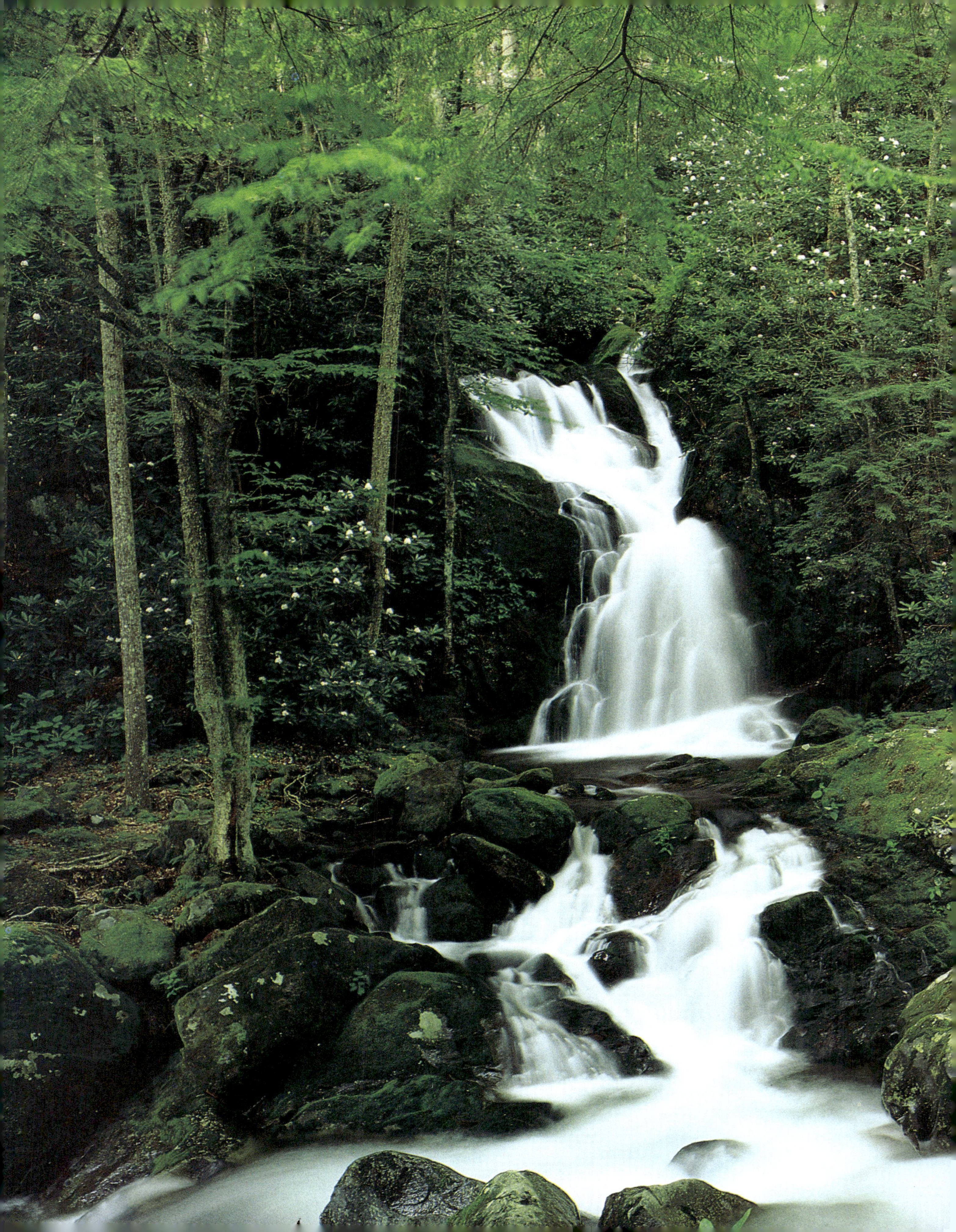

A Mother's Teachings

George Wendell Knight

As Mother's Day is drawing near,
I think of days gone by
And hear the words of singing cheer
That take away my sighs—
For through these eyes I now can see
My dear mother who cares for me.

And though my steps may wander wide
And far away from home,
My thoughts will never leave the side
Of her great queenly throne—
For earthly wealth can give no more
Than what she taught me in great store.

She taught me first of God above,
Who cares for struggling man,
And pointed me to His great love
To grasp His mighty hand;
And next she taught me of His Son,
Who is the world's Beloved One.

And then she taught this growing boy
Of kindness, mercy, peace,
And cautioned me to smile with joy
And never let it cease;
But most of all she taught my soul
To pay life's price with honest toll.

So on this day, all Mother's own,
I pledge my life anew
To honor, however far I roam,
Her strong faith and virtue true;
And may my life forever show
The lessons she taught me long ago.

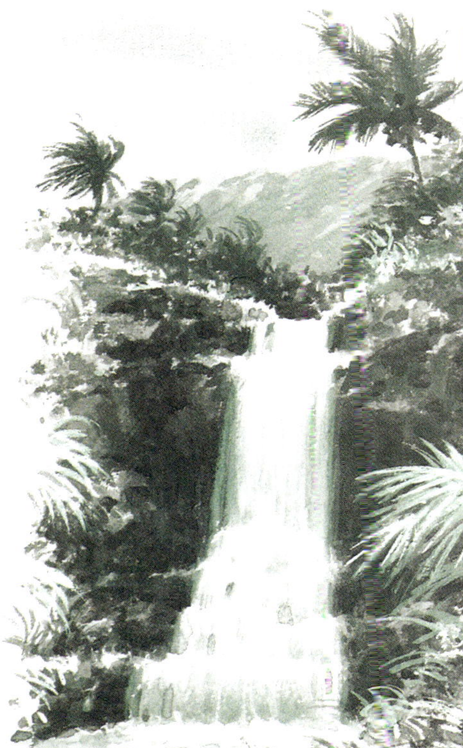

The pleasant splashing of Mouse Creek Falls echoes through Great Smoky Mountains National Park in North Carolina. Photograph by Daniel E. Dempster.

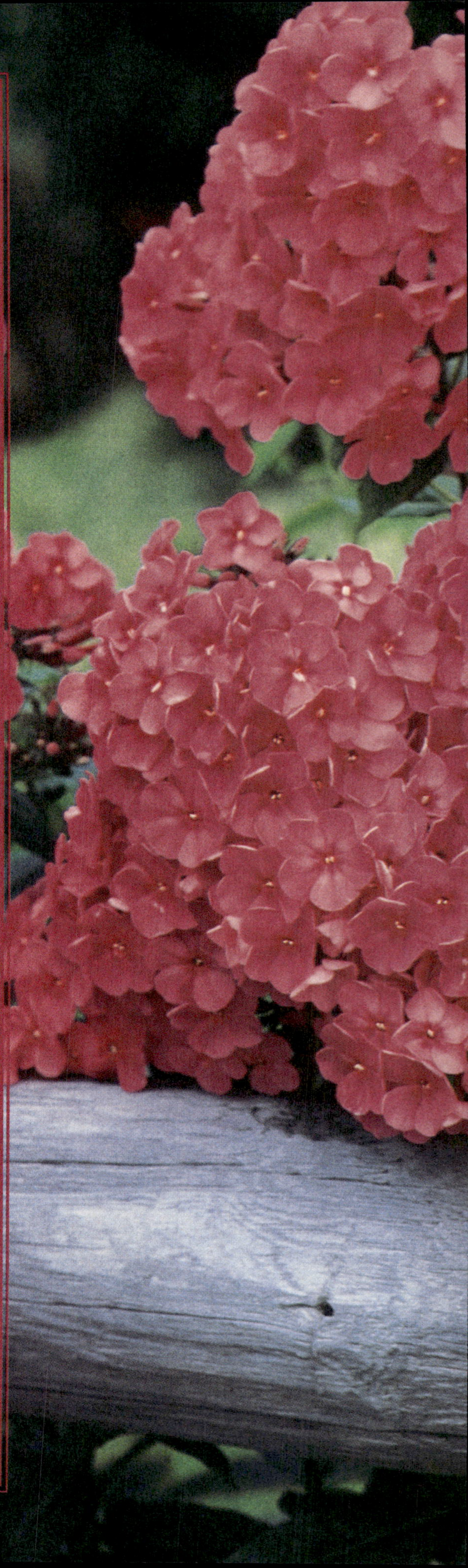

Mother's Day Gifts

Wendy Wagner Tousignant

When Mother's Day is being observed
And spring is here to stay,
God blesses each of us with gifts
Of nature, in His special way.

Fruit trees wear frills of pink and white;
Sweet lilacs bow with grace;
Upon their branches songbirds light
To seek a nesting place.

These gifts of life on Mother's Day
Are priceless gifts to me,
For they express the miracles
God gives so lovingly.

The Gift of Mothers

Inez Franck

He gives the soft moonbeams at night
That linger for a while,
But there is nothing like the glow
Of Mother's touching smile.

He makes the rose to grace the day,
The stars to light above.
Of all the gifts, the dearest one
Is Mother's faithful love.

He cares for us in many ways
And fills our vast demands;
He sends our mothers for the tasks,
With sure and willing hands.

He brings the leaders in their strength
With guidance for our fears;
Yet mothers rule with words so wise,
They live throughout the years.

Vibrant pink hydrangeas drape a fence post in Peachman, Vermont. Photograph by Dick Dietrich.

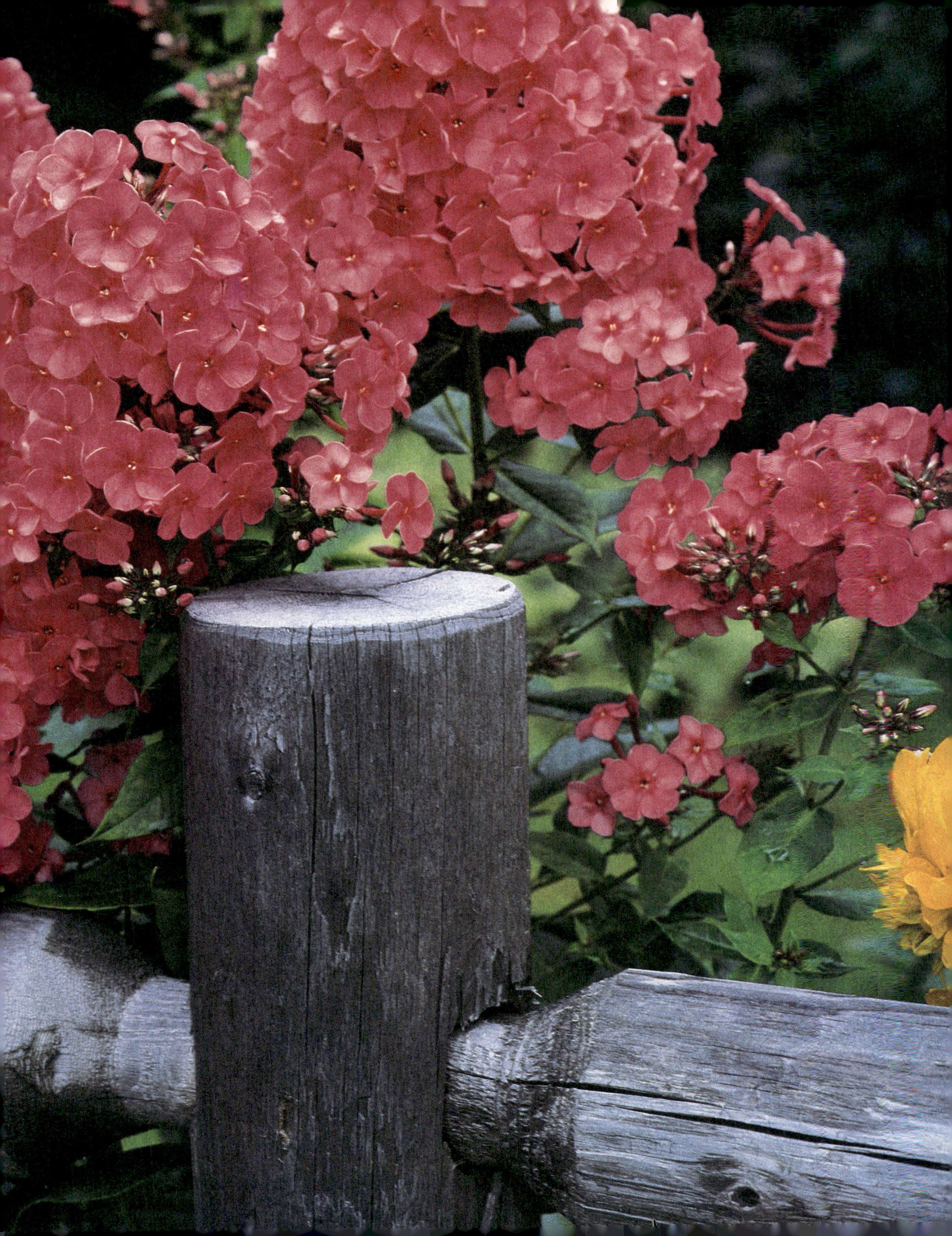

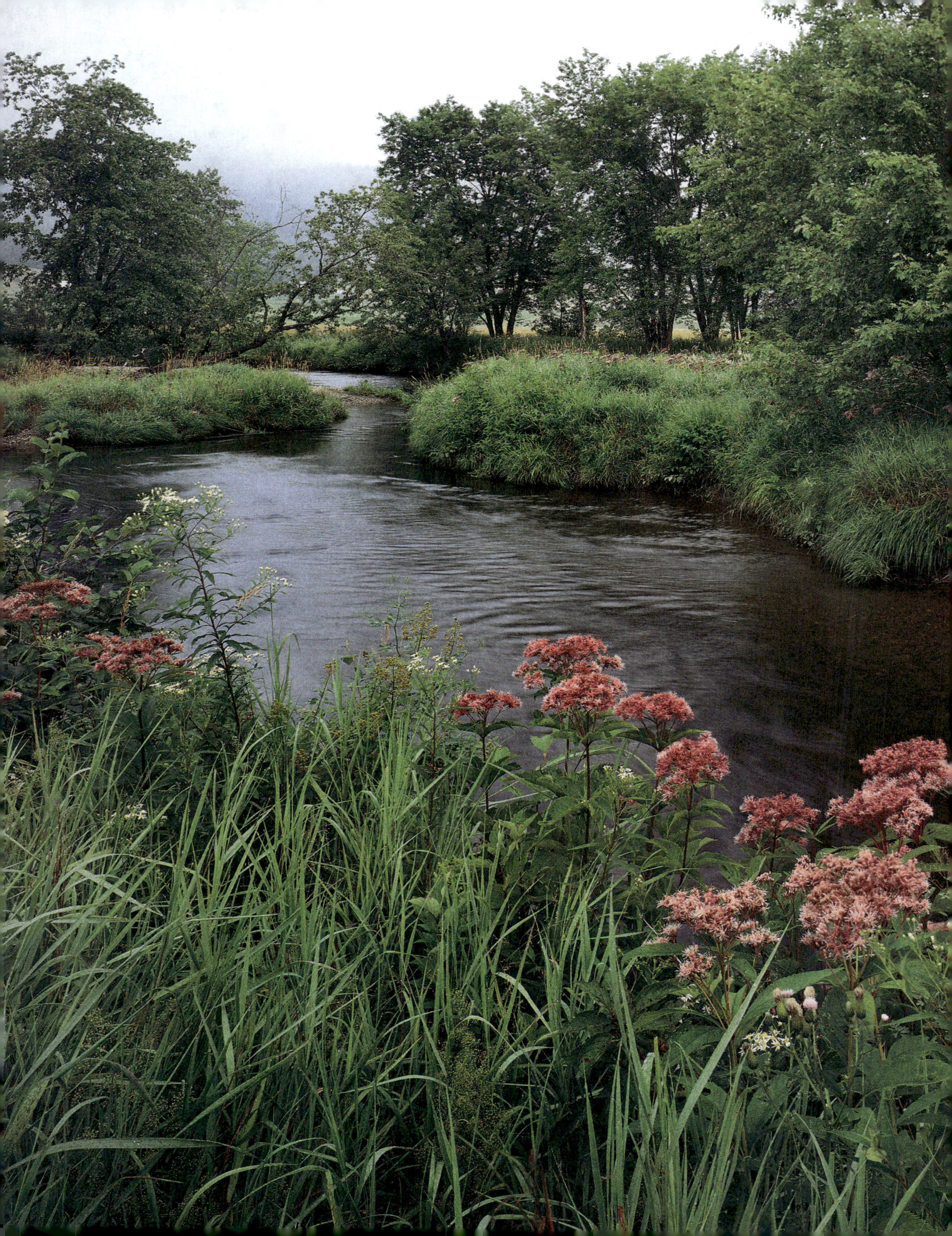

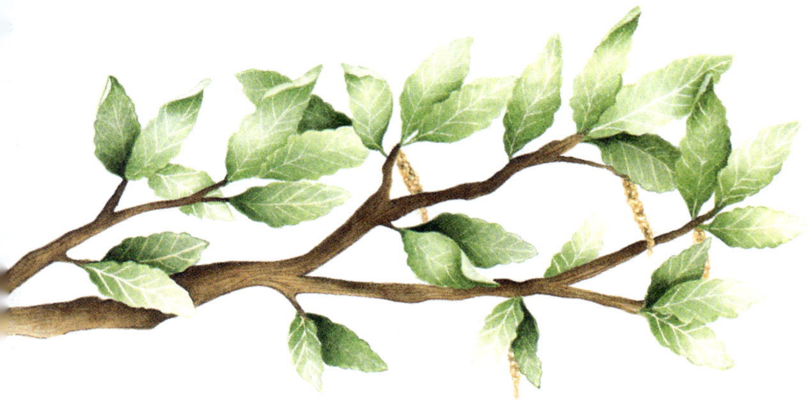

Mother's Day Tribute

Rudolph N. Hill

To what shall I compare you, Mother?
The rose is not so sweet, I vow;
Nor will there ever bloom another
As sweet to me as you are now.

The daffodil is not so golden
As treasured love within your breast;
Even honeysuckle is beholden
To the lesson of your hands' caress.

Yes, you are yet the sweetest flower
That blooms upon this lovely earth;
And I would send back to you, this hour,
The love you gave me from my birth.

Springtime

Ellen Martin

The world is bright and all aglow;
Buds are bursting free;
New leaves have started forming—
There's fruit upon our apple tree.

Newborn lambs and baby ducklings
Bless our nursery;
God chose the perfect season
For Mother's Day to be.

Joe-Pye weed decorates the border of Indian Stream as it slowly meanders through Pittsburg, New Hampshire. Photograph by William H. Johnson.

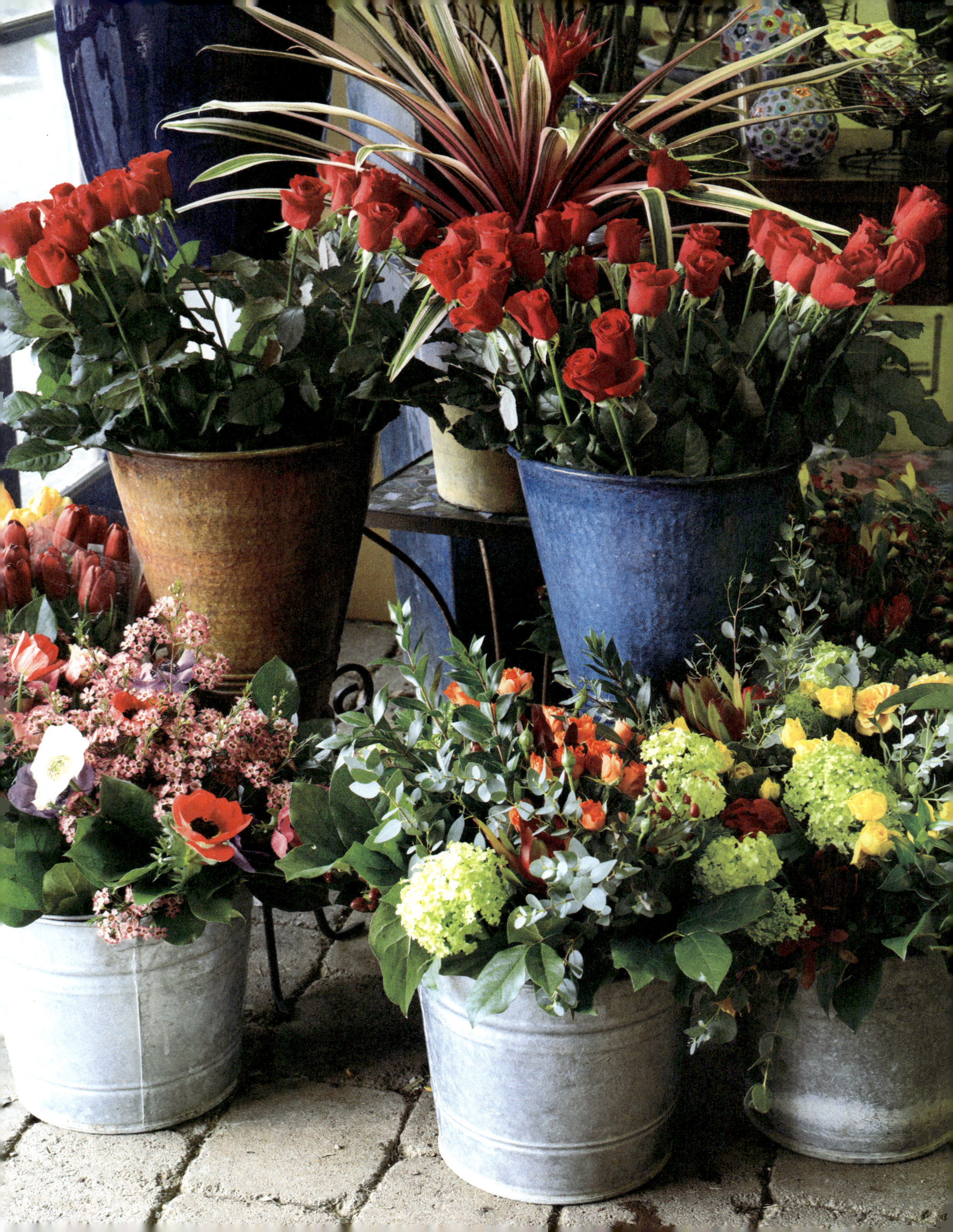

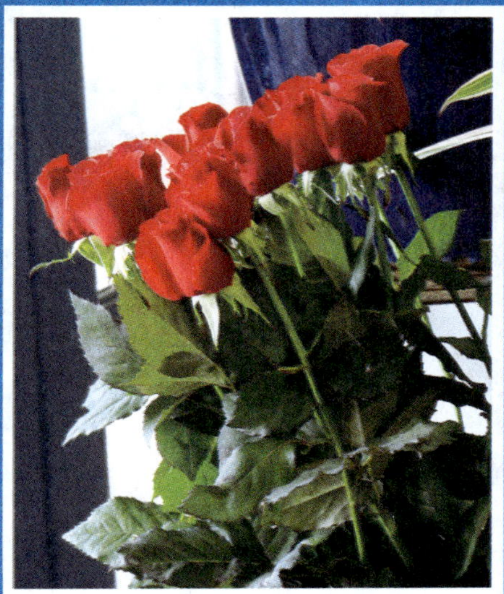

I've been very near to heaven in the race of falling sands,
Kneeling beside an angel, as I kissed my mother's hands.

—Josh Higgins

Mother's Hands

Margaret Krebs Lohr

Their beauty lies
within the gentle way
She strokes a kitten,
arranges a bouquet;
Their tenderness is a part
of all the kindness
flowing from her heart.

The Touch of Mother's Hands

Madge Downs

My mother's hands—how gentle
Their touch upon my hair,
As she smoothed it from my brow
And pressed her soft lips there—
Oft soothing childish trouble
Or easing hurt and pain.

Oh, that I might recall the years
And her hands' touch again,
Not soft, nor white and shapely,
And not so very small.
Perhaps an artist's fancy
Would not picture them at all
Yet, to me, a treasured memory,
Which from childhood days outstands:
When ailing, I sought comfort
In the touch of Mother's hands.

Brilliant-hued roses and other flowers await arranging. Photograph by Mary Liz Austin.

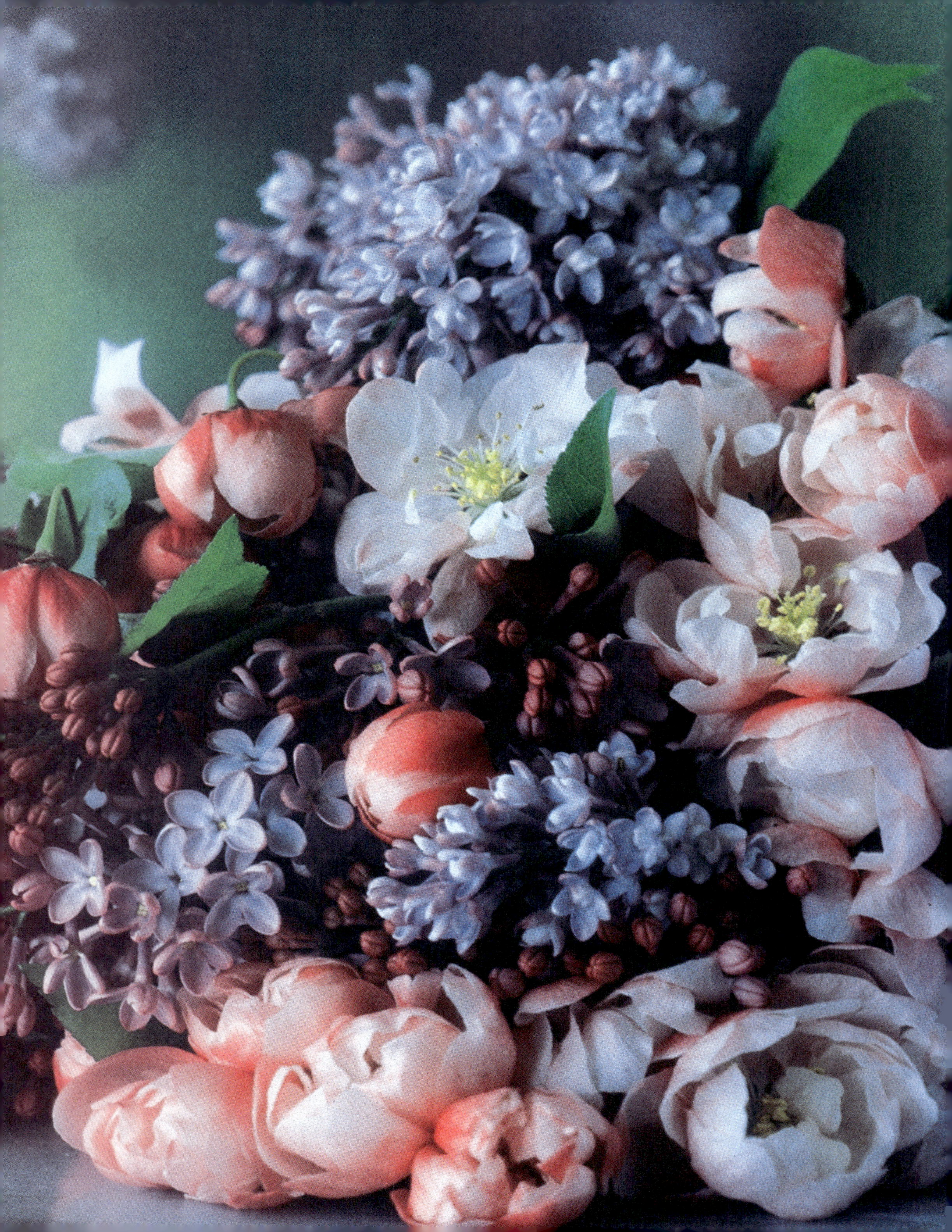

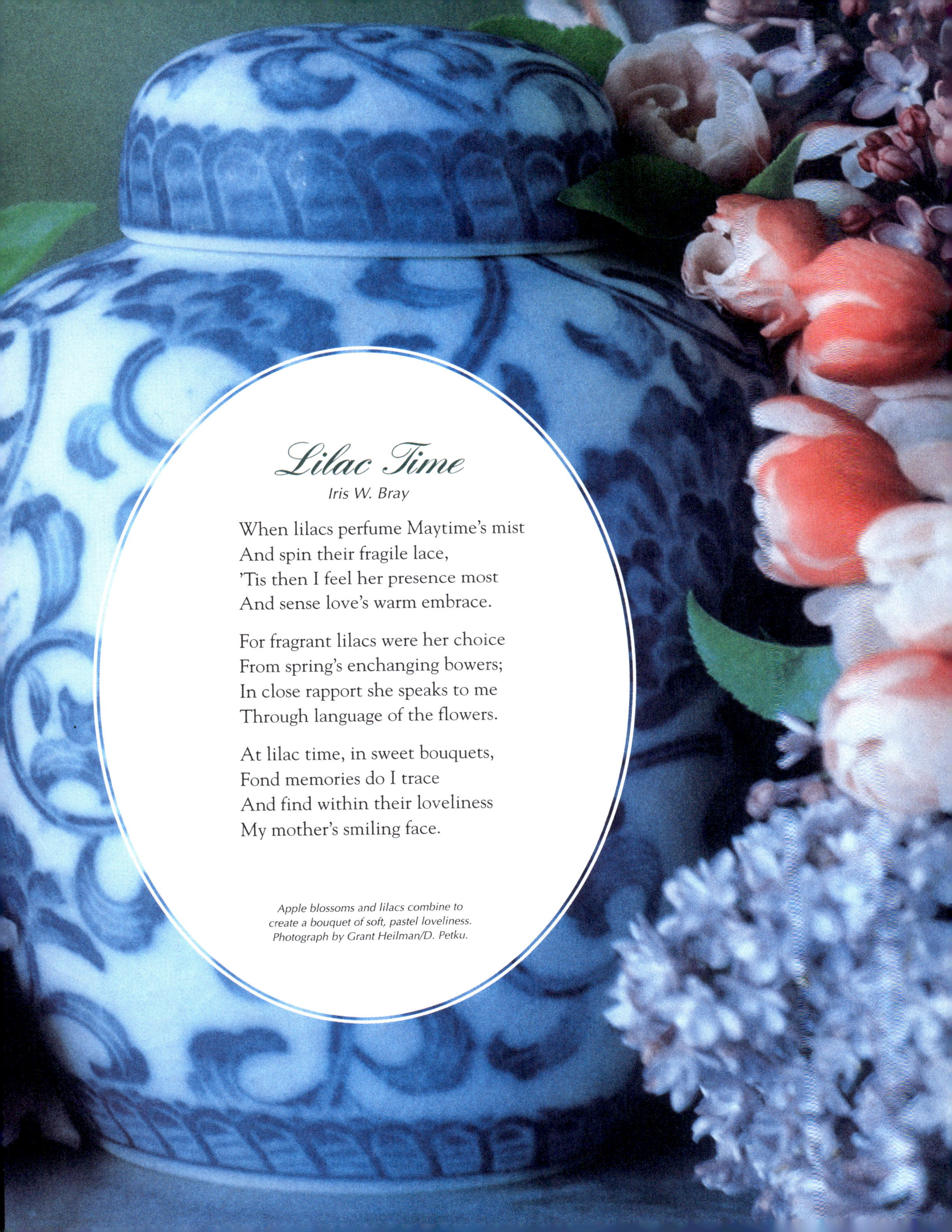

Lilac Time

Iris W. Bray

When lilacs perfume Maytime's mist
And spin their fragile lace,
'Tis then I feel her presence most
And sense love's warm embrace.

For fragrant lilacs were her choice
From spring's enchanging bowers;
In close rapport she speaks to me
Through language of the flowers.

At lilac time, in sweet bouquets,
Fond memories do I trace
And find within their loveliness
My mother's smiling face.

Apple blossoms and lilacs combine to create a bouquet of soft, pastel loveliness. Photograph by Grant Heilman/D. Petku.

Mother's Garden

Janet Arnold Lietz

I remember Mother's garden;
She had a special touch.
She toiled there with loving care;
Of self she gave so much.

She planned each row in early spring,
Prepared the soil just so.
The seeds were set in carefully;
They could not help but grow.

For there, between the vegetables—
Every other row—
Grew a myriad of flowers
To make a lovely show.

Orange nasturtiums blossomed there,
Providing bold relief
Between the lowly cabbages
And crispy lettuce leaf.

Purple pansies in the onions
Smiled their secret smile;
While white petunias entertained
In captivating style.

I loved to sit there, in the sun,
Tomatoes all around.
Right off the vine, they tasted good,
A banquet on the ground.

I have these happy memories
'Cause Mother made it so.
She nurtured me with that same care
That made her garden grow.

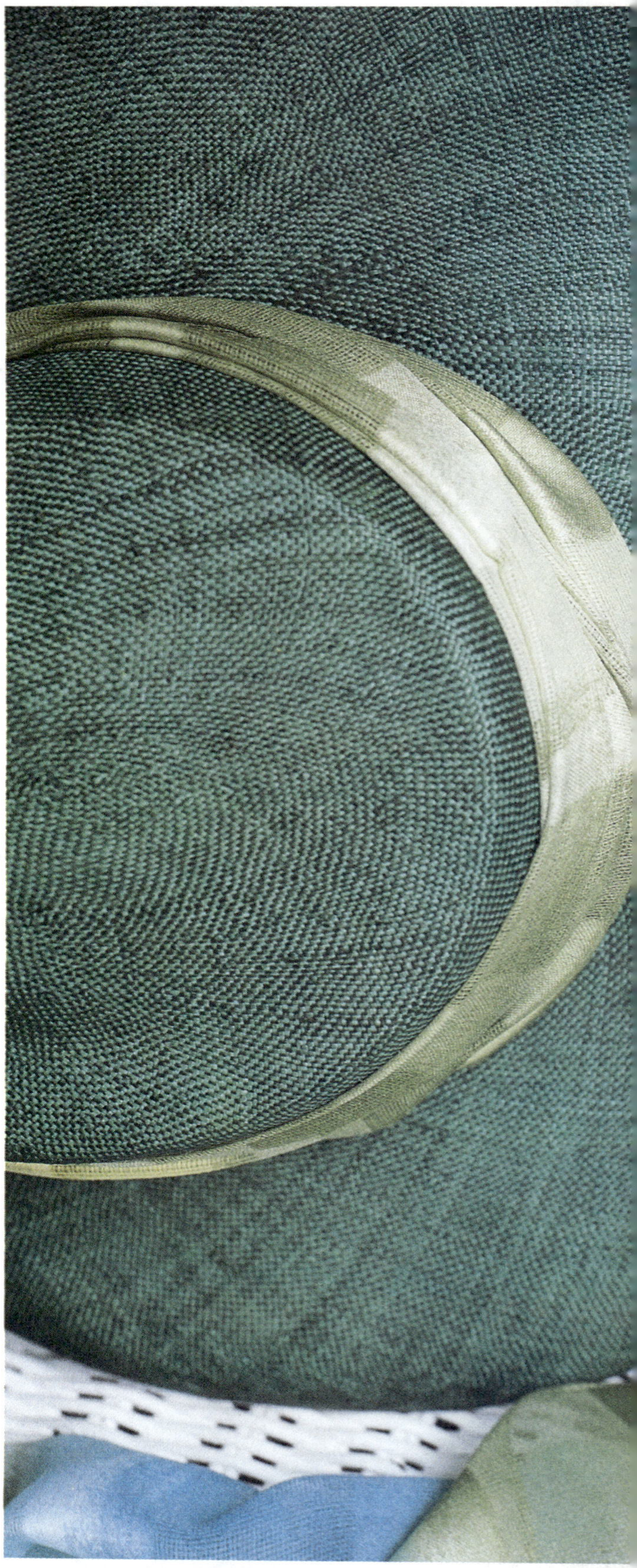

Here is an inviting respite to share on a spring day—enjoying the outdoors and sampling fresh strawberries. Photograph by Dianne Dietrich Leis.

Border: Strawberries tempt with vivid color and sweet flavor. Photograph by Daniel E. Dempster.

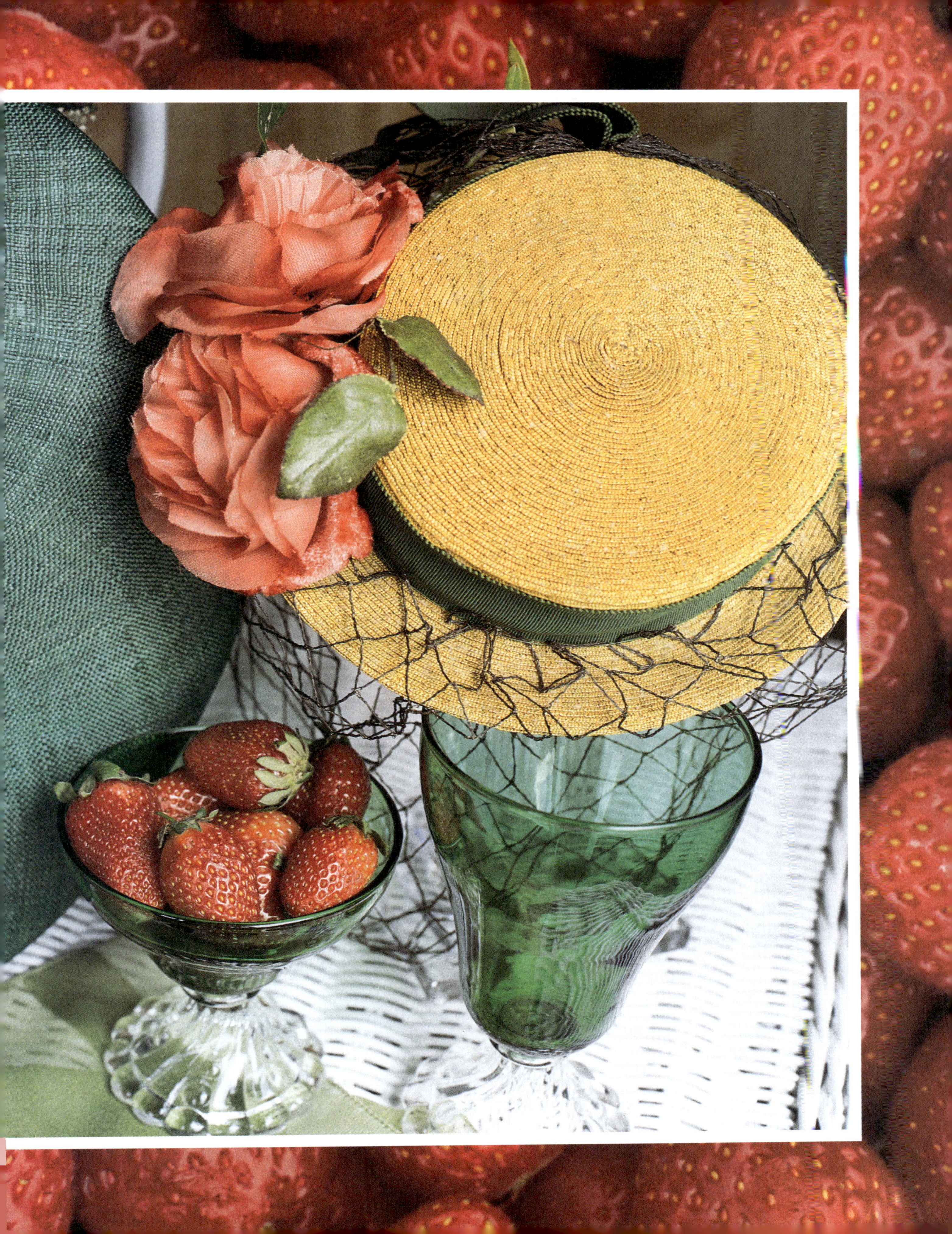

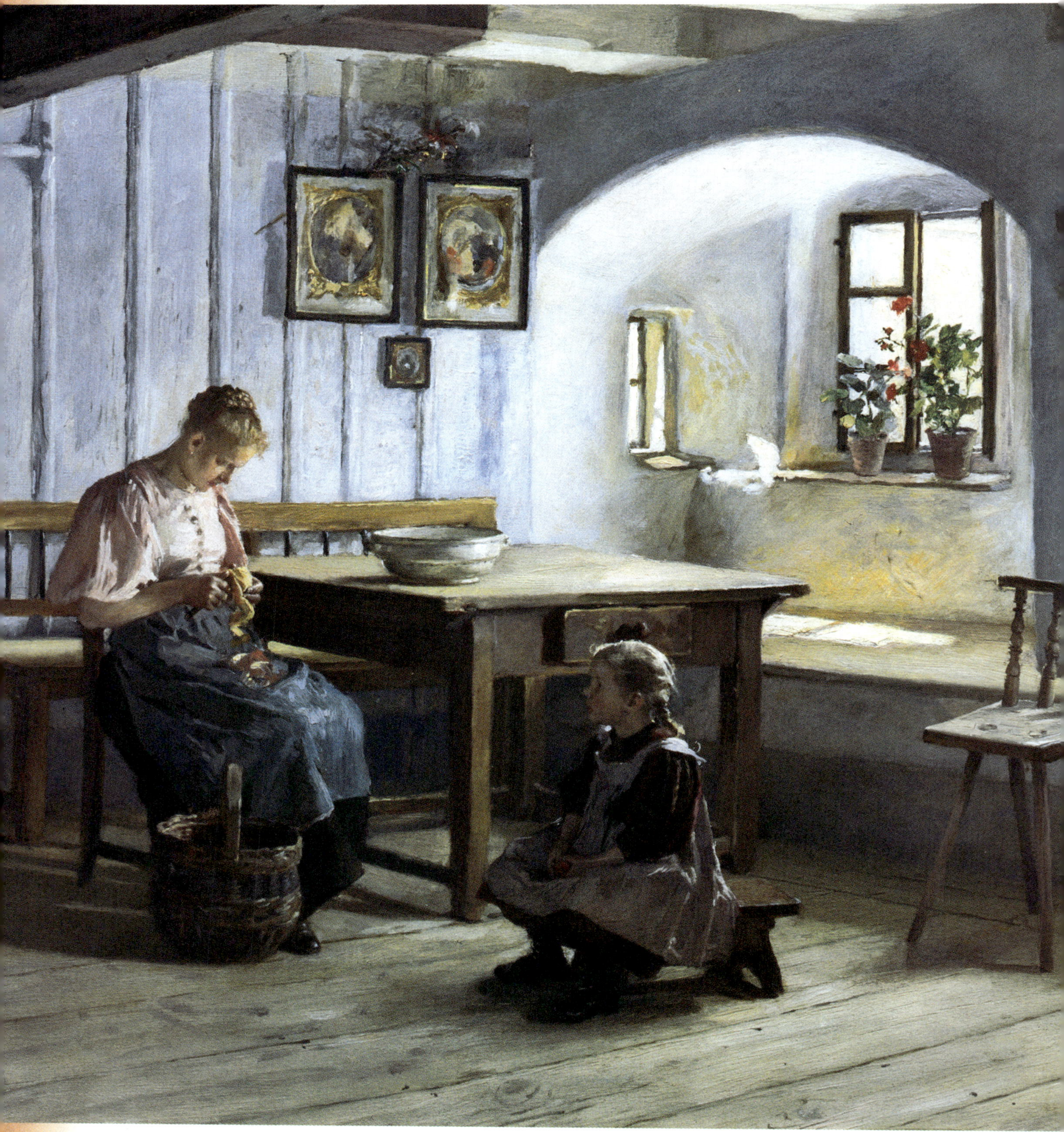

A lesson in kitchen wisdom is depicted in the painting, Making Apple Pie, *by Gustave Auguste Hessl (1849-1926). Image from Fine Art Photographic Library, Ltd., London/Polak Gallery.*

REMEMBER WHEN

Laura Ingalls Wilder

LITTLE HOUSE IN THE OZARKS: THE REDISCOVERED WRITINGS

May 1923

"The days are just filled with little things, and I am so tired of doing them," wailed a friend recently. Since then I have been thinking about little things or these things we are in the habit of thinking small, although I am sure our judgment is often at fault when we do so.

Working in the garden; taking care of the poultry, calves, and lambs; milking the cows; and all the other chores that fall to the lot of farm women may each appear small in itself, but the results go a long way in helping to "feed the world." Sometimes I try to imagine the people who will eat the eggs I gather or the butter from my cream and who will wear the clothes made from the wool of the lambs I help to raise.

Doing cut up fingers, kissing hurt places, and singing bedtime songs are small things by themselves; but they will inculcate a love for home and family that will last through life and help to keep America a land of homes.

Putting up the school lunch for the children or cooking a good meal for the family may seem insignificant tasks as compared with giving a lecture, writing a book, or doing other things that have a larger audience; but I doubt very much if, in the ultimate reckoning, they will count for as much.

When cooking, think of yourself as a chemist, combining different ingredients into a food that will properly nourish human bodies—then the work takes on dignity and interest. Surely a family well-nourished with healthful food so that the boys and girls grow up strong and beautiful while their elders reach a hale old age, is no small thing.

It belittles us to think of our daily tasks as small things, and, if we continue to do so, it will

We will feel an added dignity and poise from the fact that our everyday round of duties is as important as any other part of the work of the world.

in time make us small. It will narrow our horizon and make of our work just drudgery.

There are so many little things that are really great, and when we learn to look beyond the insignificant-appearing acts themselves to their far-reaching consequences, we will "despise not the day of small things." We will feel an added dignity and poise from the fact that our everyday round of duties is as important as any other part of the work of the world.

And just as a little thread of gold, running through a fabric, brightens the whole garment, so women's work at home, while only the doing of little things, is like the golden gleam of sunlight that runs through and brightens all the fabric of civilization.

Readers' Reflections

Readers are invited to submit original poetry for possible publication in future issues of IDEALS. *Please send typed copies only; manuscripts will not be returned. Writers receive payment for each published submission. Send material to Readers' Reflections, Ideals Publications, 535 Metroplex Drive, Suite 250, Nashville, Tennessee 37211.*

Rose

Mary Beth Bracy
Plattsburgh, New York

My flower of love,
My child of grace,

My sun through the clouds,
My rose in a vase,

My own precious gift,
The greatest ever—

My little girl,
I'll love you forever.

Nuptials

Karen A. Baughan
Luray, Virginia

Bower of roses, candles of irises,
Perfume of lilac walls,
Carpet of violets, ceiling of sunshine,
Tender green shrubbery halls–
These form the setting, the chancel awaiting
The mystical, seasonal vows
Spoken in hush at a marriage event
That June alone allows.
This wedding of spring and summer occurs
Under new warmth of the sun,
But deep in in their hearts the seasons know
That love has just begun.

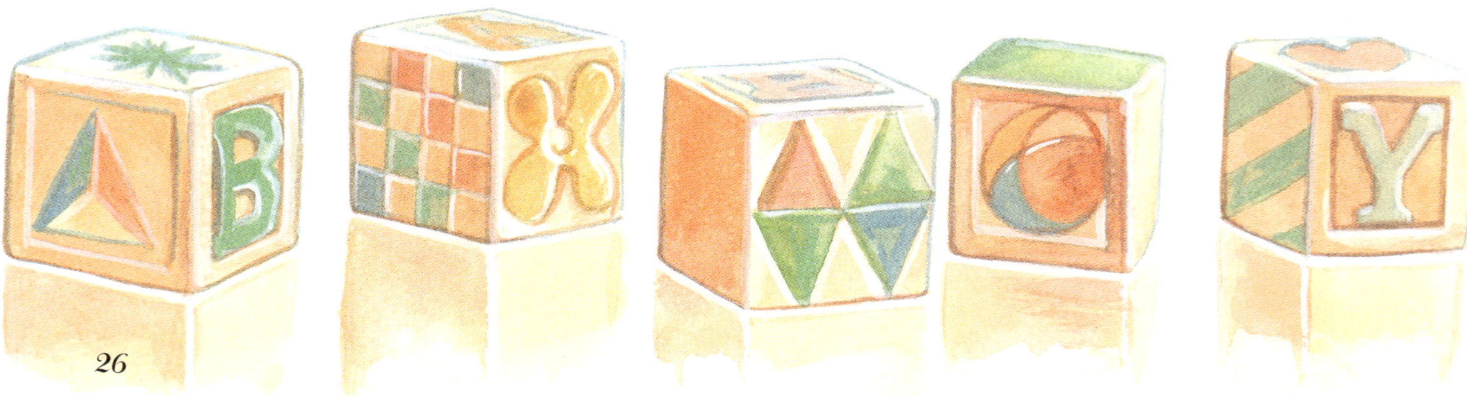

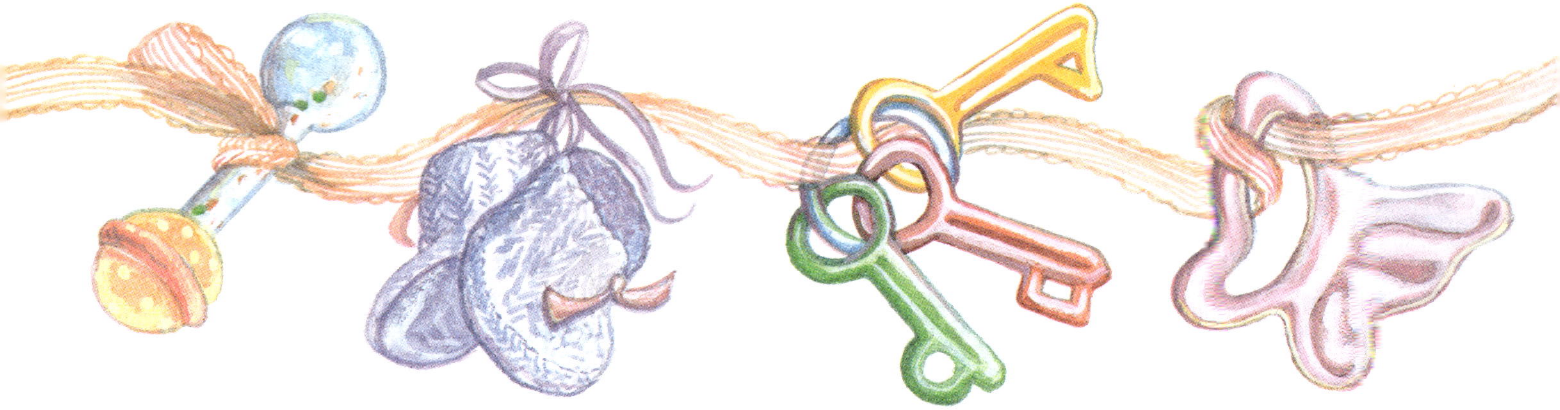

My Mother Taught Me

Irene K. Palko
Botkins, Ohio

My mother taught me:
Wake up with a smile,
Walk at least a mile,
Drink juice, eat toast,
Try hard not to boast.
Think with a clear head,
Wear a dash of red,
Smile.
Give a friend a helping hand,
From your socks shake the sand.
Feel the warm sun,
Get to know the trees,
Appreciate little things,
Especially honeybees.
When the day is done,
Ask yourself,
"Did I have fun?"

Hello, It's Spring

Charlotte Partin
Sumter, South Carolina

Spring can't come to the phone right now;
She's flown to distant hills
To dabble speckles on the fawn
And fling out daisy spills.

When she re-mosses forest floors
And pulls back winter's pall,
She'll batten down a daffodil
And then return your call.

To teach the wren a little song
Will take an hour or two;
And stripping birches lasts a while,
So wait, and she'll call you.

You'll know when Spring comes again,
On gentle breezes blown.
Close your eyes and smell the air,
And listen for her tone.

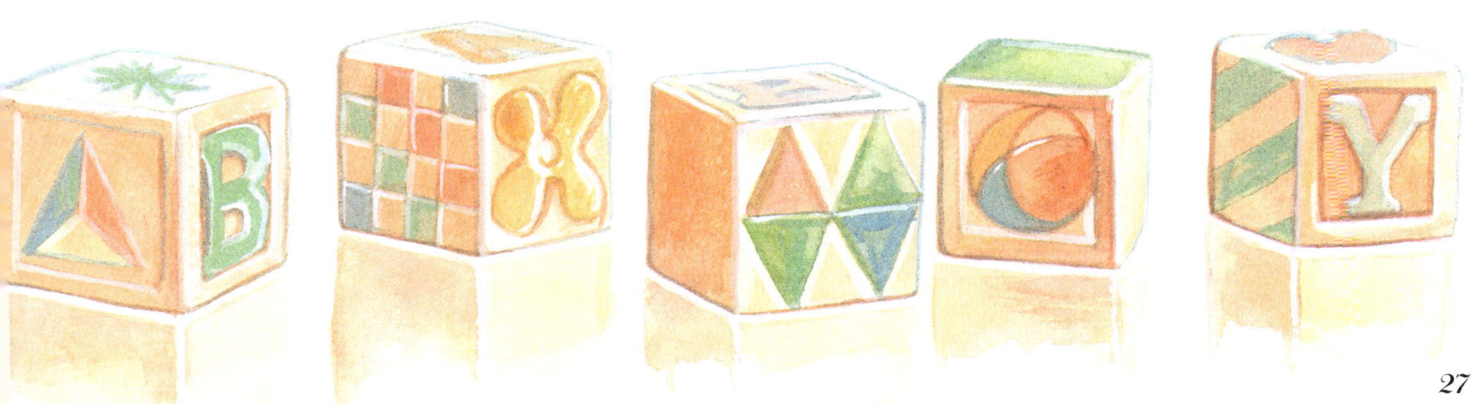

Family Recipes

Strawberry Cobbler

Faye Field, Longview, Texas

- 1/2 cup butter
- 3/4 cup flour
- pinch salt
- 2 teaspoons baking powder
- 1 3/4 cups sugar
- 3/4 cup milk
- 1 quart strawberries, sliced

Preheat oven to 350°F. Melt butter in an 8-by-8-inch baking pan. Set aside. In a medium bowl, sift together flour, salt, baking powder, and sugar. Stir milk into dry mixture just until ingredients are moistened. Fold in strawberries. Pour batter slowly into pan. Bake 1 hour. Makes 9 servings.

Strawberry-Rhubarb Pie

Marjorie Goodall, Stillwell, Oklahoma

- 1 1/2 cups rhubarb, sliced
- 1 1/2 cups strawberries, sliced
- 1 cup sugar
- 1/4 cup flour
- 2 9-inch unbaked pie crusts
- 1 teaspoon grated orange rind
- 2 tablespoons butter, cut up
- 1 tablespoon sugar, optional

Preheat oven to 425°F. In a large bowl, combine rhubarb and strawberries. Sprinkle sugar with flour over fruit. Fold in. Pour into one unbaked pie crust. Sprinkle with orange rind. Dot with butter. Cover with remaining pie crust; seal and crimp edge. Cut several slits in top crust. Sprinkle with sugar, if desired. Protect edges of crust with aluminum foil. Bake 40 minutes or until crust is slightly browned. Makes 6 to 8 servings.

Company Strawberry Pie

Tara Boswell, Nineveh, Indiana

- 1 cup sugar
- 2½ tablespoons cornstarch
- 1½ cups water
- 2 drops red food coloring
- 1 3-ounce package strawberry gelatin mix
- 1 quart strawberries, sliced
- 1 8-inch prepared pie shell
- 1 8-ounce package frozen whipped topping, thawed

In a medium saucepan, mix sugar and cornstarch. Add water and stir in food coloring to desired color. Boil over medium heat until mixture coats spoon, stirring occasionally. Remove from heat. Stir in gelatin mix until dissolved and mixture becomes the consistency of pudding. Fold in strawberries and pour into prepared pie crust. Refrigerate until firm. Serve with a dollop of whipped topping. Makes 6 to 8 servings.

Easy Strawberry Preserves

Pearl Craig, Fort Smith, Arkansas

- 4 cups sugar
- ½ cup water
- 2 cups strawberries, hulled and crushed
- 2 cups small strawberries, whole

In a medium saucepan, combine 2 cups sugar with water. Boil over medium-high heat until clear, stirring constantly. Stir in crushed strawberries and cook until juice turns red. Add remaining 2 cups sugar and whole strawberries. Boil slowly for 8 minutes, stirring occasionally. Set aside to cool. Once cool, store covered in refrigerator. Keeps 2 to 3 days. Use as a topping for waffles, ice cream or angel-food cake. Makes approximately 3 cups.

Tempt your family and friends with the unique sweetness of fresh strawberries in these favorite recipes. We would love to try your favorite recipe too. Send a typed copy to Ideals Publications, 535 Metroplex Drive, Suite 250, Nashville, Tennessee 37211. Payment will be provided for each recipe published.

For My Mother

Emily Sargent Councilman

I think true mothers everywhere
Are gently brushed by angel wings,
And in some stillness hear God speak,
"Your child can do great things."

And so a mother dreams her dreams
And has the love to see,
In every stumbling, struggling child,
What God knows he can be.

How can I fail to seek His will
And follow in His way,
When I have known my mother's prayer
Lifting me to heaven each day?

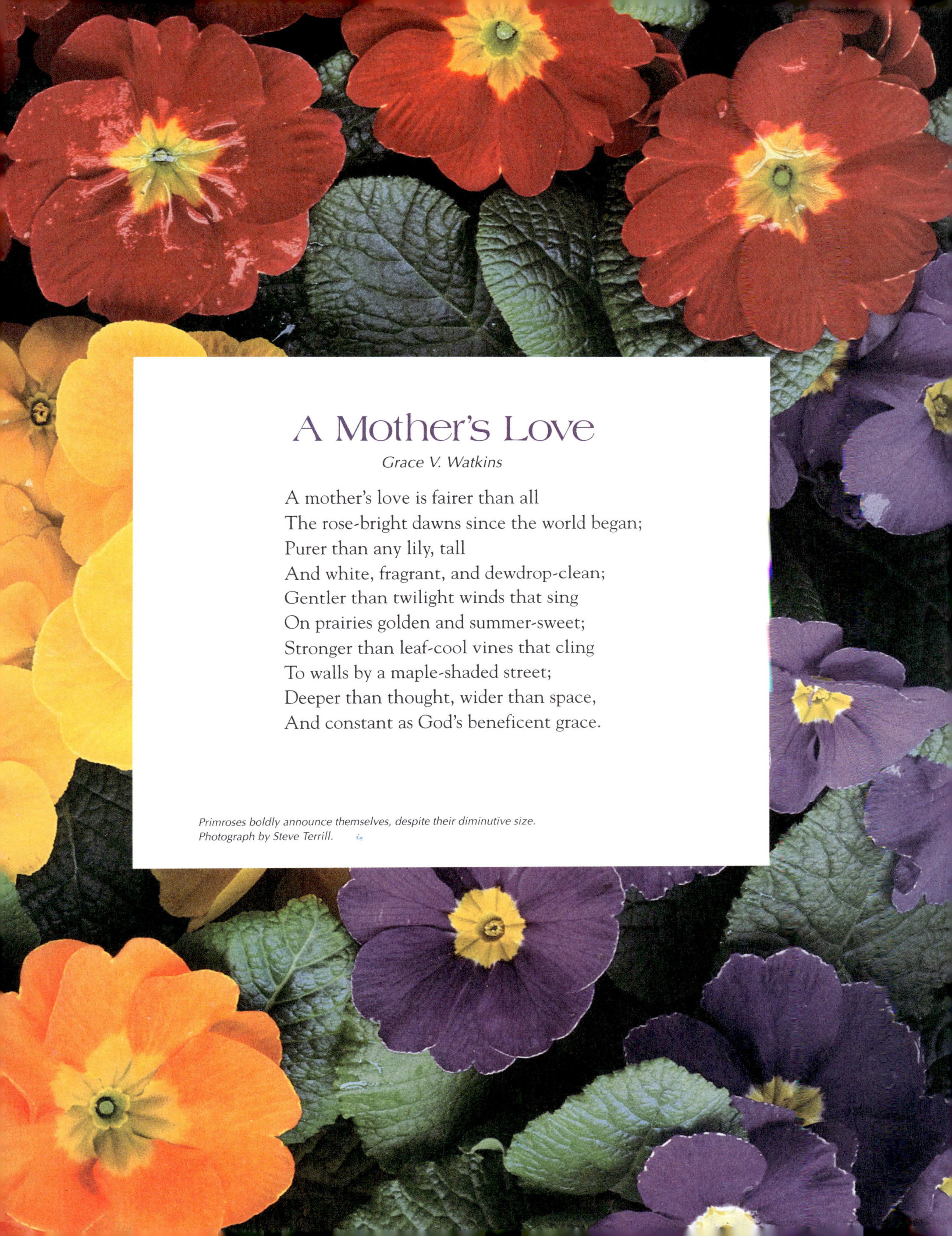

A Mother's Love

Grace V. Watkins

A mother's love is fairer than all
The rose-bright dawns since the world began;
Purer than any lily, tall
And white, fragrant, and dewdrop-clean;
Gentler than twilight winds that sing
On prairies golden and summer-sweet;
Stronger than leaf-cool vines that cling
To walls by a maple-shaded street;
Deeper than thought, wider than space,
And constant as God's beneficent grace.

Primroses boldly announce themselves, despite their diminutive size.
Photograph by Steve Terrill.

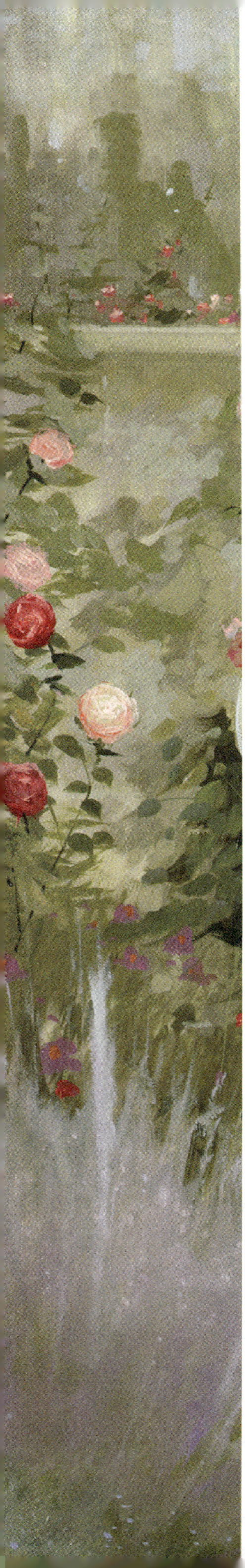

For the Children

Come Dance with Me, Mama

Eileen Spinelli

Come dance with me, Mama;
This step isn't hard.
We'll tap through the kitchen
And twirl through the yard.

Come swing with me, Mama;
The sky is so blue.
I think we can touch it
Together, don't you?

Come bake with me, Mama,
A mud pie supreme.
We'll frost it with moss
That we find by the stream.

And next we'll pretend
There's a wedding today.
You'll be the bride
With a daisy bouquet.
I'll be the flower girl.
I'll fix your hair.
Whom will you marry?
Of course—Teddy Bear.

Come play with me, Mama;
Come skip in the sun.
You've worked long enough, now
It's time for some fun.

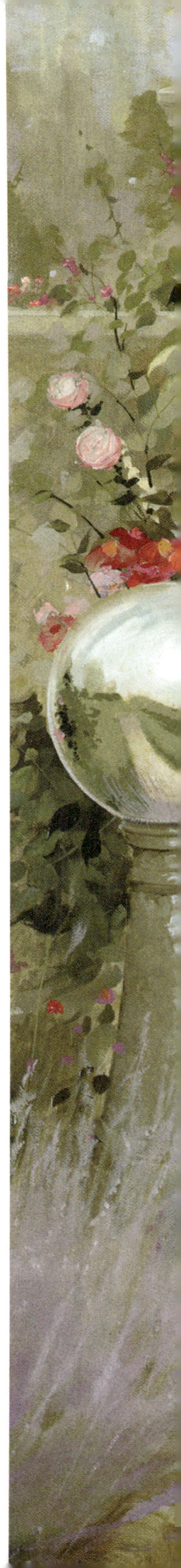

A sweet young girl offers an irresistible invitation to play make-believe in an original oil painting, entitled Wingless Angel, *by Donald Zolan.*

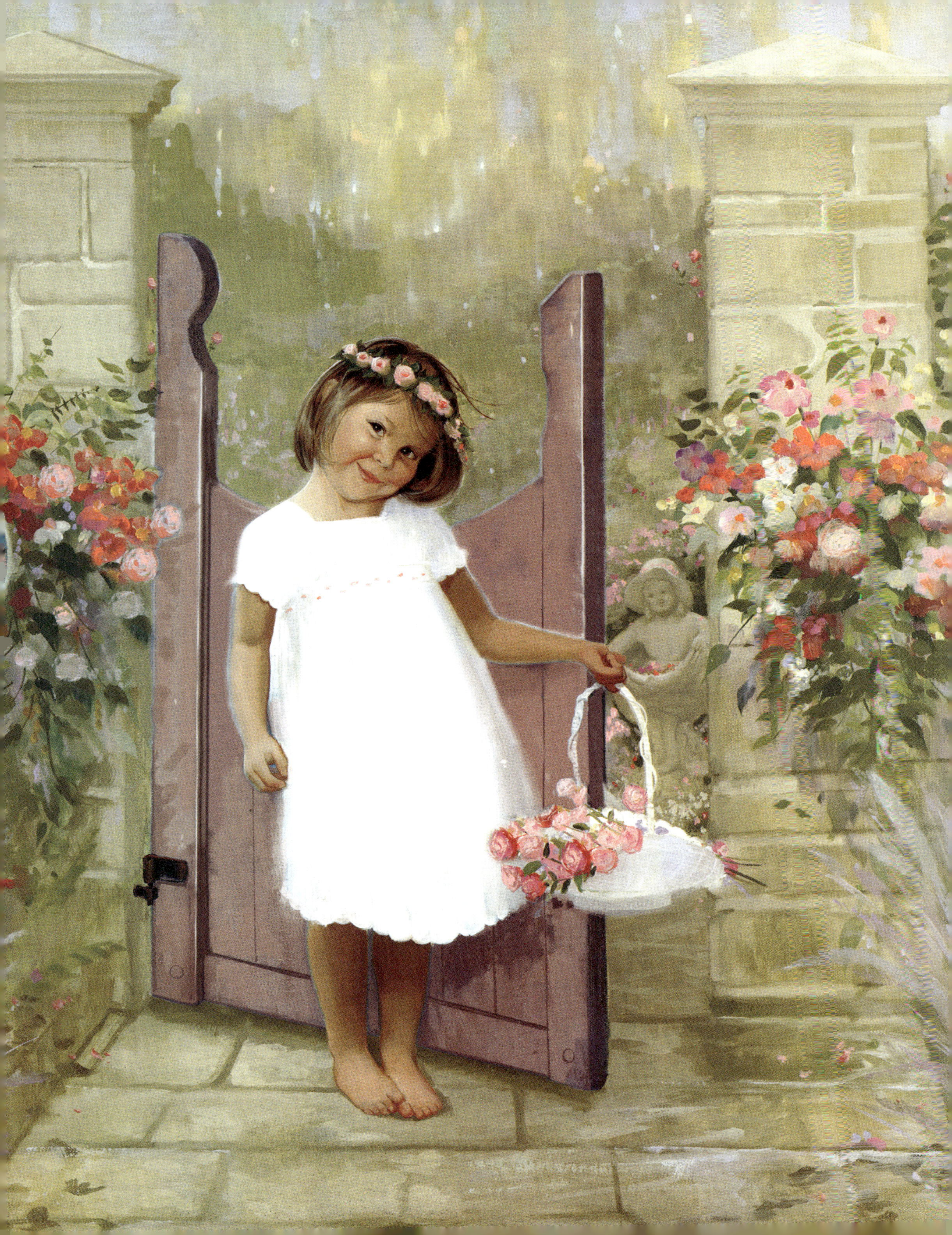

Collector's Corner

Laurie Hunter

Tussie-Mussie Holders

I began a tradition of giving certain unique gifts to friends and family right after my engagement. I was looking through a magazine in search of ideas for the wedding when a picture of a beautiful bride caught my eye. It was not her dress or hairstyle or veil that enchanted me. It was an exquisitely detailed vase pinned at the waist of her gown that held a tiny bridal bouquet—a tussie-mussie holder that secured a posy of snowdrops, symbolizing hope for a wonderfully happy married life.

I ordered the precise one for my wedding—a sterling silver holder, intricately designed, with a heart-shaped handle and an engravable charm. I loved the idea of selecting meaningful flowers for my own bridal tussie-mussie bouquet, as the Victorians had done, and binding the stems into a special holder that could be passed down the generations.

Bridesmaids gifts—why couldn't these precious miniature vases be the special gifts for my bridemaids? I selected tiny vials in a satin pewter finish for the bridesmaids to wear in their hair, naturally ordering an extra one as a keepsake for myself. The mothers, I decided, would also need tussie-mussie holders. I found striking cobalt-blue glass holders encased in silver for the mothers to pin on their dresses, again ordering just one more for myself. After much hunting, I found the perfect centerpiece for the reception as well. It was a silver filigree Victorian bridal tussie-mussie holder, with a large holder at the center surrounded by a ring of six bridesmaids holders.

And the tradition continues—for bridal showers I often give a milk-glass tussie-mussie, knowing it is a thoughtful and much-appreciated gift. For the babysitter's prom, a silver-plated brooch for the corsage was perfect. I have one, too, which I wear to weddings, christenings, showers, and other special events. My collection also includes a trumpet-shaped tussie-mussie stand I found at a Victorian bridal boutique; it beautifully displays anniversary flowers from my husband on our dining or bedside table. My favorite one is a pink, diamond-studded, tussie-mussie brooch, given to me by my husband on Mother's Day. The diamonds form tiny rosebuds encircling the holder. Each year it holds a meaningful tussie-mussie: one year jonquils for affection, another year lilies for sweetness, but every year a red rose at the center for pure and ardent love.

My favorite one is a pink tussie-mussie brooch given to me by my husband on Mother's Day.

Say It with Flowers

If you would like to collect tussie-mussie holders, the following information may be helpful.

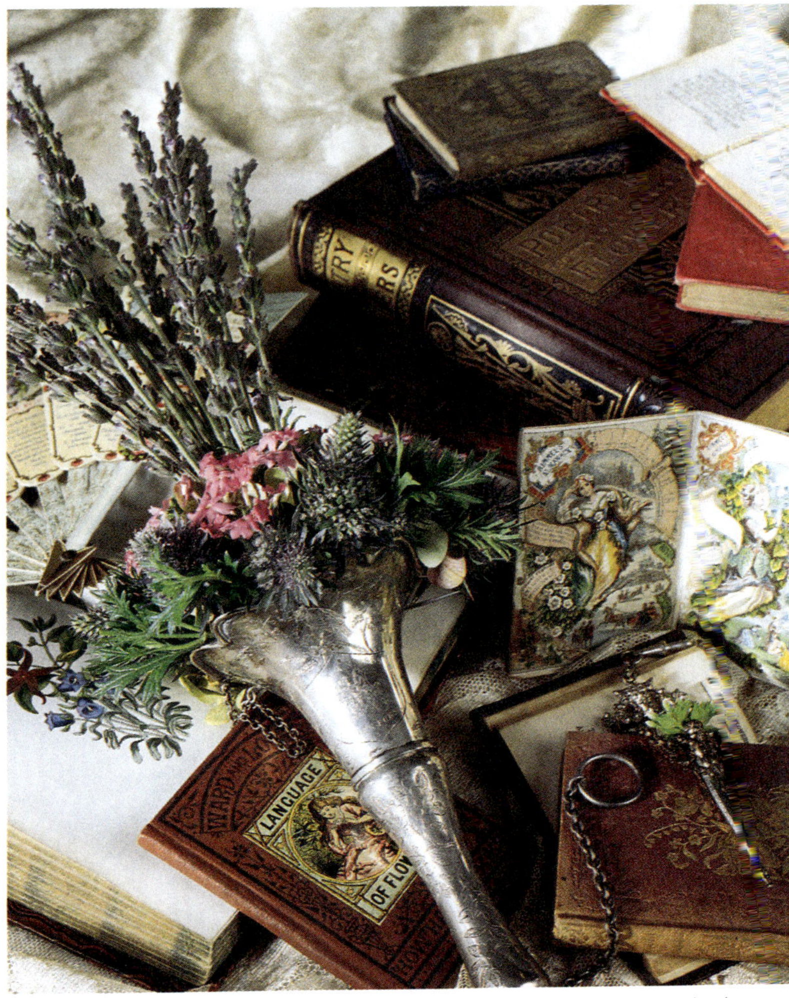

A sterling silver tussie mussie, filled with lavender and sea holly, rests upon antique books on the language of flowers. Photograph by Jessie Walker.

What Is a Tussie-Mussie?

- A tussie-mussie is a little cluster of sweet-smelling herbs and flowers tied together. It may also be called a *posy* or a *nosegay*, and there are several spellings of the term itself.
- The word *tussie* refers to the knot of flowers. The word *mussie* refers to the holder, originally damp moss that kept the flowers and herbs fresh.

Tussie and Mussie History

- The earliest tussie-mussies were used for medicinal purposes. Judges carried herbs wrapped in moss holders en route to the courts to keep contagious diseases at bay. Brides carried posies of fragrant flowers bound in damp moss to create a protective aura around themselves.
- In the 1800s, ladies used diminutive cone vases to hold their dainty bouquets.
- Moss holders were cumbersome to hold or wear during dinner or dancing; they also did not last long. By Victorian times, tussie-mussie holders were created by jewelry makers. Some were exquisitely detailed and others were simple.

Tussie-Mussie Holders

- Well-made tussie-mussie holders are like tiny works of art, each one lovingly fashioned to convey heartfelt sentiments and wishes.
- During the nineteenth century, it was considered more suitable for young women to wear flowers than jewelry.
- Some tussie-mussie holders were tiny glass vials tucked into the bosom of a dress. Others were worn in a lady's hair, at her waist, or pinned onto her dress like a brooch.

Modern Tussie-Mussie Holders May Be:

- Porcelain adorned with crystals
- Engraved with a couple's initials or full names
- Larger than antique ones in order to accommodate modern bouquet styles
- Remarkable reproductions of vintage holders.

Some collectors also branch out to include hanging tussie-mussie holders and centerpiece stands.

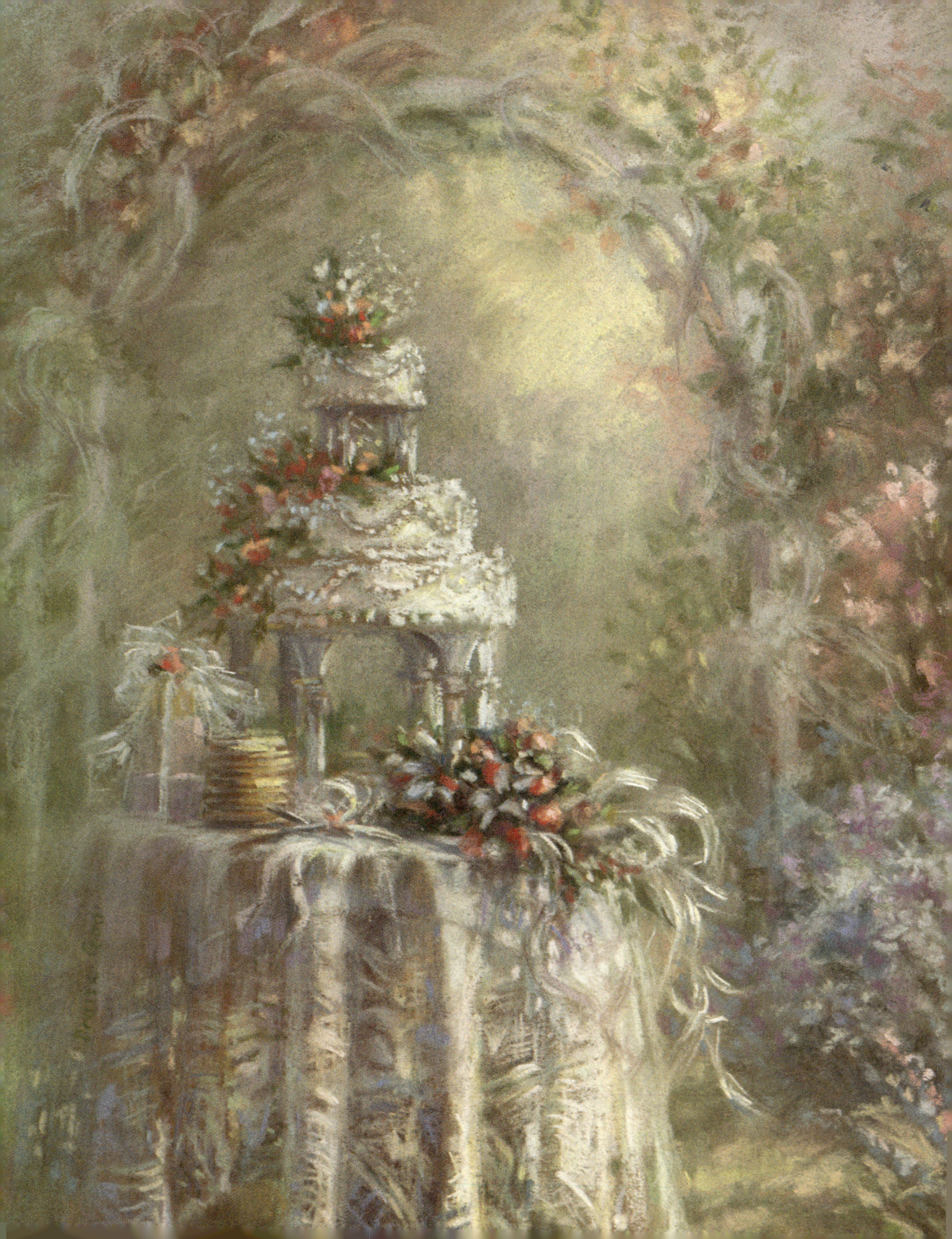

Only Daughter

D. A. Hoover

What little girl is this
Who lifts her veil to kiss
The handsome groom?
Why do we gather here
And drop a silver tear
In this candlelit room?
Is it that we must know
Our little girl will go?
Her blossoming
Will not be ours alone.
The golden sun that shone
And made us sing
Joins us to bless
Her happiness,
Like a warm and gentle flame.
She's no less ours now, we know,
Yet time that life bestows
In days ahead will never be the same.

Mother of the Groom

E. K. Alaskey

As he comes down the aisle, his bride on his arm,
The tears I held back start to flow.
Am I crying with happiness for them
Or with sadness for me? I don't know.
Oh, yes, I am pleased that they have wed,
And I share in their obvious joy;
But I remember not so long ago
This broad-shouldered man was my little boy.
Where did the time go—the days and the years—
When did all these changes take place?

How could so many seasons have passed
Since I adored the smile on his sweet baby face?
The little dirt-covered boy, where did he go—
With mud-spattered shoes and holes in his pants,
The ball-player, tree-climber, neighborhood menace,
The fresh-scrubbed teenager at his first dance?
I must not have noticed the clock ticking away
As the precious moments slipped by;
So swiftly, too quickly, he became this man—
Perhaps that's the reason I smile as I cry.

The honored tradition of the wedding cake, designed for the pleasure of the family and friends of the bride and groom, is delicately portrayed in this painting by Kathryn Andrews Fincher, entitled simply THE WEDDING.

Through My Window

Pamela Kennedy

The Wedding Shower

We were opening the mail together after dinner. There was a semi-transparent parchment envelope. Inside was a frosty card with green engraved script attached to an ivory liner with a narrow, organdy ribbon. It said:

Please join us Saturday.

It's a Wedding Shower for Kim and Harold.

Buffet Lunch at the Moana Surfrider Hotel.

P.S. It's a surprise!

"This one's for you," my husband said, tossing it to my side of the table.

I picked up the envelope and glanced at the address. "It's for us," I corrected. "Look, both our names are here. And the invitation says the shower is for Kim and Harold."

"It has ribbons," my husband said. "It's green and frilly and practically see-through. It's a girl thing. Besides, guys don't do wedding showers."

"But this is definitely a couple's shower, and it's given by the people at your office. You're stuck, Sweetie!"

I laughed. "Hey, big guy, you've navigated a warship through hostile waters, changed a tire on a stormy freeway, rebuilt your deck board by board. What's the big deal about a wedding shower? Look at it this way—there's food."

"Yeah, that's how they get you there, they offer food. And then when you're full, they make you do weird stuff. I've heard about these things."

"What, there's a male warning system out there sending periodic wedding shower bulletins?" I inquired.

"We have an information network," he offered. "I think I need to go to the hardware store."

"I'll RSVP to say we're coming," I called after him as he headed for the car. I think I heard a groan just before the garage door closed.

The groom looked shell-shocked. I could tell this was going to be a great event.

We entered the private dining room reserved for the wedding shower. The women were happily chatting about the bride and groom and the impending nuptials. The men were looking around uneasily, no doubt checking for booby traps and escape routes.

"Ever been to one of these before?" one asked.

"Are you kidding?" my uncomfortable spouse replied. The fellow nodded in solemn agreement. They joined some other males clustered together at the side of the room, looking with skepticism at the tables adorned with flowers, candles, balloons, and organza bags filled with potpourri. One guy picked up a bag and opened it, dumping a few of the multicolored balls into his palm.

"Herb! Don't eat those, they're for smelling," his wife shouted from across the room. Herb sheepishly returned the balls to the bag and retied the

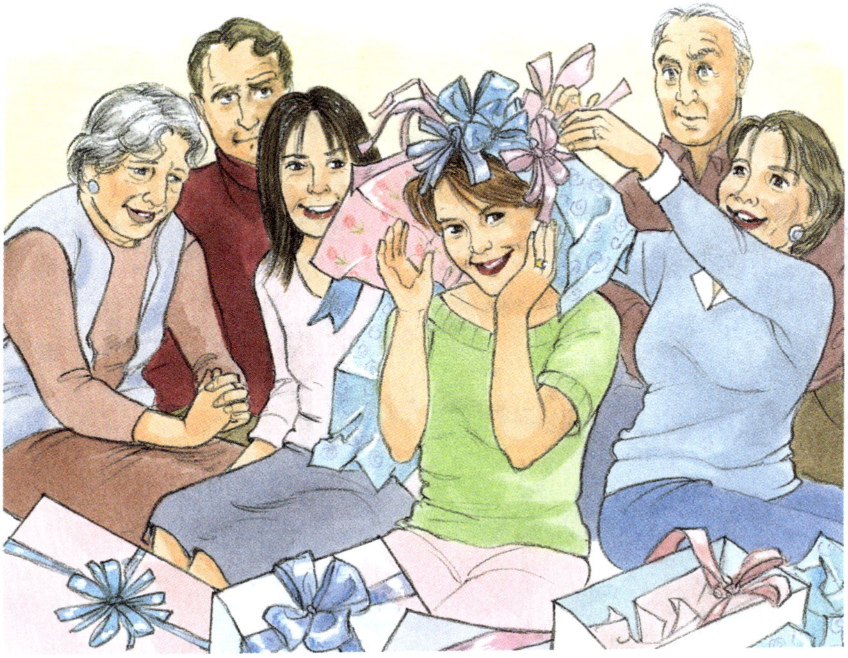

satin ribbon. Then he dangled it in front of his friends knowingly. "Look guys, car deodorizer!"

"SURPRISE!!!" we called as the happy couple entered the room. The bride blushed with shy pleasure. The groom looked shell-shocked. I could tell this was going to be a great event.

The food was wonderful and the conversation great. Even the men were beginning to feel comfortable, bantering back and forth across the beautifully decorated tables.

"Time for games!!" announced Lynn, one of the hostesses. My husband shot me a knowing look.

"I told you so," he whispered, swallowing his last bite of cake.

"This is called 'Wedding Whites'," the hostess said. We were grouped into teams of three and given ten small plastic bags filled with white substances. "You have five minutes to figure out what's in each bag—but you can't open the bags. Here's a hint. They are things found in a kitchen."

"Oh, sure," said my husband, the ultimate competitor, "It would have to be the kitchen!"

Despite his initial reluctance, he became a very enthusiastic participant, and, when the game ended, his team had won, correctly identifying seven of the ten items and winning their choice of colorful kitchen gadgets. The next game involved unscrambling wedding words. He did pretty well on that one too, despite the fact that he unscrambled *"sromongem"* to spell "moon germs" instead of "groomsmen."

"Moon germs?" I asked. He just shrugged.

When the bride and groom opened their gifts, my husband leaned over and whispered, "Why doesn't she just rip open the paper—this is taking way too long!"

"Just wait," I replied. "You'll see."

The women at the shower began constructing a bridal gown for Kim from the wrapping paper and ribbons. As she laughed, posing for photos in her tissue paper veil, I glanced at my husband. He was incredulous.

"I told you they'd do weird stuff," he muttered.

After some good-natured joking, folks started to drift away. We also said our goodbyes and headed for home. After a few miles, my eyes started to water. I sniffed a bit.

"What's that smell?" I asked, rolling down the window.

My husband opened the small storage compartment between our seats and reached inside. He pulled out a handful of emerald green organza bags.

"Car deodorizers!" he announced with a grin

Pamela Kennedy is a freelance writer of short stories, articles, essays, and children's books. Wife of a retired naval officer and mother of three children, she currently resides in Honolulu, Hawaii.

Original artwork by Meredith Johnson.

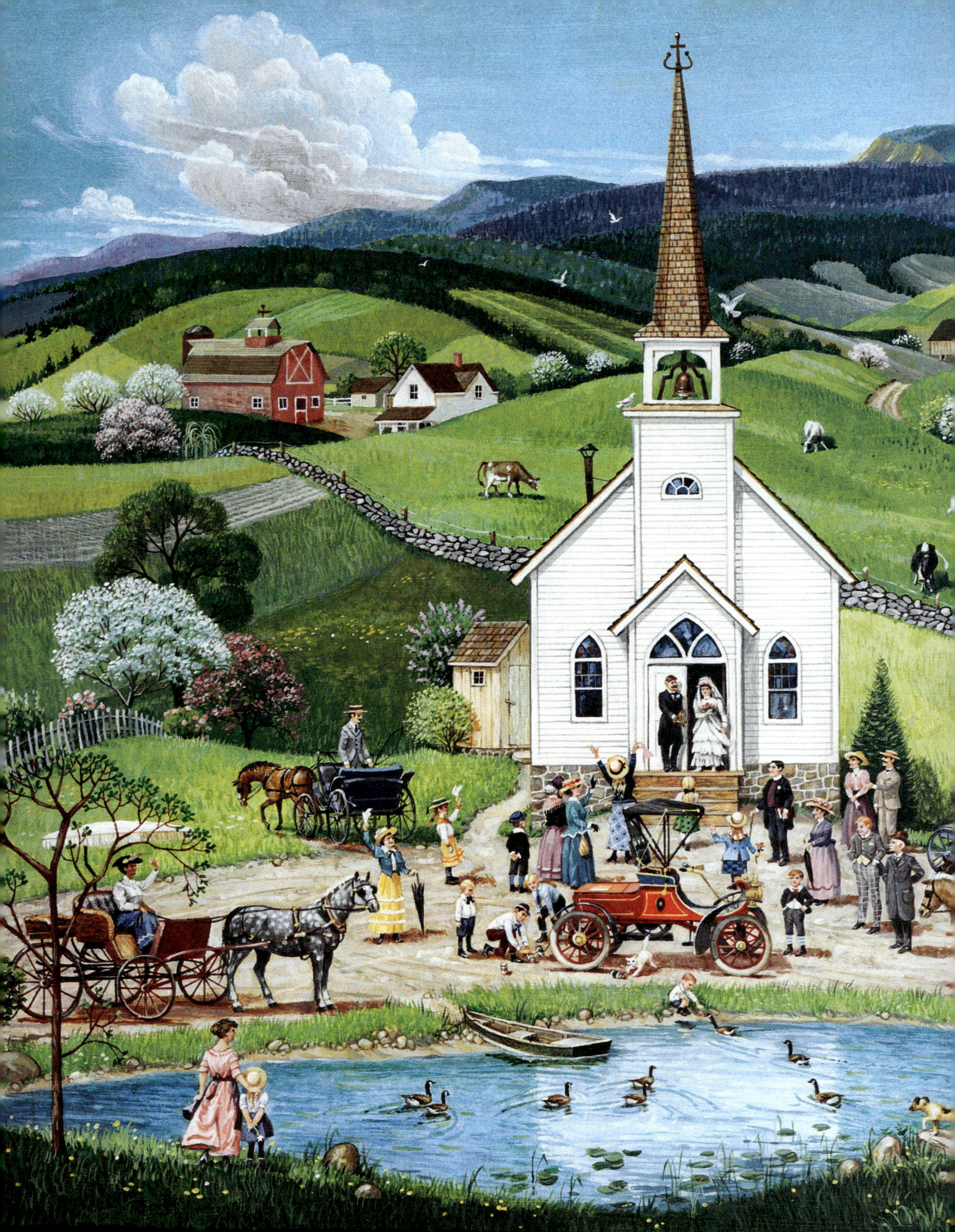

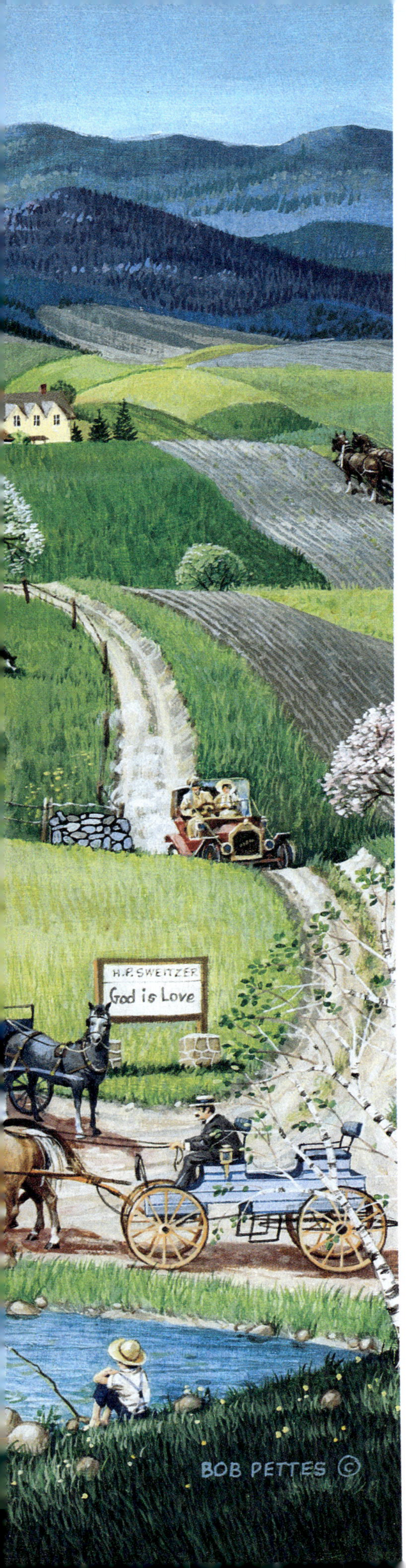

My Daughter's Wedding

Louise Weibert Sutton

It was a day of soft, pink-rose perfume
And clover-scents which lavished peace distilled.
No season ever lovelier, such bloom
In generous proportions ever freer-willed,
Than on that day when love's long dream came true
At last, in answer to my heart's sweet search.
Everything I sought is here for you—
The man, your vows, and a little country church.

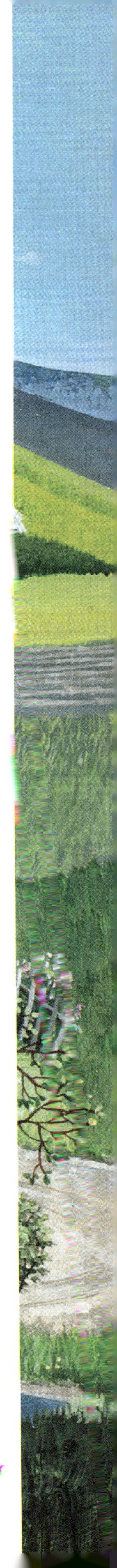

The activities of the community surrounding a young couple's wedding are presented in a painting by Bob Pettes, entitled Spring Wedding.

HANDMADE HEIRLOOM

Melissa Lester

WEDDING-RING PILLOWS

My brother's wedding will soon be here. This is the baby boy I have loved from his birth as if he were my own child. Seven years my junior, Nathan was born approximately nine months after I wished for him at Thanksgiving. Crouched in the bushes outside our home, wishbone in hand, I asked God to give me a baby boy. After some serious thought, however, I realized that I still had responsibilities, especially finishing elementary school. Perhaps Mommy could have the baby, but I would know in my heart that he was really mine. And mine he was. I adored Nathan and reported his progress daily to teachers and classmates. My heart still swells with pride when I talk about my Nathan.

As my brother takes the important life step of marriage, I want him to know that my prayers and good wishes go with him and his new bride, Shana. As a token of blessing, I have made a wedding-ring pillow for the ceremony. I hope the pillow will be a keepsake Nathan and Shana will display in their home for years to come.

As I watch the ring bearer make his way down the aisle with the wedding-ring pillow carefully held in his small hands, I know I will see flashes of the little boy I loved so dearly. I am sure I will also reflect on the generations of little boys who have accepted this responsibility in earlier weddings. Including children in the wedding party became customary during Victorian times. The children would precede the bride and her escort, following behind the rest of the bridal party. Flower girls scattered rose petals along the bridal path, and little boys carried the rings to the altar as ring bearers. Sometimes children walked in pairs behind the bride as trainbearers. The children who participated in Victorian weddings were attired formally. In particular, the ring bearer's costume

As I watch the ring bearer make his way down the aisle with the wedding-ring pillow carefully held in his small hands, I know I will see flashes of the little boy I loved so dearly.

hearkened back to the days of royal pages during the Middle Ages. Just as his predecessor carried a crown as part of a coronation, the ring bearer carries the most precious wedding symbols to the altar on a pillow trimmed with lace and ribbons.

A handmade wedding-ring pillow can add a personal touch to the modern wedding accouterments. Traditional fabric choices include white or off-white satin, silk, or brocade. Use of the same fabric and lace as the wedding dress

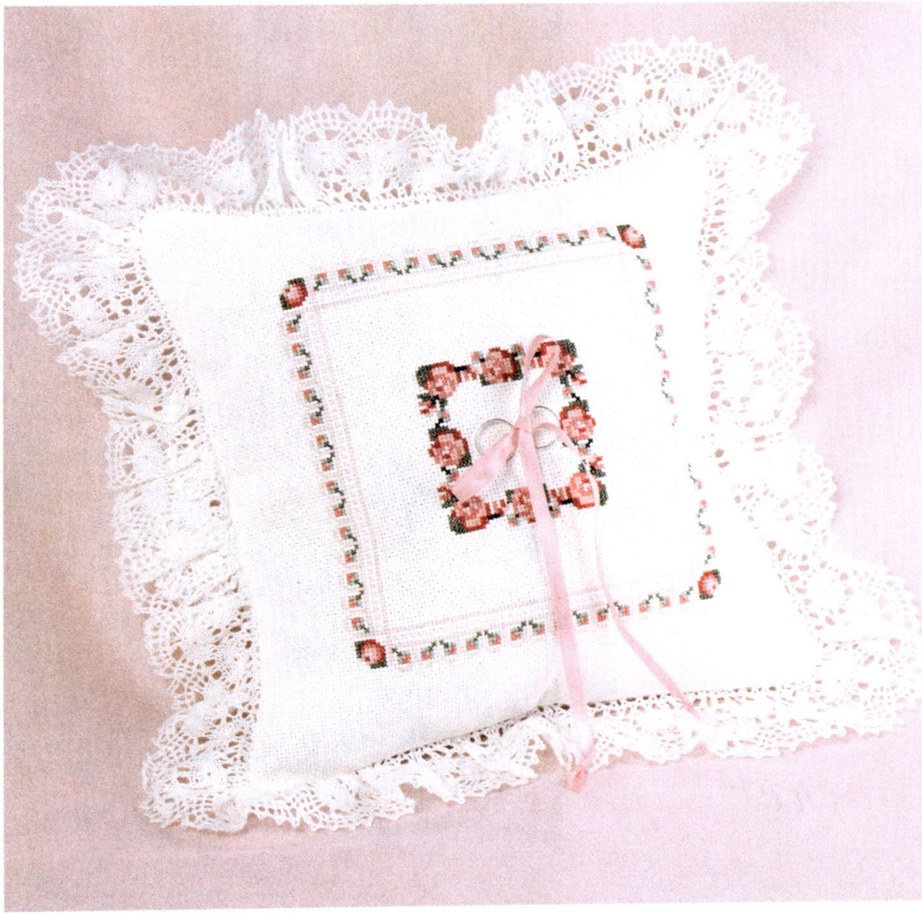

This lovely wedding ring pillow awaits the hands of the young ring bearer. Design and construction courtesy of DMC Corporation. Photograph by Jerry Koser.

makes the pillow even more special. Wedding-ring pillows are usually eight to ten inches in diameter and can be round, square, or heart-shaped. Ribbons or pieces of lace can be woven across the top of the pillow for a lovely design. A hand-sewn monogram or embroidery design adds a classic touch; pretty trims add elegance.

To make a simple wedding-ring pillow, cut two squares of fabric and two or three pieces of polyester batting. All these pieces should be the same size. Cut lengths of lace, ribbon, or other trims to decorate the pillow as desired. Some embellishments, such as embroidered designs, need to be completed before the pillow is sewn. Next, pin the chosen trim to the top square of the pillow, with right sides together and edges lined up evenly. Then pin the two fabric pieces, right sides together. Sew three sides of the pillow, and turn the design right-side out. Stuff the pillow with batting, fold the unstitched edges into the pillow, and hand-sew the remaining seam. Ribbon hand-sewn to the top of the pillow, or small decorative pockets, can hold the wedding rings in place for the ceremony; although many couples choose to attach decorative rings instead.

When Nathan and Shana walk down the aisle, I hope they will see my love for them in the wedding-ring pillow I have made for them out of silk shantung with a cluster of silk roses in the center. When the ring bearer carries the pillow to the altar, I alone will know about the secret it contains. Sewn into one of the corners is a tiny charm. The little silver wishbone is my way of reflecting on the hope that preceded my brother's arrival and the love that has watched him become the man he is today. But this small token is also my way of letting go, happy in the knowledge that his wedding day is the culmination of dreams for all who love these two special people.

Melissa Lester is a freelance writer living in Wetumpka Alabama, with her husband, two sons, and a new daughter. She contributes to a number of magazines and authored the book Giving for All It's Worth.

Dearest Mother

Kathleen S. Kelley

As I think of all you've meant to me,
I remember myself upon your knee;
Only a child, and yet I knew
That home itself was made by you.

As years have come and years have flown,
I find myself, your daughter, grown—
Realizing the price of love you pay
To keep me safe as I live each day.

So Mother, though words aren't often spoken,
You have this promise yet unbroken:
"The love you've shown along the way,
I return to you today."

Thank You, Mother

Dottlee Duggan Reid

If I had all of earth's roses
In one giant bouquet,
Mother, they could never tell you
The things I want to say.

Your love has sustained me
As a boy changed to a man;
I often took you for granted,
But you seemed to understand.

Your smile is always tender;
Your voice is sweet and kind.
The world is full of mothers,
But none's as great as mine.

I will always love you,
For time and all of eternity.
And I'll forever be grateful
For the mother God gave to me!

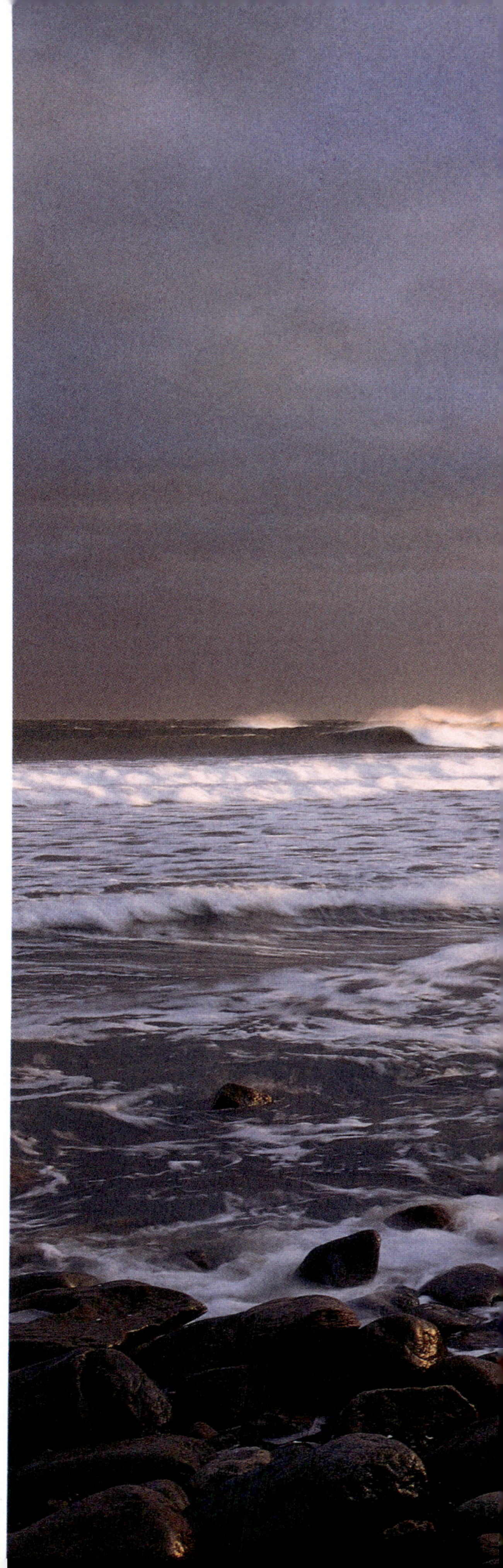

A gentle sunrise softens the morning's arrival in York, Maine. Photograph by William H. Johnson.

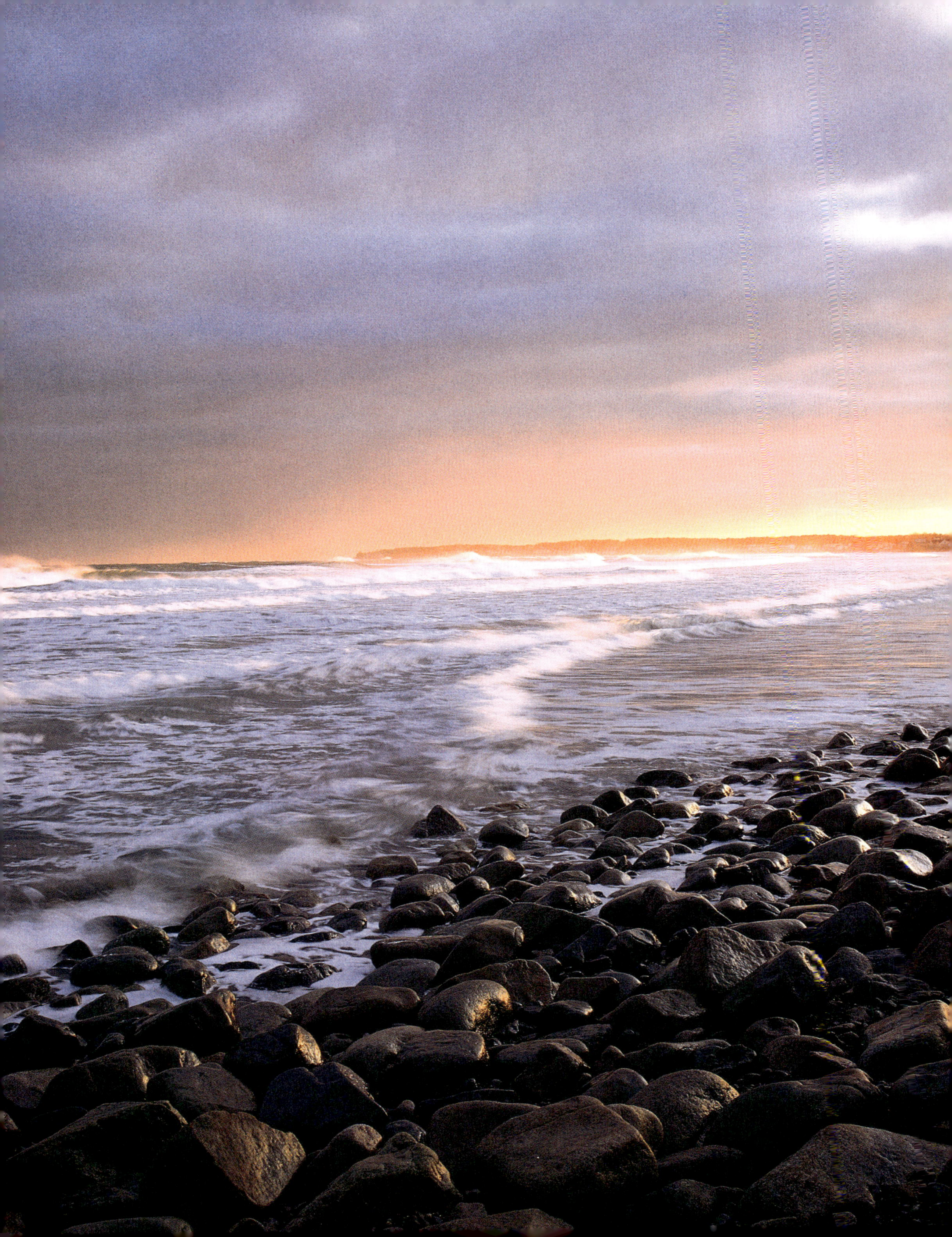

Traveler's Diary

D. Fran Morley

Niagara Falls

New York / Ontario

My first visit to Niagara Falls taught me that this display of nature's power is more impressive in reality than our meager imaginations can conceive.

Europeans arrived at the falls as long ago as 1626. The earliest "travel writer" to visit was Father Louis Hennepin, traveling the wilderness with French explorer LaSalle in 1678. The descriptive stories and sketches in his book, *A New Discovery*, no doubt relied on many of the same superlatives that writers still use today to describe the spectacle.

My visit to Niagara Falls had many conveniences that Father Hennepin's did not, and it had one big advantage—I could explore the entire history of the falls by watching a film at the Visitor's Center.

The first thing I learned from the film is that Niagara Falls is actually two separate falls, the American Falls (which includes Bridal Veil Falls) and the Canadian Horseshoe Falls. Ninety percent of the water that makes the tumble from Niagara River flows over Horseshoe Falls, falling nearly two hundred feet to the bottom. The American Falls are narrower and slightly higher, but with shorter uninterrupted drops because of large boulders that are scattered along the bottom.

I further learned that Niagara Reservation State Park became America's first state park in 1885, a designation aimed at preserving its natural beauty. The law that created the park set a precedent for the protection of the nation's natural areas. It didn't halt commercial progress, however; the falls were used to generate long distance electric current just ten years later.

I had always wondered how the falls came to be a popular wedding and honeymoon destination, and the film supplied that answer too. Napoleon's younger brother, Jerómê, brought his American bride to the falls by packhorse in 1804. I imagine their experience was quite different from today's honeymooners.

My first glimpse of Niagara Falls was breathtaking.

After the film, I strolled through the Great Lakes Garden just outside the Visitor's Center. The garden covers more than an acre and is cleverly designed to resemble a map; the Great Lakes and other waterways are represented by grassy paths. The surrounding terrain is depicted with thousands of flowers and plants. It was fun to walk along the grass and follow the route of the water from the northernmost point of Lake Superior to the falls. After that, I wanted to see the real thing.

My first glimpse of Niagara Falls was breathtaking—the falls were even bigger and more beautiful than I had thought possible. I leaned into the mist at the rail, lulled into a meditative state by the continuous rush of water. I could have stayed there all day; however, I wanted to get even nearer to the impressive torrents. So I pulled myself away to go find the Maid of the Mist boat; boats by this name have been taking visitors by the falls since 1846.

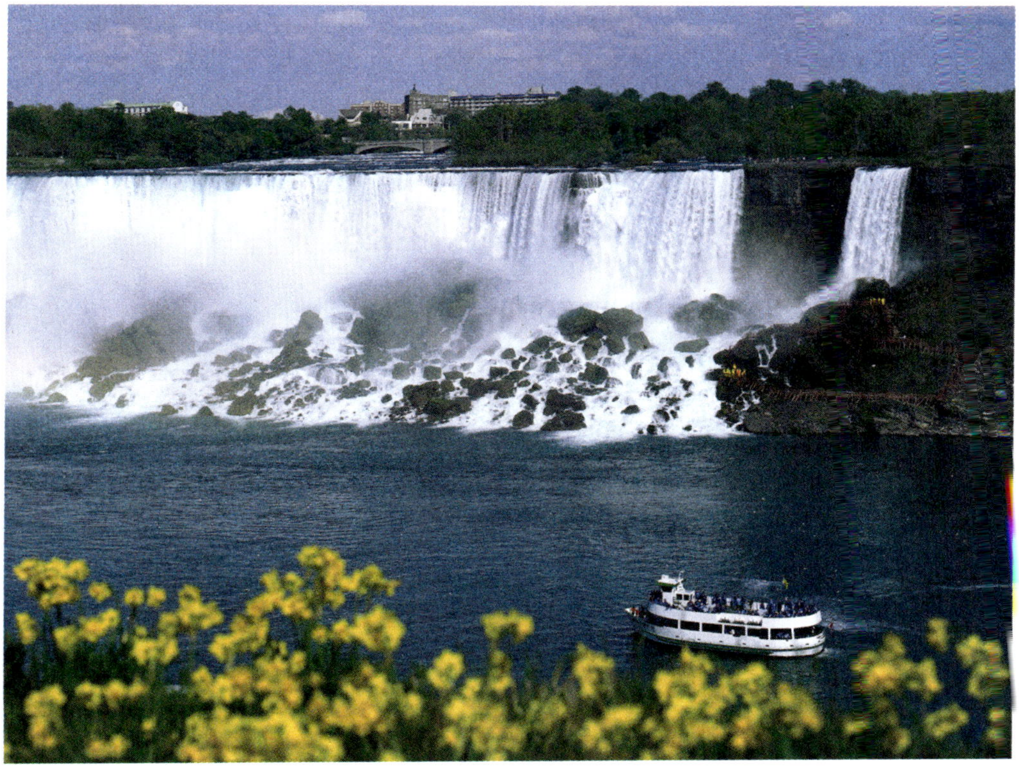

The American side of Niagara Falls continues to offer a breathtaking experience for visitors.
Photograph by Steve Vidler/Superstock.

After taking an elevator down to the water's edge, I donned a protective poncho, boarded, and the boat moved into the churning water. The sturdy boat chugged right into the rainbow that floats in the spray on sunny days. It was a thrilling and very wet ride; my view looking up toward the top of the falls was almost as grand as my view looking down had been.

Back on shore, I boarded the tram for a ride to Goat Island, in the middle of Niagara River. Although I was already soaking wet from the boat ride, I dutifully donned another poncho for my climb along the path and up the wooden stairs to the Hurricane Deck, a mere twenty feet from Bridal Veil Falls. Here the flow seems so powerful that I was surprised when a guide explained that more than half of the water in Niagara River is diverted for electric power before it even reaches the falls.

The return tram ride left me at the American Falls just in time to witness a wedding that was taking place at the very spot I had stood earlier in the day. The eternal rush of water, without beginning or end, was a fitting backdrop, and I understood why some fifty thousand couples choose to marry or honeymoon here every year. A park guide told me that most couples marry at the overlook, in the gardens, or at a nearby chapel, but some daring couples have exchanged their vows over the falls in a helicopter or hot-air balloon!

That night, as I considered my plans to hike the miles of trails throughout the Niagara River Gorge the next day, new images of Niagara Falls filled my mind. I fell into a restful sleep, lulled by the distant sound of rushing waters.

When not gallivanting around the country, travel writer Fran Morley spends time with her husband and their cat, Gracie, in beautiful Fairhope, Alabama.

Music

R. Armistead Grady

I've heard the woodwinds and the trees
Whisper a duet, and thund'ring seas
In deep-toned symphony I've heard,
And also flute-note of a mother bird.
Heard too a sweet, exotic strain
Played in a forest by the rain,
Accompanied by mountain stream—
Exquisite music—yet these seem
To fade as I turn in the path
To home and hear a baby laugh.

At Baby's Bed

Betty W. Stoffel

Child of my heart, so fast asleep,
Why do I tiptoe back to peep
Through shadowed light at your little bed
And venture a hand to your pillowed head,
Drawn by your features calm and sweet,
Wrapped in your peace that is so complete?

Child of my heart, tucked in with care,
Why do I stand so quietly there,
Hushed in your every breath so deep,
Loving you silently in your sleep,
Warmed in a special wondrous way,
Thinking what only the heart can say?

Child of my heart, it must be true
That God stands there and watches too,
For I feel as I study your little face
That reverence felt in a holy place.
Can it be that a mother's heart is led
To know God best at a baby's bed?

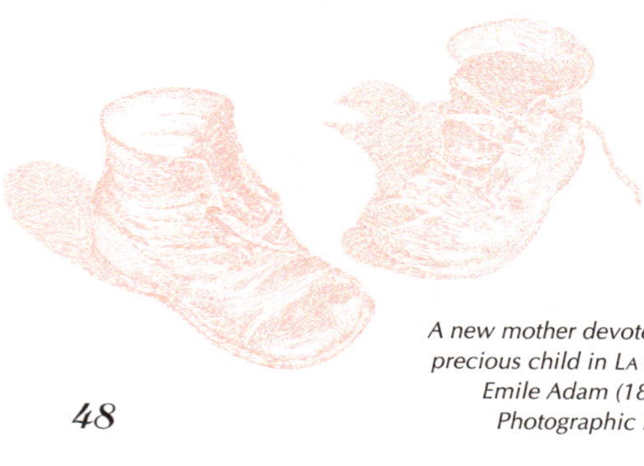

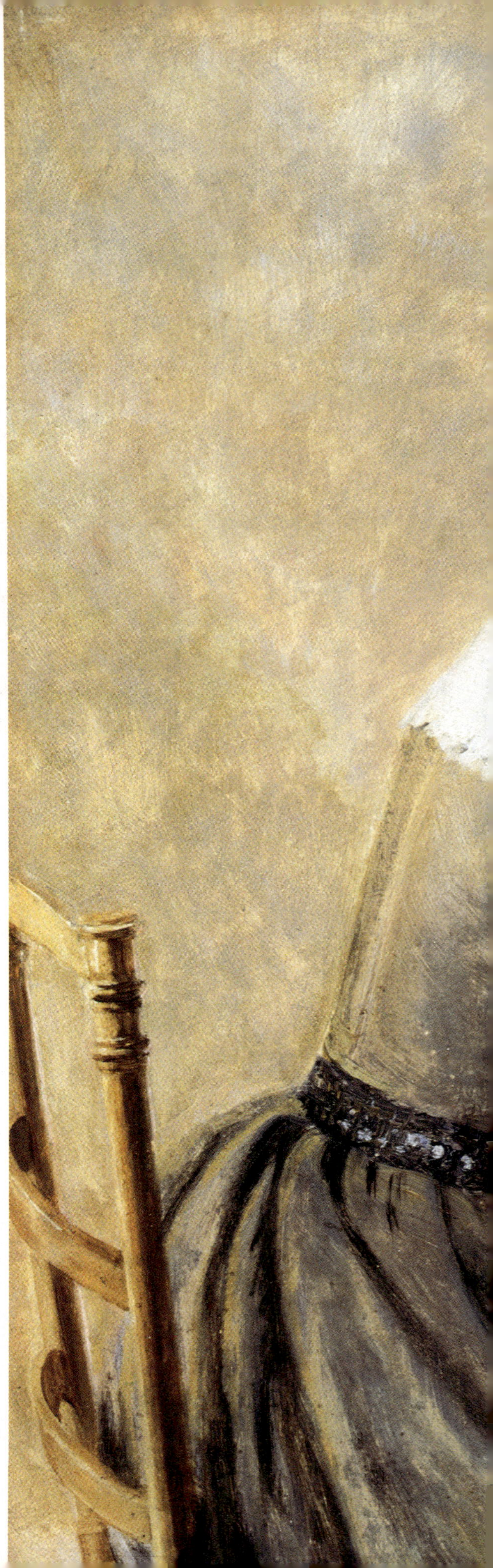

A new mother devotes her love and attention to her precious child in LA MATERNITE, *a painting by Louis-Emile Adam (1839-1937). Image from Fine Art Photographic Library, Ltd./Private Collection.*

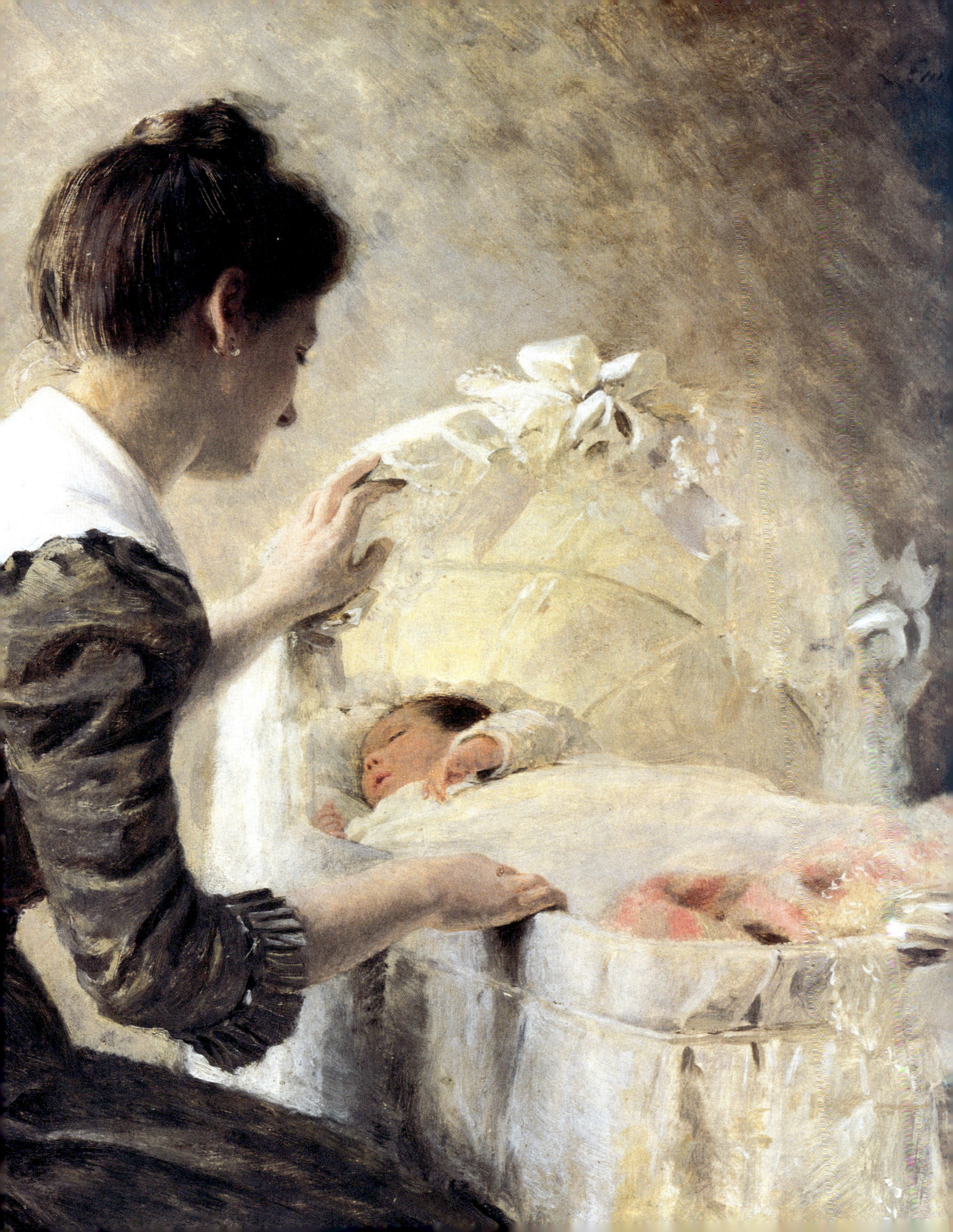

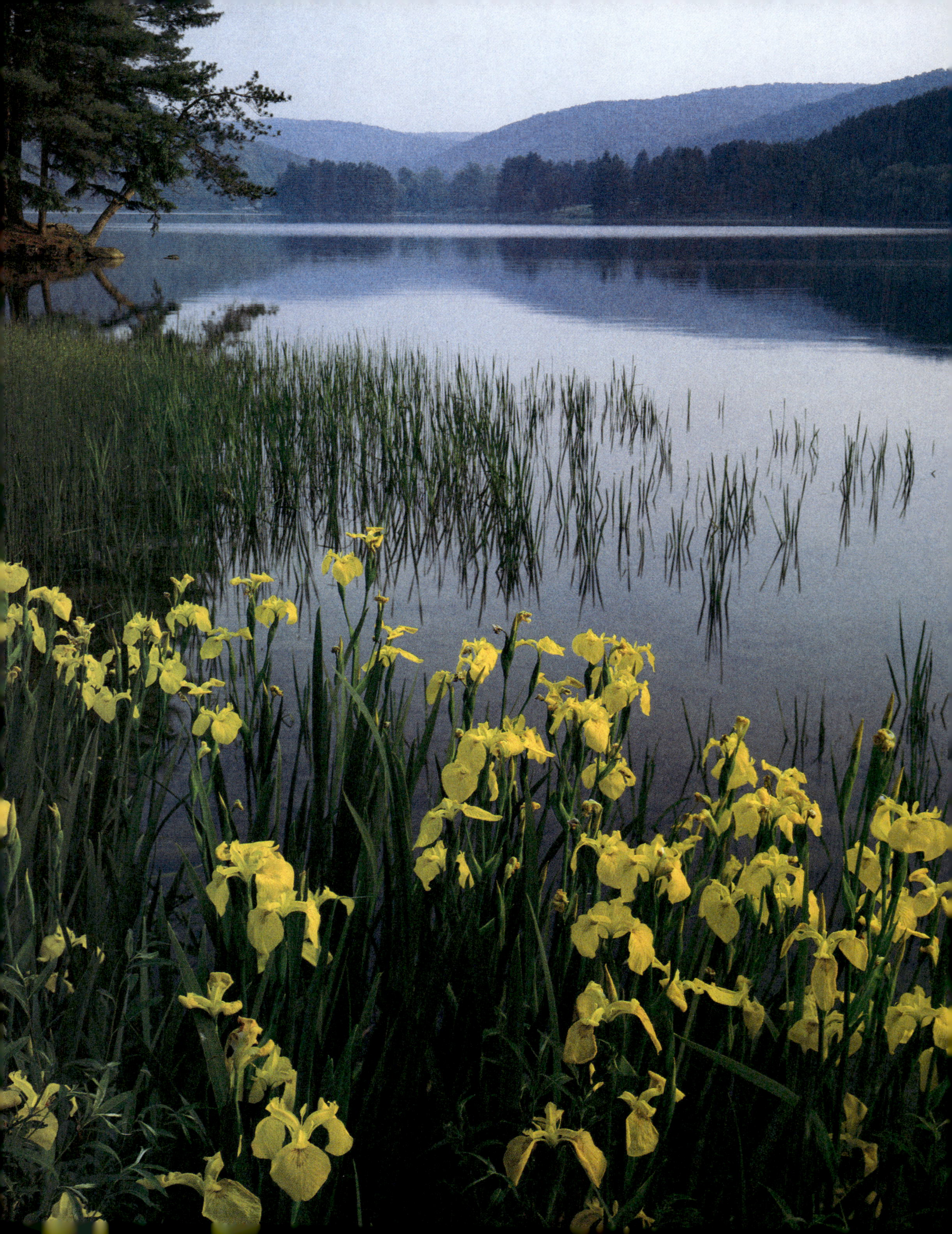

New Son

Maud Dawson

You came so quietly,
With that confident air—
Not like your sister,
Who wiggled and whooped
And kept us flustered.
Your voice very gently
Spoke to all of us there.
Then you were scooped
Into the arms of your mother
And gave to us another
Word for sweet love—"brother."

Adopting a Child

Lisa C. Ragan

Though I was not the chosen vessel,
I have waited just the same.
Pregnant only with anticipation—
Praying, dreaming, planning.

And when you come I will know
You are so much mine for this
Too-short moment. And in the next,
A grown being set free again.

And I will praise God for your coming—
An angel in my life.

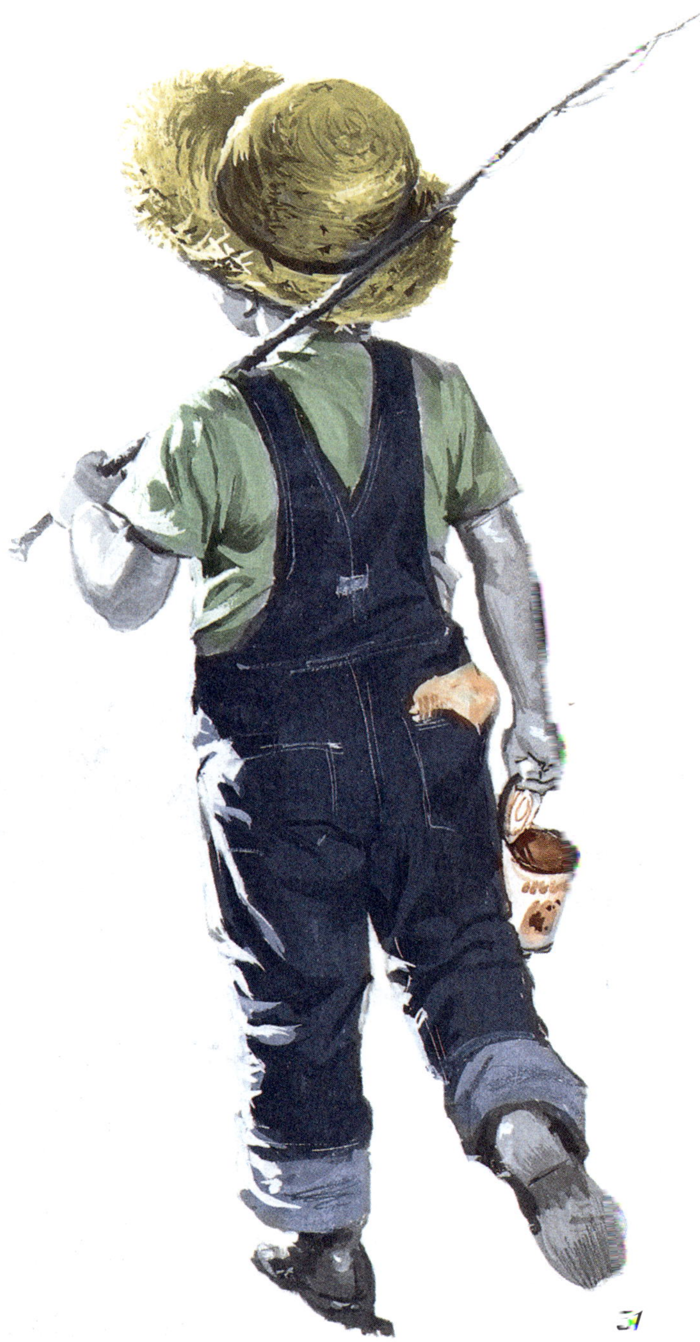

Red House Lake, Allegheny State Park, New York, is skirted by yellow irises. Photograph by Carr Clifton.

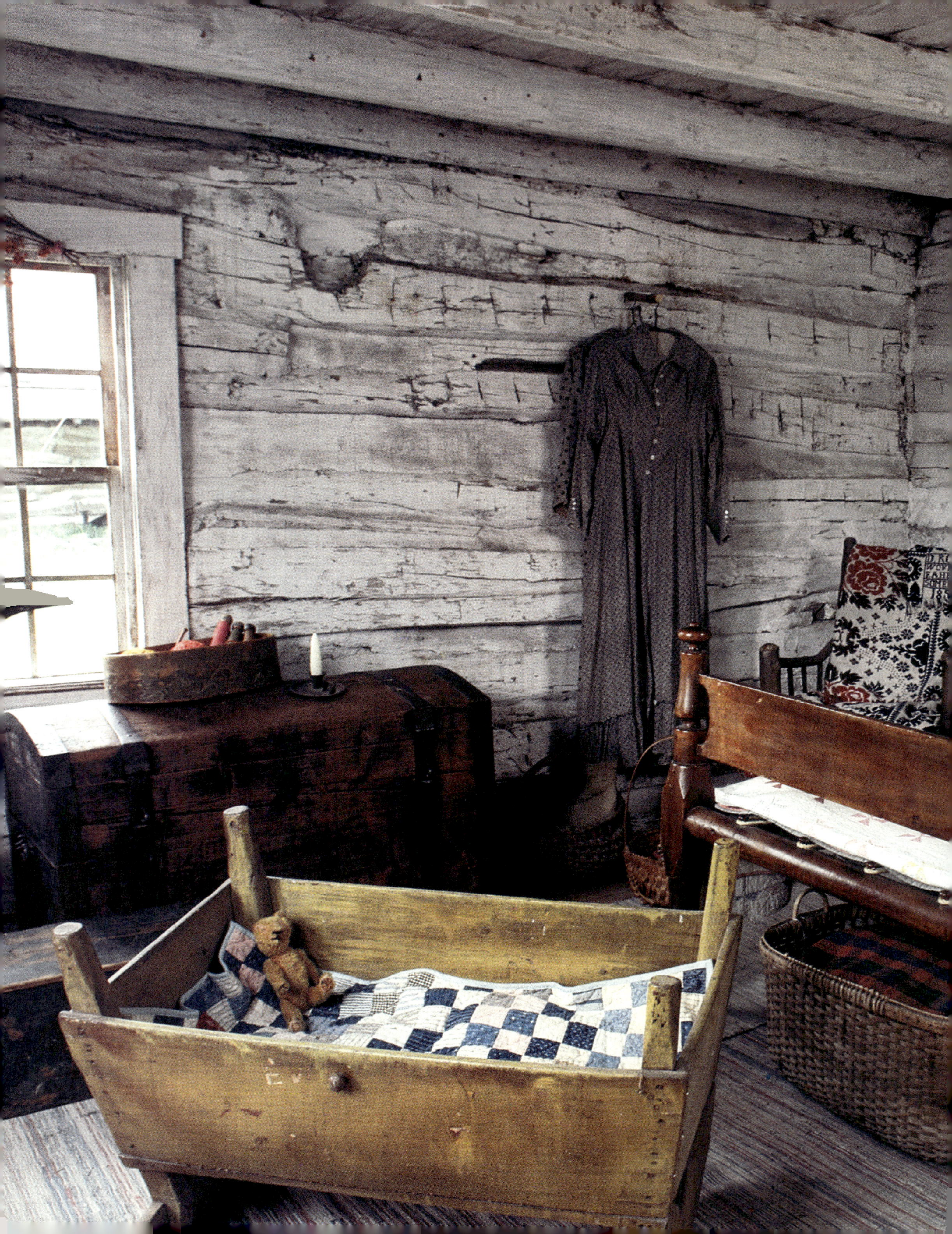

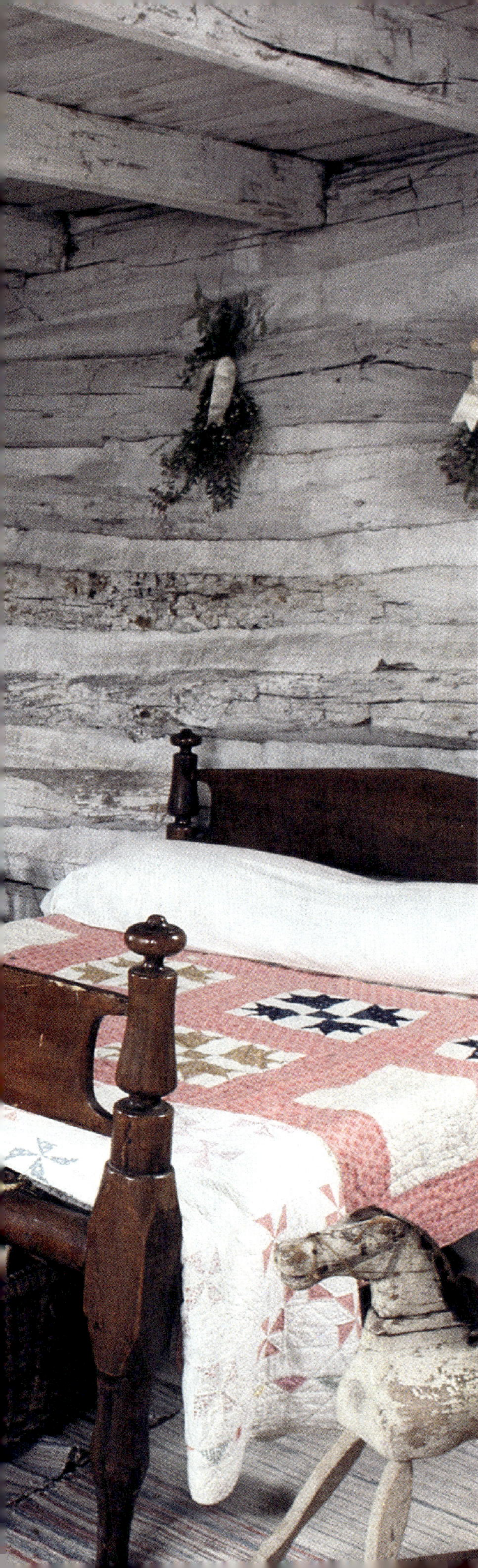

Country Chronicle

Lansing Christman

Harbor for Nine

I wonder where it is today, the cradle in the alcove from which I embarked on the sea of life more than ninety years ago. I was not the only one to make a departure from this harbor of infancy—six brothers and two sisters were ahead of me, each in his or her own time.

Of course, I don't remember how long I occupied that cradle, just three short steps from my mother's bed. She was the guardian angel of each little bundle that was kept in the crib, near enough to hear the slightest sound or cry.

I do remember when the cradle was stored in the attic above the farmhouse kitchen. As a boy I enjoyed inspecting and rocking that cradle as streams of sunlight streamed in through a small window on the attic's south side. It had been my bed, my baby bed.

My father told me how he used hammerstones picked up in the fields to keep the cradle from rocking. He placed them under the rockers. No jiggling jouncing baby could bounce those rocks away.

The cradle was moved away some years after my tenancy, to the home of an older brother and his wife. I do not know what distant ports it visited next.

The cradle in the alcove . . . eight "sailors" ahead of me. Here I am, the last of the line, still sailing along on the sea of time.

The author of four books, Lansing Christman has contributed to Ideals *for more than thirty years. Mr. Christman has also been published in several American, international, and Braille anthologies. He lives in rural South Carolina.*

A primitive cradle awaits its latest newborn in the bedroom of this white-washed log cabin. Photograph by Jessie Walker.

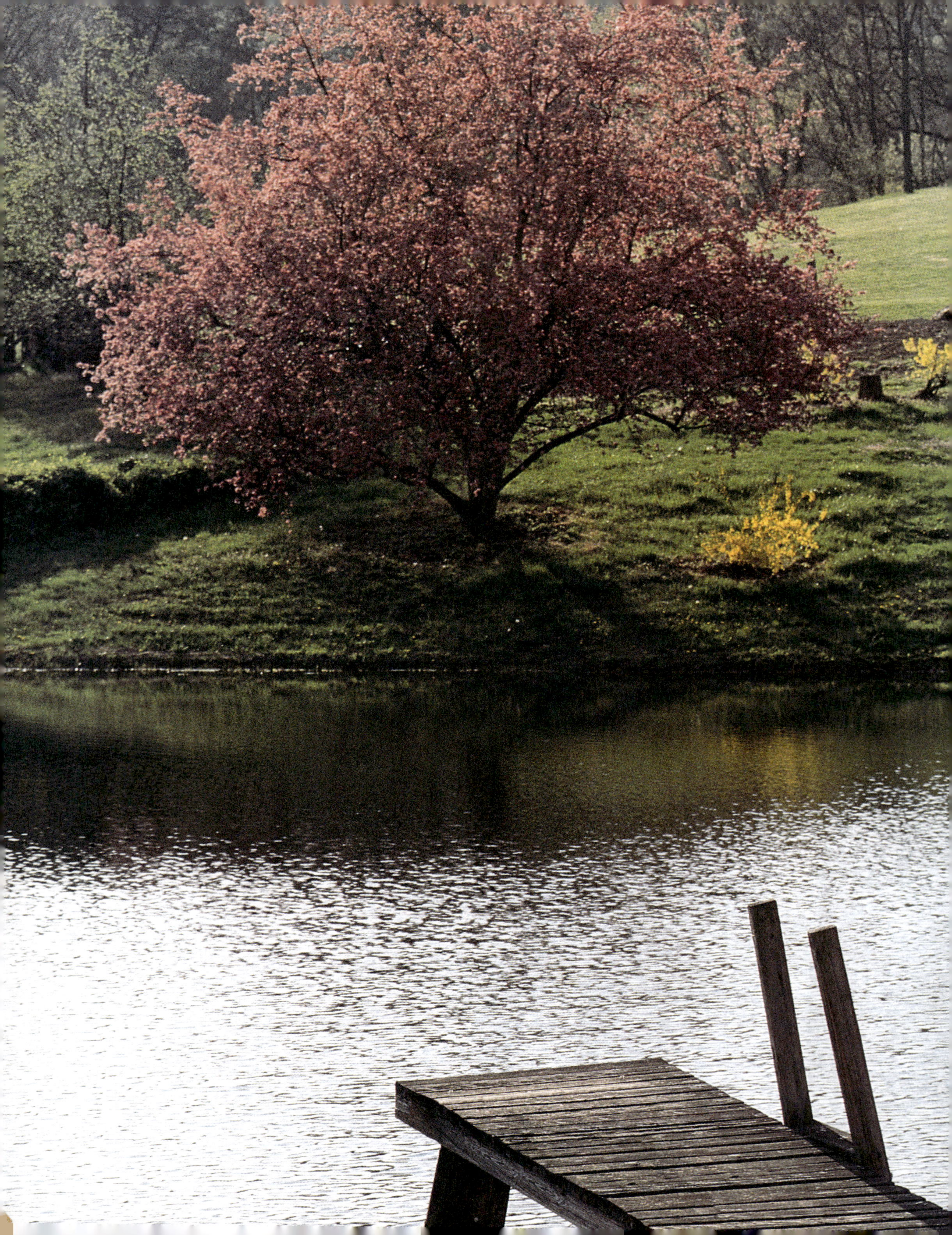

On Our Daughter Becoming a Mother

Wesley H. Hager

O Lord,
I pray for her and her beloved,
And for that unknown other,
That soon Thy love will give to them—
The child who'll call her "Mother."

Keep all of them within Thy care;
Bring safely girl or boy;
And as Thou gavest much to us,
So bless their home with joy.

Grant my prayers for these, my children,
And then I ask another:
Give me the common sense to be
A wise and good grandfather.

Young Mother

Elinor Lennen

But yesterday she was a child;
An infant, scarcely days before.
How can this change be reconciled?
Swiftly, as through a secret door,
Come ancient wisdom, utmost grace,
And womanhood as her bequest.
She holds the promise of our race
Like a medallion at her breast.

A lake and a warm afternoon offer a quiet refuge.
Photograph by Daniel E. Dempster.

LEGENDARY AMERICANS

Melinda Rathjen

VIRGINIA APGAR

"Every baby born in a modern hospital anywhere in the world is looked at first through the eyes of Virginia Apgar," a physician once said, referring to the universal newborn health assessment invented by Apgar. Apgar's impressive contributions to medicine have saved countless lives and revolutionized delivery room practices. The most well-known of these contributions is the Apgar Score, a test of a newborn's adjustment to life outside the womb. Although Apgar was personally present for more than seventeen thousand births, her legacy, the Apgar Score, has been used in millions more deliveries throughout the world.

The Apgar Score is a test of the baby's condition at one and again at five minutes after birth. Five observations, which can be made without special equipment, are each rated from zero to two, for a total of ten possible points. A mnemonic based on Dr. Apgar's name lists each observation:

A—Appearance. Is the baby's color normal?

P—Pulse. Is the baby's heart rate above one hundred beats per minute?

G—Grimace. What is the baby's response to stimuli?

A—Activity. Are the baby's arms and legs flexed or actively moving?

R—Respiration. What is the baby's breathing rate and depth?

A score of seven or higher indicates that the danger to the infant is minimal, while a total score of less than four is a sign that the infant needs resuscitation or other medical intervention.

The Apgar Score was the highlight in the medical career of an accomplished and dedicated physician. Virginia Apgar was a brilliant doctor and researcher, a champion of public awareness about birth defects, and an unforgettable personality. Known to friends and family as "Ginny," she was born to Helen Clarke and Charles Emory Apgar in Westfield, New Jersey, in 1909. Virginia began taking violin lessons at age six, beginning a life-long love of music. Her brother Lawrence played the piano, and the pair would often give concerts for their family. Virginia's father had many hobbies, including astronomy and wireless telegraphy. These early years with her family instilled in her a love of learning and an intellectual curiosity.

Both Apgar's high school and college experiences show evidence of a variety of interests, athletic as well as academic, including participating in the orchestra. She also worked part-time to help pay for her education.

At a time when it was unusual for a female to pursue higher education, Apgar aspired to become a doctor. She received a bachelor's degree in zoology from Mount Holyoke in 1929, and, in 1933, earned her M.D. at Columbia University's College of Physicians and Surgeons.

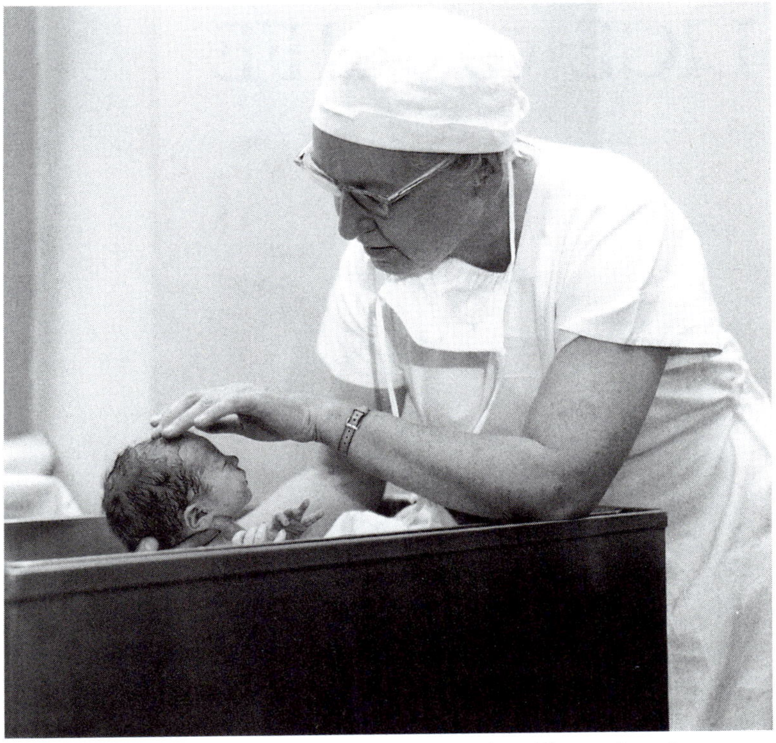

Dr. Virginia Apgar applies the Apgar Score to a newborn. Photograph courtesy Columbia University Medical Center.

While completing a very prestigious surgical internship at Columbia–Presbyterian Hospital, Apgar became interested in the new medical field of anesthesiology. In 1939, Apgar was only the fiftieth physician in the country certified as an anesthesiologist. Soon afterwards, she was appointed the director of anesthesiology at Columbia–Presbyterian Hospital.

Apgar's work eventually focused on obstetric anesthesia. Many women at the time were experiencing serious problems during or just after giving birth, even to the point of losing their lives. By 1949, this area had become Apgar's specialty. Her observations led her to question such traditional practices as giving women general anesthesia for childbirth. Apgar helped to demonstrate that local anesthesia was not only just as effective as general anesthesia, but better for the mother and the baby as well.

After studying the effects of anesthesia on newborns, Apgar became aware of another problem and the means of resolving it. Realizing that birth can be the most hazardous time of life, Apgar recognized the need for an immediate, standardized measure of how well an infant was adapting to life outside the womb. Prior to this time, too many newborns in need of immediate resuscitation or other life-saving procedures were not given attention until it was too late. When a medical student asked Apgar if such an evaluation existed, she used a napkin to jot down the notes for observations that would later be called the Apgar Score. Apgar presented her assessment thesis in 1952, at a meeting of the International Anesthesia Research Society. The Newborn Scoring System was soon put into practice in delivery rooms around the globe, and, in 1962, the newborn test was arranged by two pediatricians as an acronym using Apgar's name.

The Apgar Score as a test of newborn health is still, half a century later, trusted. Since its inclusion in immediate post-birth procedures, the infant mortality rate in the United States has declined from 29.20 percent in 1950 to just 6.75 percent. Virginia Apgar's contributions played a heroic part in that dramatic drop, saving countless lives.

NAME: Virginia Apgar

BORN: June 7, 1909, Westfield, New Jersey

DIED: August 7, 1974, New York City

ACCOMPLISHMENTS: Created the Apgar Score; co-author of *Is My Baby All Right?*

QUOTE: "Nobody, but nobody, is going to stop breathing on me."

SLICE OF LIFE

Edna Jaques

SHE'S MOTHERLY

She's motherly—what lovelier praise
Could e'er be said of one whose days
Are filled from morning until night,
Keeping the lamp of joy alight,
Like a small candle's golden glow
In a vast world of want and woe.

She's motherly—and looks the part,
As if the cockles of her heart
Were warm and red like glowing coals
That cheer the very hearts and souls
Of lucky folk who came to share
The tiny orbit of her care.

She loves to cook and have things nice;
Her kitchen smells of sage and spice,
The fragrance of fresh applesauce
And warm buns with a sticky gloss,
Cookies spread out to cool, and pies
That are a treat for hungry eyes.

There is no trait in womankind
That is more beautiful to find
Than that deep instinct from above
To mother and protect and love
Those who are ill-equipped to bear
Their heavy load of grief and care.

She's motherly—what kindlier praise,
Could e'er be heard to crown her days?

A young mother and her son share a quiet, early-morning moment in an original painting, MOTHER AND SON, by Robert Duncan. Copyright © Robert Duncan. All rights reserved. Image provided by Robert Duncan Studios.

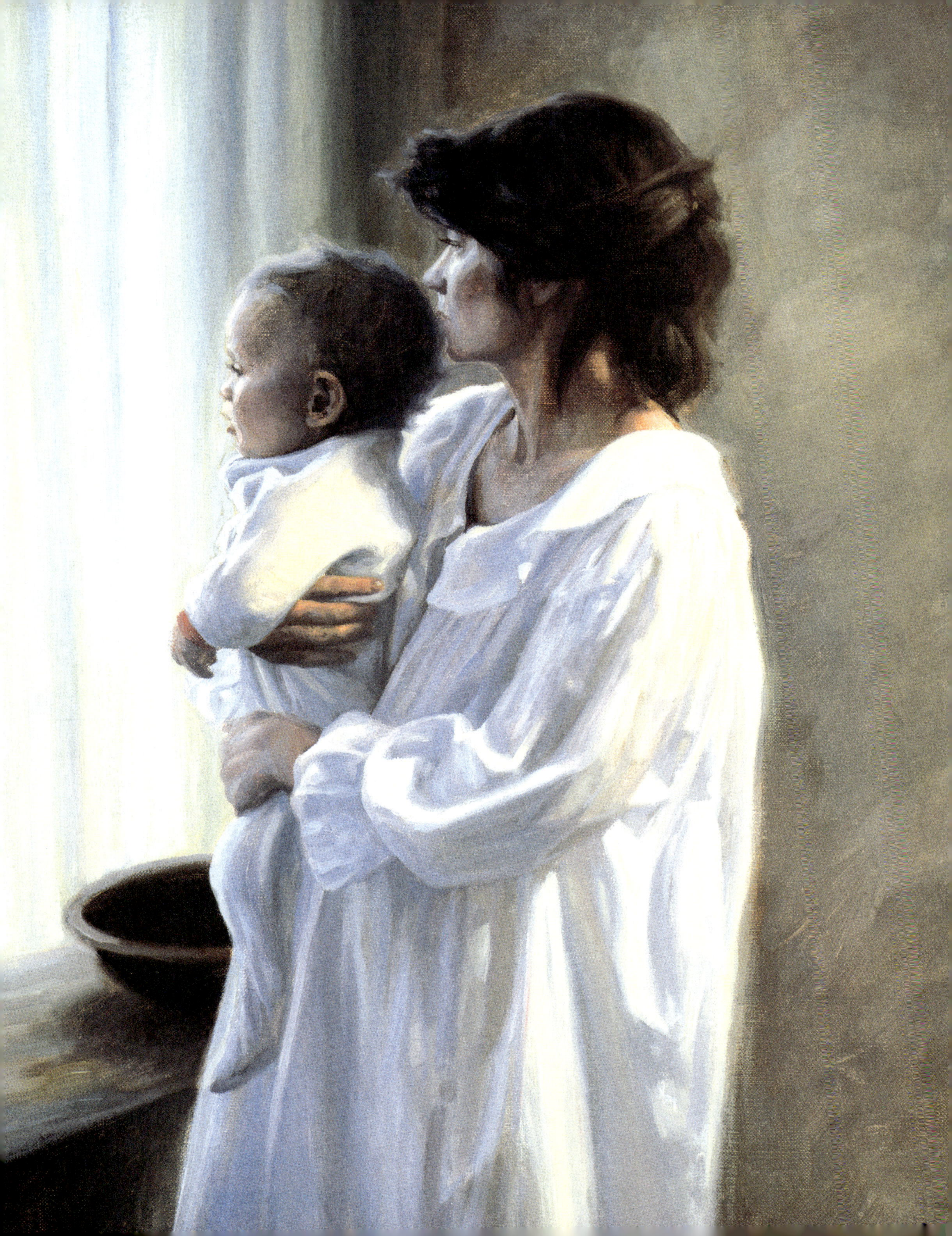

DEVOTIONS FROM THE HEART

Pamela Kennedy

These commandments that I give you today are to be upon your hearts. Impress them on your children. Talk about them when you sit at home and when you walk along the road, when you lie down and when you get up. Tie them as symbols on your hands and bind them on your forehead.
—Deuteronomy 6:6–8 (NIV)

TEACHING OUR CHILDREN

I teach teenagers these days, but before I returned to the classroom, I had over twenty-five years of teaching experiences at home. I was a full-time mother. As most mothers know, we fulfill myriad roles, from taxi driver to first-aid worker, from costume designer to psychologist; but the role we are most often called upon to play is that of teacher.

"Mama, why is the sky blue?"

"Mommy, how do you build a fort?"

"Mom, what's the hypotenuse of a right triangle?"

"Mother, how do I let a girl know I like her without sounding stupid?"

There's always something new to teach our children, and it often seems a daunting task. Methods that work with one child don't always work with another. Attention spans and interests vary, and even some subject matter changes over time. But there are some things our children need to know that never change. Mothers, grandmothers, and aunts have the precious opportunity and the sometimes awesome challenge of teaching children about God.

In the Bible, Moses records God's instructions above quoted from the book of Deuteronomy. For millennia, Orthodox Jews have taken these instructions quite literally. In their communities, it is not unusual to see a man wearing two small leather cases, one strapped to the forehead and the other to the upper left arm. In these are deposited four passages of Scripture from the books of Exodus and Deuteronomy—reminders of the commandments of God. The point of these leather phylacteries is to fulfill God's laws by keeping them near one's mind and heart.

Dear Lord, You have promised to be both my counselor and teacher. Grant me creativity as I reach out to the children You have placed in my life to teach them about Your commandments and love.

Most mothers would not choose to take this command so literally, but the importance of keeping the words of God in our hearts and minds and passing along their truths to our children cannot be denied. Today, so many voices tell

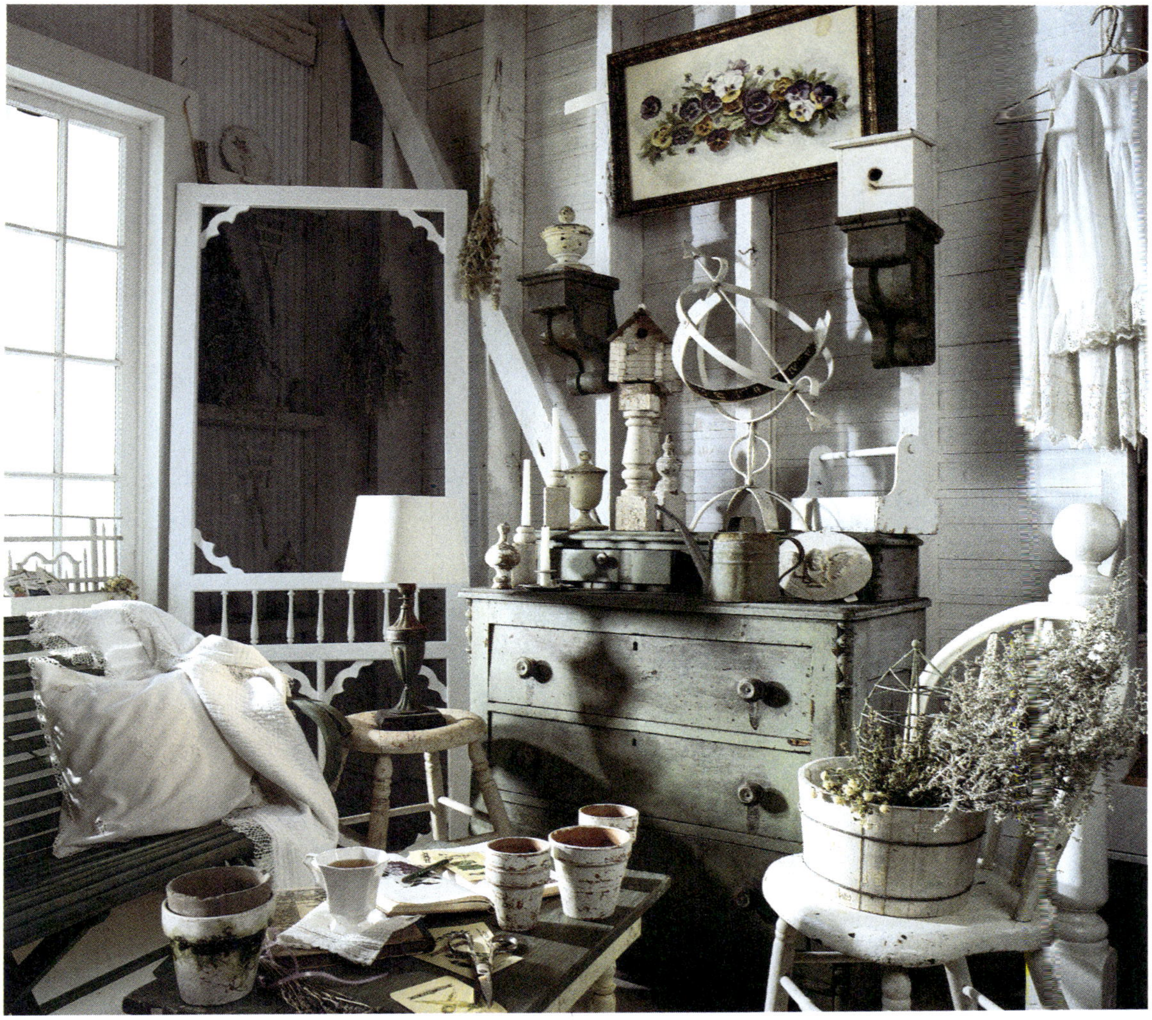

This garden room offers many opportunities for a family to share pleasurable tasks and memorable times together. Photograph by Jessie Walker.

our youngsters what to do. And some of these voices are not at all helpful. Who will teach little ones to distinguish right from wrong, encourage school-aged children to treat each other with kindness, and help adolescents and young adults make wise and moral choices?

When we are with our children, grandchildren, nephews, and nieces, we have wonderful opportunities to impact their hearts and minds with godly lessons. We can talk about God's creation as we observe with a little one the diligence of an ant or the beauty of a bird in flight. When we help young students with their schoolwork, we can point out the magnificent order of the universe or the moral character of the protagonist in a novel. Sharing lessons from our own lives, telling our own stories of failure and faith, can inspire a young man or woman to trust in prayer and persevere in times of trial. Their hearts and minds are open to us in ways a professional teacher may never experience, and thus we can encourage them through lessons laced with love.

There are stories to be read and told, movies and videos to be watched, music to be heard. And all of these are teaching tools. Today, we have an abundance of materials and methods at our disposal to help the commandments of God penetrate the hearts and minds of our children. All it takes is time and a little patience. Who knows our children better than we? Who loves them more? Who, then, could be a better teacher?

My Daughter's Gift

Jill Noblit MacGregor

My daughter brings me flowers
of vast and many hues—
Long and short, bright and quaint,
of pink and white and blue.

My daughter brings me flowers,
in this her heart delights—
To gather all God's budded treasures,
come the morning light.

My daughter brings me flowers
as she skips across the lawn,
Leaving footprints fast upon the grass
as night's dew graces dawn.

My daughter brings me flowers;
a bouquet of love she bears,
Fragrant offerings of thanksgiving
to disarm my every care.

My daughter brings me flowers,
yet how fleeting are these days,
Like the flowers she brings and simple things,
they too shall pass away.

My daughter brings me flowers;
it sometimes makes me cry,
For with flowers we say "I love you,"
and with flowers we say "Goodbye."

Small Son

Mary Turton Johnson

I watch him playing in the meadow, enraptured
By his new world and its exciting charms—
A small world, still, but with horizons wider
Than sighted from the circle of my arms.

He chases butterflies and leaps to catch a leaf,
Sniffs all the pretty flowers; then, rolling in the grass,
Exuberant, inebriate with freedom,
Supernal innocence looks up at me and laughs.

With manly pride, he scrambles up. I think, "How short
The moments he will need me; oh, how few the years."
And then he comes, largess in hands, proclaiming
His own heart's choice for now, and stays the starting tears.

"For you, Mom." Dandelions, a bit of crumpled fern,
Presented with a hug and smudgy kiss.

Queen Anne's lace, daisies, yarrow, and other flowers fill a meadow near Poultney, Vermont. Photograph by William H. Johnson.

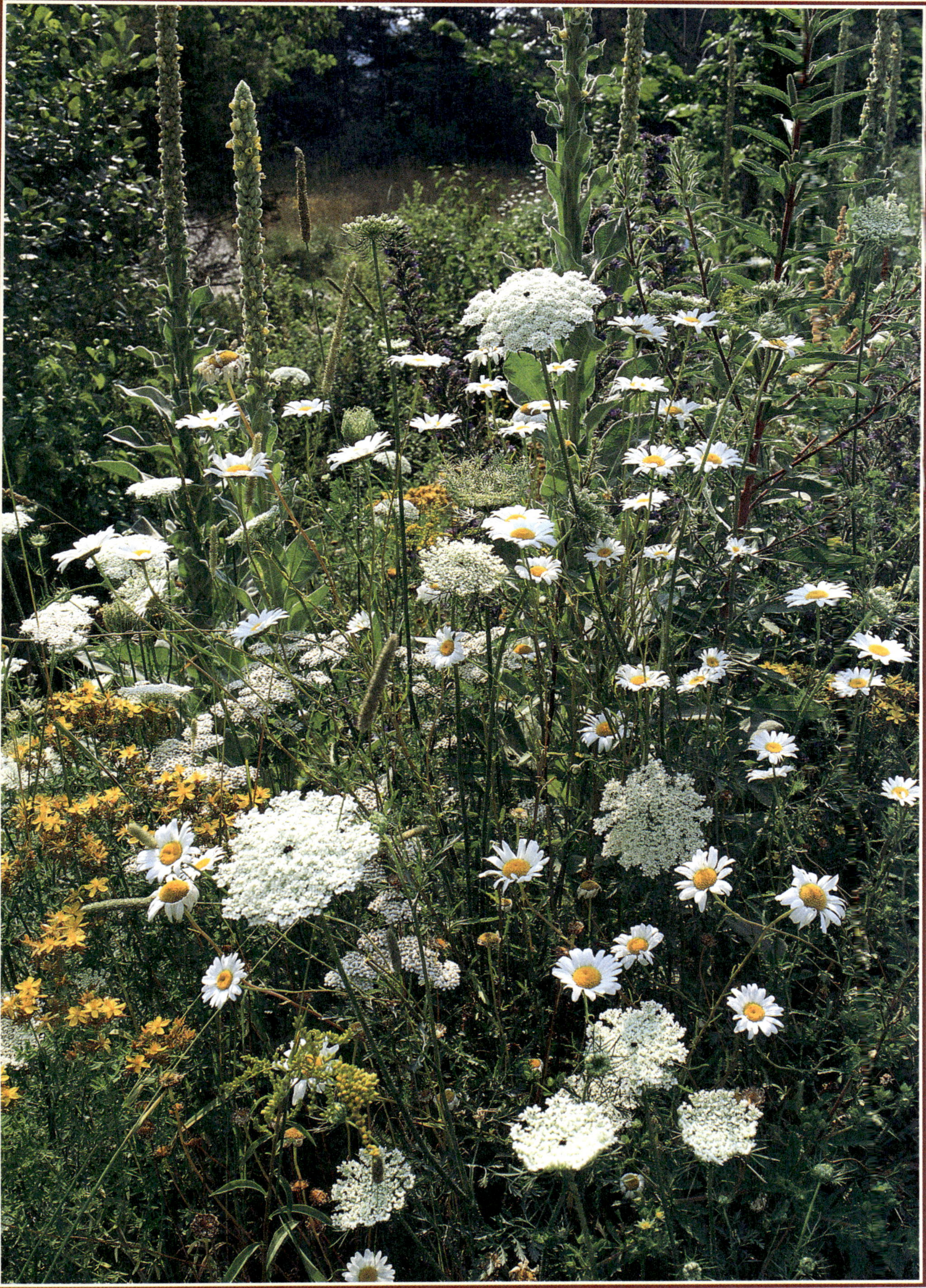

BITS & PIECES

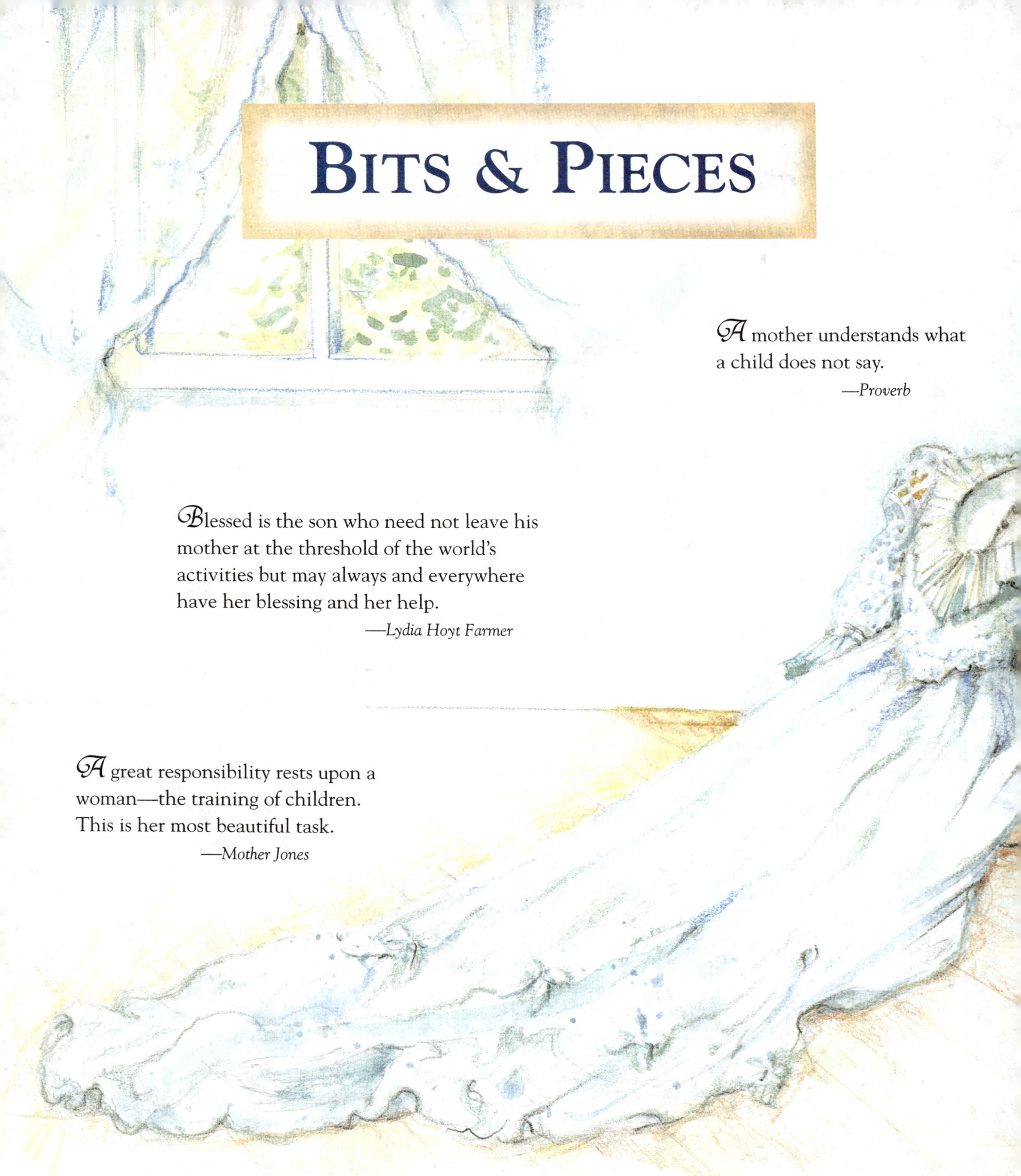

A mother understands what a child does not say.

—*Proverb*

Blessed is the son who need not leave his mother at the threshold of the world's activities but may always and everywhere have her blessing and her help.

—*Lydia Hoyt Farmer*

A great responsibility rests upon a woman—the training of children. This is her most beautiful task.

—*Mother Jones*

Mother's arms are made of tenderness,
And sweet sleep blesses the child who lies therein.

—*Victor Hugo*

Good mothers are married over again at their daughters' weddings.

—*William Makepeace Thackery,* Vanity Fair

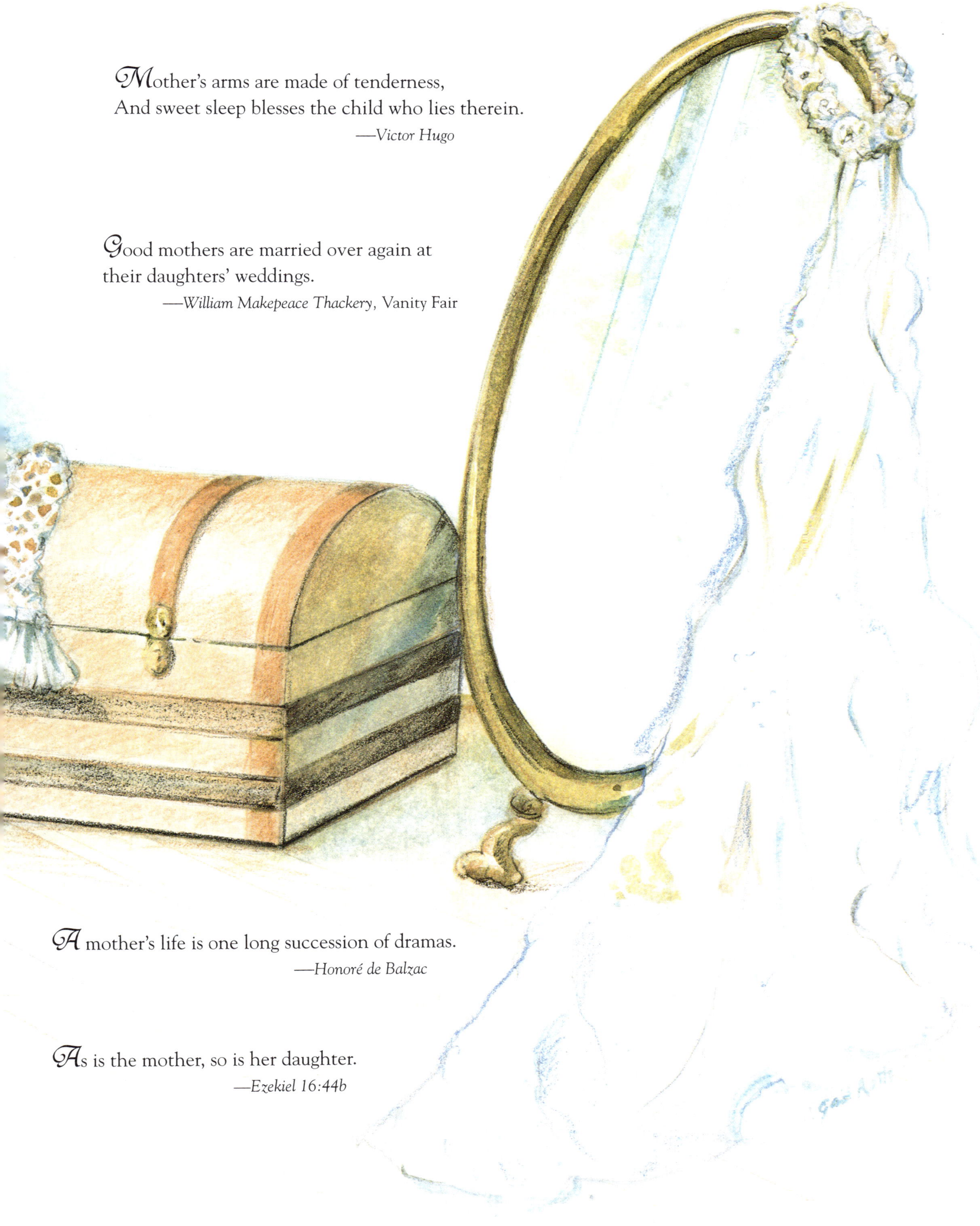

A mother's life is one long succession of dramas.

—*Honoré de Balzac*

As is the mother, so is her daughter.

—*Ezekiel 16:44b*

Upon My Mother's Knee

Reginald Holmes

If I could turn life's pages back
And time would set me free,
I'd like to be a child again
Upon my mother's knee.
Could I but know the loving care
That banished all my fears
And feel the soft and sweet caress
That brushed aside my tears.

If I could see her tender smile
Or gaze upon her charms;
And know the calm contentment found
Within her loving arms;
Or hear again the wondrous tales
That only she could tell;
And listen to the slumber song
She sang when twilight fell.

If I could hear her fervent prayer
As she knelt beside my bed,
When she with gentleness would place
Her hand upon my head;
If I could journey back once more
To days of used-to-be,
I'd like to be a child again
Upon my mother's knee.

The timeless beauty of roses is joyously multiplied in this photograph by Nancy Matthews.

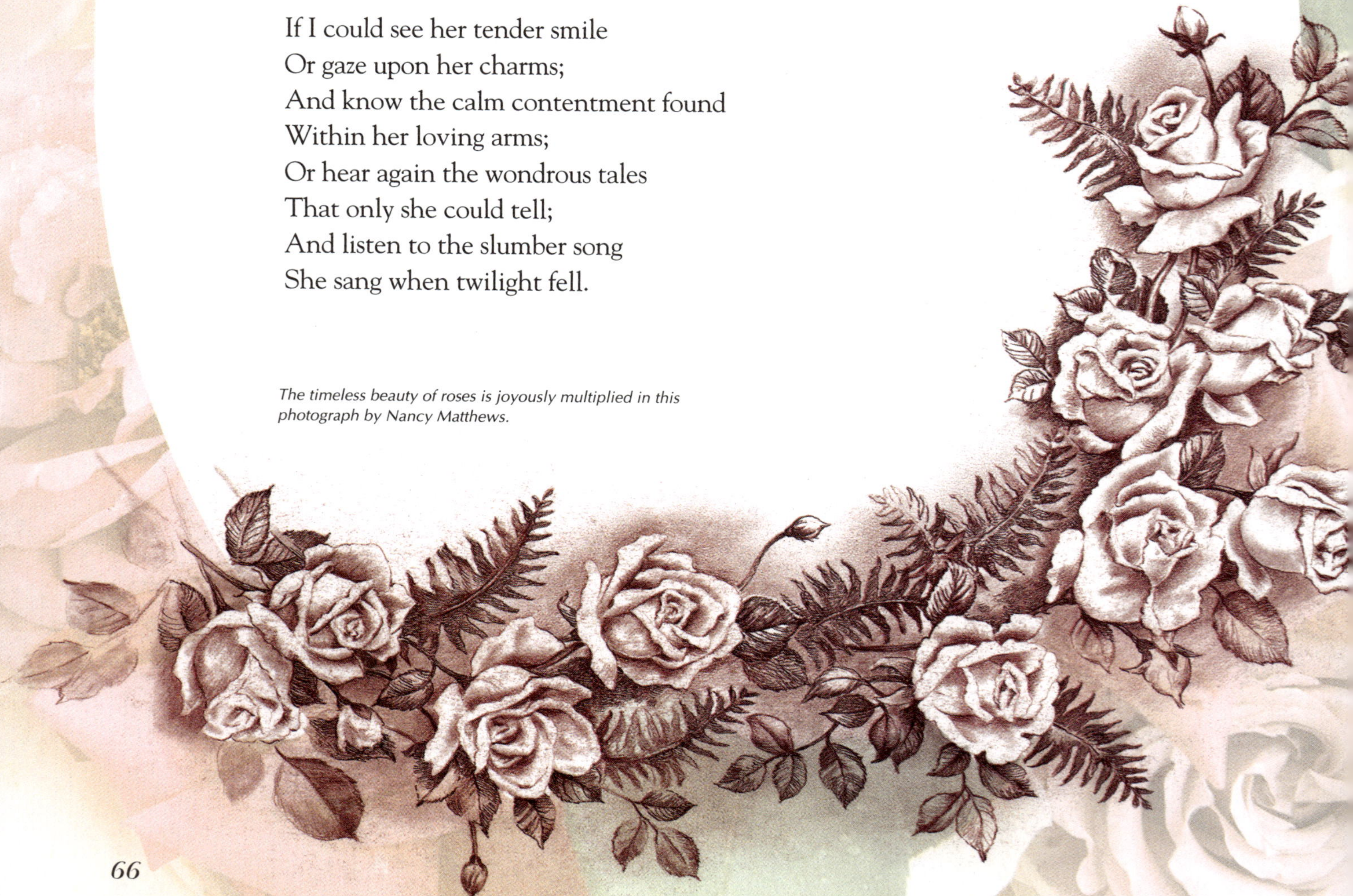

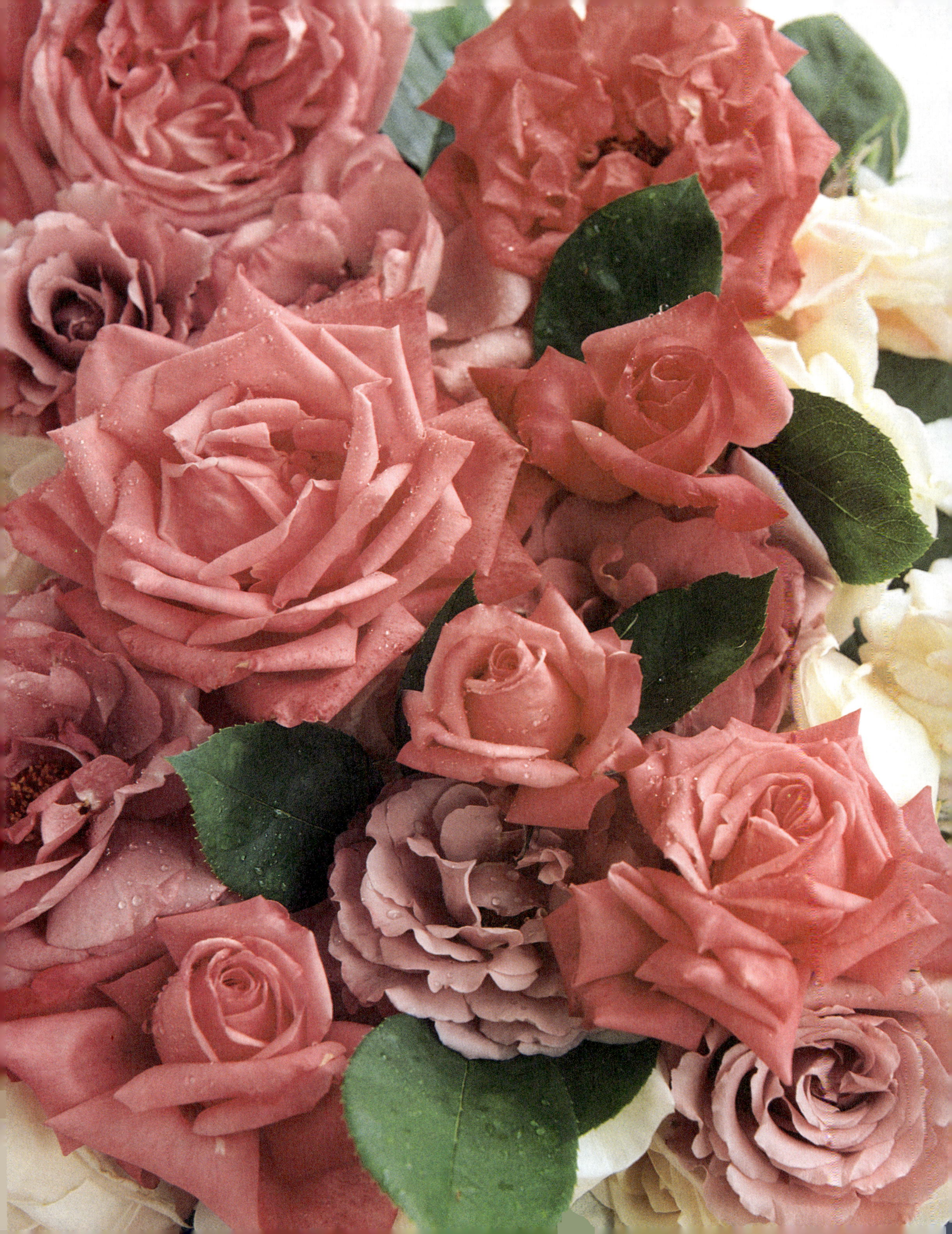

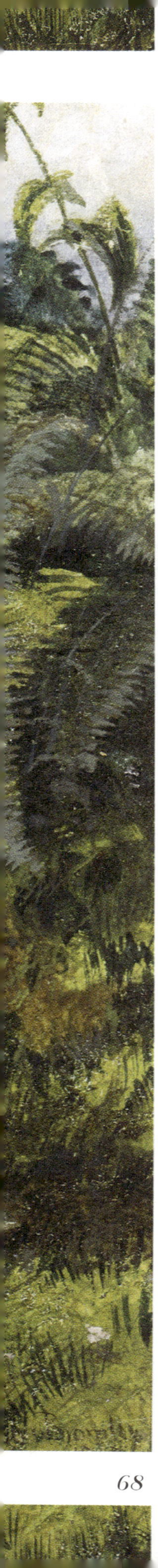

from Abigail Adams' Letter to her son, John Quincy Adams

JUNE 1778

Great Learning and superior abilities, should you ever possess them, will be of little value and small Estimation, unless Virtue, Honour, Truth and Integrity are added to them. Adhere to those religious Sentiments and principles which were early instilled into your mind, and remember that you are accountable to your Maker for all your words and actions.

There is an endearing tenderness in the love of a mother to a son that transcends all other affections of the heart. It is neither to be chilled by selfishness nor daunted by danger, nor weakened by worthlessness, nor stifled by ingratitude. She will sacrifice every comfort to his convenience; she will surrender every pleasure to his enjoyment; she will glory in his fame and exult in his prosperity; and if adversity overtake him, he will be the dearer to her by misfortune; and if disgrace settle upon his name, she will still love and cherish him; and if all the world beside cast him off, she will be all the world to him.

—WASHINGTON IRVING

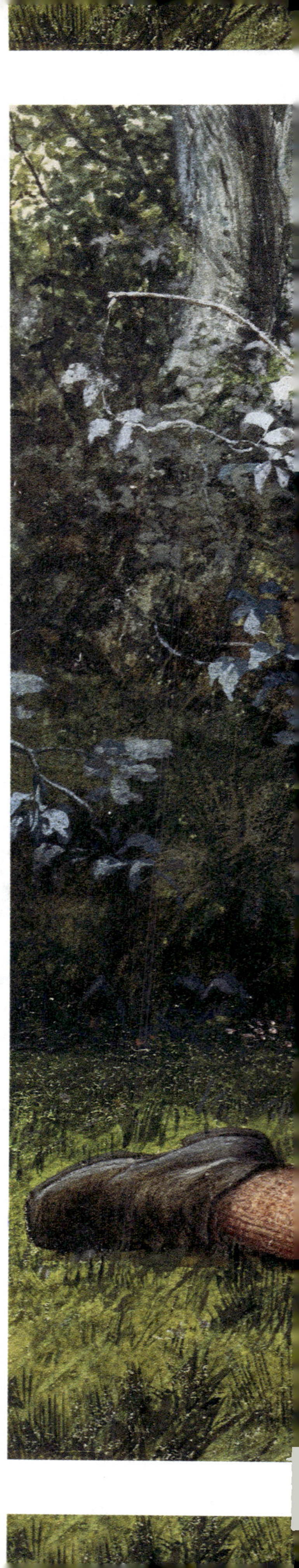

A young boy has the best of two different worlds, the imagination of the printed word and the freshness of the outdoors. Painting, A QUIET READ, by William Bromly (1855–1888). Image from Fine Art Photographic Library, Ltd., London/Haynes Fine Art.

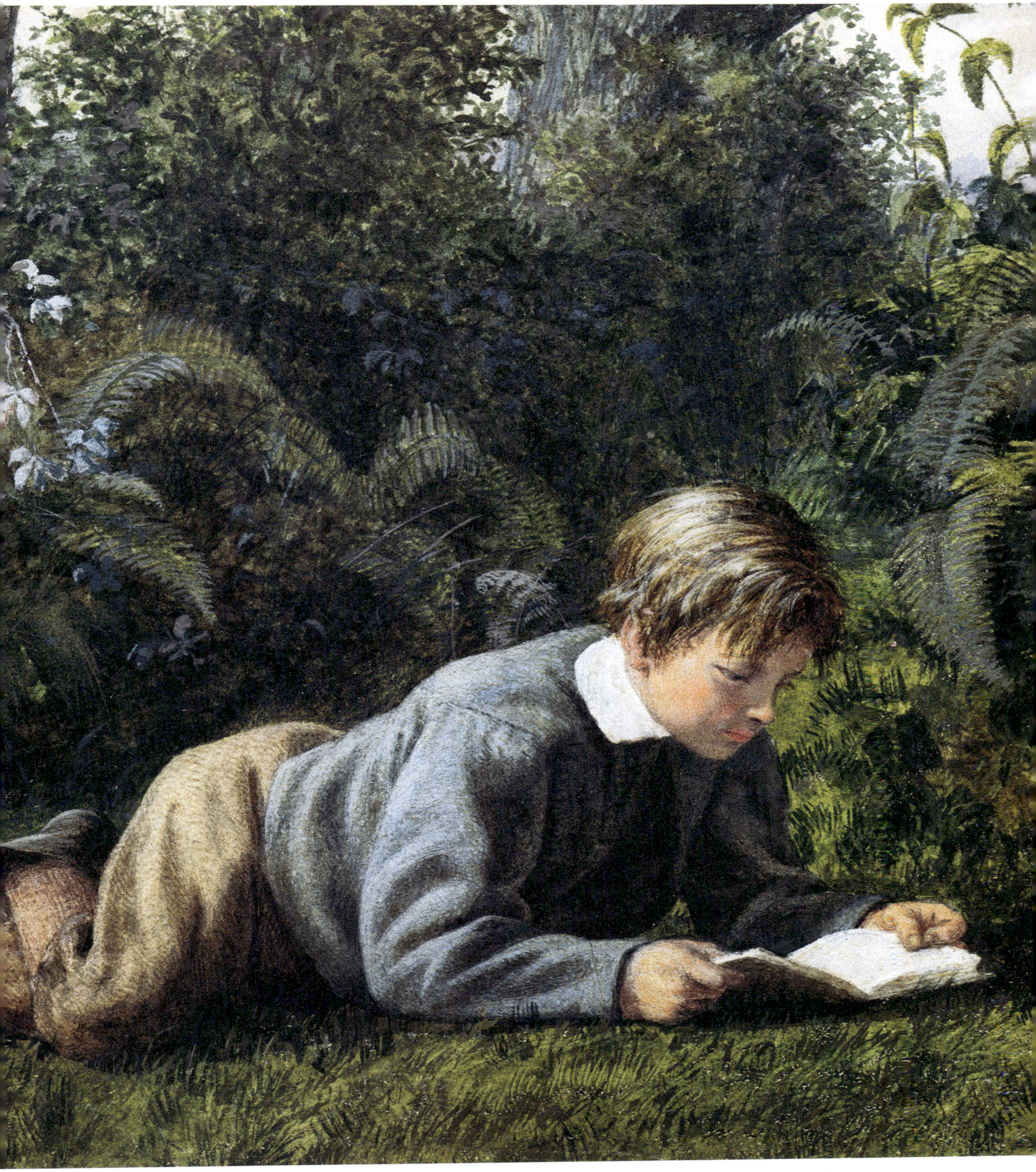

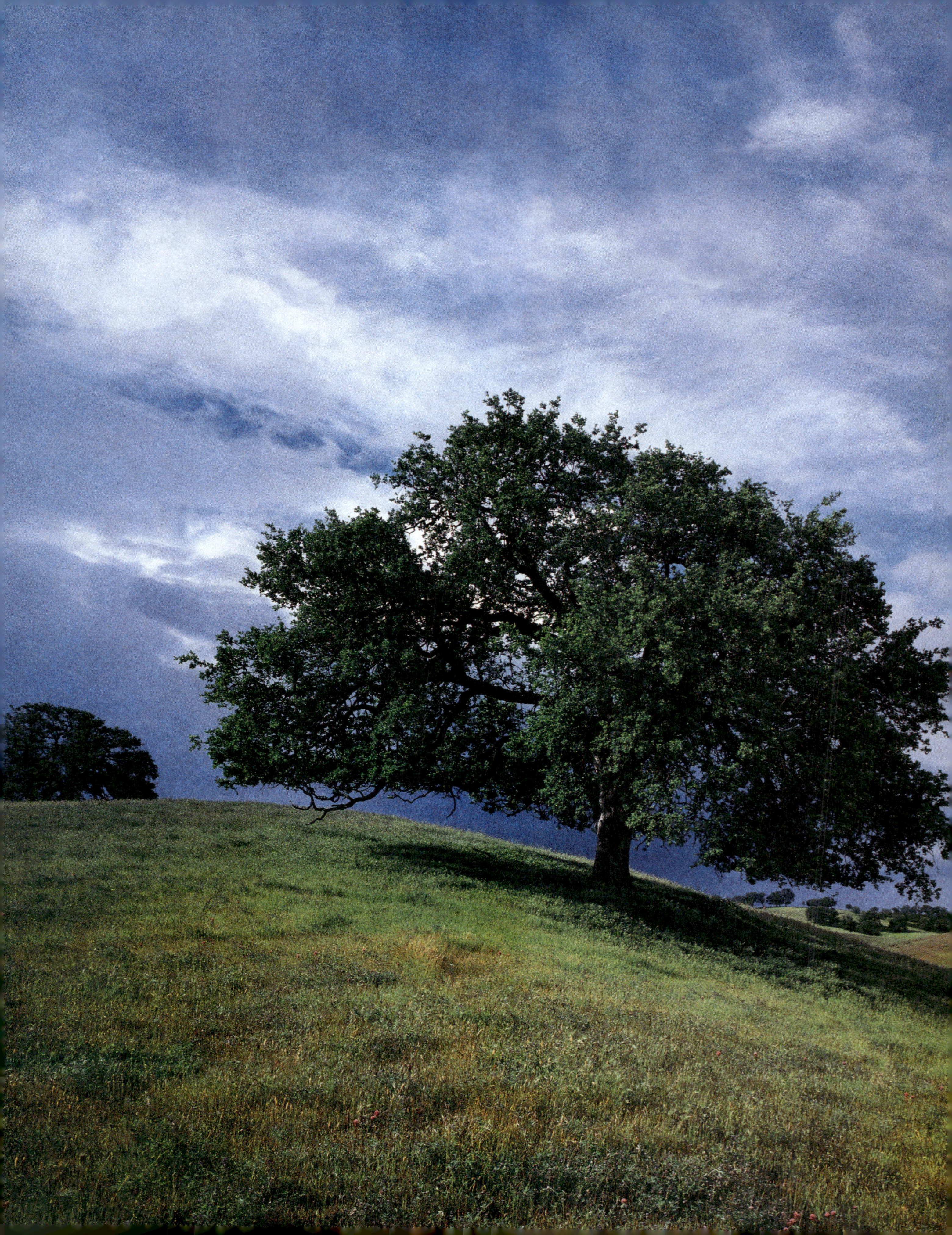

Boy in April

Grace V. Watkins

Beyond the radius of map and chalk,
His heart has climbed a greening April hill,
Above a glade where nesting robins talk
And violets are blooming, azure still.
It may be I should call him back again
To rendezvous with adjective or noun
Or half-forgotten laws devised by men
In senate chambers of an ancient town.

And yet I visualize a future spring
And see a man with blue dreams in his eyes
Look over city roofs remembering
A country hill where green enchantment lies
And bless this hour, tasting a timeless joy
More honey-sweet than all the fame of Troy.

My mother had a great deal of trouble with me, but I think she enjoyed it.

—MARK TWAIN

An old oak and a green hillside of the Tremblor Range, California, beckon to be explored. Photograph by Carr Clifton.

Overleaf: Dwarf fireweed and Indian paintbrush dramatically frame the Saint Elias Mountains in Glacier Bay National Park and Preserve, Alaska. Photograph by Carr Clifton.

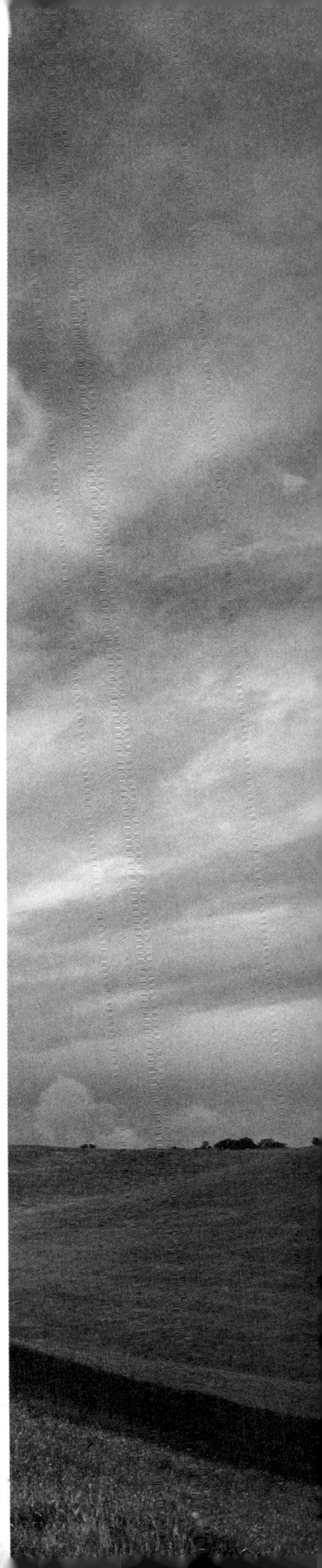

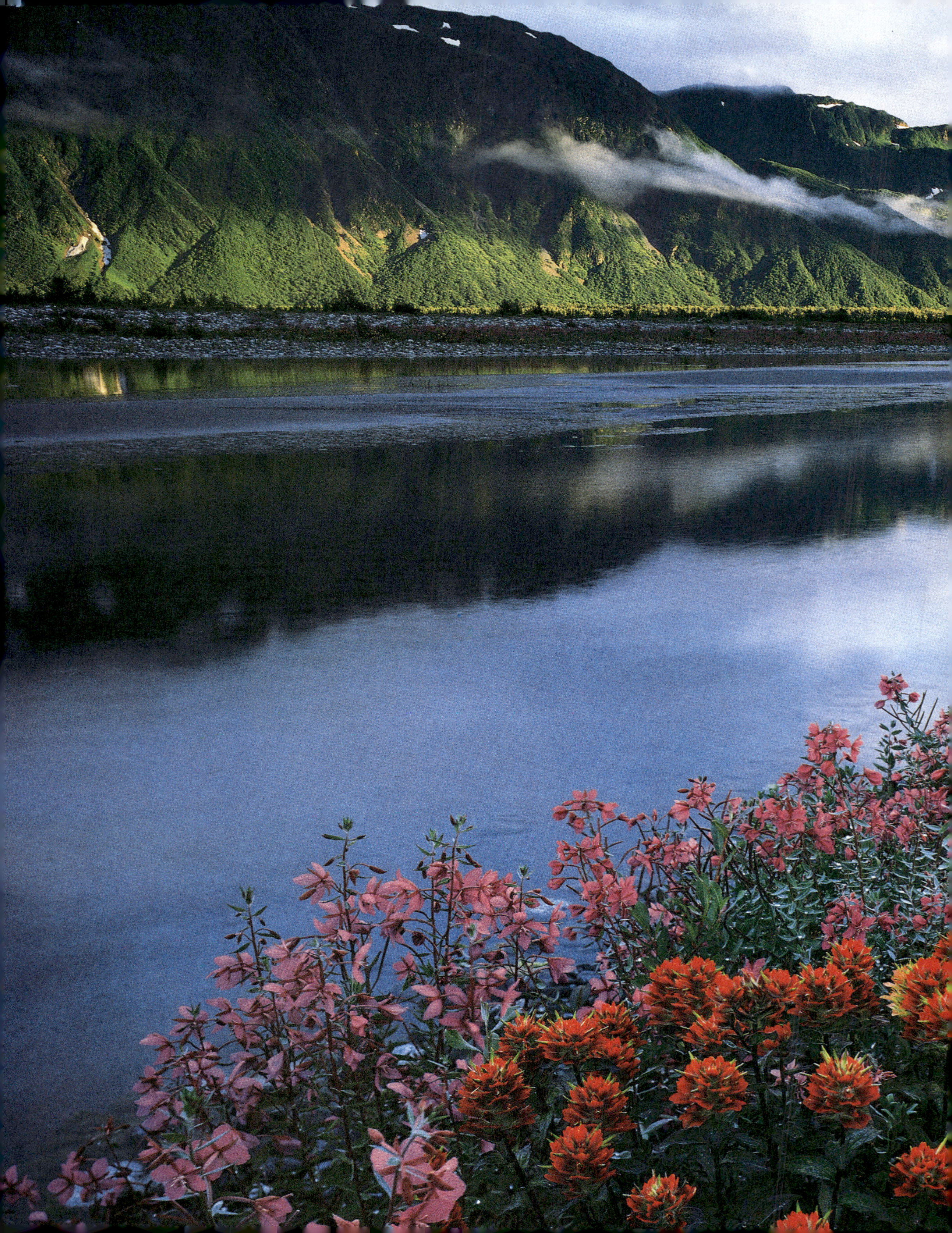

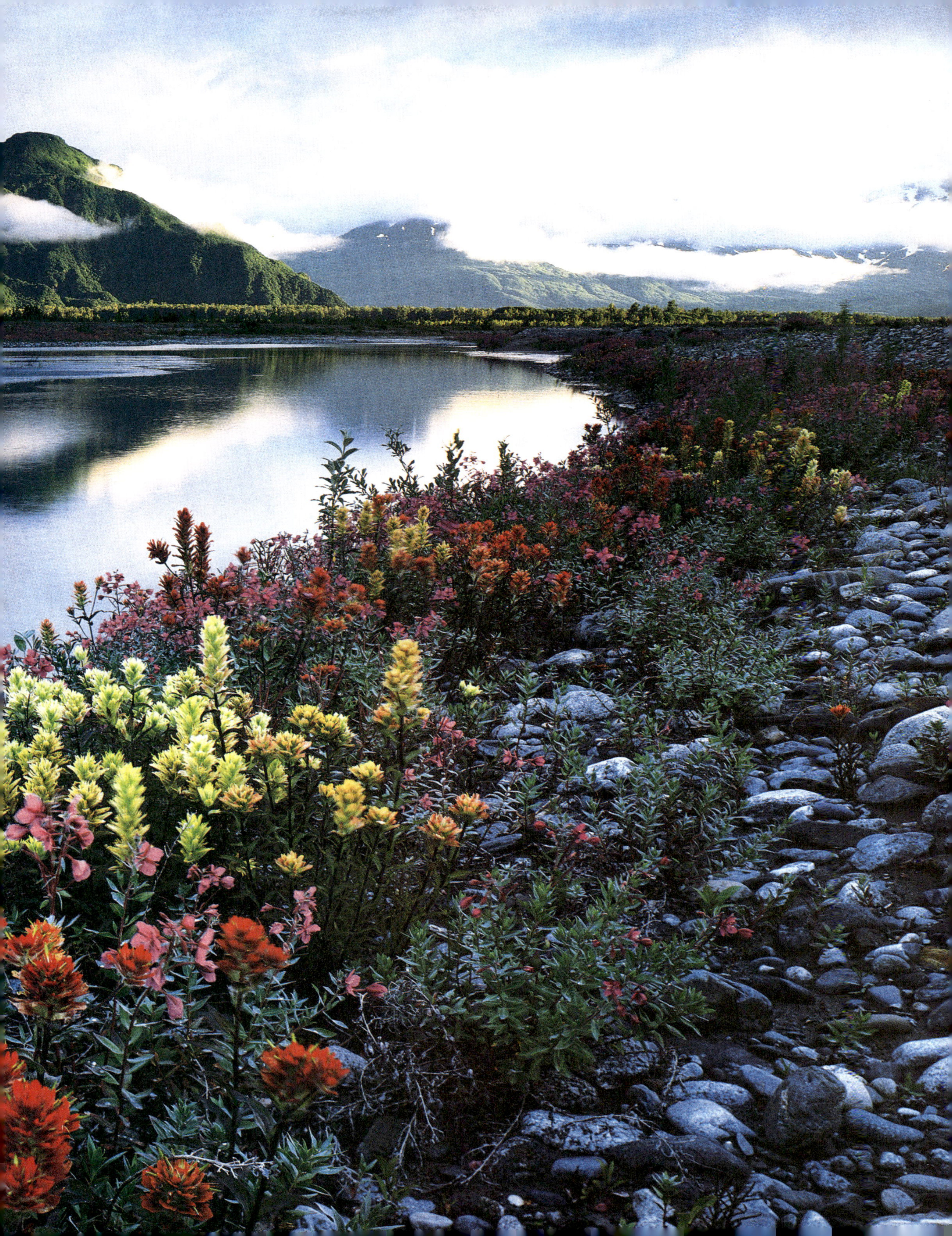

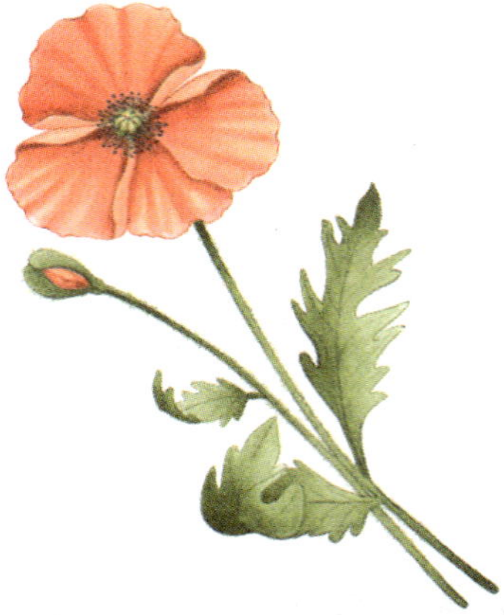

Mother's Care

Penny McGinnis

A time would come around each year
When warmth would fill the air.
I'd run out to the flower bed,
So free, without a care.

There I would find my mother,
Bent down to tend the plants
That grew in this bright garden
Where the orange poppies danced.

The poppies were my favorite,
Though they did not last for long.
Their swaying in the breeze
Was like a gentle song.

Mother nurtured the young flowers
Each year with loving care,
The way that she would care for us—
Patiently, and with prayer.

The poppy blooms have faded;
The garden's turned to grass.
But Mother's love has lasted
Through all the years that've passed.

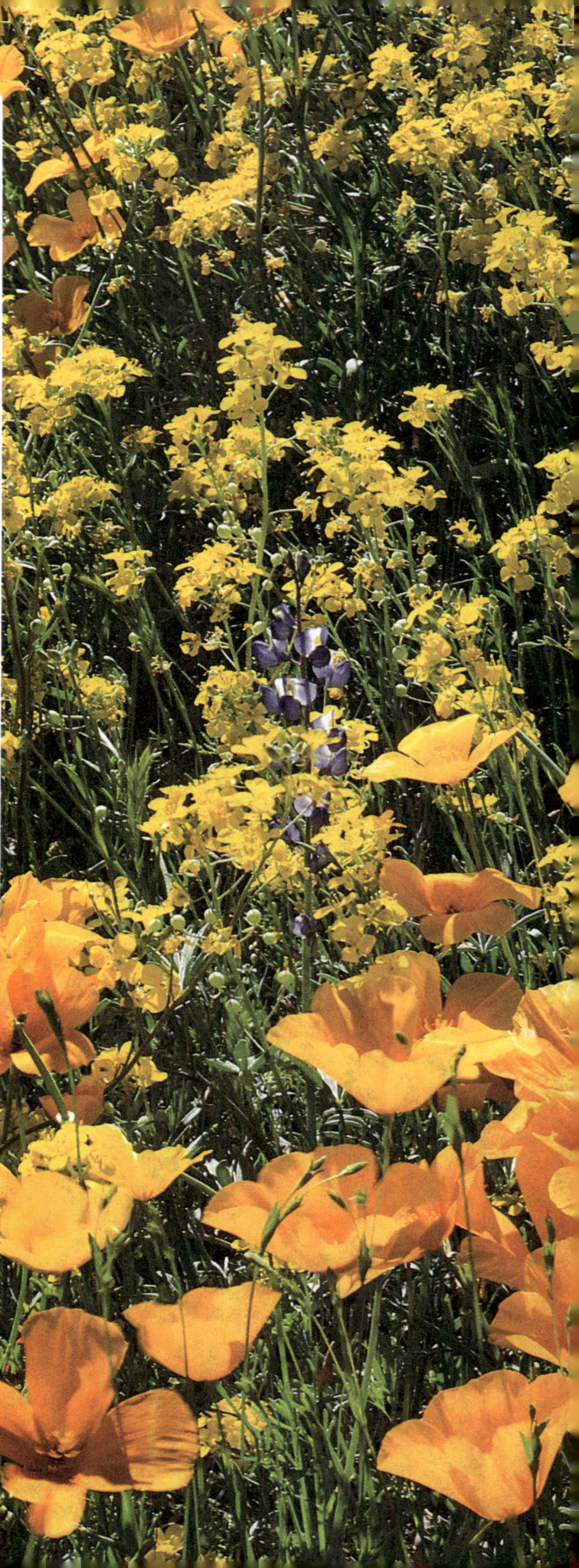

The desert floor of Organ Pipe Cactus National Monument, Arizona, is decorated with Mexican gold poppies and other wildflowers. Photograph by Terry Donnelly.

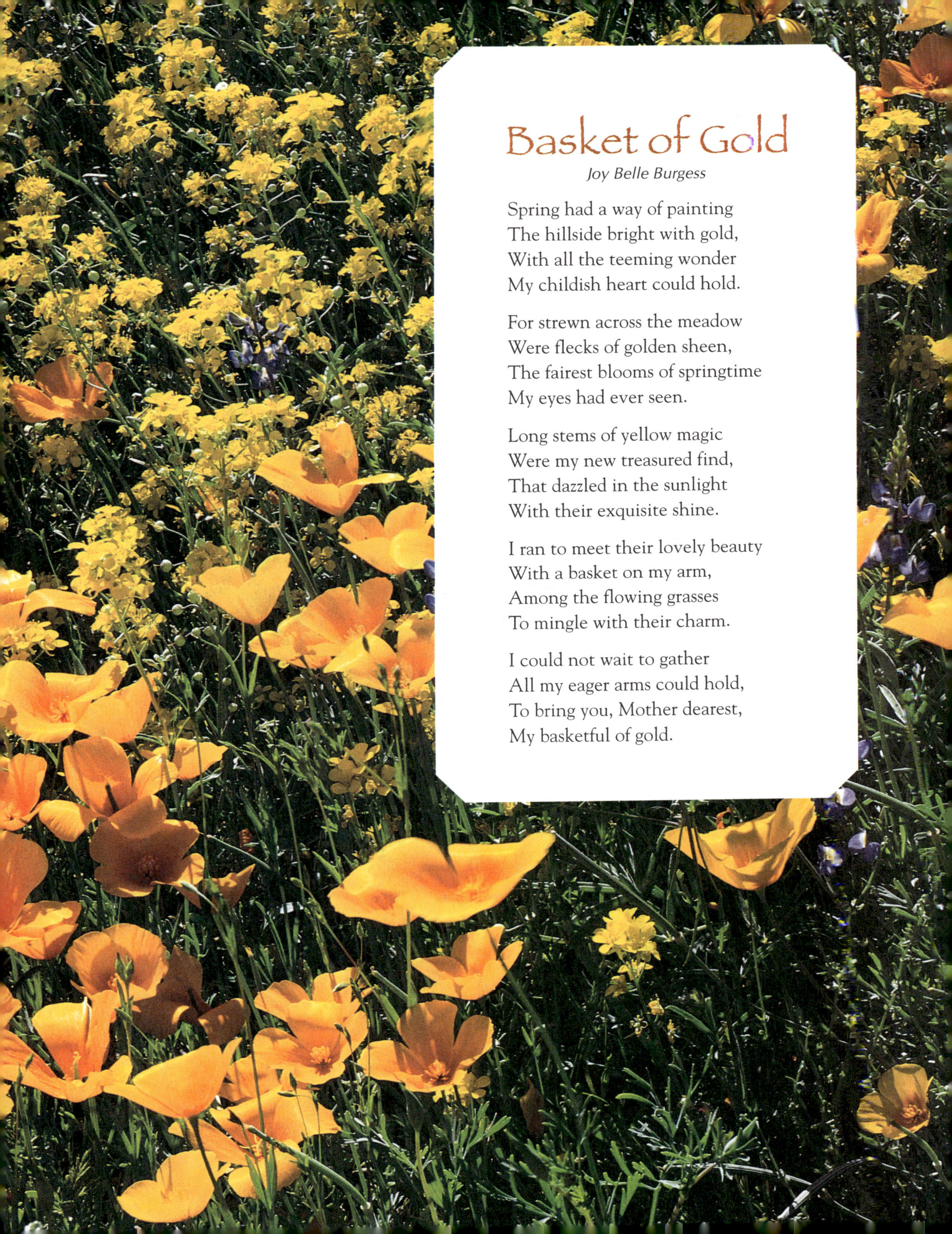

Basket of Gold

Joy Belle Burgess

Spring had a way of painting
The hillside bright with gold,
With all the teeming wonder
My childish heart could hold.

For strewn across the meadow
Were flecks of golden sheen,
The fairest blooms of springtime
My eyes had ever seen.

Long stems of yellow magic
Were my new treasured find,
That dazzled in the sunlight
With their exquisite shine.

I ran to meet their lovely beauty
With a basket on my arm,
Among the flowing grasses
To mingle with their charm.

I could not wait to gather
All my eager arms could hold,
To bring you, Mother dearest,
My basketful of gold.

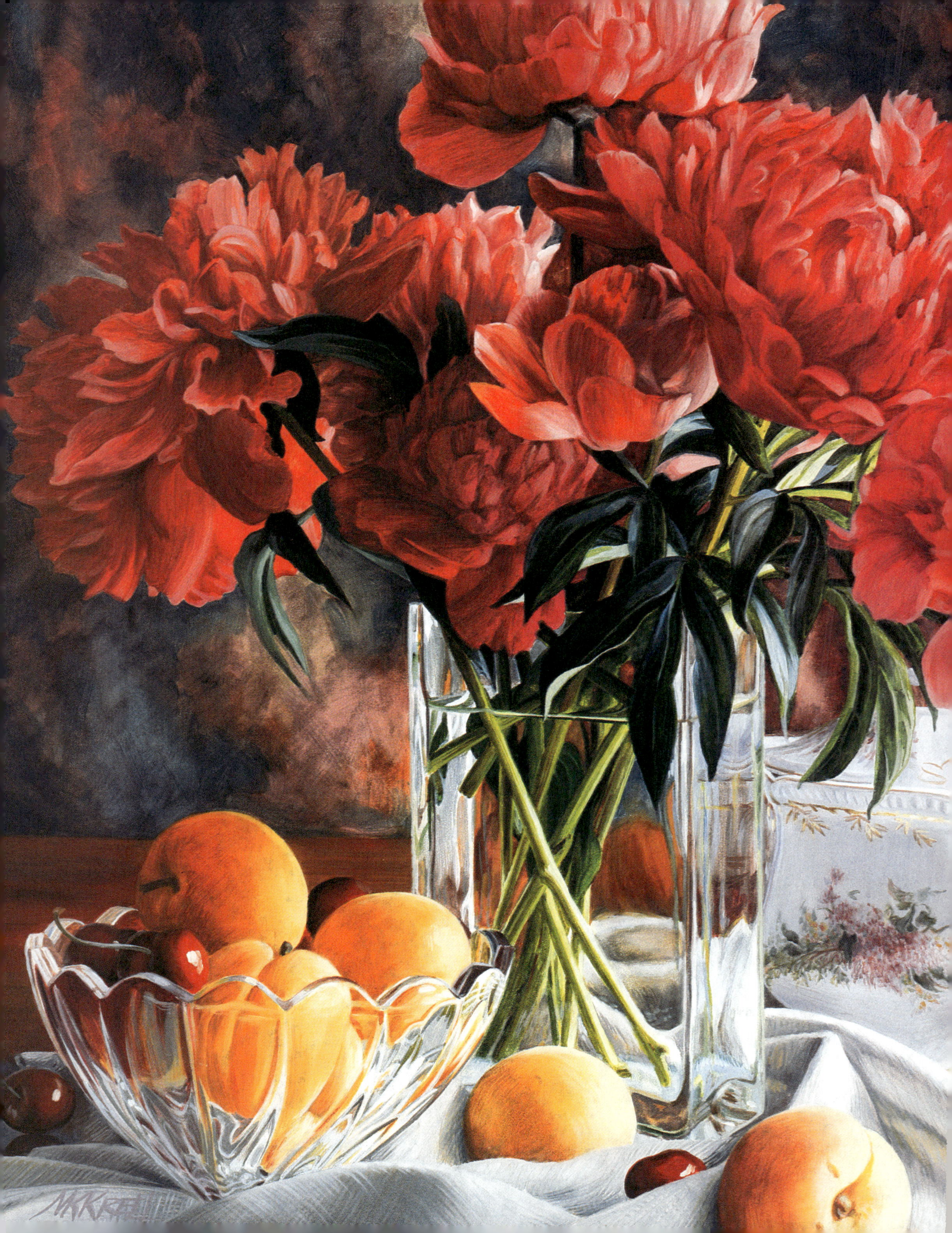

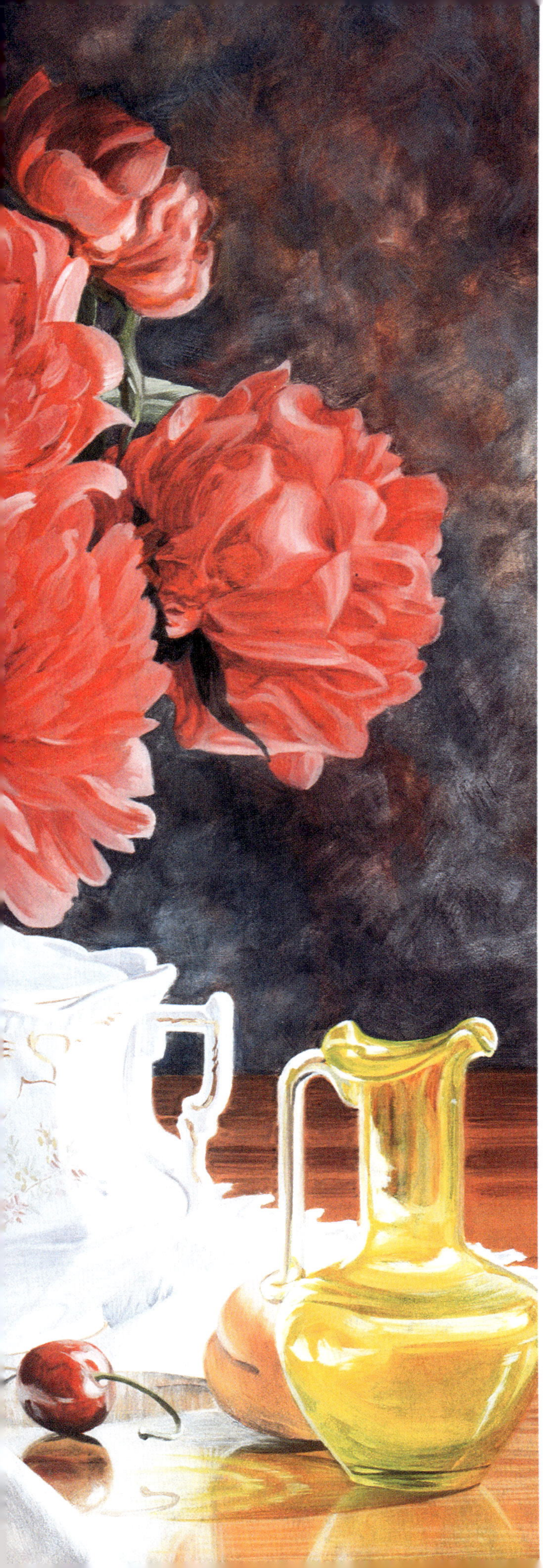

To My Mother's Memory

R. H. Grenville

Like treasures in a teakwood chest,
Rich souvenirs of life remain
In memory—all I could wrest
From love and longing, joy and pain.
There beauty is, and youth, and spring;
Old dreams, like tatters of fine lace;
And one incomparable thing,
One flawless cameo—your face.

To My Mother

Oreon Marie McKee

Your love is the moonlight,
Shimmering silvery rays,
Lighting up the darkest night
Of life's tempestuous days.

Your love is the North Star,
Gleaming so pure and white,
Shining down from up afar
To guide my steps aright.

Your love is the golden sun,
My cloak of warmth and life
That bursts asunder clouds that come
In times of care and strife.

Your love is all the heaven's blue
That holds moon, stars, and sun,
Heaven that brings the rainbow hue
When the rain of tears is done.

The vivid colors of flowers and fruit brighten a table in a painting by Mary Kay Krell, entitled PEONIES AND APRICOTS. *Photograph by Steve Beasley.*

Rock Me to Sleep

Elizabeth Akers Allen

Backward, turn backward, O Time, in your flight,
Make me a child again just for tonight!
Mother, come back from the echoless shore,
Take me again to your heart as of yore;
Kiss from my forehead the furrows of care,
Smooth the few silver threads out of my hair;
Over my slumbers your loving watch keep;
Rock me to sleep, Mother—rock me to sleep.

Tired of the hollow, the base, the untrue,
Mother, O Mother, my heart calls for you!
Many a summer the grass has grown green,
Blossomed and faded, our faces between.
Yet, with strong yearning and passionate pain
Long I tonight for your presence again.
Come from the silence so long and so deep;
Rock me to sleep, Mother—rock me to sleep.

Over my heart, in the days that are flown,
No love like mother-love ever has shone;
No other worship abides and endures—
Faithful, unselfish, and patient like yours.
None like a mother can charm away pain
From the sick soul and the world-weary brain.
Slumber's soft calms o'er my heavy lids creep;
Rock me to sleep, Mother—rock me to sleep.

Come, let your brown hair, just lighted with gold,
Fall on your shoulders again as of old;
Let it drop over my forehead tonight,
Shading my faint eyes away from the light;
For with its sunny-edged shadows once more
Haply will throng the sweet visions of yore;
Lovingly, softly, its bright billows sweep;
Rock me to sleep, Mother—rock me to sleep.

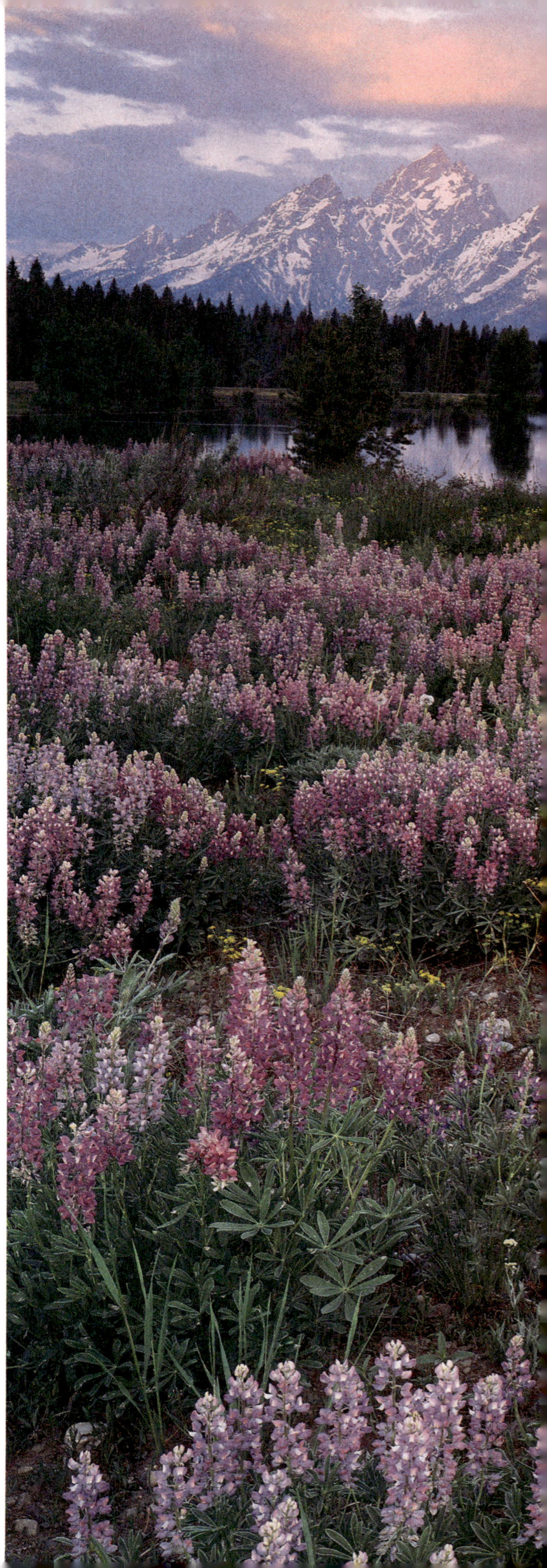

A lupine meadow borders a pond, reflecting the Grand Teton Range at dawn. Photograph by Mary Liz Austin.

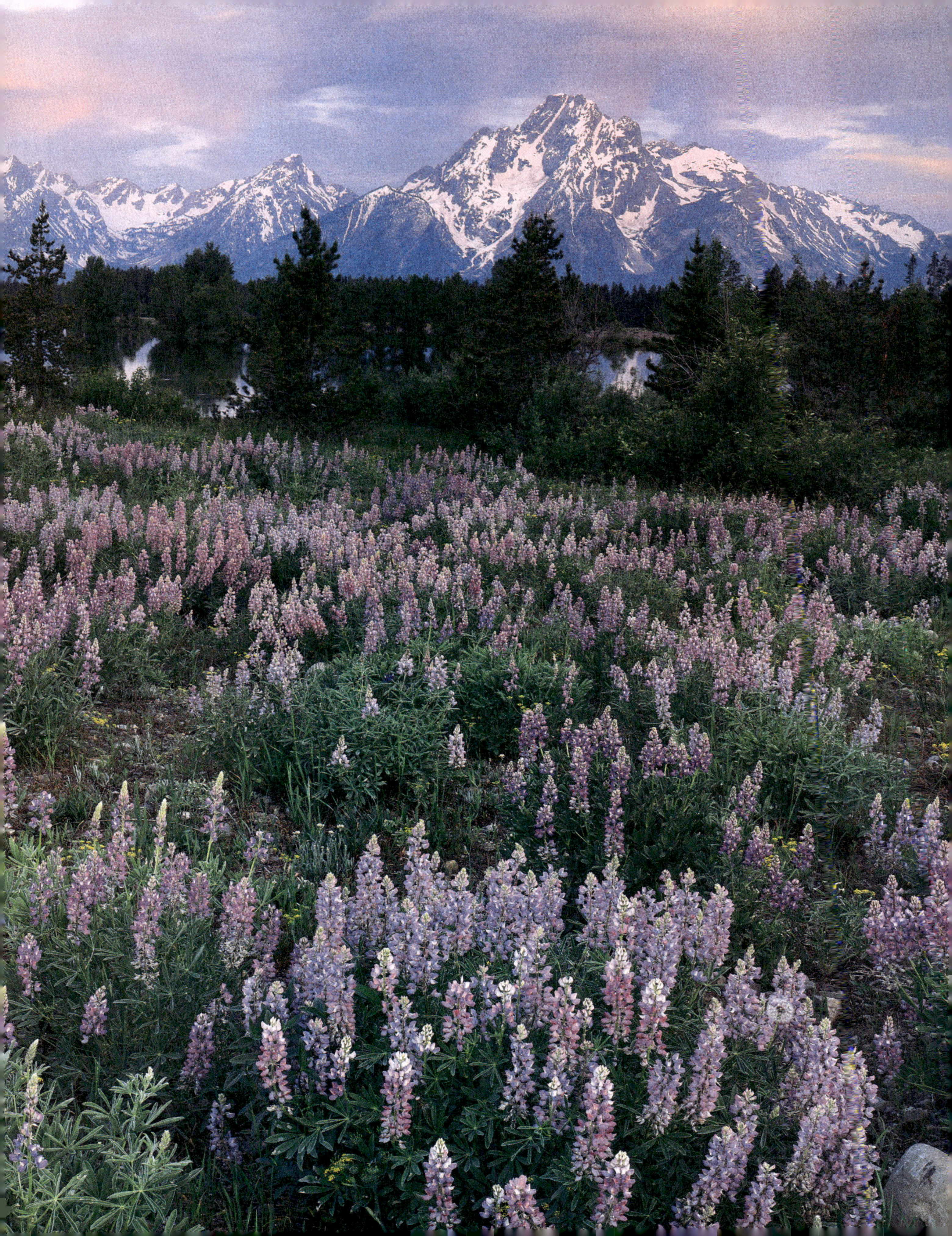

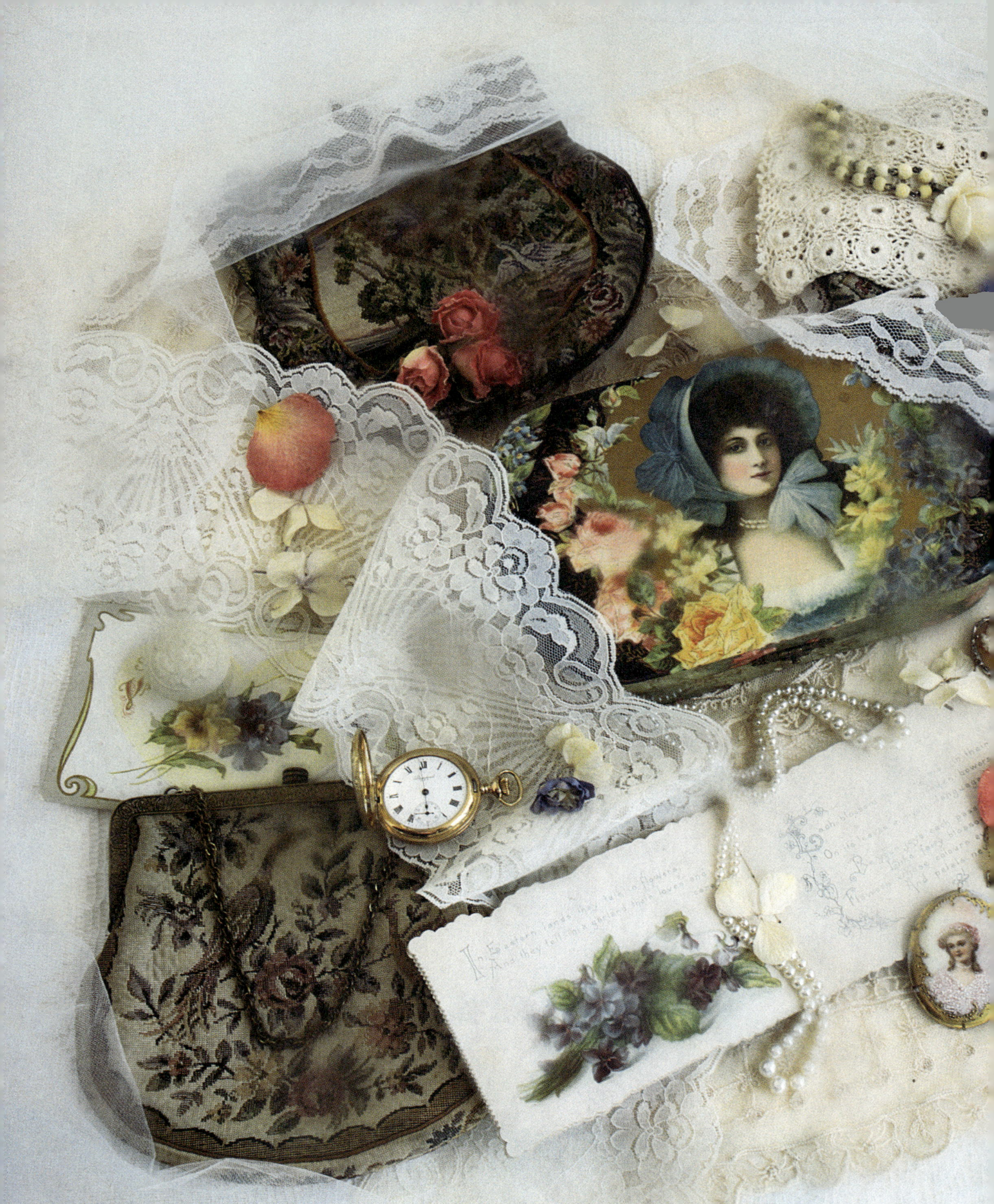

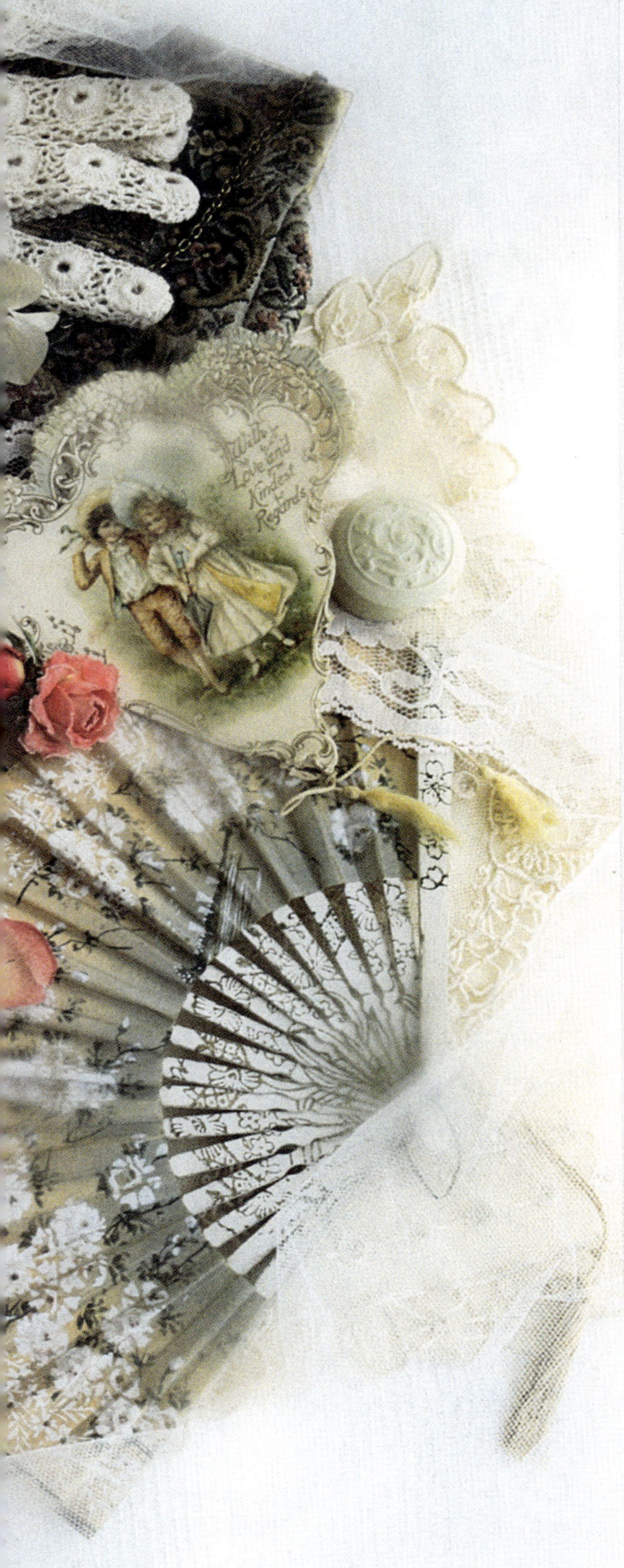

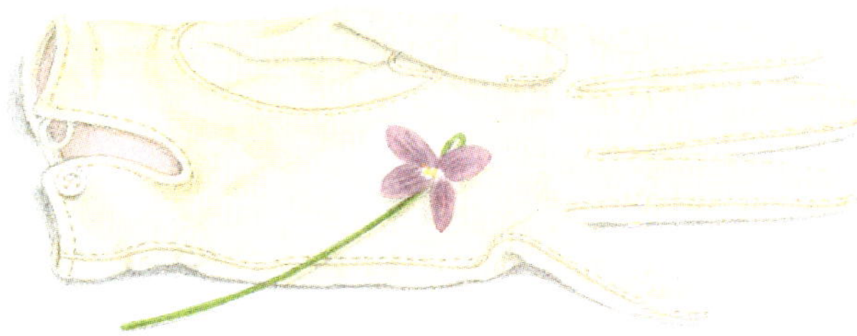

Mother's Legacy

Kay Hoffman

She left behind a legacy
Of finest homepsun lace,
For this my mother loved to do
When she found a little space.

She never could sit idly;
Her hands had work to do.
It mattered not the time or place
The crochet needle flew.

Lace tablecloths and doilies
In most every shape and size,
Afghans, and lap robes she'd make
For someone's warm surprise.

Once I thought her art old-fashioned,
Not keeping with the style,
But, oh, how wisely do the years
Teach of the things worthwhile.

Though Mother's no longer with us
Her unselfish legacy lives on,
As her children's children cherish
Lace gifts she passed along.

A fan, lace, and other dainty possessions are displayed in this photograph by Nancy Matthews.

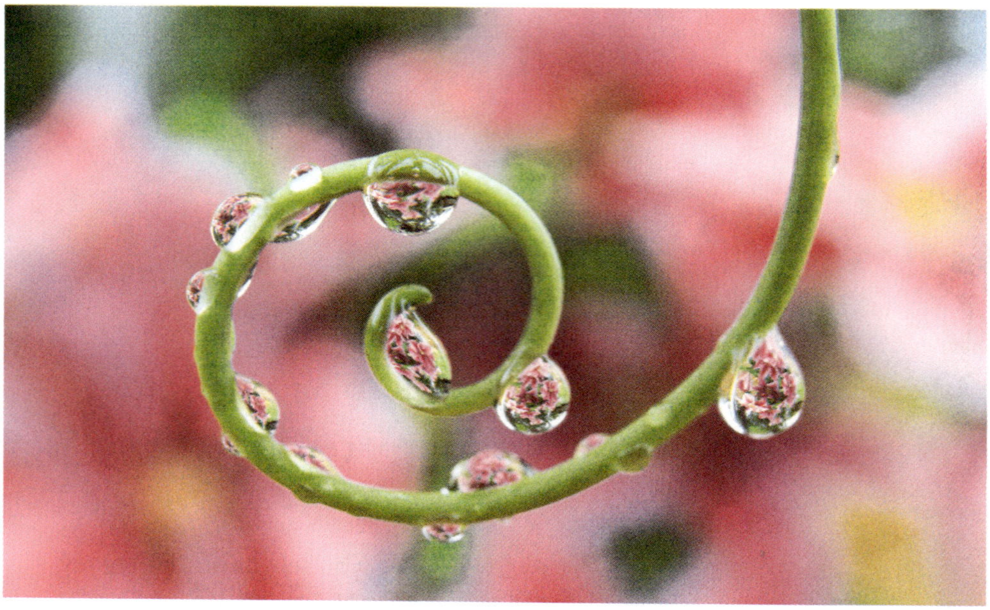

My Mother

Thelma Anna Street

It's true, there seems a lasting charm
In the woman of quiet way.
A resource shared from a spirit rich,
She is gentle day by day.

It's true, we all could learn from her
Life's riches which endure.
The wellspring of a loving heart
Where speech is soft and pure.

A Sketch of Mother

Cleone Montgomery

She turns to tending flower beds,
From plumping downy pillows,
And stoops to kiss a tear-stained face
Beneath the weeping willows;

Returns to kitchen's ordered hush,
With wifely skill to bake
A flower-fragrant, leaf-brown loaf,
Or white-rose angel-cake.

Her flying fingers make, and mend,
And iron crisp, dainty frocks;
While through the shining pane she sees
Their sisters, hollyhocks.

In row on row shy infant bulbs
And seedling hopes she nurses
With one hand, while the other writes
Delightful flower verses.

Serene, she fills a brimming cup
For each demanding hour;
Yet walks in ways of garden paths
With every thought a flower.

Clematis and rockcress accompany passionflowers in a garden in Clackamas County, Oregon. Photograph by Steve Terrill.

Above: The pale pink of clematis is seen through the water beads on a tendril of a passionflower. Photograph by Dennis Frates.

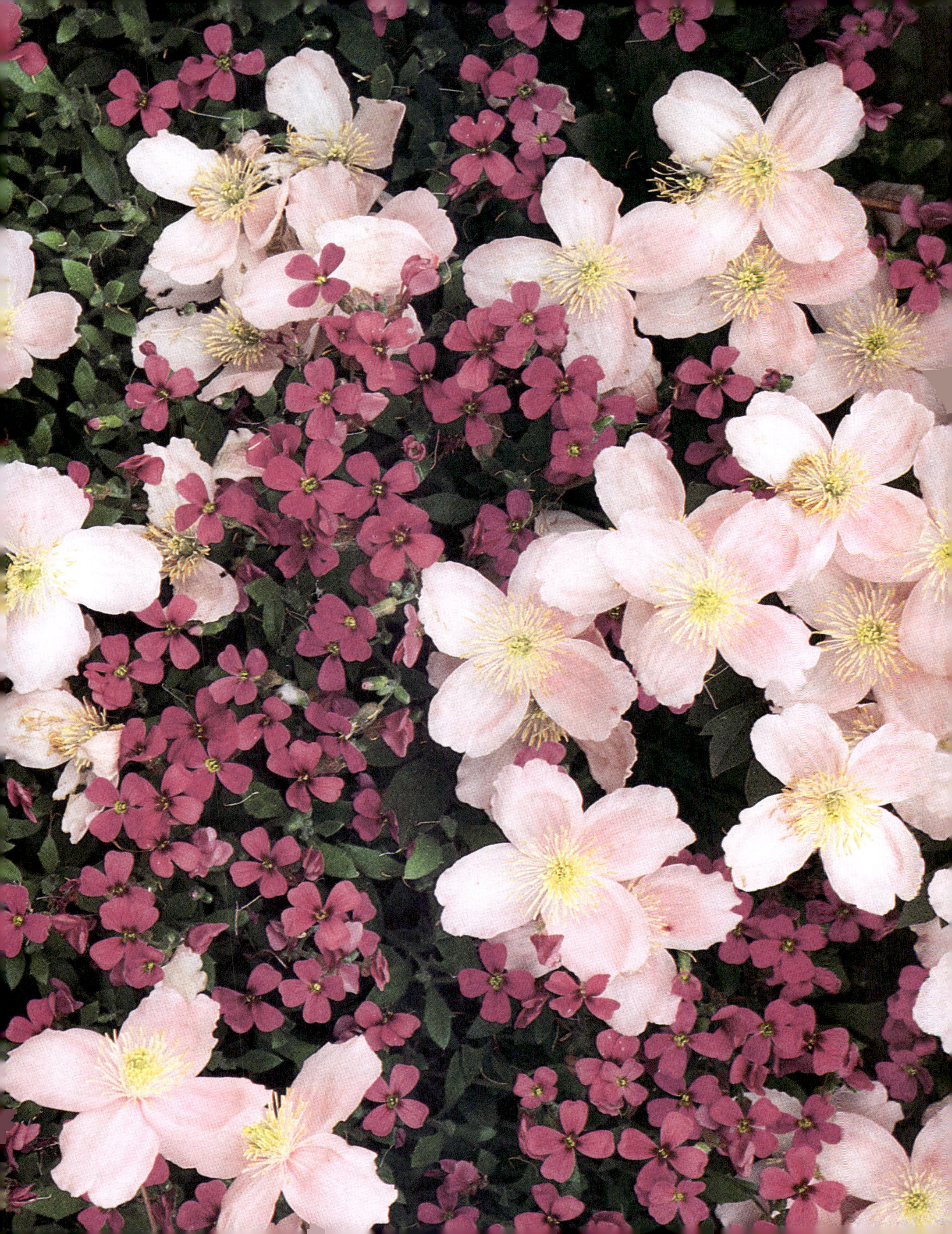

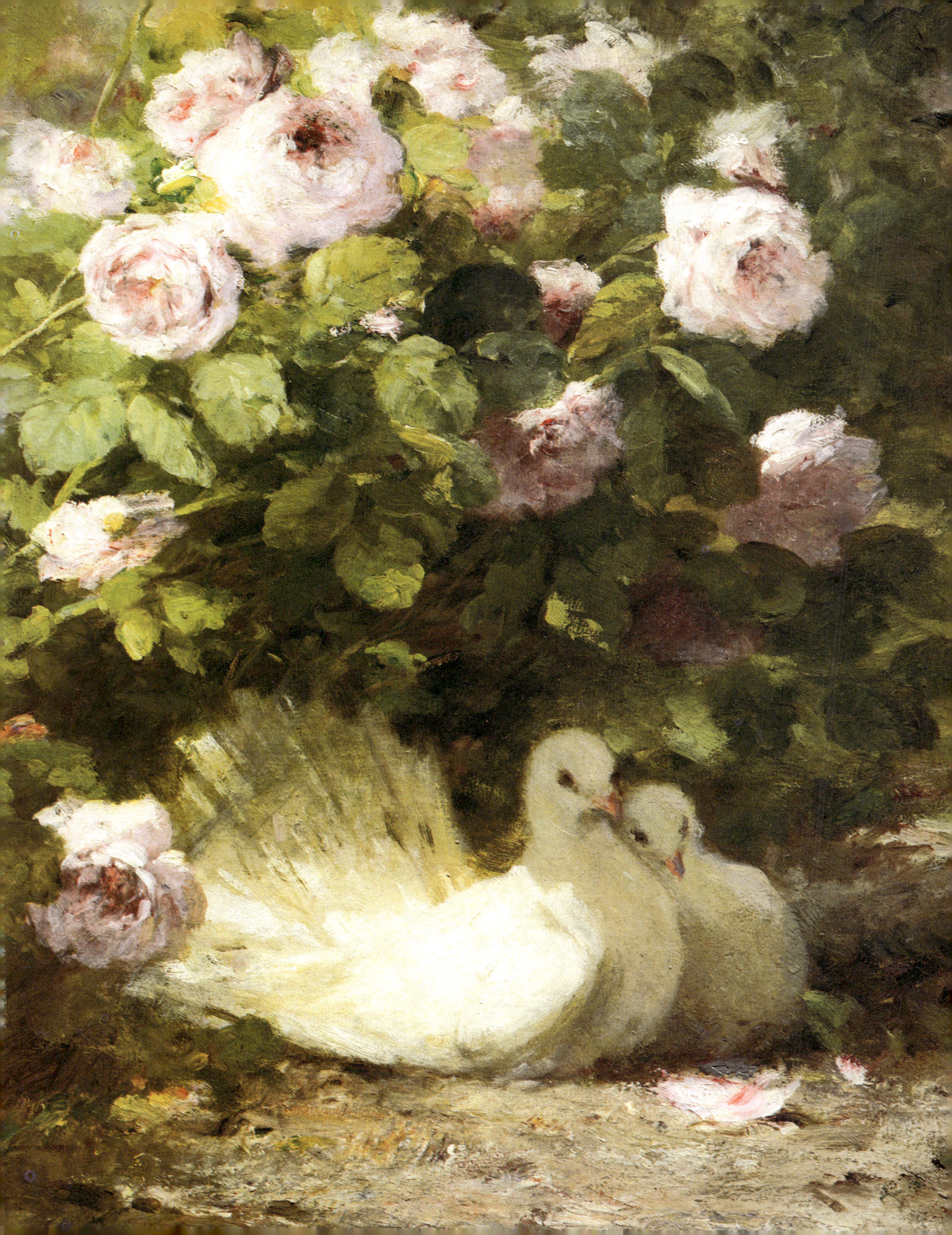

A Mother's Song

Jessie Cannon Eldridge

Love taught me beauty—
Peace on starlit nights,
The glowing magic of each sunlit day,
The gentle wonder of the silver rain,
The rapture of homecoming, when away.

Love taught me dreams—
The loveliness in pain,
How faith's bright candle will burn far and long,
The satisfaction of a giving hand,
The good comfort of knowing you belong.

Love taught me hope—
Deep joy in simple things,
The precious music of a small child's care,
That want makes need, and, in the trembling dark,
The sweet sound of forgiveness, waiting there.

Love taught me this—that all my days I'd know,
This is the way I would have my life go.

LES DEUX COLOMBES, a painting by Alphonse Frederic Murton (1824–1911), expresses the commitment of love and companionship. Image from Fine Art Photographic Library, Ltd., London/Waterhouse & Dodd.

READERS' FORUM

Snapshots from our IDEALS *readers*

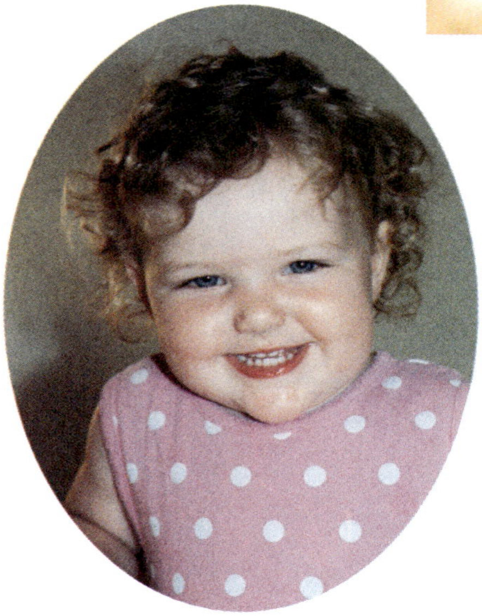

Left: The busy polka dots on Madeline Kate Skena's dress match the playfulness of her smile. Madeline lives in Chicago, Illinois. Her grandmother, Dorothy Schultz, of Hereford, Pennsylvania, shares this photograph.

Right: Enjoying a ride through their hometown of Pennington, New Jersey, are nine-month-old twins, Georgia and Trevor Daniel. Their grandparents, Juanita and George Fodor of Pittsburgh, Pennsylvania, are proud of their double blessing.

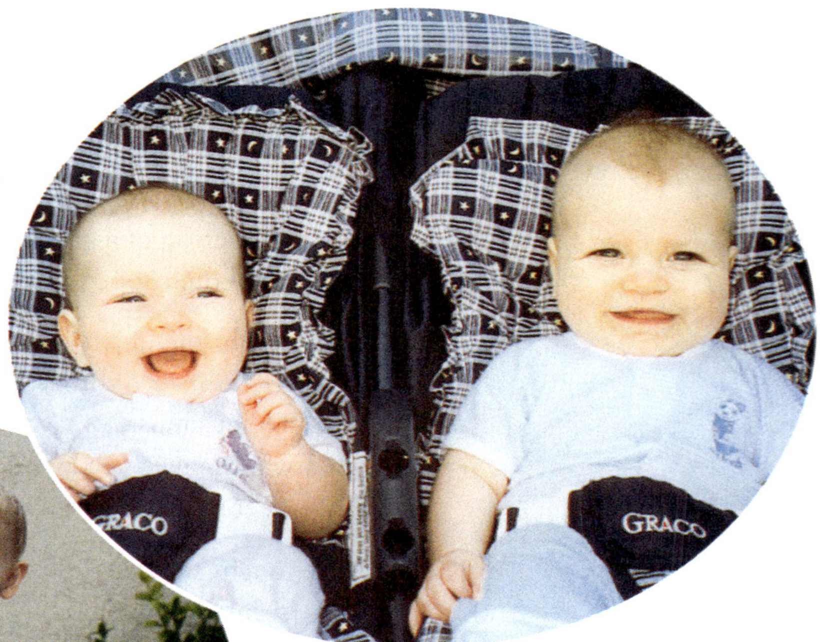

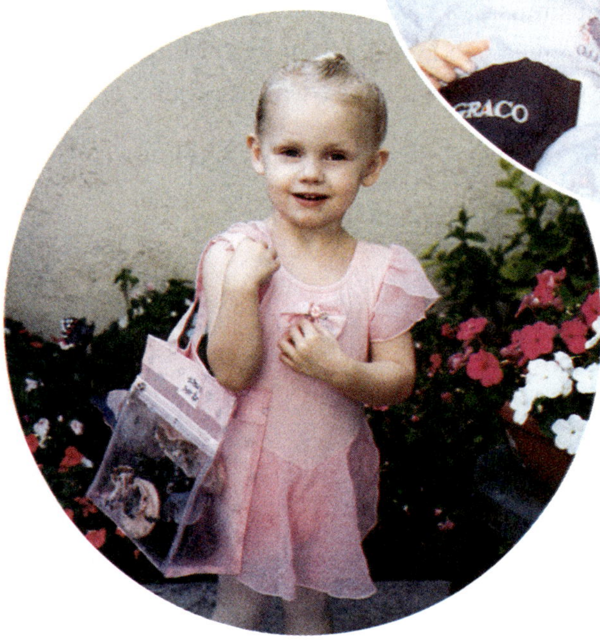

Left: Hayley Ann Ireland is "pretty in pink" and ready for her first ballet lesson. Her parents are Jarrod and Christa Ireland, of Garden Grove, California.

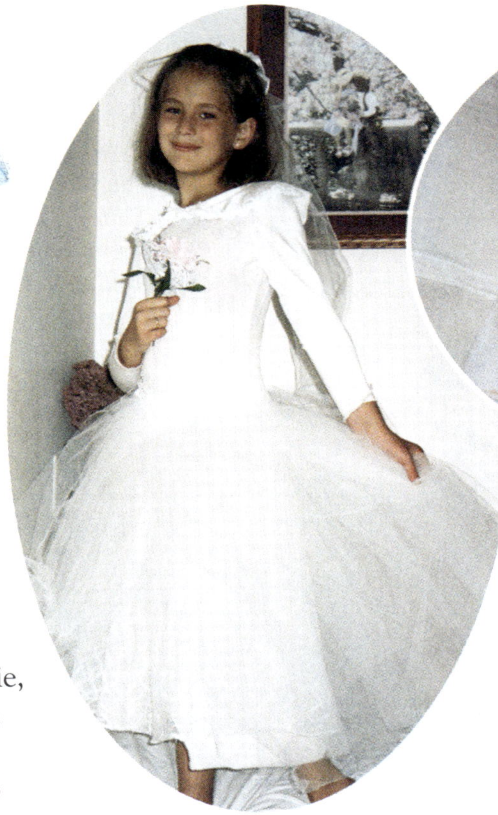

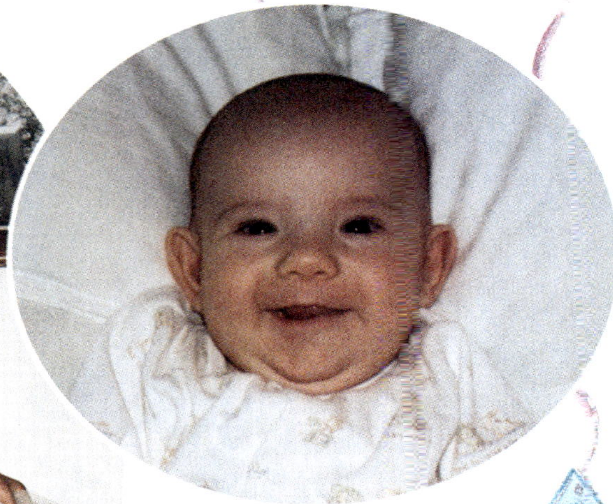

Right: Tonielle Sparkes, of Medicine Hat, Alberta, Canada, wrote a special poem at age seven for her grandmother, Dorothy Michie, in which she states, "I always like your special letters, / But visiting you is always better!"

Far right: Four-month-old John "Jack" Henry Friendt, son of David and Angel Friendt of Blue Earth, Minnesota, is the "happiest little guy you'd want to meet," according to his grandmother, Mrs. Ada DeRemer. She writes that Jack returns the love of his family with big smiles.

Below: Seven-month-old Madelyn Grace Wall is lovingly held by her second cousins Hannah and Lauren Richardson. Boaz, Alabama, is their home.

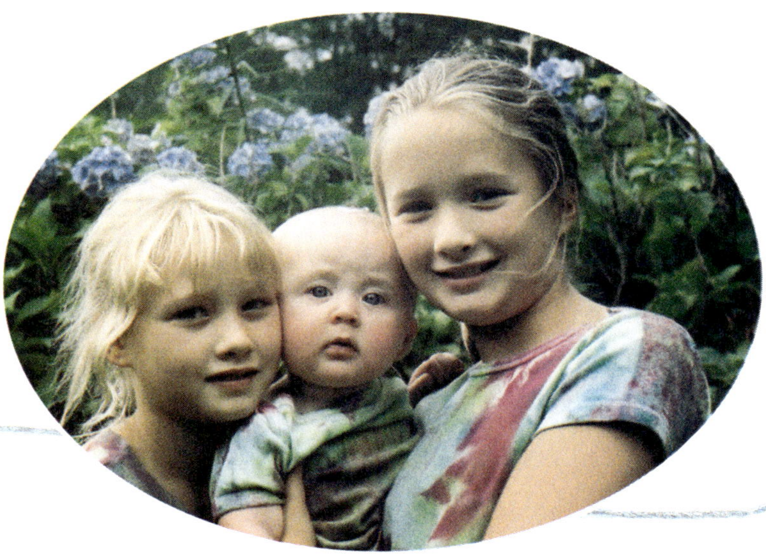

THANK YOU for sharing your family photographs with *Ideals*. We hope to hear from other readers who would like to share snapshots with the *Ideals* family. Please include a self-addressed, stamped envelope if you would like the photos returned. Keep your original photographs for safekeeping and send duplicate photos along with your name, address, and telephone number to:

Readers' Forum
Ideals Publications
535 Metroplex Drive, Suite 250
Nashville, Tennessee 37211

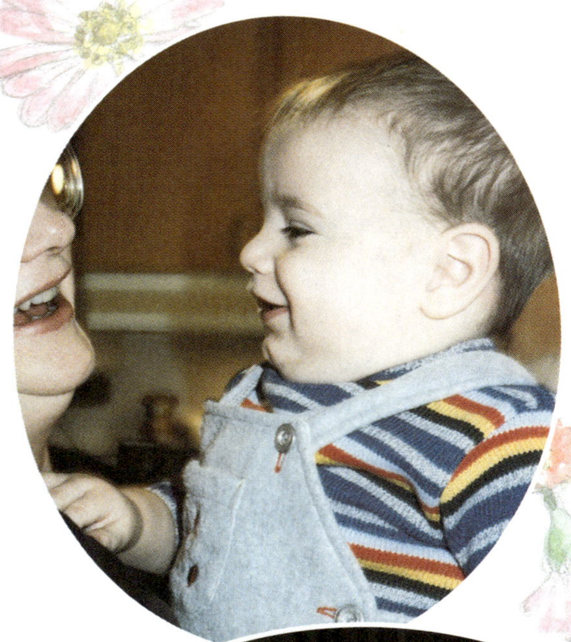

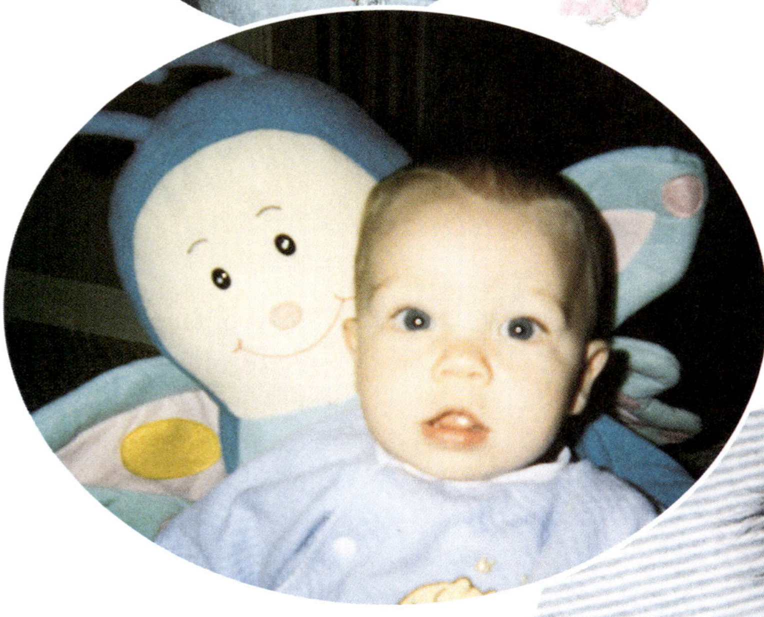

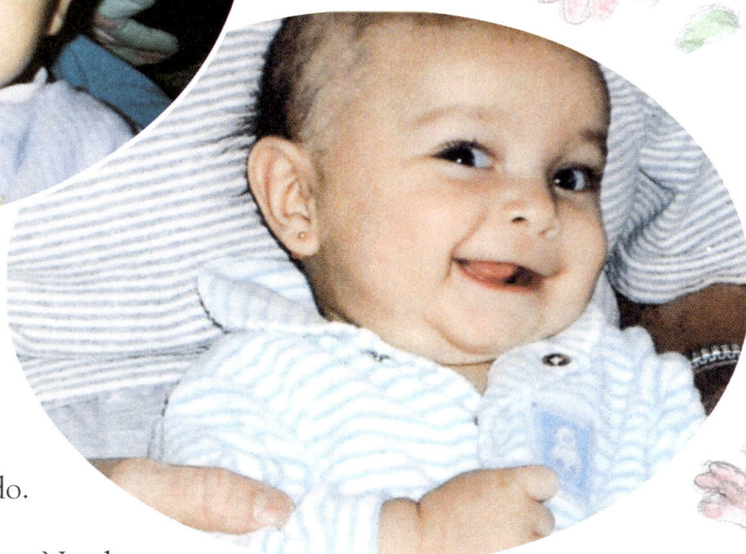

ideals®

Publisher, Patricia A. Pingry
Editor, Marjorie Lloyd
Designer, Marisa Calvin
Copy Editor, Melinda Rathjen
Permissions Editor, Patsy Jay
Contributing Writers, Lansing Christman, Laurie Hunter, Pamela Kennedy, Melissa Lester, Fran Morley, Lisa Ragan, and Melinda Rathjen

ACKNOWLEDGMENTS

BORLAND, HAL. An excerpt from *This Hill, This Valley.* Copyright © 1957 by Hal Borland, renewed 1985 by Barbara Dodge Borland. Published by John Hopkins University Press. Used by permission of Frances Collin Literary Agent. HOOVER, DAN A. "Only Daughter." Used by permission of Golde Hoover. JAQUES, EDNA. "She's Motherly" from *The Golden Road,* published by Thomas Allen, Ltd, 1953. Used by permission of Louise Bonnell. STOFFEL, BETTY W. "At Baby's Bed." Used by permission of E. Lee Stoffel. WILDER, LAURA INGALLS. "Daily Tasks Are Not Small Things, May 1923" from *Little House in the Ozarks.* Copyright © 1991 by Stephen W. Hines, editor. Published by Thomas Nelson, Inc. Used by permission of Stephen W. Hines. Our thanks to Mrs. Walter Kurz for submitting "Mother's Hands." Copyright © 1939. From "By the Bend O' the River" with Josh Higgins. Our sincere thanks to those authors whom we were unable to locate.

Top: One-year-old Collin Ray of Council Bluffs, Iowa, enjoys the company of his grandmother, Mrs. Julie Lee Smith. This charming photograph was sent to us by Collin's great-aunt, Sara Beddow, of Colorado Springs, Colorado.

Middle: Doris Smith of Lake Waccamaw, North Carolina, writes us that her grandson, eight-month-old Jackson Smith, is her "precious angel from heaven." He is perched in a beanbag chair, a special gift from his grandmother.

Right: Mrs. Geraldine Finch, of West Bend, Wisconsin, shares this photograph of her smiling five-month-old great-granddaughter, Rachel Adela Sepulveda.

Fill Your Heart with Fun, Laughter and Faith!

Laughter is good for the soul...and the three-volume *Hearts Full of Laughter* collection proves it. You'll laugh your troubles away as you share the real-life antics of the funny Women of Faith who contribute their zany anecdotes to these fun-filled books. These life lessons of laughter will help you see the humor in your own life, and will help you to cope with your own burdens—and see the joyful side of life.

The three softcover books—*She Who Laughs, Lasts!...Don't Stop Laughing Now!...and Faith, Hope & Hilarity*—contain original first-person stories filled with joy and hope. They are a reminder that God wants us to see the healing humor in the world around us. From the minute you open the first volume in this series you're going to find yourself laughing with great Women of Faith who share their funniest moments with you.

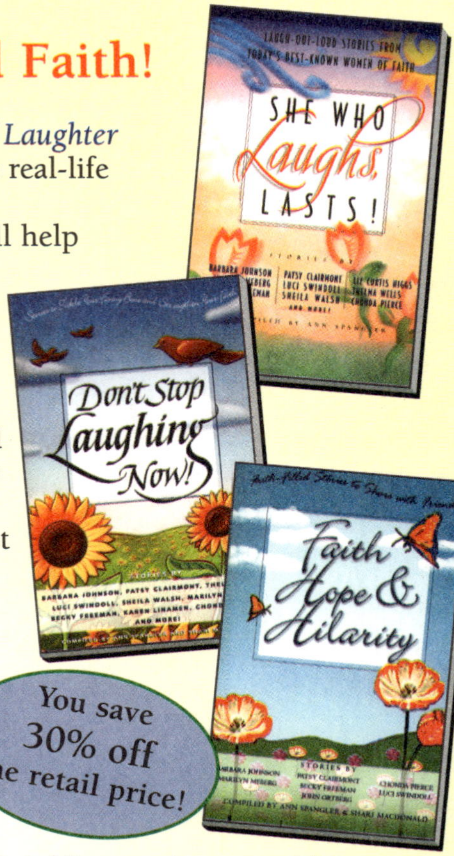

You save 30% off the retail price!

Rib-tickling stories on real-life issues help you see the humor all around you!

- Marriage
- Church going
- Children
- Getting older
- Bad haircuts
- Losing weight
- Vacations
- and more!

NO POSTAGE NECESSARY IF MAILED IN THE UNITED STATES

BUSINESS REPLY MAIL
FIRST-CLASS MAIL PERMIT NO. 38 CARMEL NY

POSTAGE WILL BE PAID BY ADDRESSEE

IDEALS PUBLICATIONS
A Division of GUIDEPOSTS
PO BOX 797
CARMEL NY 10512-9905

Free Bookmark with order!

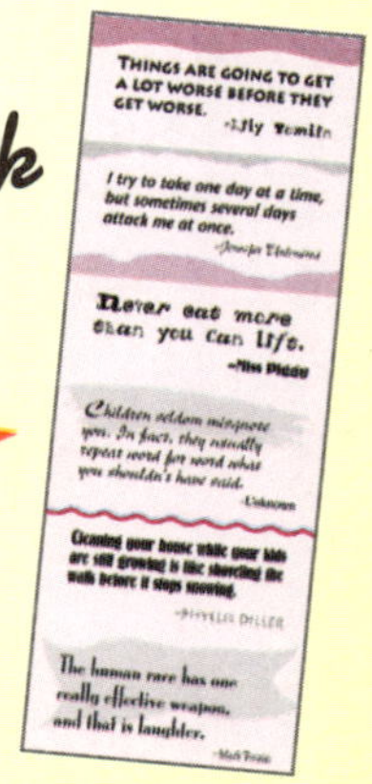

Your exclusive Guideposts price!

FREE EXAMINATION CERTIFICATE

YES! I'd like to examine ***Hearts Full of Laughter***, a three-volume collection, at no risk or obligation. If I decide to keep the set, I will be billed later at the low Guideposts price of only $22.98, payable in 3 installments of $7.66 each, plus shipping and processing. If not completely satisfied, I may return the set within 30 days and owe nothing. The FREE bookmark is mine to keep no matter what I decide.

Total sets ordered: ___________

Please print your name and address:

NAME

ADDRESS APT#

CITY STATE ZIP

Allow 4 weeks for delivery. Orders subject to credit approval.
Send no money now. We will bill you later.
www.guidepostsbooks.com

Printed in USA
11/202187821

Only $22.98

payable in three installments of $7.66 each, plus shipping and processing.

Complete the Free Examination Certificate and mail today for your 30-Day Preview.

No need to send money now!